WORLD TRADE ORGANIZATION

Dispute Settlement Reports

2001
Volume I

Pages 1-409

CAMBRIDGE
UNIVERSITY PRESS

PUBLISHED BY THE PRESS SYNDICATE OF THE UNIVERSITY OF CAMBRIDGE
The Pitt Building, Trumpington Street, Cambridge, United Kingdom

CAMBRIDGE UNIVERSITY PRESS
The Edinburgh Building, Cambridge CB2 2RU, UK
40 West 20th Street, New York, NY 10011–4211, USA
477 Williamstown Road, Port Melbourne, VIC 3207, Australia
Ruiz de Alarcón 13, 28014 Madrid, Spain
Dock House, The Waterfront, Cape Town 8001, South Africa

http://www.cambridge.org

First published 2003

Printed in the United Kingdom at the University Press, Cambridge

French edition and Spanish edition paperbacks of this title are both available directly from WTO Publications, World Trade Organization, Centre William Rappard, 154 rue de Lausanne, CH-1211 Geneva 21, Switzerland http://www.wto.org

ISBN 0 521 82978 X hardback

THE WTO DISPUTE SETTLEMENT REPORTS

The *Dispute Settlement Reports* of the World Trade Organization (the "WTO") include panel and Appellate Body reports, as well as arbitration awards, in disputes concerning the rights and obligations of WTO Members under the provisions of the *Marrakesh Agreement Establishing the World Trade Organization.* The *Dispute Settlement Reports* are available in English, French and Spanish. Starting with 1999, the first volume of each year contains a cumulative index of published disputes.

This volume may be cited as DSR 2001: I

TABLE OF CONTENTS

KOREA – MEASURES AFFECTING IMPORTS OF FRESH, CHILLED AND FROZEN BEEF

Report of the Appellate Body

WT/DS161/AB/R, WT/DS169/AB/R

Korea, *Appellant*
Australia, *Appellee*
United States, *Appellee*
Canada, *Third Participant*
New Zealand, *Third Participant*

Present:
Ehlermann, Presiding Member
Abi-Saab, Member
Feliciano, Member

TABLE OF CONTENTS

I. INTRODUCTION

1. Korea appeals certain issues of law and legal interpretations in the Panel Report, *Korea – Measures Affecting Imports of Fresh, Chilled and Frozen Beef* (the "Panel Report").[1] The Panel was established to consider a complaint by Australia and the United States with respect to Korean measures that affect the importation of certain beef products. The aspects of these measures relevant for this appeal relate to, first, domestic support provided to the beef industry and to the Korean agriculture sector more generally, and, second, the separate retail distribution channels that exist for certain imported and domestic beef products (the so-called "dual retail system") and related measures. The dual retail system is given legal effect by the *Management Guideline for Imported Beef* (the "*Management Guideline*").[2] The factual aspects of this dispute are described in detail in paragraphs 8 through 29 of the Panel Report.

2. The Panel considered claims by Australia that the requirements imposed on the retail sale of imported beef are contrary to Articles III and XI of the *General Agreement on Tariffs and Trade 1994* (the "GATT 1994"); that the tendering process adopted by the Livestock Products Marketing Organization (the "LPMO") results in quantitative restrictions being applied to grass-fed beef, con-

---

[1] Panel Report, *Korea – Measures Affecting Imports of Fresh, Chilled and Frozen Beef* ("*Korea – Various Measures on Beef*"), WT/DS161/R, WT/DS169/R, adopted 10 January 2001.

[2] The essential features of the Korean dual retail system for beef are found in the *Guidelines Concerning Registration and Operation of Specialized Imported Beef Stores,* (61550-81) 29 January 1990, modified on 15 March 1994; and the *Regulations Concerning Sales of Imported Beef,* (51550-100), modified on 27 March 1993, 7 April 1994, and 29 June 1998. On 1 October 1999, these two instruments were replaced by the *Management Guideline for Imported Beef,* (Ministry of Agriculture Notice 1999-67), which maintained, however, the basic principles of the dual retail system. The *Management Guideline* is an elaboration of Article 25 of the *Livestock Act (Revised)*, as amended by Act No. 5720 on 29 January 1999.

trary to Articles II:1, III:4, XI:1 and XVII of the GATT 1994; that discharge procedures for LPMO beef are contrary to Articles III, XI and XVII of the GATT 1994 and Article 4.2 of the *Agreement on Agriculture*; that restrictions on sales of beef imported by the LPMO are contrary to Article III:4 of the GATT 1994; that Korea applies a mark-up on beef imported under the "Simultaneous Buy/Sell" ("SBS") system which is inconsistent with Korea's obligations under Articles II or III of the GATT 1994; that the SBS system applies limitations on the import and distribution of imported beef, and imposes labelling, reporting and record-keeping requirements, that are contrary to Articles III and XI of the GATT 1994; and that, in 1997, Korea provided domestic support to its beef industry which resulted in Korea's Current Total Aggregate Measurement of Support ("AMS") for 1997 being in excess of its reduction commitments for that year, contrary to Articles 3, 6 and 7 of the *Agreement on Agriculture*. [3]

3. The Panel also considered claims by the United States that Korea's requirement that imported beef be sold only in specialized imported beef stores, and its laws and regulations restricting the resale and distribution of imported beef by SBS super-groups, retailers, customers, and end-users are inconsistent with its obligations under Article III:4 of the GATT 1994; that Korea's discretionary import regime, as well as the LPMO's establishment of minimum import prices and delay of both invitations to tender as well as quota allocations, are inconsistent with its obligations under Article XI:1 of the GATT 1994, Article 4.2 of the *Agreement on Agriculture*, and Articles 1 and 3 of the *Agreement on Import Licensing Procedures*; that Korea's imposition of other duties or charges in the form of a mark-up not provided for in Korea's Schedule LX is inconsistent with its obligations under Article II:1 of the GATT 1994; and that Korea has failed to fulfill its reduction commitment for domestic support for 1997 and 1998, and has, thus, acted inconsistently with its obligations under Articles 3, 6, and 7 of the *Agreement on Agriculture*. [4]

4. The Panel Report was circulated to the Members of the World Trade Organization (the "WTO") on 31 July 2000.

5. The Panel concluded that certain of the measures at issue are included in "the remaining restrictions" within the meaning of Note 6(e) of Korea's Schedule and thus benefit from a transitional period until 1 January 2001, by which date they shall be eliminated or otherwise brought into conformity with the *Marrakesh Agreement Establishing the World Trade Organization* (the "*WTO Agreement*"); that the dual retail system for beef (including the obligation for department stores and supermarkets authorized to sell imported beef to hold a separate display, and the obligation for foreign beef shops to bear a sign with the words "Specialized Imported Beef Store") is inconsistent with the provisions of Article III:4 of the GATT 1994 in that it treats imported beef less favourably than domestic beef,

3 Panel Report, *Korea – Various Measures on Beef*, *supra*, footnote 1, para. 49.

4 *Ibid*., para. 51.

and cannot be justified pursuant to Article XX(d) of the GATT 1994; that the requirement that the supply of beef from the LPMO's wholesale market be limited to specialized imported beef stores is inconsistent with Article III:4 of the GATT 1994 and cannot be justified pursuant to Article XX(d) of the GATT 1994; that the imposition of more stringent record-keeping requirements on those who purchase foreign beef imported by the LPMO than on those who purchase domestic beef is inconsistent with Article III:4 of the GATT 1994; that the prohibition against cross-trading between end-users of the SBS system is inconsistent with Article III:4 of the GATT 1994; that any additional labelling requirements imposed on foreign beef imported through the SBS system that are not also imposed on domestic beef, such as the requirement that the end-consumer, the contract number and super-group importer be identified and indicated on the imported beef, are inconsistent with Article III:4 of the GATT 1994; that the LPMO's lack of, and delays in, calling for tenders, and its discharge practices between November 1997 and the end of May 1998, constitute import restrictions on foreign beef, inconsistent with Article XI of the GATT 1994, and the same practices are also inconsistent with Article 4.2 of the *Agreement on Agriculture* and its footnote; that even if the LPMO had not had monopoly rights over the import and distribution of its share of Korea's beef import, the LPMO's lack of, and delays in, calling for tenders during the same period constituted an import restriction inconsistent with Article XI of the GATT 1994 through the application of the Ad Note to Articles XI, XII, XIII, XIV and XVIII of the GATT 1994, and that the LPMO's discharge practices during the same period were inconsistent with Article XVII:1(a) of the GATT 1994; that the LPMO's calls for tenders that are made subject to grass-fed or grain-fed distinctions impose import restrictions inconsistent with Article XI of the GATT 1994, and treat imports of grass-fed beef less favourably than is provided for in Korea's Schedule, contrary to Article II:1(a) of the GATT 1994; that Korea's domestic support for beef for 1997 and 1998 was not correctly calculated and exceeded the *de minimis* level, contrary to Article 6 of the *Agreement on Agriculture*, and was not included in Korea's Current Total AMS, contrary to Article 7.2(a) of the *Agreement on Agriculture*; that Korea's total domestic support (Current Total AMS) for 1997 and 1998 exceeded Korea's commitment levels, as specified in Part IV, Section I of its Schedule, contrary to Article 3.2 of the *Agreement on Agriculture*. [5]

6. The Panel recommended that the Dispute Settlement Body ("DSB") request Korea to bring its measures into conformity with its obligations under the *WTO Agreement*. [6]

7. On 11 September 2000, Korea notified the DSB of its intention to appeal certain issues of law covered in the Panel Report and certain legal interpretations developed by the Panel, pursuant to paragraph 4 of Article 16 of the *Understand-*

[5] Panel Report, para. 845.
[6] Panel Report, para. 847.

ing on Rules and Procedures Governing the Settlement of Disputes (the "DSU"), and filed a Notice of Appeal pursuant to Rule 20 of the *Working Procedures for Appellate Review* (the "*Working Procedures* "). On 21 September 2000, Korea filed its appellant's submission.[7] on 6 October 2000, Australia and the United States [8] each filed an appellee's submission. On the same day, Canada and New Zealand each filed a third participant's submission.[9]

8. The oral hearing in the appeal was held on 23 and 24 October 2000. The participants and third participants presented oral arguments and responded to questions put to them by the Members of the Division hearing the appeal.

II. ARGUMENTS OF THE PARTICIPANTS AND THE THIRD PARTICIPANTS

A. Korea – Appellant

1. Terms of Reference

9. Korea claims that the Panel erred by making two findings that were outside its terms of reference. First, the Panel erred by ruling on Part IV, Section I of Korea's Schedule LX, in particular by considering which set of numbers in Schedule LX constitutes Korea's commitment levels. Neither the United States nor Australia challenged Korea's Schedule LX in their requests for the establishment of a panel. As Schedule LX is not mentioned in these panel requests, the complaining parties have not met the "minimum prerequisite" established by the Appellate Body for panel requests under Article 6.2 of the DSU, that treaty provisions claimed to have been violated must be identified, and, therefore, Korea should be considered *per se* to have suffered prejudice.

10. Second, neither the United States nor Australia, in their panel requests, identified Annex 3 of the *Agreement on Agriculture* as a treaty provision claimed to have been violated in the context of Korea's calculation methodology for domestic support to the cattle industry. Consequently, the Panel acted outside its terms of reference when it ruled that Annex 3 provided the basis for calculating Korea's current domestic support for beef. Further, the complaining parties have not met the "minimum prerequisite" established by the Appellate Body for panel requests under Article 6.2 of the DSU.

2. Domestic Support Under the Agreement on Agriculture

11. Korea believes the Panel erred in finding that, by virtue of Articles 1(a)(ii) and 1(h)(ii) of the *Agreement on Agriculture*, Korea is bound by the provisions

---

7 Pursuant to Rule 21(1) of the *Working Procedures*.

8 Pursuant to Rule 22 of the *Working Procedures*.

9 Pursuant to Rule 24 of the *Working Procedures*.

of Annex 3 of that Agreement in its calculation of Current AMS for beef, since it did not have any "constituent data and methodology" for beef in its Schedule. The Panel's interpretation of Articles 1(a)(ii) and 1(h)(ii) leads to an unfair outcome and ignores the object and purpose of the *Agreement on Agriculture*. WTO Members' Schedules on the reduction of subsidies for agricultural products can be understood as multi-year equations. One side of the equation includes the commitment level for a given year, while the other side of the equation includes the actual AMS provided for the same year. Thus, for the equation to be meaningful, both sides of the equation should be based on the same set of data and methodology. Using one methodology for commitment levels and another methodology for actual AMS undermines comparability between the two, and leads to unfair results. All the commitment levels set out in Korea's Schedule and all the actual AMS provided by Korea are calculated on the basis of a consistent methodology, which relies on the base years of 1989-1991 (with an exception for rice) and an "actual purchase" definition of eligible production. However, according to the Panel's ruling, Korea should calculate its Current AMS for beef according to different base years and a different definition of eligible production than was used for calculating commitment levels. Korea argues that this leads to unfair results.

12. Furthermore, Korea contends the Panel's interpretation would frustrate the object and purpose of the *Agreement on Agriculture*, which is, in part, to provide for substantial progressive reduction in agricultural support and protection over an agreed period of time. The Panel's interpretation would make it impossible correctly to determine whether a Member has abided by its reduction commitments or not.

13. Moreover, the Panel's interpretation of Articles 1(a)(ii) and 1(h)(ii) of the *Agreement on Agriculture* would render inutile important parts of these provisions. If the calculation methods of Annex 3 were mandatory, as the Panel suggests, the reference in Articles 1(a)(ii) and 1(h)(ii) to the constituent data and methodology in the tables of supporting material would be reduced to redundancy and inutility. The Panel found that support to Korea's cattle industry should be calculated solely on the basis of Annex 3, because support to the cattle industry was not included in Korea's Schedule. However, Articles 1(a)(ii) and 1(h)(ii) do not make a distinction between products which are already contained in the Schedule of a Member and those which are not.

14. In addition, in Korea's view, the Panel erred in finding that Korea's annual AMS commitment levels in its Schedule LX were not the figures in brackets, but rather the figures not in brackets. The Panel was fundamentally in error when it found that "Korea did not identify" which of the two sets of figures for annual commitment levels (figures in brackets or figures not in brackets) constitutes Korea's obligation. The Panel failed to apply the general rule of interpretation ex-

pressed in Article 31 of the *Vienna Convention on the Law of Treaties* [10] (the "*Vienna Convention*") by not taking into account the context of the terms of Korea's Schedule LX, in particular Note 1 to Korea's Schedule LX, which refers to Note 1 of Supporting Table 6. In addition, the Panel's finding on this point would reduce the figures in brackets, Note 1 to Schedule LX, and Note 1 in Supporting Table 6 to inutility, again contrary to the customary rules of treaty interpretation and previous Appellate Body rulings.

15. Korea also submits that Korea's commitment levels were "public knowledge". Korea's Schedule, including Part IV, Section I, was reviewed by all the negotiating parties during the Uruguay Round. Also, the amount of Korea's subsidy to agricultural products was notified to the Committee on Agriculture every year since 1996. In each notification, Korea used the figures within brackets as Korea's commitment level for the given year. Korea considers that its consistent and amply documented position on this issue has been a matter of public record since 1996 and the very first meeting of the Committee on Agriculture to review Members' notifications under the *Agreement on Agriculture*. Thus, the "subsequent practice" of the parties following the Uruguay Round sustains Korea's position on this point of interpretation. Korea also believes that its position is supported by the manner in which the United States and Australia treated this issue in their first submissions to the Panel.

3. *Dual Retail System*

(a) Article III:4 of the GATT 1994

16. To Korea, the Panel fundamentally misinterpreted and misapplied Article III:4 of the GATT 1994 when it concluded that the dual retail system maintained by Korea is inconsistent with that provision. Article III:4 requires that WTO Members provide equal conditions of competition to both domestic and foreign like products. Article III:4 is an "obligation of result": the result that must be achieved is "no less favourable treatment for foreign goods". The particular method of achieving this result is irrelevant. Article III:4 neither imposes nor prohibits any particular means that Members employ to provide equal conditions of competition. According to Korea, its dual retail system does provide "no less favourable treatment to foreign goods", and, therefore, achieves the result required by Article III:4. The Panel erroneously concluded that the dual retail system "constitutes in itself differential treatment."

17. Korea submits that a proper analysis of Korea's obligation under Article III:4 requires review of both *de jure* and *de facto* discrimination. The dual retail system does not amount to either *de jure* or *de facto* discrimination. With regard to *de jure* discrimination, Korea's dual retail system assures perfect regulatory symmetry between imports and domestic products. Imported beef is sold only in

---

[10] Done at Vienna, 23 May 1969, 1155 U.N.T.S. 331; 8 International Legal Materials 679.

stores that choose to sell imported beef, and domestic beef is sold only in stores choosing to sell domestic beef. In addition, there is total freedom on the part of retailers to switch from one category of shops to the other. Thus, the Panel failed to demonstrate that there is any discrimination "demonstrated on the basis of the words of the relevant legislation, regulation or other legal instrument," the standard for a finding of *de jure* discrimination.

18. To demonstrate the presence or absence of *de facto* discrimination, the Panel should have undertaken an analysis of the market as part of an examination of the "total configuration of the facts". Instead, the Panel resorted to "speculation". An examination of the facts of the Korean beef market demonstrates that imported and domestic goods experience equal competitive conditions. The absence of such a factual analysis means that the Panel's finding on the dual retail system under Article III:4 is in error.

19. Korea also argues that the Panel erred in finding the display sign requirement to be inconsistent with Article III:4. The first ground offered by the Panel is that the display sign requirement would necessarily be inconsistent with Article III:4 since the dual retail system had already been found to be inconsistent. However, the Panel itself stated that the display sign requirement is a related measure "which the Panel addresses separately in Section 3 thereinafter." In other words, the Panel did not include the display sign requirement in its review of the dual retail system.

20. The second ground cited by the Panel is that the display sign requirement goes beyond the indication of origin of goods. Quoting from a 1956 Working Party Report, the Panel argues that such requirements are inconsistent with Article III:4 of the GATT. To Korea, the legal status of this report is unclear. The language of the report suggests that it was not intended to be binding or to provide an authoritative interpretation of the GATT.

(b) Article XX(d) of the GATT 1994

21. Should the Appellate Body disagree with Korea's claim that the dual retail system is consistent with Article III:4, then Korea submits that the Panel erred in ruling that the dual retail system was not justified under Article XX(d) of the GATT 1994.

22. The Panel found that Korea did not apply a dual retail system for other products in respect of which fraudulent sales have occurred. According to the Panel, such failure was evidence that the dual retail system was not "necessary to secure compliance with laws or regulations which are not inconsistent with the provisions of this Agreement" under Article XX(d). Korea submits that to decide whether a particular measure is necessary under Article XX(d), panels must simply examine whether another means exists which is less restrictive than the one used, and which can reach the objective sought. Consistency among regulations applicable to different products is irrelevant for establishing whether the means chosen by a WTO Member is necessary to achieve the objective of the regulation.

23. Furthermore, the Panel, in analyzing alternative, less restrictive means, did not take into account the level of enforcement sought. Korea's goal is not simply the "reduction or limitation" of deceptive practices, but their "elimination". The Panel considered four less trade-restrictive alternatives, which are investigations, fines, record-keeping and policing. In view of the fact that all four alternatives already comprise a package of policy tools used by Korea, along with the dual retail system, the Panel should have examined the facts to see whether, if the dual retail system were withdrawn, Korea's regulatory goal of the *elimination* of deceptive practices would be satisfied. Instead, the Panel narrowly focused its review on whether the less restrictive option is reasonably available. The Panel failed to link the means of implementation used to the objective sought.

24. Korea's dual retail system satisfies the requirements of the introductory clause of Article XX of the GATT 1994 as well. As the Appellate Body has held, the introductory clause of Article XX is concerned with the "even-handedness" underlying the application of national legislation. In other words, national legislation must be applied "even-handedly" between and among trading partners. Korea's dual retail system does not differentiate between Korea's trading partners. In fact, the dual retail system imposes, in practice, a much heavier burden on domestic beef producers.

25. Furthermore, in Korea's view, the display sign requirement is justified under Article XX(d) of the GATT 1994 as it is "necessary to secure compliance with laws or regulations which are not inconsistent with the provisions of this Agreement". To require shop-owners to display a sign that their store engages in selling imported beef imposes a "proportional burden" in view of the objective sought. Korea considered an alternative measure, but it would not have achieved Korea's objective.

26. Finally, Korea argues that the Panel failed to examine whether the display sign requirement was justified under Article XX(d) of the GATT 1994. The Panel did not explain its failure to examine the display sign requirement under Article XX(d), despite the fact that Korea had made clear that its Article XX defense extended to the display sign requirement as well. Korea submits that, were the Appellate Body to complete the analysis left undone by the Panel, the Appellate Body will find that the display sign requirement is fully justified under Article XX.

B. *Australia – Appellee*

1. *Terms of Reference*

27. Australia considers that Korea's claim that the Panel ruled outside its terms of reference in making findings as to the commitment levels and the AMS calculation methodology used by Korea to calculate the Current AMS, is unfounded. In Australia's view, the Panel correctly ruled that Australia's panel request meets the requirements of Article 6.2 of the DSU because Australia identi-

fied the specific measures at issue and provided a brief summary of the legal basis of the complaint sufficient to present the problem clearly.

28. In respect of the commitment levels, Australia argues that as Articles 3, 6 and 7 of the *Agreement on Agriculture* specifically refer to a Member's Schedule, consideration of Korea's commitment levels contained in Part IV, Section I of Korea's Schedule was within the Panel's terms of reference. A determination as to which of Korea's two sets of commitment levels constituted the figures against which its Current Total AMS should be compared was necessary to the Panel's legal examination of claims under Articles 3, 6 and 7 of the *Agreement on Agriculture*.

29. With regard to the AMS calculation methodology, Australia submits that the Panel took into account the linkages between the obligations contained in Articles 3, 6 and 7 of the *Agreement on Agriculture* and the relevant definitions contained in Article 1 of that Agreement, which include specific reference to methodologies contained in Annex 3. The Panel correctly concluded that it could not assess whether Korea had met its obligations under Articles 3, 6 and 7 without examining the calculation prescriptions for AMS contained in Annex 3.

30. Furthermore, Australia contends that Korea has failed to show any prejudice arising from a deficiency in Australia's request for a panel. Korea appears to have been informed sufficiently well of the claims being made to prepare a defence. Korea seems to have understood the nature of the legal claims sufficiently well for the purposes of its first submission, in which it argued at length that its calculation methodology was in fact consistent with the *Agreement on Agriculture*. It was not until the final meeting with the Panel that Korea claimed that its ability to defend itself had been prejudiced. Korea has also not shown that third parties were prejudiced.

2. *Domestic Support under the Agreement on Agriculture*

31. Australia submits that Korea's argument, that the Panel's interpretation of Articles 1(a)(ii) and 1(h)(ii) of the *Agreement on Agriculture* is unfair, illogical and results in inappropriate comparisons between a WTO Member's reduction commitments and support provided, is without substance. Korea's arguments evidence a misunderstanding of the concepts of Current AMS, Current Total AMS and Annual and Final Bound Reduction Commitments, as defined in the *Agreement on Agriculture*. Australia states that the two figures involved in the comparison will not necessarily be based on the same product mix, as the categories of products that are subsidized may change from year to year.

32. Australia considers that Korea's interpretation that Current AMS should be calculated based on the constituent data and methodology in Korea's Schedule would render the reference to Annex 3 in Articles 1(a)(ii) and 1(h)(ii) inutile. The Panel correctly found that for products where no support was included in the base period, there is no relevant "constituent data or methodology" in the tables of supporting material. Calculations based on Annex 3 are, therefore, mandatory.

33. With regard to the two sets of commitment levels in Korea's Schedule, Australia argues that a treaty interpreter is not required to give effect to treaty terms which are invalid. The Panel noted that Korea is the only WTO Member whose Part IV domestic support Schedule contains two sets of annual commitment levels, and that no provision of the *Agreement on Agriculture* authorizes such a departure from the norm or practice. For this reason, the Panel was under no obligation to give effect to the commitment level figures in brackets.

34. Australia also contends that the question of whether Korea's commitment levels were "public knowledge" is beyond the Appellate Body's mandate under Article 17.6 of the DSU to address "issues of law covered in the panel report and legal interpretations developed by the panel", as Korea did not present any such evidence to the Panel. In any case, public knowledge of a WTO-inconsistent Schedule commitment does not validate that commitment. Finally, Korea did not meet its burden of demonstrating that "subsequent practice" of WTO Members establishes the agreement of Members regarding the interpretation of Korea's Schedule.

3. *Dual Retail System*

(a) Article III:4 of the GATT 1994

35. In Australia's view, Korea's claim that proper analysis of its obligation under Article III:4 requires a two-step review of whether *de jure* or *de facto* discrimination is at issue is legally flawed and should be rejected. According to Australia, the legal standard imposed by the phrase "less favourable treatment" has long been settled: a panel must consider whether imported products are being accorded effective equality of competitive opportunities.

36. Australia contends that the Panel was correct when it found that the design and architecture of the dual retail system and related measures clearly provide less favourable treatment for imported beef. Australia states that stores selling imported beef face restrictions on volumes, price and types of beef available for sale, additional record-keeping, recording and signage requirements, and the commercial disadvantage of having to dismantle their current business in domestic beef if they wish to test the market for imported beef. Fundamentally, imported beef is prevented from being sold in the same stores, under the same conditions, as domestic beef. Thus, the claim by Korea that "regulatory symmetry" exists cannot be sustained.

37. In Australia's view, the Panel correctly concluded that the dual retail system constitutes, in and of itself, differential treatment. This differential treatment unavoidably results in imported beef being less favourably treated on the Korean market than like domestic products, and the segregation of imported beef provides the domestic product with a competitive advantage over the imported product.

(b) Article XX(d) of the GATT 1994

38. Australia claims the Panel was correct in finding that, even if the dual retail system had been instituted to prevent the fraudulent misrepresentation of imported beef as domestic beef, the measure was not "necessary" to accomplish that purpose, within the meaning of Article XX(d). The Panel explored the alternatives available to Korea, including alternatives currently applied to situations of alleged country of origin fraud involving other foodstuffs where price differentials prevail. This approach reflects the ordinary meaning of the term "necessary" that no reasonable alternative exists, as well as past GATT and WTO practice.

39. Australia submits that the burden is on Korea to demonstrate a *prima facie* case that the dual retail system falls within one of the exceptions of Article XX, and that it meets the requirements of the introductory clause. Korea has to demonstrate that there was no other alternative measure it could reasonably employ, which was WTO-consistent or less WTO-inconsistent, to secure compliance with the *Unfair Competition Act*. In the particular circumstances of the Korean market for imported beef, where it is otherwise impossible to distinguish between domestic and imported beef, where there is no dual wholesale system and where no record-keeping by stores selling domestic beef is required, it is impossible to conclude that the dual retail system has any serious impact on the prevention or elimination of fraud.

40. Even if the Panel erred in law in finding that the dual retail system did not qualify for the exception provided by Article XX(d), the Appellate Body has sufficient facts and legal argument to complete the Panel's inquiry. In doing so, the Appellate Body should find that the dual retail system does not meet the requirements of the introductory clause of Article XX. Australia considers relevant the fact that Korea only applies the dual retail system to imported beef, despite the fact that the problem of fraud also exists in relation to different types of beef and to a range of other agricultural products where a price differential exists between imported and domestic products. Furthermore, the dual retail system is not an isolated measure in an otherwise non-discriminatory environment for imported beef. Rather, the dual retail system is part of the regulatory framework for imported beef under which the importation, distribution and sale of imported beef is tightly regulated and heavily restricted by the Korean government, and substantial subsidies are provided to domestic producers, consistent with the government's stabilisation policies for domestic beef. Consideration of the dual retail system in this context reveals its protective purpose.

41. According to Australia, Korea is incorrect when it asserts that the Panel did not consider the display sign requirement in its review of the dual retail system. The Panel agreed with Korea that the sign requirement was "essentially ancillary to the dual retail system", and considered the two requirements together under Article XX(d). Thus, the Panel subsumed its findings related to the display sign requirement within its findings related to the dual retail system as a whole.

C. *United States – Appellee*

1. *Terms of Reference*

42. According to the United States, its panel request clearly states its claim that Korea has increased the level of domestic support for its cattle industry to the point that the total domestic support provided by Korea exceeds its AMS commitment levels. Based on Articles 3, 6 and 7 of the *Agreement on Agriculture*, Korea's current total domestic support is greater than the AMS commitment levels set out in the *Agreement on Agriculture*. All of the pertinent provisions of the *Agreement on Agriculture*, including Annex 3, had to be examined. The determination of the level of Current Total AMS, requires the application of the provisions of Annex 3, as Annex 3 is "intrinsic" to the calculation of the Current Total AMS.

43. Similarly, the commitment levels in Korea's Schedule also had to be examined. As the Current Total AMS was to be compared to Korea's commitment levels, it was first necessary to determine which set of figures in Korea's Schedule constituted Korea's commitment levels.

44. The United States notes that the Appellate Body has previously stated that a panel is obliged to consider provisions that are "directly linked" to the provisions cited in the panel request. In this case, Annex 3 and the commitment levels in Korea's Schedule are "directly linked" to the claim set out in the panel request, and therefore must be considered.

45. Furthermore, Korea suffered no prejudice on this issue as a result of the complaining parties' panel requests. In fact, Korea, in its first submission, submitted detailed explanations on how it had calculated its AMS for beef. Thus, Korea clearly understood the matter at issue.

2. *Domestic Support under the Agreement on Agriculture*

46. According to the United States, the Panel was correct in its finding that Korea's Current AMS for beef must be calculated in accordance with the requirements of Annex 3 of the *Agreement on Agriculture*. The specific language of Article 1(a)(ii) makes clear that the Current AMS calculation must be made in accordance with the provisions of Annex 3. While additional guidance is provided in this provision, to the effect that the "constituent data and methodology" in Korea's Schedule must be taken into account, this cannot be construed to nullify the express requirement that the Current AMS calculation be performed in accordance with Annex 3.

47. If Korea's Current AMS for beef is calculated correctly, it is more than *de minimis* under Article 6.4 of the *Agreement on Agriculture*, and must therefore be included in the calculations for Current Total AMS. When Current AMS for beef is included in Current Total AMS, Current Total AMS exceeds Korea's AMS commitment levels set out in its Schedule.

48. The United States contends that Korea, by including an alternative set of commitment levels in its Schedule, is trying to modify unilaterally the terms of the *Agreement on Agriculture* to substitute a domestic support commitment that is not in accordance with Annex 3. In effect, by claiming that the figures in brackets represent its commitment levels, Korea is attempting to inflate the amount of its annual AMS commitment level. The methodology used by Korea is not consistent with the obligations under the *Agreement on Agriculture*. The United States notes that a WTO Member may not, in its Schedule, act inconsistently with its WTO obligations. WTO Members may yield rights and grant benefits in their Schedules, but may not diminish their obligations.

49. Korea has argued that WTO Members knew of the contents of Korea's Schedule, and, therefore, they implicitly accepted the figures in the Schedule. The United States contends that this argument is untenable, for two reasons. First, in making this argument, Korea raises new factual allegations, which may not be addressed by the Appellate Body on appeal. Second, WTO Members did not waive their rights to dispute settlement with regard to other Members' Schedules as a result of the signing of the *WTO Agreement*.

3. *Dual Retail System*

(a) Article III:4 of the GATT 1994

50. According to the United States, the Panel correctly found that the dual retail system in itself constituted "less favourable treatment" inconsistent with Article III:4. Article III:4 is concerned with preserving the "effective equality of opportunities" for imported products. With regard to the dual retail system, the notion of effective equality of opportunities means that there must be a possibility for imported beef to be physically present with "like" domestic beef at the point of sale to the consumer. By excluding imported beef from the existing retail system for domestic beef, the dual retail system limits the potential market opportunities for imported beef. Since imported beef does not enjoy the same competitive opportunity to be sold in the same manner and in the same stores in which Korean beef is sold, it is treated less favourably than domestic beef.

51. The United States argues that Korea's defense of the dual retail system as providing "regulatory symmetry" between imported and domestic beef must fail. The Panel found that, in fact, the dual retail system, in conjunction with certain restrictions on imports, more onerous record-keeping requirements for imported beef sellers, and the display sign requirement imposed on imported beef sellers, resulted in less favourable treatment for imported beef.

52. Furthermore, the United States contends, the Panel's additional conclusion that the dual retail system involves *de facto* discrimination against imported beef was also correct. The Panel noted the following factors as relevant: the separate store requirement limits the ability of consumers to make side-by-side comparisons of imported and domestic beef and to make purchasing decisions based on differences in quality, characteristics and prices of the respective products; im-

ported beef is segregated due to the obstacles confronted by a store owner who wishes to sell imported beef; and there are fewer imported than domestic beef stores. The Panel found that the segregation of domestic and imported beef provides domestic beef with a competitive advantage over the imported product. In the view of the United States, this finding of the Panel should be upheld.

53. Article 9 of the *Management Guideline* requires that imported beef stores display a sign indicating that the beef sold in the store is imported. According to the United States, given the undisputed difference in treatment resulting from Article 9 of the Guidelines, Korea bears the burden of demonstrating that the dual retail system does not result in less favourable treatment, and Korea has failed to meet its burden. The Panel's finding that the display sign requirement was "ancillary" to the dual retail system was accurate. The 1956 Working Party Report was simply invoked to "reinforce" the Panel's view, not as a basis for its finding.

(b) Article XX(d) of the GATT 1994

54. The United States argues that the Panel correctly concluded that Korea failed to sustain its burden of justifying its dual retail system under Article XX(d) of the GATT 1994. The Panel determined that in order to benefit from the Article XX(d) exception, Korea had to demonstrate that its dual retail regime: (1) was in place in order to "secure compliance" with laws or regulations that are themselves not inconsistent with the GATT 1994; (2) was "necessary" to secure compliance with those laws or regulations; and (3) was applied in conformity with the requirements of the introductory clause of Article XX. The Panel found that the dual retail system was in place in order to "secure compliance" with laws or regulations that are themselves not inconsistent with the GATT 1994, in particular, the *Unfair Competition Act*. However, the Panel found that Korea did not demonstrate that the dual retail system is "necessary" to secure compliance with Korea's *Unfair Competition Act*.

55. In particular, Korea failed to demonstrate that the WTO-consistent alternatives shown by the complaining parties to be available were inadequate to secure compliance with the *Unfair Competition Act* with regard to imported beef. The Panel found that Korea employed traditional and WTO-consistent means, such as inspections, investigations and prosecutions, to enforce the *Unfair Competition Act* with respect to other imported food products. The Panel regarded this as evidence that Korea could eliminate any fraud involving beef with the same measures.

56. The United States contends that, contrary to Korea's claims, the Panel did not establish a "consistency" standard requiring that uniform measures be used to secure compliance. Rather, the Panel properly examined the enforcement practices used generally by Korea to obtain compliance with the *Unfair Competition Act* to determine whether means other than the dual retail system were reasonably available. Korea's practice with regard to other products was simply one factor to be taken into account as part of this analysis.

57. In addition, the United States argues that if the Appellate Body finds Korea's dual retail system to be "necessary" in terms of Article XX(d), Korea still cannot benefit from the Article XX exception, as Korea has failed to demonstrate that the dual retail system was designed to "secure compliance" with the *Unfair Competition Act*. The dual retail system does not prevent actions that would be illegal under the provisions of the *Unfair Competition Act* relating to fair trade practices. At most, the dual retail system serves the same objectives as the *Unfair Competition Act*.

58. The United States also submits that the dual retail system does not satisfy the requirements of the introductory clause of Article XX. For reasons of judicial economy, the Panel did not consider this issue. However, if the Appellate Body were to reverse the Panel's finding regarding whether the dual retail system is "necessary" to secure compliance with the *Unfair Competition Act*, the Appellate Body should then complete the legal analysis and find that the dual retail system does not satisfy the requirements of the introductory clause, as that system constitutes "unjustifiable discrimination" within the meaning of the introductory clause.

59. Korea criticizes the Panel for not separately addressing Korea's assertion that the display sign requirement is entitled to an exception under Article XX(d). However, the Panel concluded that the display sign requirement is ancillary to the separate store requirement, and therefore is subject to the same analysis and legal conclusions. Thus, in the view of the United States, the Panel's examination of the dual retail system under Article XX(d) is pertinent to both the separate store requirement and to the display sign requirement.

60. Finally, the United States argues, it was for Korea to demonstrate that the display sign requirement was justified under Article XX(d). However, Korea offered no evidence or reasoning to support a finding that the display sign requirement is independently necessary to secure compliance with the *Unfair Competition Act*.

D. *Arguments of the Third Participants*

1. *Canada*

(a) Dual Retail System

(i) Article III:4 of the GATT 1994

61. Canada agrees with the Panel's finding that the dual retail system constitutes in itself differential treatment which leads to "less favourable treatment" for imported products under the terms of Article III:4 of the GATT 1994. The dual retail system reduces "direct competition" between imported and domestic beef. In effect, only domestic beef can compete directly against other domestic beef. In these circumstances, imported beef does not benefit from "equal conditions of competition" as compared to domestic beef.

62. Canada supports the Panel's finding that the display sign requirement is "ancillary" to the dual retail system, and thus is also inconsistent with Article

III:4 of the GATT 1994. The measure would be inconsistent even if it existed independently of the dual retail system, as it treats imported beef differently than domestic beef, in contravention of Article III:4.

(ii) Article XX(d) of the GATT 1994

63. Canada also agrees with the Panel's finding with regard to Article XX(d).

2. *New Zealand*

(a) Terms of Reference

64. In New Zealand's view, it is within the Panel's terms of reference to examine the calculation methodology of AMS in order to determine whether Korea's Current Total AMS exceeds its commitment levels, in violation of Articles 3, 6 and 7 of the *Agreement on Agriculture*. Although Annex 3 of the *Agreement on Agriculture* is not specifically referred to in the complaining parties' panel requests in this dispute, Article 6 of the *Agreement on Agriculture*, which is referred to in the panel requests, defines AMS by reference to Article 1. Article 1, in turn, refers to the calculation of AMS in terms of Annex 3. Thus, the provisions of Annex 3 are necessary to determine whether Korea has met its domestic support commitments under Articles 3, 6 and 7.

65. Furthermore, the complaining parties have not made a separate claim regarding Annex 3. Rather, the claim they have made is under Articles 3, 6 and 7 of the *Agreement on Agriculture*, and the references to Annex 3 are simply arguments in support of this claim. Since the claim under Articles 3, 6 and 7 of the *Agreement on Agriculture* is within the Panel's terms of reference, arguments in support of that claim are within the terms of reference as well.

66. New Zealand also argues that Korea has failed to demonstrate that it has been prejudiced by the omission of a reference to Annex 3 in the panel request. The calculation methods set out in Annex 3 are linked to Articles 3, 6 and 7 of the *Agreement on Agriculture*. New Zealand, as a third party to the dispute, was able to determine the measure and claims at issue and respond accordingly based on the reference in the panel request to "domestic support". Korea has not demonstrated that it could not do the same.

67. Finally, New Zealand contends that Korea failed to bring its procedural objections before the Panel in a timely manner.

(b) Domestic Support under the *Agreement on Agriculture*

68. New Zealand notes that, according to Article 1(a)(ii) of the *Agreement on Agriculture*, the AMS is to be calculated "in accordance with" Annex 3, but "taking into account" the constituent data and methodology in the supporting tables in a Member's Schedule. Thus, a Member is to calculate the AMS according to An-

nex 3, but may also use the relevant and applicable constituent data and methodology set out in the supporting tables of its Schedule. However, resort to such data and methodology does not absolve a Member of the obligation of correctly calculating the AMS in a manner consistent with Annex 3.

69. New Zealand further submits that a Member can only take into account the constituent data and methodology where it exists. As there was no data or methodology for beef set out in the supporting tables of Part IV of Korea's Schedule, the Panel was correct to calculate AMS by relying on Annex 3 exclusively.

70. Finally, New Zealand argues that AMS calculations under Annex 3 are based on "eligible" production, as required by that provision. Thus, the argument of Korea that "actual" purchases are properly the basis of its AMS calculation should be rejected.

(c) Dual Retail system

(i) Article III:4 of the GATT 1994

71. New Zealand submits that the term "less favourable treatment" under Article III:4 requires that imported and domestic goods receive "effective equality of opportunities". New Zealand supports the Panel's finding that, in the circumstances of this case, Korea's dual retail system for beef results in competitive disadvantages for imported beef, as imported beef is denied the opportunity to compete in the framework of an integrated market. As the Panel concluded, the existence of a dual retail system, in circumstances where there is an extensive existing retail system, in itself constitutes a violation of Article III:4.

72. Furthermore, New Zealand agrees with the Panel's finding that the display sign requirement, being ancillary to the dual retail system, is also inconsistent with Article III:4. While the Panel chose to consider this aspect of the dual retail system separately, it is nevertheless one of the components of the dual retail system.

(ii) Article XX(d) of the GATT 1994

73. New Zealand supports the Panel's finding that Korea failed to show that the dual retail system was "necessary" within the meaning of Article XX(d) to accomplish Korea's desired level of fraud prevention. As stated by the Panel, practices used in other sectors to address deceptive practices are relevant for a determination of whether certain practices are "necessary" in the beef sector.

74. New Zealand also contends that the dual retail system is not consistent with the requirements of the introductory clause of Article XX. The dual retail system enables the Korean Government to protect Korea's domestic beef producers from import competition by limiting the terms on which imported products may be sold in the market, and therefore constitutes a means of arbitrary or unjustifiable discrimination between countries where the same conditions prevail, or

a disguised restriction on international trade, within the meaning of the introductory clause of Article XX.

III. ISSUES RAISED IN THIS APPEAL

75. The issues raised in this appeal are the following:

(a) whether examination of Korea's Schedule LX and Annex 3 of the *Agreement on Agriculture* was within the Panel's terms of reference;

(b) whether the Panel erred in calculating Korea's Current AMS for beef based on Annex 3 of the *Agreement on Agriculture*, and whether the resulting Current Total AMS exceeded Korea's AMS commitment levels for 1997 and 1998;

(c) whether the "dual retail system", which requires the sale of imported beef in specialized stores, was inconsistent with Article III:4 of the GATT 1994; and

(d) whether the "dual retail system", if inconsistent with Article III:4 of the GATT 1994, can nevertheless be justified under Article XX(d).

IV. TERMS OF REFERENCE

76. Before the Panel, Korea argued that its Schedule LX is not mentioned in the complaining parties' panel requests and, therefore, no violation can be claimed with regard to the Schedule.[11] Korea further contended that the panel requests were insufficiently detailed and specific to encompass the complaining parties' claims based on Annex 3 of the *Agreement on Agriculture*.[12]

77. The Panel held that, when examining claims regarding Articles 3, 6 and 7 of the *Agreement on Agriculture*, "its terms of reference require it to examine Korea's Schedule LX to assess whether its domestic support in 1997 and 1998 exceeded the reduction commitments contained in its Schedule"[13], and that "its assessment of the compatibility of Korea's domestic support with Articles 3, 6 and 7 requires that the Panel compares the effective support provided by Korea as determined using the calculation parameters of Annex 3."[14] Therefore, an examination of Korea's Schedule LX and Annex 3 of the *Agreement on Agriculture* for this purpose was not outside the Panel's terms of reference.

---

11 Panel Report, para. 787.

12 *Ibid.*

13 *Ibid.*, para. 803.

14 *Ibid.*, para. 815.

78. On appeal, Korea argues that the Panel erred by ruling on two claims that were outside of its terms of reference. In particular, Korea refers to the Panel's finding as to which set of numbers in its Schedule LX constitutes Korea's levels of commitment[15]; and to the Panel's finding that Korea's methodology for calculating Current Aggregate Measurement of Support ("AMS") for beef was not consistent with the methodology provided in Annex 3 of the *Agreement on Agriculture.*[16]

79. In this dispute, the Panel's terms of reference were defined as follows:

> To examine, in the light of the relevant provisions of the covered agreements cited by the United States in document WT/DS/161/5 and by Australia in document WT/DS/169/5, the matter referred to the DSB by the United States and Australia in those documents and to make such findings as will assist the DSB in making the recommendations or in giving the rulings provided for in those agreements.[17]

Thus, the Panel's terms of reference required it to examine the "matter" referred to the DSB by the complaining parties in the requests for the establishment of a panel by the United States and Australia, respectively.[18] The "matter" referred to the DSB is the set of claims made in these requests..[19]

80. In its panel request, Australia stated, in respect of Korea's agricultural domestic support, that:

> Korea has also increased the level of domestic support for its cattle industry in amounts which result in the total domestic support provided by Korea exceeding its Aggregate Measurement of Support (AMS) under the Agreement on Agriculture.

Australia went on to state that Korea was acting inconsistently with obligations under, *inter alia*, Articles 3, 6 and 7 of the *Agreement on Agriculture.*

81. The United States, in its panel request, stated, in very similar terms:

> At the same time, Korea has increased the level of domestic support for its cattle industry to the point that the total domestic support provided by Korea exceeds its Aggregate Measurement of Support (AMS) under the Agreement on Agriculture.

The United States also referred to Korea's measures as being inconsistent with, *inter alia*, Articles 3, 6, and 7 of the *Agreement on Agriculture.*

---

15 Korea's appellant's submission, paras. 15-25.

16 *Ibid.*, paras. 65-70.

17 WT/DS161/6, WT/DS169/6; see also Article 7.1 of the DSU.

18 WT/DS161/5, WT/DS169/5.

19 See Appellate Body Report, *Brazil – Measures Affecting Desiccated Coconut* ("*Brazil – Desiccated Coconut*"),WT/DS22/AB/R, adopted 20 March 1997, DSR 1997:I, 167, at 186; Appellate Body Report, *Guatemala – Anti-Dumping Investigation Regarding Portland Cement from Mexico*, WT/DS60/AB/R, adopted 25 November 1998, DSR 1998:IX, 3767, para. 72.

82. Thus, the claim made by both complaining parties was that Korea's domestic support for its cattle industry had increased to the point that Korea exceeded its AMS commitment levels for certain years, in contravention of Articles 3, 6 and 7 of the *Agreement on Agriculture*.

83. With respect to Korea's claim that the Panel acted outside its terms of reference in examining the "commitment levels" in Korea's Schedule, the following paragraphs of Articles 3 and 6 of the *Agreement on Agriculture* are of particular importance. Article 3.2 obligates Members not to exceed the support levels they had specified in their Schedules:

> Subject to the provisions of Article 6, a *Member shall not provide support* in favour of domestic producers in excess of the *commitment levels specified in Section I of Part IV of its Schedule*. (emphasis added)

Article 6.3 in turn states:

> A Member shall be considered to be in compliance with its domestic support reduction commitments in any year in which *its domestic support* in favour of agricultural producers expressed in terms of Current Total AMS *does not exceed* the corresponding *annual or final bound commitment level specified in Part IV of the Member's Schedule*. (emphasis added)

Articles 3.2 and 6.3 both refer explicitly to the "commitment level" specified in Part IV of a Member's Schedule. In order to make a finding on the complaining parties' claim, the Panel had no choice but to determine the appropriate "commitment levels" in Korea's Schedule.

84. With respect to Korea's claim[20] that the Panel acted outside its terms of reference in examining Annex 3 of the *Agreement on Agriculture*, we note that Article 6.4 provides:

> (a) A Member shall not be required to include in the calculation of its Current Total AMS and shall not be required to reduce:
>
> (i) product-specific domestic support which would otherwise be required to be included in a Member's calculation of its Current AMS where such support does not exceed 5 per cent of that Member's total value of production of a basic agricultural product during the relevant year;
>
> ...
>
> (b) For developing country Members, the *de minimis* percentage under this paragraph shall be 10 per cent.

---

20 *Supra*, para. 78.

Article 7.2(a) states:

> Any domestic support measure in favour of agricultural producers, including any modification to such measure, and any measure that is subsequently introduced that cannot be shown to satisfy the criteria in Annex 2 to this Agreement or to be exempt from reduction by reason of any other provision of this Agreement shall be included in the Member's calculation of its Current Total AMS.

Both Articles 6 and 7, claimed by the complaining parties to have been violated by Korea, refer explicitly to Current AMS and/or Current Total AMS.

85. AMS and Total AMS are defined in Article 1 of the *Agreement on Agriculture*, entitled "Definition of Terms". According to Article 1(a)

> "*Aggregate Measurement of Support*" and "*AMS*" mean the annual level of support, expressed in monetary terms, provided for an agricultural product in favour of the producers of the basic agricultural product ... which is:
>
> ...
>
> (ii) with respect to support provided during any year of the implementation period and thereafter, *calculated in accordance with the provisions of Annex 3 of this Agreement* and taking into account the constituent data and methodology used in the tables of supporting material incorporated by reference in Part IV of the Member's Schedule; (emphasis added)

According to Article 1(h)

> "*Total Aggregate Measurement of Support*" and "*Total AMS*" mean the sum of all domestic support provided in favour of agricultural producers, calculated as the sum of all aggregate measurements of support for basic agricultural products, ... which is:
>
> ...
>
> (ii) with respect to the level of support actually provided during any year of the implementation period and thereafter (i.e. the "Current Total AMS"), *calculated in accordance with the provisions of this Agreement*, including Article 6, and with the constituent data and methodology used in the tables of supporting material incorporated by reference in Part IV of the Member's Schedule; (emphasis added)

86. While Article 1(h)(ii) uses the terms "provisions of this Agreement", Article 1(a)(ii) is more specific and refers precisely to "*the provisions of Annex 3 of this Agreement*". Annex 3 is entitled "Domestic Support: Calculation of Aggregate Measurement of Support". Through the definitions set out in Article 1, Annex 3 thus becomes part of Articles 6 and 7. In examining the claims under Articles 3, 6 and 7, the Panel, therefore, had to examine the terms of Annex 3 as well. The Panel had to calculate Current AMS for beef "*in accordance with the provi-*

sions of Annex 3 ... and taking into account the constituent data and methodology ..." to determine whether Current AMS for beef was to be included in Current Total AMS. Thus, in order to reach a finding on the complaining parties' claim, the Panel in this case had to ascertain the appropriate "commitment levels" in Korea's Schedule, and had to calculate Current AMS for beef "in accordance with the provisions of Annex 3 ... " to determine whether Current AMS for beef was to be included in Current Total AMS.

87. It is true that, as Korea states, the panel requests in this dispute do not explicitly refer to the "commitment levels" in Korea's Schedule or to "Annex 3" of the *Agreement on Agriculture*. In *Argentina – Safeguard Measures on Imports of Footwear*, however, we held that the "terms of Article 4.2(c) of the *Agreement on Safeguards* expressly incorporate the provisions of Article 3" of that Agreement.[21] In that case, we stated that "we find it difficult to see how a panel could examine whether a Member had complied with Article 4.2(c) without also referring to the provisions of Article 3 of the *Agreement on Safeguards*."[22] We believe the same approach appropriately applies here. Although the "commitment levels" in Korea's Schedule and "Annex 3" of the *Agreement on Agriculture* were *not explicitly* referred to in the panel requests in this dispute, it is clear that Articles 3 and 6 of the *Agreement on Agriculture*, which *were referred* to in the panel requests, incorporate those terms, either directly through Articles 3.2 and 6.3, in the case of the "commitment levels", or indirectly through Article 1(a)(ii), in the case of "Annex 3". In our view, the commitment levels in Korea's Schedule and the provisions of Annex 3 were in effect referred to in the complaining parties' panel requests, and were, therefore, within the Panel's terms of reference.

88. It is useful to add that, in deciding which set of figures in Korea's Schedule constituted the true and effective commitment levels of Korea and in determining how Current AMS should be calculated under Annex 3, the Panel did not rule on a separate "claim".[23] Rather, it examined specific arguments related to the claim that Korea's domestic support exceeded its AMS commitment levels. In this context, it seems useful to recall our statement in *European Communities – Regime for the Importation, Sale and Distribution of Bananas* that:

> ... there is a significant difference between the *claims* identified in the request for the establishment of a panel, which establish the panel's terms of reference under Article 7 of the DSU, and the *arguments* supporting those claims, which are set out and progres-

21 Appellate Body Report, In *Argentina – Safeguard Measures on Imports of Footwear*, ("*Argentina – Footwear (EC)*"), WT/DS121/AB/R, adopted 12 January 2000, DSR 2000:I, 515. para. 74.

22 *Ibid.*

23 We note that in para. 800 of its Report, the Panel addressed the United States' "claim" that the Base Total AMS specified in Part IV, Section I of Korea's Schedule was initially miscalculated. The Panel considered that this "claim" was not properly before it. It concluded "that the only measure at issue is Korea's current domestic support for its beef industry in the context of Korea's scheduled commitment levels on domestic support under the *Agreement on Agriculture*". This conclusion of the Panel has not been appealed and is not before us.

> sively clarified in the first written submissions, the rebuttal submissions and the first and second panel meetings with the parties.[24]

The claim of the complaining parties was that Korea's domestic support for beef had increased to the point that this support exceeded Korea's commitment levels for certain specified years. This claim was made under Articles 3, 6 and 7 of the *Agreement on Agriculture*, as stated in both panel requests, and was clearly within the Panel's terms of reference. The Panel's examination of the commitment levels in Korea's Schedule and the calculation methodology in Annex 3 was carried out in the course of assessing arguments related to the complaining parties' claim.

89. For these reasons, we conclude that the Panel did not err in finding that the issue of which set of figures constituted Korea's commitment levels and the issue of whether Current AMS for beef must be calculated in accordance with Annex 3 were within its terms of reference.

V. DOMESTIC SUPPORT UNDER THE *AGREEMENT ON AGRICULTURE*

90. In the Panel proceedings, the complaining parties claimed that Korea provided domestic support to its beef industry, measured by Current AMS, in amounts which exceeded *de minimis* levels in 1997 and 1998 and which, therefore, were required to be included in Korea's calculation of Current Total AMS for those years. When domestic support for beef was included in Current Total AMS, they contended, Korea's Current Total AMS exceeded its commitment levels set out in Part IV of its Schedule for those years, contrary to Articles 3 and 6 of the *Agreement on Agriculture*.[25]

91. In addressing the above claim, the Panel ascertained both Korea's commitment levels for 1997 and 1998 and Korea's Current Total AMS for those years. With regard to Korea's commitment levels, the Panel noted that there were two sets of figures in Korea's Schedule in the column entitled "Annual and final bound commitments level 1995-2004", with one set in brackets and the other set not in brackets. The Panel concluded that the figures *not* in brackets constituted Korea's commitment levels.[26] With regard to Current Total AMS for 1997 and 1998, the Panel first examined whether Current AMS for beef exceeded the 10 per cent *de minimis* level set out in Article 6.4 of the *Agreement on Agriculture*. The Panel found that Current AMS for beef exceeded the *de minimis* level, and,

---

[24] *European Communities – Regime for the Importation, Sale and Distribution of Bananas* ("*EC – Bananas III*"), WT/DS27/AB/R, adopted 25 September 1997, DSR 1997:II, 591, para. 141.

[25] See Panel Report, paras. 49, 51 and 818. Australia argued that Korea exceeded its commitment levels only for 1997, whereas the United States argued that Korea exceeded its commitment levels for both 1997 and 1998.

[26] Panel Report, para. 821.

therefore, was required to be included in Current Total AMS, and that Korea's failure to include Current AMS for beef in Current Total AMS was inconsistent with Article 7.2(a) of the *Agreement on Agriculture*.[27] The Panel then compared Current Total AMS for 1997 and 1998 with Korea's commitment levels for those years, and concluded that Current Total AMS exceeded the commitment levels, contrary to Article 3.2 of the *Agreement on Agriculture*.[28]

92. On appeal, Korea argues that the Panel's conclusion that Korea exceeded its commitment levels for 1997 and 1998 was in error, for two reasons. First, Korea's view is that the Panel's finding that Korea's commitment levels, as set out in its Schedule, comprise the figures not in brackets is wrong. According to Korea, the commitment levels are, in fact, embodied in the figures in brackets, as Note 1 of Supporting Table 6 of Korea's Schedule makes clear.[29] Second, Korea contends that the Panel's conclusion that Current AMS for beef must be included in Current Total AMS was also wrong. According to Korea, the Panel mistakenly looked to Annex 3 of the *Agreement on Agriculture* in order to calculate the Current AMS for beef, failing to rely instead on the "constituent data and methodology" provided in Korea's Schedule, as required by Articles 1(a)(ii) and 1(h)(ii). Korea claims that its Current AMS for beef was properly calculated, on the basis of "constituent data and methodology" in its Schedule, and is less than the *de minimis* level established in Article 6.4 of the *Agreement on Agriculture*. Therefore, Korea argues, Current AMS for beef need not be included in Current Total AMS.[30]

93. The issue before us on appeal has two parts: did the Panel err in finding, firstly, that Korea failed to include Current AMS for beef in Current Total AMS, contrary to Article 7.2(a) of the *Agreement on Agriculture*, and in finding, secondly, that, contrary to Article 3.2 of the *Agreement on Agriculture*, Korea's Current Total AMS exceeds the commitment levels in Part IV of its Schedule for 1997 and 1998? In examining the component parts of this issue, it is necessary for us to ascertain two sets of figures: the figures which constitute Korea's commitment levels for 1997 and 1998, and the figures for Korea's Current Total AMS for 1997 and 1998. We turn first to an examination of Korea's commitment levels for 1997 and 1998.

A. *Korea's Commitment Levels for 1997 and 1998*

94. In Korea's Schedule LX, Part IV, Section I, entitled "Domestic Support: Total AMS Commitments", Korea has provided annual bound commitment levels for domestic support for agriculture for the period 1995-2004. The Schedule contains three columns, as follows:

---

27 *Ibid.*, para. 841.
28 *Ibid.*, para. 843.
29 Korea's appellant's submission, paras. 26-54.
30 *Ibid.*, paras. 79-90.

₩ = Korean Won

Base Total AMS	Annual and final bound commitments level 1995 - 2004			Relevant Supporting Tables and document reference
1	2			3
bil. ₩	bil. ₩			
1,718.6	1995:	1,695.74	(2,182.55) *Note 1	AGST/KOR (Supporting Table 4, 5, 6, 7, 8 and 10)
	1996:	1,672.90	(2,105.60)	
	1997:	1,650.03	(2,028.65)	
	1998:	1,627.17	(1,951.70)	
	1999:	1,604.32	(1,874.75)	
	2000:	1,581.46	(1,797.80)	
	2001:	1,558.60	(1,720.85)	
	2002:	1,535.74	(1,643.90)	
	2003:	1,512.89	(1,566.95)	
	2004:	1,490.00	(1,490.00)	

*Note 1: Refer to Note 1 of Supporting Table 6 about the numbers in parentheses.

Korea's commitment levels are in Column 2, entitled "Annual and final bound commitments level 1995-2004". This column contains two sets of figures pertaining to the years 1995-2004: one set in brackets, and one set not in brackets.

95. In its findings, the Panel referred to part of Korea's Schedule. In particular, the Panel referred to the figures in Column 1 and Column 2. However, the Panel did not refer to "* Note 1" in Column 2, nor to the explanatory information set out in Note 1, and did not reprint Column 3.[31] The Panel concluded that the set of figures not in brackets constitutes Korea's commitment levels. In support of its conclusion, the Panel noted that "the unbracketed figures in Korea's Schedule are derived from, and directly linked to, the 'Base Total AMS'". By contrast, the figures in the column with brackets "bear no such relationship to the specified 'Base Total AMS' of 1,718.60 billion won."[32] Therefore, Korea's commitment level for 1997 is 1,650.03 billion won, while the commitment level for 1998 is 1,627.17 billion won.[33] On appeal, Korea argues that the Panel's conclusion was in error.[34]

96. Examining this issue requires us to interpret Korea's Schedule. At the outset, we note, as we have previously stated in *European Communities – Customs Classification of Certain Computer Equipment*, that:

> A Schedule is ... an integral part of the GATT 1994 ... . Therefore, the concessions provided for in that schedule are part of the

[31] Panel Report, para. 820.

[32] *Ibid.*, para. 822.

[33] See Panel Report, para. 843.

[34] Korea's appellant's submission, paras. 26-54.

> terms of the treaty. As such, the only rules which may be applied in interpreting the meaning of a concession are the general rules of treaty interpretation set out in the *Vienna Convention*.[35]

Thus, we now examine Korea's Schedule in light of the rules of treaty interpretation. We begin with the ordinary meaning of the terms of the Schedule, in their context and in the light of the object and purpose of the treaty, in accordance with Article 31(1) of the *Vienna Convention*.

97. The Panel examined the two sets of figures provided by Korea, as well as the figure for "Base Total AMS". However, as is clear from the table in Korea's Schedule LX, Part IV, Section I, which has been reprinted in paragraph 94 above, the two sets of figures do not exist in isolation. Rather, to the right of the two sets of figures is the notation "* Note 1". At the bottom of Korea's Schedule, there is "* Note 1" which states: "Refer to Note 1 of Supporting Table 6 about the numbers in parentheses." The Panel, in its reasoning, referred to the set of figures in Column 1 and Column 2, but did *not* refer to "* Note 1", nor did it consider the terms of "* Note 1".[36] An examination of the ordinary meaning of the terms of a treaty must take into account *all* of those terms, and, accordingly, we proceed with an examination of Korea's Schedule, including Note 1 of Supporting Table 6. In our view, the Panel's examination of the "ordinary meaning" of Korea's Schedule was not done in accordance with the rules of interpretation of general international law as codified in the *Vienna Convention*.

98. Supporting Table 6 is entitled "Aggregate Measurements of Support: Market Price Support". This table provides the supporting figures for the commitment levels set out in Part IV, Section I of Korea's Schedule LX, that is, the figures used to calculate the commitment levels. Supporting figures are provided for rice, barley, soybean, maize (corn) and rape seeds. In respect of each product, the AMS for each of the years 1989-1991 is provided, along with an average AMS level for the years 1989-1991. For rice, AMS figures for 1993 are given as well. The figures for each product were combined in order to obtain a Base Total AMS figure which could then be used to determine commitment levels for the years 1995-2004.

99. Note 1 of Supporting Table 6 reads as follows:

> The AMS for rice has been calculated based on 1993 market price support instead of 1989-1991 average. The Final Bound Commitment level in 2004, however, is the level reduced by 13.3% from the 1989-1991 average Base Total AMS.[37]

35 Appellate Body Report, *European Communities – Customs Classification of Certain Computer Equipment ("EC – Computer Equipment")*, WT/DS62/AB/R, WT/DS67/AB/R, WT/DS68/AB/R, adopted 22 June 1998, DSR 1998:V, 1851, para. 84.

36 See Panel Report, paras. 820-823.

37 G/AG/AGST/KOR, p. 8.

As the Panel did not consider Note 1 at the bottom of Korea's Schedule LX, Part IV, Section I, it did not consider Note 1 of Supporting Table 6 either.

100. In interpreting Note 1 of Supporting Table 6, we look again at its ordinary meaning. The first sentence of this Note indicates that the AMS calculations for *rice* are based on 1993 figures, whereas for products other than rice, the AMS figures are based on the 1989-1991 average amounts.

101. The second sentence of Note 1 of Supporting Table 6 makes clear that the final bound commitment level for 2004 has been determined by reducing the 1989-1991 average Base Total AMS by 13.3 per cent.

102. We note that the use of the term "however" ordinarily indicates a contrast between two things, and lends support to Korea's position. The contrast here is the following: whereas the starting AMS amount is calculated using the 1989-1991 figures for products other than rice and the 1993 figures for rice, the Final Bound Commitment level for 2004 is calculated based on the 1989-1991 average Base Total AMS, which relies on 1989-1991 figures for *all* products, including rice. It appears to us that what Korea stated in Note 1 of Supporting Table 6 was this: the starting AMS commitment level for 1995 is determined by using AMS calculations relying on base years of 1989-1991 for all products except rice, and 1993 for rice; "however", the final target commitment level for 2004 is based on the Base Total AMS figure which was derived by using the base years 1989-1991 for *all* products. The starting AMS commitment level figure for 1995 (2182.55 billion won) was reduced in equal annual amounts over the period from 1995 to 2004 in order to reach the final target commitment level for 2004 (1490.00 billion won). The reduced commitment levels for each year over the period 1995-2004, the calculation of which has been described by Korea in Note 1 of Supporting Table 6, are set out in the figures in brackets. It follows from the wording of Korea's Schedule LX, Part IV, Section I, read together with Note 1 of the Supporting Table 6, that Korea's AMS commitment levels for 1995-2004 are not represented, as the Panel concluded, by the figures not in brackets, but, rather, as Korea contends, by the figures in brackets.

103. The above view is reflected in Korea's subsequent statements before the Committee on Agriculture. At a November 1996 Committee on Agriculture meeting, New Zealand asked Korea this question: "Noted that Korea's Schedule contains two sets of figures regarding annual and final bound commitment levels. Which set is accurate?" Korea responded as follows:

> *The figures in brackets correspond to Korea's real annual commitment level, using the 1993 base period for rice and the 1989-1991 base period for other products*, as indicated in the footnote of Korea's Schedule LX. The said calculation and annual commitment level of AMS were already reviewed and agreed upon by Member countries in March 1994. *The other set of figures corresponds to*

the annual commitment using the base period of 1989-1991 for all the products.[38] (emphasis added)

104. Furthermore, in its official annual Notifications to the Committee on Agriculture concerning domestic support commitments for 1995 to 1998, Korea made reference to its commitment level for the period in question. In each Notification, the figure Korea provided was the relevant commitment level from Korea's Schedule set out in the figures in brackets. Next to the AMS figure in each Notification is a note which says "See Note 1 of Supporting Table 6 in G/AG/AGST/KOR".[39]

105. For these reasons, we conclude that Korea's commitment levels in Part IV, Section I of its Schedule LX are denoted by the figures in the Column entitled "Annual and final bound commitments level 1995-2004" which are in brackets. Thus, Korea's commitment level is 2,028.65 billion won for the year 1997, and 1,951.70 billion won for the year 1998.

106. We turn next to an examination of Korea's Current Total AMS for 1997 and 1998, to determine whether Korea's Current Total AMS for these years exceeded its commitment levels for those same years.

B. *Korea's Current Total AMS for 1997 and 1998*

107. In its Notifications to the Committee on Agriculture for 1997 and 1998, Korea provided figures for the Current Total AMS for those years. Korea claimed that for 1997 it provided Current Total AMS of 1,936.95 billion won, and for 1998 it provided 1,562.77 billion won.[40] The complaining parties argue that Korea's Current Total AMS as provided in its Notifications was calculated improperly, as Korea did not include Current AMS for beef in its Current Total AMS. The United States contends that when Current AMS for beef is included in Current Total AMS, as required, Current Total AMS for both 1997 and 1998 exceeded Korea's commitment levels for 1997 and 1998, whereas Australia limits its contention to 1997.[41]

108. The Panel found that Korea's Current AMS for beef did exceed the *de minimis* level for 1997 and 1998, and, therefore, was required to be included in Current Total AMS, under Article 7.2(a) of the *Agreement on Agriculture*.[42] The Panel then compared Korea's Current Total AMS to Korea's commitment levels for 1997 and 1998, and concluded that Current Total AMS exceeded the commitment levels, contrary to Article 3.2 of the *Agreement on Agriculture*.[43]

---

38 G/AG/R/9, 17 January 1997.

39 See G/AG/N/KOR/24, 25 August 1999; G/AG/N/KOR/18, 16 September 1998; G/AG/N/KOR/14, 15 September 1997; G/AG/N/KOR/7, 18 November 1996.

40 See G/AG/N/KOR/24, 25 August 1999; G/AG/N/KOR/18, 16 September 1998.

41 See *supra*, footnote 25.

42 Panel Report, para. 841.

43 *Ibid.*, para. 843.

109. On appeal, Korea contends that the Panel's conclusion that Current AMS for beef must be included in Current Total AMS is incorrect. According to Korea, the Panel mistakenly looked to Annex 3 of the *Agreement on Agriculture* in order to calculate the Current AMS for beef, while failing to take into account the "constituent data and methodology" provided in Korea's Schedule, as required by Articles 1(a)(ii) and 1(h)(ii) of the *Agreement on Agriculture*. Korea claims that its Current AMS for beef was properly calculated in its Notifications to the Committee on Agriculture, based on the "constituent data and methodology" in its Schedule, and that consequently this Current AMS fell below the *de minimis* level established in Article 6.4 of the *Agreement on Agriculture*. Therefore, Korea argues, the Current AMS for beef need not be included in the Current Total AMS, and Current Total AMS was properly calculated in its Notifications.[44]

110. In examining this issue, we need to determine first whether Current AMS for beef for 1997 and 1998 must be included in Korea's Current Total AMS for those years. We recall that Article 6.4 of the *Agreement on Agriculture* states that:

> A Member shall not be required to include in the calculation of its Current Total AMS and shall not be required to reduce:
>
> (i) product-specific domestic support which would otherwise be required to be included in a Member's calculation of its Current AMS where such support does not exceed 5 per cent of that Member's total value of production of a basic agricultural product during the relevant year;
>
> ...

For developing country Members the *de minimis* percentage level under this paragraph is 10 per cent.[45] Thus, Korea's Current AMS for beef must be included in Current Total AMS only if the Current AMS for beef exceeds the 10 per cent *de minimis* requirement applicable in respect of developing country Members.

111. To determine whether Korea's Current AMS for beef exceeds 10 per cent of total value of beef production, we refer again to Article 1(a)(ii) of the *Agreement on Agriculture*, which defines Current AMS. Under this provision, Current AMS is to be

> calculated *in accordance with* the provisions of Annex 3 of this Agreement and *taking into account* the constituent data and methodology used in the tables of supporting material incorporated by reference in Part IV of the Member's Schedule; ... (emphasis added)

Article 1(a)(ii) contains two express requirements for calculating Current AMS. First, Current AMS is to be "calculated *in accordance with* the provisions of An-

44 Korea's appellant's submission, paras. 79-90.
45 Article 6.4(b) of the *Agreement on Agriculture*.

nex 3 of this Agreement". The ordinary meaning of "accordance" is "agreement, conformity, harmony".[46] Thus, Current AMS must be calculated in "conformity" with the provisions of Annex 3. Second, Article 1(a)(ii) provides that the calculation of Current AMS is to be made while "taking into account the constituent data and methodology used in the tables of supporting material incorporated by reference in Part IV of the Member's Schedule." "Take into account" is defined as "take into consideration, notice".[47] Thus, when Current AMS is calculated, the "constituent data and methodology" in a Member's Schedule must be "taken into account", that is, it must be "considered".[48]

112. Looking at the wording of Article 1(a)(ii) itself, it seems to us that this provision attributes higher priority to "the provisions of Annex 3" than to the "constituent data and methodology". From the viewpoint of ordinary meaning, the term "in accordance with" reflects a more rigorous standard than the term "taking into account".

113. We note, however, that the Panel did not base its reasoning on this apparent hierarchy as between "the provisions of Annex 3" and the "constituent data and methodology".[49] Instead, the Panel considered that where no support was included in the base period calculation for a given product, there is no "constituent data or methodology" to refer to, so that the only means available for calculating domestic support is that provided in Annex 3.[50] As beef had not been included in Supporting Table 6 of Korea's Schedule LX, Part IV, Section I, the Panel concluded that Annex 3 alone is applicable for the purposes of calculating current non-exempt support in respect of Korean beef.[51]

114. In the circumstances of the present case, it is not necessary to decide how a conflict between "the provisions of Annex 3" and the "constituent data and methodology used in the tables of supporting material incorporated by reference in Part IV of the Member's Schedule" would have to be resolved in principle. As the Panel has found, in this case, there simply are no constituent data and methodology for beef.[52] Assuming *arguendo* that one would be justified – in spite of the wording of Article 1(a)(ii) – to give priority to constituent data and method-

---

46 *The New Shorter Oxford English Dictionary*, (Clarendon Press, 1993), Vol. I, p. 15.

47 *Ibid.*

48 We note that this difference is not reflected in the wording of the definition of Current Total AMS in Article 1(h). Article 1(h)(ii) provides that Current Total AMS is to be calculated "in accordance with the provisions of this Agreement, including Article 6, *and* with the constituent data and methodology used in the tables of supporting material incorporated by reference in Part IV of the Member's Schedule". (emphasis added)

49 On the contrary, the Panel opines that the "constituent data and methodology" has an important role to play in ensuring that the calculation of support to any given product is calculated in subsequent years consistently with support calculated in the base period. Panel Report, para. 811.

50 *Ibid.*

51 *Ibid.*, para. 812.

52 *Ibid.* In other words, there is no *data* (product) in respect of which the *methodology* of Schedule LX of Korea (that is, the use of figures for the years 1989-1991) could be applied, in so far as beef is concerned.

ology used in the tables of supporting material over the guidance of Annex 3, for products entering into the calculation of the Base Total AMS, such a step would seem to us to be unwarranted in calculating Current AMS for a product which did *not* enter into the Base Total AMS calculation. We do not believe that the *Agreement on Agriculture* would sustain such an extrapolation. We, therefore, agree with the Panel that, in this case, Current AMS for beef has to be calculated in accordance with the provisions of Annex 3, and with these provisions alone.

115. Korea has argued that:

> National schedules on the reduction of subsidies in favour of agricultural products ... can be understood as multi-year equations. One side of the equation includes the commitment level for a given year, while the other side of the equation includes the actual AMS for the same year. Thus, for the equation to be meaningful, both sides of the equation should be based on the same sets of data and methodology. ... Using one methodology for commitment levels and another methodology for actual AMS undermines comparability between the two, and leads to unfair results.[53]

We believe that it is not necessary or appropriate to conceive of the pertinent provisions of the *Agreement on Agriculture* as establishing "multi-year equations". The treaty definitions of both AMS and Total AMS, set out in Articles 1(a) and 1(h) respectively, do provide a specific methodology for calculating Current AMS and Current Total AMS in respect of a particular year during the implementation period. However, with respect to the other side of a hypothetical equation, the relevant treaty provisions do *not* provide for any particular mode of calculation of the "Base Total AMS", from which figure the commitment levels for particular years of the implementation period are arithmetically derived. Article 1(a)(i) of the *Agreement on Agriculture* dealing with AMS states that "with respect to support provided during the base period", a treaty interpreter needs only to go to "the relevant tables of supporting material incorporated by reference *in Part IV of a Member's Schedule* ... ". (emphasis added) Similarly, Article 1(h)(i) dealing with Total AMS, states that "with respect to support provided during the base period (i.e., the 'Base Total AMS') and the maximum support permitted to be provided during any year of the implementation period or thereafter (i.e., the 'Annual and Final Bound Commitment Levels')", a treaty interpreter needs only to go to what is "*specified in Part IV of a Member's Schedule* ... ". (emphasis added) Thus, for purposes of determining whether a Member has exceeded its commitment levels, Base Total AMS, and the commitment levels resulting or derived therefrom, are not themselves formulae to be worked out, but simply absolute figures set out in the Schedule of the Member concerned. As a result, Current Total AMS which is calculated according to Annex 3, is compared

[53] Korea's appellant's submission, para. 63.

to the commitment level for a given year that is already specified as a given, absolute, figure in the Member's Schedule.

116. We examine next Annex 3, entitled: "Domestic Support: Calculation of Aggregate Measurement of Support". Paragraphs 8 and 9 of Annex 3 provide the following definition of "market price support", the particular form of domestic support at issue here:

> ... *market price support* shall be calculated using the gap between a fixed external reference price and the applied administered price multiplied by the *quantity of production eligible to receive* the applied administered price. Budgetary payments made to maintain this gap, such as buying-in or storage costs, shall not be included in the AMS.
>
> The *fixed external reference price shall be based on the years 1986 to 1988* and shall generally be the average f.o.b. unit value for the basic agricultural product concerned in a net exporting country and the average c.i.f. unit value for the basic agricultural product concerned in a net importing country in the base period. The fixed reference price may be adjusted for quality differences as necessary. (emphasis added)

Thus, under Annex 3, "market price support" is calculated by taking the difference between a fixed external reference price and the applied administered price, and multiplying that difference by "the quantity of *production eligible* to receive the applied administered price". (emphasis added) The fixed external reference price "shall be *based on the years 1986 to 1988*". (emphasis added)

117. The Panel found that in both 1997 and 1998 Korea miscalculated its fixed external reference price, contrary to Article 6 and paragraph 9 of Annex 3, by using a fixed external reference price based on data for 1989-1991. [54] Korea justifies this choice by invoking the "constituent data and methodology" used in its Supporting Table 6 for all products other than rice, i.e., for barley, soybean, maize (corn) and rape seeds. In Supporting Table 6, all these products use the period 1989-1991 for the fixed external reference price. [55]

118. We have already explained above that we share the Panel's view with respect to Korea's argument on "constituent data and methodology" used in the table of supporting material. We agree with the Panel that, in this case, Current AMS for beef has to be calculated in accordance with Annex 3. According to Annex 3, "[t]he fixed external reference price shall be based on the years 1986 to 1988". We, therefore, also agree with the Panel that in calculating the product specific AMS for beef for the years 1997 and 1998, Korea should have used an

54 Panel Report, para. 830.
55 Korea's appellant's submission, paras. 79-80.

external reference price based on data for 1986-1988, instead of data for 1989-1991.

119. The Panel found that, in calculating the Current AMS for beef for the years 1997 and 1998, Korea made a further mistake. In determining its market price support for beef, Korea used the quantity of Hanwoo cattle actually purchased. The Panel found that "[t]he actual quantity of purchases is not relevant in the calculation of market price support. Korea, by indicating its intent to purchase specified quantities, made them eligible to receive the applied administered price, and consequently affected and supported the price of all such products". [56]

120. We share the Panel's view that the words "production *eligible* to receive the applied administered price" in paragraph 8 of Annex 3 have a different meaning in ordinary usage from "production *actually purchased* ". The ordinary meaning of "eligible" is "fit or *entitled* to be chosen". [57] Thus, "production eligible" refers to production that is "fit or entitled" to be purchased rather than production that was actually purchased. In establishing its program for future market price support, a government is able to define and to limit "eligible" production. Production actually purchased may often be less than eligible production.

121. In the present case, Korea, in effect, declared the quantity of "eligible production" when it announced in January, 1997, that it would purchase 500 head per day of Hanwoo cattle above 500 kg within the 27 January to 31 December 1997 period, which would be 170,000 head of cattle for the 1997 calendar year. [58] That figure, under paragraph 8 of Annex 3, accordingly constitutes the quantity of "eligible production". While there may be nothing under the *Agreement on Agriculture* to prevent Korea from changing the quantity of "eligible production", Korea did not do so, so far as the record of this case shows. Korea instead simply purchased a lesser number of cattle by ceasing its purchases.

122. Korea argues that it is entitled to calculate market price support in 1997 and 1998 by using actual purchases, because it used actual purchases in its calculations in the tables of supporting material in its Schedule. We recall that we share the Panel's view that for beef, "constituent data and methodology" do not exist in the Schedule, as beef did not enter into the calculation of Korea's initial Base Total AMS. We, therefore, agree with the Panel's finding that Korea erred in calculating market price support in 1997 and 1998 by using the amount of production actually purchased, instead of production declared eligible to receive the applied administered price, according to the provisions of paragraph 8 of Annex 3.

123. Having reached the conclusion that Korea had miscalculated its market price support in 1997 and 1998, the Panel attempted to evaluate correctly Korea's Current AMS for beef. In doing so, the Panel stated that "[f]or reasons of clarity

---

[56] Panel Report, para. 831.

[57] *The Concise Oxford English Dictionary*, (Clarendon Press, 1995), p. 438.

[58] Panel Report, para. 834.

and simplicity", it would rely on market price support calculations submitted by New Zealand for Korea's Current AMS for beef.[59] Based on these calculations, the Panel found that Korea's AMS for beef had exceeded the 10 per cent *de minimis* threshold referred to in Article 6.4(b) of the *Agreement on Agriculture* in 1997 and 1998.[60]

124. We note that in calculating Korea's Current AMS for beef, New Zealand uses – like Korea – a fixed external reference price based on 1989-1991 data. As we have found above, the use of such an external reference price is incompatible with paragraph 9 of Annex 3, which requires an external reference price based on the years 1986-1988.

125. The Panel was aware of this incompatibility, but seemed to assume that New Zealand's reference to 1989-1991 data benefitted, rather than harmed, Korea.[61] This could be the case if the 1989-1991 data would result in a higher external reference price than the one prescribed by paragraph 9 of Annex 3, i.e., the external reference price based on the years 1986-1988. There is, however, no indication in the Panel Report of the level of the external reference price for the years 1986-1988. Furthermore, neither the Panel Report nor the Panel record contain any elements which might allow us to determine the level of such an external reference price.[62]

126. We, therefore, must reverse the Panel's finding that Korea exceeded the 10 per cent *de minimis* threshold of Current AMS for beef in 1997 and 1998, and the consequent finding that the failure to include Current AMS for beef in Current Total AMS in these years is inconsistent with Articles 6 and 7.2(a) of the *Agreement on Agriculture*.

127. As a consequence, we must also reverse the Panel's finding that, in 1997 and 1998, Korea's Current Total AMS exceeded Korea's commitment levels, as specified in Part IV, Section I of its Schedule, in violation of Article 3.2 of the *Agreement on Agriculture*.

---

[59] Panel Report, para. 838.

[60] *Ibid.*, para. 840.

[61] This seems to be the meaning of the words "inflating Korea's legitimate level of domestic support" in footnote 442 of the Panel Report which reads as follows:

> The Panel notes that for this recalculation of Korea's FERP, New Zealand even used 1989-1991 data (inflating Korea's legitimate level of domestic support), contrary to the Panel's conclusion that pursuant to Annex 3 a 1986-1988 FERP should have been employed.

[62] In *Australia – Measures Affecting the Importation of Salmon* we stated that where we have reversed a finding of a panel, we should attempt to complete a panel's legal analysis "to the extent possible on the basis of the factual findings of the Panel and/or of undisputed facts in the Panel record". Appellate Body Report, *Australia – Measures Affecting the Importation of Salmon* ("*Australia – Salmon*"), WT/DS18/AB/R, adopted 6 November 1998, DSR 1998:VIII, 3327, para. 118. See also, Appellate Body Report, *Canada – Certain Measures Affecting the Automotive Industry* ("*Canada – Autos*"), WT/DS139/AB/R, WT/DS142/AB/R, adopted 19 June 2000, DSR 2000:VI, 2995, para. 133.

128. We should, however, stress that, as there is insufficient information in the Panel record to allow determination of whether Current AMS for beef exceeded the *de minimis* threshold in 1997 and 1998, and, therefore, had to be included in Current Total AMS, we reach no conclusion as to whether or not Korea acted inconsistently with Articles 6 and 7.2(a) of the *Agreement on Agriculture*.

129. Furthermore, as a determination of Current Total AMS cannot be made without first ascertaining Current AMS for beef, no Current Total AMS can be calculated for 1997 and 1998. As a result, there is no basis on which we can reach a conclusion on the issue of whether or not Korea exceeded its commitment levels in Part IV of its Schedule for 1997 and 1998, contrary to Article 3.2 of the *Agreement on Agriculture*.

VI. DUAL RETAIL SYSTEM

A. *Article III:4 of the GATT 1994*

130. The Panel found that Korea's dual retail system for beef accords treatment less favourable to imported beef than to like Korean beef, and is, thus, inconsistent with Article III:4 of the GATT 1994. This finding was based on the Panel's view that any measure based exclusively on criteria relating to the origin of a product is inconsistent with Article III:4. [63] The finding was also based on the Panel's assessment of how the dual retail system modifies the conditions of competition between imported and like domestic beef in the Korean market. [64]

131. Korea argues on appeal that the dual retail system does not accord treatment less favourable to imported beef than to like domestic beef. For Korea, the dual retail system does not *on its face* violate Article III:4, since there is "perfect regulatory symmetry" in the separation of imported and domestic beef at the retail level, and there is "no regulatory barrier" which prevents traders from converting from one type of retail store to another. [65] Nor, Korea argues, does the dual retail system violate Article III:4 *de facto*, and the Panel's conclusion to the contrary was not based on a proper empirical analysis of the Korean beef market. [66]

132. Article III:4 of the GATT 1994 reads in relevant part:

> The products of the territory of any Member imported into the territory of any other Member shall be accorded *treatment no less favourable* than that accorded to like products of national origin in respect of all laws, regulations and requirements affecting their in-

---

63 Panel Report, para. 627.
64 *Ibid.*, paras. 631-637.
65 Korea's appellant's submission, paras. 119-126.
66 *Ibid.*, paras. 127-156.

> ternal sale, offering for sale, purchase, transportation, distribution or use. (emphasis added)

133. For a violation of Article III:4 to be established, three elements must be satisfied: that the imported and domestic products at issue are "like products"; that the measure at issue is a "law, regulation, or requirement affecting their internal sale, offering for sale, purchase, transportation, distribution, or use"; and that the imported products are accorded "less favourable" treatment than that accorded to like domestic products. Only the last element – "less favourable" treatment – is disputed by the parties and is at issue in this appeal.

134. The Panel began its analysis of the phrase "treatment no less favourable" by reviewing past GATT and WTO cases. It found that "treatment no less favourable" under Article III:4 requires that a Member accord to imported products "effective equality of opportunities" with like domestic products in respect of the application of laws, regulations and requirements.[67] The Panel concluded its review of the case law by stating:

> Any regulatory distinction that is based exclusively on criteria relating to the nationality or the origin of the products is incompatible with Article III and this conclusion can be reached even in the absence of any imports (as hypothetical imports can be used to reach this conclusion) confirming that there is no need to demonstrate the actual and specific trade effects of a measure for it to be found in violation of Article III. The object of Article III:4 is, thus, to guarantee effective market access to imported products and to ensure that the latter are offered the same market opportunities as domestic products.[68]

135. The Panel stated that "any regulatory distinction that is based exclusively on criteria relating to the nationality or origin" of products is incompatible with Article III:4. We observe, however, that Article III:4 requires only that a measure accord treatment to imported products that is "no less favourable" than that accorded to like domestic products. A measure that provides treatment to imported products that is *different* from that accorded to like domestic products is not necessarily inconsistent with Article III:4, as long as the treatment provided by the measure is "no less favourable". According "treatment no less favourable" means, as we have previously said, according *conditions of competition* no less favourable to the imported product than to the like domestic product. In *Japan – Taxes on Alcoholic Beverages*, we described the legal standard in Article III as follows:

> The broad and fundamental purpose of Article III is to avoid protectionism in the application of internal tax and regulatory measures. More specifically, the purpose of Article III "is to ensure that

67 Panel Report, para. 624.

68 *Ibid.*, para. 627. (footnotes omitted)

> internal measures 'not be applied to imported or domestic products so as to afford protection to domestic production'". Toward this end, Article III obliges Members of the WTO to provide *equality of competitive conditions* for imported products in relation to domestic products. "[T]he intention of the drafters of the Agreement was clearly to treat the imported products in the same way as the like domestic products once they had been cleared through customs. Otherwise indirect protection could be given". [69] (emphasis added)

136. This interpretation, which focuses on the *conditions of competition* between imported and domestic like products, implies that a measure according formally *different* treatment to imported products does not *per se*, that is, necessarily, violate Article III:4. In *United States – Section 337*, this point was persuasively made. In that case, the panel had to determine whether United States patent enforcement procedures, which were formally different for imported and for domestic products, violated Article III:4. That panel said:

> On the one hand, contracting parties may apply to imported products *different* formal legal requirements if doing so would accord imported products more favourable treatment. On the other hand, it also has to be recognised that there may be cases where the application of formally *identical* legal provisions would in practice accord less favourable treatment to imported products and a contracting party might thus have to apply different legal provisions to imported products to ensure that the treatment accorded them is in fact no less favourable. For these reasons, the mere fact that imported products are subject under Section 337 to legal provisions that are different from those applying to products of national origin is in itself not conclusive in establishing inconsistency with Article III:4. [70] (emphasis added)

137. A formal difference in treatment between imported and like domestic products is thus neither necessary, nor sufficient, to show a violation of Article III:4. Whether or not imported products are treated "less favourably" than like domestic products should be assessed instead by examining whether a measure

---

[69] Appellate Body Report, *Japan – Taxes on Alcoholic Beverages* ("*Japan – Alcoholic Beverages II*"), WT/DS8/AB/R, WT/DS10/AB/R, WT/DS11/AB/R, adopted 1 November 1996, DSR 1996:I, 97, at 109-110. The original passage contains footnotes. The second sentence is footnoted to *United States - Section 337 of the Tariff Act of 1930* ("*United States – Section 337*"), BISD 36S/345, para. 5.10. The third sentence is footnoted to *United States – Taxes on Petroleum and Certain Imported Substances*, BISD 34S/136, para. 5.1.9; and *Japan – Customs Duties, Taxes and Labelling Practices on Imported Wines and Alcoholic Beverages*, BISD 34S/83, para. 5.5(b). The fifth sentence is footnoted to *Italian Discrimination Against Imported Agricultural Machinery*, BISD 7S/60, para. 11.

[70] *United States – Section 337*, *supra*, footnote 69, para. 5.11.

modifies the *conditions of competition* in the relevant market to the detriment of imported products.

138. We conclude that the Panel erred in its general interpretation that "[a]ny regulatory distinction that is based exclusively on criteria relating to the nationality or the origin of the products is incompatible with Article III." [71]

139. The Panel went on, however, to examine the conditions of competition between imported and like domestic beef in the Korean market. The Panel gave several reasons why it believed that the dual retail system alters the conditions of competition in the Korean market in favour of domestic beef. First, it found that the dual retail system would "limit the possibility for consumers to compare imported and domestic products", and thereby "reduce opportunities for imported products to compete directly with domestic products". [72] Second, the Panel found that, under the dual retail system, "the only way an imported product can get on the shelves is if the retailer agrees to substitute it, not only for one but for all existing like domestic products." This disadvantage would be more serious when the market share of imports (as is the case with imported beef) is small. [73] Third, the Panel found that the dual retail system, by excluding imported beef from "the vast majority of sales outlets", limits the potential market opportunities for imported beef. This would apply particularly to products "consumed on a daily basis", like beef, where consumers may not be willing to "shop around". [74] Fourth, the Panel found that the dual retail system imposes more costs on the imported product, since the domestic product will tend to continue to be sold from existing retail stores, whereas imported beef will require new stores to be established. [75] Fifth, the Panel found that the dual retail system "encourages the perception that imported and domestic beef are different, when they are in fact like products belonging to the same market", which gives a competitive advantage to domestic beef, "based on criteria not related to the products themselves". [76] Sixth, the Panel found that the dual retail system "facilitates the maintenance of a price differential" to the advantage of domestic beef. [77]

140. On appeal, Korea argues that the Panel's analysis of the conditions of competition in the Korean market is seriously flawed, relying largely on speculation rather than on factual analysis. Korea maintains that the dual retail system does not deny consumers the possibility to make comparisons, and the numbers of outlets selling imported beef, as compared with outlets selling domestic beef, does not support the Panel's findings. Korea argues, furthermore, that the dual

---

71 Panel Report, para. 627.
72 *Ibid.*, para. 631.
73 *Ibid.*, para. 632.
74 Panel Report, para. 633.
75 *Ibid.*, para. 634.
76 *Ibid.*
77 *Ibid.*

retail system neither adds to the costs of, nor shelters high prices for, domestic beef.[78]

141. It will be seen below that we share the ultimate conclusion of the Panel in respect of the consistency of the dual retail system for beef with Article III:4 of the GATT 1994. Portions, however, of the Panel's analysis *en route* to that conclusion appear to us problematic. For instance, while limitation of the ability to compare visually two products, local and imported, at the point of sale may have resulted from the dual retail system, such limitation does not, in our view, necessarily reduce the opportunity for the imported product to compete "directly" or on "an equal footing" with the domestic product.[79] Again, even if we were to accept that the dual retail system "encourages" the perception of consumers that imported and domestic beef are "different", we do not think it has been demonstrated that such encouragement necessarily implies a competitive advantage for domestic beef.[80] Circumstances like limitation of "side-by-side" comparison and "encouragement" of consumer perceptions of "differences" may be simply incidental effects of the dual retail system without decisive implications for the issue of consistency with Article III:4.

142. We believe that a more direct, and perhaps simpler, approach to the dual retail system of Korea may be usefully followed in the present case. In the following paragraphs, we seek to focus on what appears to us to be the fundamental thrust and effect of the measure itself.

143. Korean law in effect requires the existence of two distinct retail distribution systems so far as beef is concerned: one system for the retail sale of domestic beef and another system for the retail sale of imported beef.[81] A small retailer (that is, a non-supermarket or non-department store) which is a "Specialized Imported Beef Store" may sell any meat *except domestic beef*; any other small retailer may sell any meat *except imported beef.*[82] A large retailer (that is, a supermarket or department store) may sell both imported and domestic beef, as long as the imported beef and domestic beef are sold in separate sales areas.[83] A retailer

---

78 Korea's appellant's submission, paras. 101, 127-156.

79 See Panel Report, para. 633.

80 *Ibid.*, para. 634.

81 The essential features of the Korean dual retail system for beef are found in the *Guidelines Concerning Registration and Operation of Specialized Imported Beef Stores,* (61550-81) 29 January 1990, modified on 15 March 1994; and the *Regulations Concerning Sales of Imported Beef,* (51550-100), modified on 27 March 1993, 7 April 1994, and 29 June 1998. On 1 October 1999, these two instruments were replaced by the *Management Guideline for Imported Beef,* (Ministry of Agriculture Notice 1999-67), which maintained, however, the basic principles of the dual retail system.

82 *Guidelines Concerning Registration and Operation of Specialized Imported Beef Stores* Art. 5(C); *Regulations Concerning Sales of Imported Beef,* Art. 14(5); *Management Guideline for Imported Beef,* Art. 15.

83 *Guidelines Concerning Registration and Operation of Specialized Imported Beef Stores,* Art. 3(A); *Management Guideline for Imported Beef,* Art. 9(5).

selling imported beef is required to display a sign reading "Specialized Imported Beef Store".[84]

144. Thus, the Korean measure formally separates the selling of imported beef and domestic beef. However, that formal separation, *in and of itself*, does not necessarily compel the conclusion that the treatment thus accorded to imported beef is less favourable than the treatment accorded to domestic beef.[85] To determine whether the treatment given to imported beef is less favourable than that given to domestic beef, we must, as earlier indicated, inquire into whether or not the Korean dual retail system for beef modifies the *conditions of competition* in the Korean beef market to the disadvantage of the imported product.

145. When beef was first imported into Korea in 1988, the new product simply entered into the pre-existing distribution system that had been handling domestic beef. The beef retail system was a unitary one, and the conditions of competition affecting the sale of beef were the same for both the domestic and the imported product. In 1990, Korea promulgated its dual retail system for beef.[86] Accordingly, the existing small retailers had to choose between, on the one hand, continuing to sell domestic beef and renouncing the sale of imported beef or, on the other hand, ceasing to sell domestic beef in order to be allowed to sell the imported product. Apparently, the vast majority of the small meat retailers chose the first option.[87] The result was the virtual exclusion of imported beef from the retail distribution channels through which domestic beef (and until then, imported beef, too) was distributed to Korean households and other consumers throughout the country. Accordingly, a new and separate retail system had to be established and gradually built from the ground up for bringing the imported product to the same households and other consumers if the imported product was to compete at all with the domestic product. Put in slightly different terms, the putting into legal effect of the dual retail system for beef meant, in direct practical effect, so far as imported beef was concerned, the sudden cutting off of access to the normal, that is, the previously existing, distribution outlets through which the domestic product continued to flow to consumers in the urban centers and countryside that make up the Korean national territory. The central consequence of the dual retail system can only be reasonably construed, in our view, as the imposition of a drastic reduction of commercial opportunity to reach, and hence to generate sales to, the same consumers served by the traditional retail channels for domestic beef. In 1998, when this case began, eight years after the dual retail system was first prescribed, the consequent reduction of commercial opportunity was reflected in the much smaller number of specialized imported beef shops (approximately 5,000

84 *Guidelines Concerning Registration and Operation of Specialized Imported Beef Stores*, Art. 5(A); *Regulations Concerning Sales of Imported Beef*, Art. 14(5); *Management Guideline for Imported Beef*, Art. 9(6).

85 Apart from the display sign requirement, dealt with in para. 151.

86 See Panel Report, para. 630.

87 Panel Report, para. 633.

shops) as compared with the number of retailers (approximately 45,000 shops) selling domestic beef. [88]

146. We are aware that the dramatic reduction in number of retail outlets for imported beef followed from the decisions of individual retailers who could choose freely to sell the domestic product or the imported product. The legal necessity of making a choice was, however, imposed by the measure itself. The restricted nature of that choice should be noted. The choice given to the meat retailers was *not* an option between remaining with the pre-existing unified distribution set-up or going to a dual retail system. The choice was limited to selling domestic beef only or imported beef only. Thus, the reduction of access to normal retail channels is, in legal contemplation, the effect of that measure. In these circumstances, the intervention of some element of private choice does not relieve Korea of responsibility under the GATT 1994 for the resulting establishment of competitive conditions less favourable for the imported product than for the domestic product.

147. We also note that the reduction of competitive opportunity through the restriction of access to consumers results from the imposition of the dual retail system for beef, notwithstanding the "perfect regulatory symmetry" of that system[89], and is not a function of the limited volume of foreign beef actually imported into Korea. The fact that the WTO-consistent quota for beef has, save for two years, been fully utilized does not detract from the lack of equality of competitive conditions entailed by the dual retail system.

148. We believe, and so hold, that the treatment accorded to imported beef, as a consequence of the dual retail system established for beef by Korean law and regulation, is less favourable than the treatment given to like domestic beef and is, accordingly, not consistent with the requirements of Article III:4 of the GATT 1994.

149. It may finally be useful to indicate, however broadly, what we are *not* saying in reaching our above conclusion. We are *not* holding that a dual or parallel distribution system that is *not* imposed directly or indirectly by law or governmental regulation, but is rather solely the result of private entrepreneurs acting on their own calculations of comparative costs and benefits of differentiated distribution systems, is unlawful under Article III:4 of the GATT 1994. What is addressed by Article III:4 is merely the *governmental* intervention that affects the conditions under which like goods, domestic and imported, compete in the market within a Member's territory.

---

[88] The number of imported beef shops is noted by the Panel in footnote 347 of the Panel Report; the number of domestic beef shops has been provided by the United States in para. 175 of the Panel Report, and has not been contested by Korea.

[89] The notion of "perfect regulatory symmetry" is set out in Korea's appellant's submission, para. 95. See also *supra*, para. 17.

150. Finally, we note that Korea requires that imported beef be sold in a store displaying a sign declaring "Specialized Imported Beef Store". The Panel found that the sign requirement was "essentially ancillary to the dual retail system", and, since the dual retail system was inconsistent with Article III:4, the Panel found that the sign requirement was as well. [90] The Panel found also that, since the sign requirement went beyond an obligation to indicate origin, it was inconsistent with statements contained in a 1956 GATT Working Party Report. [91] On appeal, Korea claims that the Panel used "erroneous logic" in its conclusion based on the ancillary character of the sign requirement, and that the statement in the Working Party Report did not apply to the sign requirement. [92]

151. Without a system of specialized imported beef stores, the sign requirement would have no meaning and would not be required. When considered independently from a dual retail system, a sign requirement might or might not be characterized legally as consistent with Article III:4 of the GATT 1994. On the other hand, when considered simply as a detail of the dual retail system, the sign requirement partakes of the legal characterization given to that system itself. We believe it unnecessary to pass upon separately the consistency of the display sign requirement with Article III:4 of the GATT 1994.

B. *Article XX(d) of the GATT 1994*

152. The Panel went on to conclude that the dual retail system, which it found to be inconsistent with Article III:4, could *not* be justified pursuant to Article XX(d) of the GATT 1994. The Panel found that the dual retail system is a disproportionate measure not necessary to secure compliance with the Korean law against deceptive practices. [93]

153. The Panel began its examination of Korea's dual retail system under Article XX(d) by finding that the dual retail system was designed to "secure compliance" with the *Unfair Competition Act*, a law consistent on its face with WTO provisions. [94] The Panel then focused on whether the dual retail system is "necessary" to secure compliance with that law. It examined enforcement measures taken by Korea for related products where fraudulent misrepresentation or passing of one product for another has occurred, and found that in these areas a dual retail system was not used. Instead, in respect of such product areas, Korea uses traditional enforcement measures, consistent with WTO rules, which include record-keeping, investigations, policing and fines. The Panel next inquired into whether these alternative, WTO-consistent measures were "reasonably available"

---

90 Panel Report, para. 641.

91 Working Party Report, *Certificates of Origin, Marks of Origin, Consular Formalities*, adopted 17 November 1956, BISD 5S/102, para. 13.

92 Korea's appellant's submission, paras. 206-213.

93 Panel Report, para. 675.

94 *Ibid.*, para. 658.

to Korea to meet Korea's desired level of enforcement of laws against fraudulent misrepresentation in the retail beef sector. The Panel concluded that these measures are "reasonably available" alternative measures, and that Korea therefore cannot justify the dual retail system as "necessary" under Article XX(d). [95]

154. Korea appeals the Panel's conclusion. Korea argues that the Panel incorrectly interpreted the term "necessary" in Article XX(d) as requiring *consistency* among enforcement measures taken in related product areas. [96] Further, according to Korea, the Panel neglected to take into account the *level of enforcement* that Korea sought with respect to preventing the fraudulent sale of imported beef. [97]

155. Article XX(d), together with the introductory clause of Article XX, reads as follows:

> Article XX
>
> *General Exceptions*
>
> Subject to the requirement that such measures are not applied in a manner which would constitute a means of arbitrary or unjustifiable discrimination between countries where the same conditions prevail, or a disguised restriction on international trade, nothing in this Agreement shall be construed to prevent the adoption or enforcement by any Member of measures:
>
> ...
>
> (*d*) necessary to secure compliance with laws or regulations which are not inconsistent with the provisions of this Agreement, including those relating to customs enforcement, the enforcement of monopolies operated under paragraph 4 of Article II and Article XVII, the protection of patents, trade marks and copyrights, and the prevention of deceptive practices;

156. We note that in examining the Korean dual retail system under Article XX, the Panel followed the appropriate sequence of steps outlined in *United States – Standards for Reformulated and Conventional Gasoline* ("*United States – Gasoline*"). There we said:

> In order that the justifying protection of Article XX may be extended to it, the measure at issue must not only come under one or another of the particular exceptions -- paragraphs (a) to (j) -- listed under Article XX; it must also satisfy the requirements imposed by the opening clauses of Article XX. *The analysis is, in other words, two-tiered: first, provisional justification by reason of characteri-*

95 *Ibid.*, paras. 660-674.
96 Korea's appellant's submission, paras. 166-180.
97 *Ibid.*, paras. 181-193.

zation of the measure under XX(g); second, further appraisal of the same measure under the introductory clauses of Article XX. [98] (emphasis added)

The Panel concentrated its analysis on paragraph (d), that is, the first-tier analysis. Having found that the dual retail system did not fulfill the requirements of paragraph (d), the Panel correctly considered that it did not need to proceed to the second-tier analysis, that is, to examine the application in this case of the requirements of the introductory clause of Article XX.

157. For a measure, otherwise inconsistent with GATT 1994, to be justified provisionally under paragraph (d) of Article XX, two elements must be shown. First, the measure must be one designed to "secure compliance" with laws or regulations that are not themselves inconsistent with some provision of the GATT 1994. Second, the measure must be "necessary" to secure such compliance. A Member who invokes Article XX(d) as a justification has the burden of demonstrating that these two requirements are met. [99]

158. The Panel examined these two aspects one after the other. The Panel found, "despite ... troublesome aspects, ... that the dual retail system was put in place, at least in part, in order to secure compliance with the Korean legislation against deceptive practices to the extent that it serves to prevent acts inconsistent with the *Unfair Competition Act*." [100] It recognized that the system was established at a time when acts of misrepresentation of origin were widespread in the beef sector. It also acknowledged that the dual retail system "does appear to reduce the opportunities and thus the temptations for butchers to misrepresent [less expensive] foreign beef for [more expensive] domestic beef ". [101] The parties did not appeal these findings of the Panel.

159. We turn, therefore, to the question of whether the dual retail system is "necessary" to secure compliance with the *Unfair Competition Act*. Once again, we look first to the ordinary meaning of the word "necessary", in its context and in the light of the object and purpose of Article XX, in accordance with Article 31(1) of the *Vienna Convention.*

---

98 Appellate Body Report, *United States – Standards for Reformulated and Conventional Gasoline* ("*United States – Gasoline*") WT/DS2/AB/R, adopted 20 May 1996, DSR 1996:I, 3 at 20. See also, Appellate Body Report, *United States – Import Prohibition of Certain Shrimp and Shrimp Products* ("*United States – Shrimp*"), WT/DS58/AB/R, adopted 6 November 1998, DSR 1998:VII, 2755, paras. 119-121.

99 Appellate Body Report, *United States – Gasoline*, *supra*, footnote 98, at 21; Appellate Body Report, *United States – Measure Affecting Imports of Woven Wool Shirts and Blouses from India* ("*US – Shirts and Blouses*"), WT/DS33/AB/R and Corr. 1, adopted 23 May 1997, DSR 1997:I, 323 at 335-337; Panel report, *United States – Section 337*, *supra*, footnote 69, para. 5.27.

100 Panel Report, para. 658.

101 *Ibid.*

160. The word "necessary" normally denotes something "that cannot be dispensed with or done without, requisite, essential, needful". [102] We note, however, that a standard law dictionary cautions that:

> [t]his word must be considered in the connection in which it is used, as it is a word susceptible of various meanings. It may import absolute physical necessity or inevitability, or it may import that which is only convenient, useful, appropriate, suitable, proper, or conducive to the end sought. It is an adjective expressing degrees, and may express mere convenience or that which is indispensable or an absolute physical necessity". [103]

161. We believe that, as used in the context of Article XX(d), the reach of the word "necessary" is not limited to that which is "indispensable" or "of absolute necessity" or "inevitable". Measures which are indispensable or of absolute necessity or inevitable to secure compliance certainly fulfil the requirements of Article XX(d). But other measures, too, may fall within the ambit of this exception. As used in Article XX(d), the term "necessary" refers, in our view, to a range of degrees of necessity. At one end of this continuum lies "necessary" understood as "indispensable"; at the other end, is "necessary" taken to mean as "making a contribution to." We consider that a "necessary" measure is, in this continuum, located significantly closer to the pole of "indispensable" than to the opposite pole of simply "making a contribution to". [104]

162. In appraising the "necessity" of a measure in these terms, it is useful to bear in mind the context in which "necessary" is found in Article XX(d). The measure at stake has to be "necessary to ensure compliance with laws and regulations … , *including* those relating to customs enforcement, the enforcement of [lawful] monopolies … , the protection of patents, trade marks and copyrights, and the prevention of deceptive practices". (emphasis added) Clearly, Article XX(d) is susceptible of application in respect of a wide variety of "laws and regulations" to be enforced. It seems to us that a treaty interpreter assessing a measure claimed to be necessary to secure compliance of a WTO-consistent law or regulation may, in appropriate cases, take into account the relative importance of the common interests or values that the law or regulation to be enforced is intended to protect. The more vital or important those common interests or values

---

[102] *The New Shorter Oxford English Dictionary*, (Clarendon Press, 1993), Vol. II, p. 1895.

[103] *Black's Law Dictionary*, (West Publishing, 1995), p. 1029.

[104] We recall that we have twice interpreted Article XX(g), which requires a measure "*relating* to the conservation of exhaustible natural resources". (emphasis added). This requirement is more flexible textually than the "necessity" requirement found in Article XX(d). We note that, under the more flexible "*relating to*" standard of Article XX(g), we accepted in *United States – Gasoline* a measure because it presented a "*substantial* relationship", (emphasis added) i.e., *a close and genuine* relationship of ends and means, with the conservation of clean air. *Supra*, footnote 98, p.19. In *United States – Shrimp* we accepted a measure because it was "*reasonably related*" to the protection and conservation of sea turtles. *Supra*, footnote 98, at para. 141.

are, the easier it would be to accept as "necessary" a measure designed as an enforcement instrument.

163. There are other aspects of the enforcement measure to be considered in evaluating that measure as "necessary". One is the extent to which the measure contributes to the realization of the end pursued, the securing of compliance with the law or regulation at issue. The greater the contribution, the more easily a measure might be considered to be "necessary". Another aspect is the extent to which the compliance measure produces restrictive effects on international commerce [105], that is, in respect of a measure inconsistent with Article III:4, restrictive effects *on imported goods*. A measure with a relatively slight impact upon imported products might more easily be considered as "necessary" than a measure with intense or broader restrictive effects.

164. In sum, determination of whether a measure, which is not "indispensable", may nevertheless be "necessary" within the contemplation of Article XX(d), involves in every case a process of weighing and balancing a series of factors which prominently include the contribution made by the compliance measure to the enforcement of the law or regulation at issue, the importance of the common interests or values protected by that law or regulation, and the accompanying impact of the law or regulation on imports or exports.

165. The panel in *United States – Section 337* described the applicable standard for evaluating whether a measure is "necessary" under Article XX(d) in the following terms:

> It was clear to the Panel that a contracting party cannot justify a measure inconsistent with another GATT provision as "necessary" in terms of Article XX(d) if an alternative measure which it could reasonably be expected to employ and which is not inconsistent with other GATT provisions is available to it. By the same token, in cases where a measure consistent with other GATT provisions is not reasonably available, a contracting party is bound to use, among the measures reasonably available to it, that which entails the least degree of inconsistency with other GATT provisions. [106]

166. The standard described by the panel in *United States – Section 337* encapsulates the general considerations we have adverted to above. In our view, the weighing and balancing process we have outlined is comprehended in the determination of whether a WTO-consistent alternative measure which the Member concerned could "reasonably be expected to employ" is available, or whether a less WTO-inconsistent measure is "reasonably available".

---

105 We recall that the last para. of the Preamble of the GATT of 1994 reads as follows: "Being desirous of contributing to these objectives by entering into reciprocal and mutually advantageous arrangements directed to the substantial reduction of tariffs and other barriers to trade *and to the elimination of discriminatory treatment in international commerce*". (emphasis added)

106 Panel report, *supra*, footnote 1, *United States – Section 337*, *supra*, footnote 69, para. 5.26.

167. The Panel followed the standard identified by the panel in *United States – Section 337*. It started scrutinizing whether the dual retail system is "necessary" under paragraph (d) of Article XX by stating:

> Korea has to convince the Panel that, contrary to what was alleged by Australia and the United States, no alternative measure consistent with the WTO Agreement is reasonably available at present in order to deal with misrepresentation in the retail market as to the origin of beef. [107]

168. The Panel first considered a range of possible alternative measures, by examining measures taken by Korea with respect to situations involving, or which could involve, deceptive practices similar to those which in 1989-1990 had affected the retail sale of foreign beef. The Panel found that Korea does not require a dual retail system in *related product areas*, but relies instead on traditional enforcement procedures. There is no requirement, for example, for a dual retail system separating domestic Hanwoo beef from domestic dairy cattle beef. [108] Nor is there a requirement for a dual retail system for any other meat or food product, such as pork or seafood. [109] Finally, there is no requirement for a system of separate restaurants, depending on whether they serve domestic or imported beef, even though approximately 45 per cent of the beef imported into Korea is sold in restaurants. [110] Yet, in all of these cases, the Panel found that there were numerous cases of fraudulent misrepresentation. [111] For the Panel, these examples indicated that misrepresentation of origin could, in principle, be dealt with "on the basis of basic methods ... such as normal policing under the Korean *Unfair Competition Act*." [112]

169. Korea argues, on appeal, that the Panel, by drawing conclusions from the absence of any requirement for a dual retail system in related product areas, introduces an illegitimate "consistency test" into Article XX(d). For Korea, the proper test for "necessary" under Article XX(d):

> ... is to see whether another means exists which is less restrictive than the one used and which can reach the objective sought. Whether such means will be applied *consistently* to other products or not is not a matter of concern for the necessity requirement under Article XX(d). [113]

---

[107] Panel Report, para. 659.

[108] In 1998, domestic dairy cattle beef amounted to 12 percent of total beef consumption in Korea. Panel Report, para. 661.

[109] *Ibid.*, para. 662.

[110] *Ibid.*, para. 663.

[111] *Ibid.*, paras. 661-663, including footnote 366, in which the Panel noted "that the Livestock Times reported that the deceptive beef marketing practice was widespread in restaurants (where price differential was 58 per cent)".

[112] *Ibid.*, para. 664.

[113] Korea's appellant's submission, para. 167.

170. Examining enforcement measures applicable to the same illegal behaviour relating to like, or at least similar, products does not necessarily imply the introduction of a "consistency" requirement into the "necessary" concept of Article XX(d). Examining such enforcement measures may provide useful input in the course of determining whether an alternative measure which could "reasonably be expected" to be utilized, is available or not.

171. The enforcement measures that the Panel examined were measures taken to enforce the same law, the *Unfair Competition Act.* [114] This law provides for penal and other sanctions [115] against any "unfair competitive act", which includes any:

> *Act misleading the public to understand the place of origin of any goods* either by falsely marking that place on any commercial document or communication, in said goods or any advertisement thereof *or in any manner of misleading the general public*, or by selling, distributing, importing or exporting goods bearing such mark; [116] (emphasis added)

The language used in this law to define an "unfair competitive act" – "any manner of misleading the general public" – is broad. It applies to all the examples raised by the Panel – domestic dairy beef sold as Hanwoo beef, foreign pork or seafood sold as domestic product, as well as to imported beef served as domestic beef in restaurants.

172. The application by a Member of WTO-*compatible* enforcement measures to the same kind of illegal behaviour – the passing off of one product for another – for like or at least similar products, provides a suggestive indication that an alternative measure which could "reasonably be expected" to be employed may well be available. The application of such measures for the control of the same illegal behaviour for like, or at least similar, products raises doubts with respect to the objective *necessity* of a different, much stricter, and WTO-inconsistent enforcement measure. The Panel was, in our opinion, entitled to consider that the "examples taken from outside as well as within the beef sector indicate that misrepresentation of origin can indeed be dealt with on the basis of basic methods, consistent with the *WTO Agreement*, and thus less trade restrictive and less mar-

---

[114] In GATT case law, comparisons have been made between enforcement measures taken in different *jurisdictions*. In the *United States – Measures Affecting Alcoholic and Malt Beverages* case, the panel said that "[t]he fact that not all fifty states maintain discriminatory distribution systems indicates to the Panel that alternative measure for enforcement of state excise tax laws do indeed exist." Adopted 19 June 1992, BISD 39S/206, para. 5.43. In the *United States – Section 337* case, the panel "did not consider that a different scheme for imports alleged to infringe process patents is necessary, since many countries grant to their civil courts jurisdiction over imports of products manufactured abroad under processes protected by patents of the importing country". *Supra*, footnote 69, para. 5.28.

[115] *Unfair Competition Prevention and Business Secret Protection Act*, Article 2(1)(c), Article 8.

[116] *Unfair Competition Prevention and Business Secret Protection Act*, Article 2(1)(c) (from translation provided by Korea as Exhibit 28 of its second submission to the Panel.

ket intrusive, such as normal policing under the Korean *Unfair Competition Act.*" [117]

173. Having found that possible alternative enforcement measures, consistent with the *WTO Agreement*, existed in other related product areas, the Panel went on to state that:

> ... it is for Korea to demonstrate that such an alternative measure is not reasonably available or is unreasonably burdensome, financially or technically, taking into account a variety of factors including the domestic costs of such alternative measure, to ensure that consumers are not misled as to the origin of beef. [118]

174. The Panel proceeded to examine whether the alternative measures or "basic methods" – investigations, prosecutions, fines, and record-keeping – which were used in related product areas, were "reasonably available" to Korea to secure compliance with the *Unfair Competition Act.* The Panel concluded "that Korea has not demonstrated to the satisfaction of the Panel that alternative measures consistent with the WTO Agreement were not reasonably available". [119] Thus, as noted at the outset, the Panel found that the dual retail system was "a disproportionate measure not necessary to secure compliance with the Korean law against deceptive practices". [120] The dual retail system was, therefore, not justified under Article XX(d). [121]

175. Korea also argues on appeal that the Panel erred in applying Article XX(d) because it did not "pay due attention to the level of enforcement sought." [122] For Korea, under Article XX(d), a panel must:

> ... examine whether a means reasonably available to the WTO Member could have been used in order to reach the objective sought without putting into question the level of enforcement sought. [123]

For Korea, alternative measures must not only be reasonably available, but must also *guarantee* the level of enforcement sought which, in the case of the dual retail system, is the *elimination* of fraud in the beef retail market. [124] With respect to investigations, Korea argues that this tool can only reveal fraud *ex post*, whereas the dual retail system can combat fraudulent practices *ex ante.* [125] Korea contends that *ex post* investigations do not *guarantee* the level of enforcement that Korea has chosen, and therefore should not be considered. With respect to

---

117 Panel Report, para. 664.
118 Panel Report, para. 665.
119 *Ibid.*, para. 674.
120 *Ibid.*, para 675.
121 *Ibid.*
122 Korea's appellant's submission, para. 182.
123 *Ibid.*, para. 181.
124 *Ibid.*, paras. 181, 185.
125 *Ibid.*, para. 192.

policing, Korea believes that this option is not "reasonably available", because Korea lacks the resources to police thousands of shops on a round-the-clock basis.

176. It is not open to doubt that Members of the WTO have the right to determine for themselves the level of enforcement of their WTO-consistent laws and regulations. We note that this has also been recognized by the panel in *United States – Section 337*, where it said: "The Panel wished to make it clear that this [the obligation to choose a reasonably available GATT-consistent or less inconsistent measure] does not mean that a contracting party could be asked to change its substantive patent law or its desired *level of enforcement* of that law .... ". (emphasis added) The panel added, however, the caveat that "provided that such law and such *level of enforcement* are the same for imported and domestically-produced products".[126]

177. We recognize that, in establishing the dual retail system, Korea could well have intended to secure a higher level of enforcement of the prohibition, provided by the *Unfair Competition Act*, of acts misleading the public *about the origin of beef* (domestic or imported) *sold by retailers*, than the level of enforcement of the same prohibition of the *Unfair Competition Act* with respect to *beef served in restaurants*, or the sale by *retailers* of *other meat or food products*, such as *pork or seafood*.

178. We think it unlikely that Korea intended to establish a level of protection that *totally eliminates* fraud with respect to the origin of beef (domestic or foreign) sold by retailers. The total elimination of fraud would probably require a total ban of imports. Consequently, we assume that in effect Korea intended to *reduce considerably* the number of cases of fraud occurring with respect to the origin of beef sold by retailers. The Panel did find that the dual retail system "does appear to reduce the opportunities and thus the temptations for butchers to misrepresent foreign beef for domestic beef ".[127] And we accept Korea's argument that the dual retail system *facilitates* control and permits combatting fraudulent practices *ex ante*. Nevertheless, it must be noted that the dual retail system is only an *instrument* to achieve a significant reduction of violations of the *Unfair Competition Act*. Therefore, the question remains whether other, conventional and WTO-consistent instruments can not reasonably be expected to be employed to achieve the same result.

179. Turning to investigations, the Panel found that Korea, in the past, had been able to distinguish imported beef from domestic beef, and had, in fact, published figures on the amount of imported beef fraudulently sold as domestic beef. This meant that Korea was able, in fact, to detect fraud.[128] On fines, the Panel found that these could be an effective deterrent, as long as they outweighed the

---

[126] Panel report, *United States – Section 337, supra*, footnote 69, para. 5.26.

[127] Panel Report, para. 658.

[128] *Ibid.*, para. 668.

potential profits from fraud. [129] On record-keeping, the Panel felt that if beef traders at all levels were required to keep records of their transactions, then effective investigations could be carried out. [130] Finally, on policing, the Panel noted that Korea had not demonstrated that the costs would be too high. [131] For all these reasons, the Panel considered "that Korea has not demonstrated to the satisfaction of the Panel that alternative measures consistent with the WTO Agreement were not reasonably available". [132] Thus, as already noted, the Panel found that the dual retail system was "a disproportionate measure not necessary to secure compliance with the Korean law against deceptive practices". [133]

180. We share the Panel's conclusion. We are not persuaded that Korea could not achieve its desired level of enforcement of the *Unfair Competition Act* with respect to the origin of beef sold by retailers by using conventional WTO-consistent enforcement measures, if Korea would devote more resources to its enforcement efforts on the beef sector. It might also be added that Korea's argument about the lack of resources to police thousands of shops on a round-the-clock basis is, in the end, not sufficiently persuasive. Violations of laws and regulations like the Korean *Unfair Competition Act* can be expected to be routinely investigated and detected through selective, but well-targeted, controls of potential wrongdoers. The control of records will assist in selecting the shops to which the police could pay particular attention.

181. There is still another aspect that should be noted relating to both the method actually chosen by Korea – its dual retail system for beef – and alternative traditional enforcement measures. Securing through conventional, WTO-consistent measures a higher level of enforcement of the *Unfair Competition Act* with respect to the retail sale of beef, could well entail higher enforcement costs for the national budget. It is pertinent to observe that, through its dual retail system, Korea has in effect shifted all, or the great bulk, of these potential costs of enforcement (translated into a drastic reduction of competitive access to consumers) to imported goods and retailers of imported goods, instead of evenly distributing such costs between the domestic and imported products. In contrast, the more conventional, WTO-consistent measures of enforcement do not involve such onerous shifting of enforcement costs which ordinarily are borne by the Member's public purse.

182. For these reasons, we uphold the conclusion of the Panel that Korea has not discharged its burden of demonstrating under Article XX(d) that alternative WTO-consistent measures were not "reasonably available" in order to detect and

---

[129] Panel Report, para. 669

[130] *Ibid.*, para. 672.

[131] *Ibid.*, para. 673.

[132] *Ibid.*, para. 674.

[133] *Ibid.*, para. 675.

suppress deceptive practices in the beef retail sector [134], and that the dual retail system is therefore not justified by Article XX(d). [135]

183. Korea further argues, on appeal, that the Panel did not make a separate finding on whether the display sign requirement was justified by Article XX(d), and requests that, should the Appellate Body uphold the Panel's finding that the sign requirement was inconsistent with Article III:4, it should proceed to consider the issue of its justification under Article XX(d). [136]

184. We recall that Korean law requires an imported beef retailer to display a sign reading "Specialized Imported Beef Store". [137] Since the Panel correctly regarded the sign requirement as merely ancillary to the dual retail system, we consider that it is unnecessary to examine separately whether the display sign requirement can be justified under Article XX(d).

185. In sum, we uphold the Panel's conclusion that the dual retail system, which is inconsistent with Article III:4, is not justified under Article XX(d) of the GATT 1994.

VII. FINDINGS AND CONCLUSIONS

186. For the reasons set out in this Report, the Appellate Body:

(a) upholds the Panel's conclusion that, under the Panel's terms of reference, the Panel was required to examine, pursuant to the complaining parties' claims, the commitment levels in Korea's Schedule and Annex 3 of the *Agreement on Agriculture;*

(b) upholds the Panel's conclusion that Korea's domestic support for beef for 1997 and 1998 was not correctly calculated pursuant to Article 1(a)(ii) and Annex 3 of the *Agreement on Agriculture*;

(c) reverses the Panel's finding on recalculated amounts of Korea's domestic support for beef in 1997 and 1998, as the Panel used, for these recalculations, a methodology inconsistent with Article 1(a)(ii) and Annex 3 of the *Agreement on Agriculture*; and reverses, therefore, the Panel's following conclusions, based on these recalculated amounts: (i) that Korea's domestic support for beef in 1997 and 1998 exceeded the *de minimis* level contrary to Article 6 of the *Agreement on Agriculture*; (ii) that Korea's failure to include Current AMS for beef in Korea's Current Total AMS was contrary to Article 7.2(a) of that Agreement; and (iii) that Korea's total do-

[134] Panel Report, para. 674.

[135] *Ibid.*, para. 675.

[136] Korea's appellant's submission, paras. 217-223.

[137] Panel Report,paras. 642-643.

mestic support for 1997 and 1998 exceeded Korea's commitment levels contrary to Article 3.2 of the *Agreement on Agriculture*;

(d) is unable, in view of the insufficient factual findings made by the Panel, to complete the legal analysis of: (i) whether Korea's domestic support for beef exceeds the *de minimis* level contrary to Article 6 of the *Agreement on Agriculture*; (ii) whether the failure to include Current AMS for beef in Korea's Current Total AMS was contrary to Article 7.2(a) of that Agreement; and (iii) whether Korea's total domestic support for 1997 and 1998 exceeded Korea's commitment levels contrary to Article 3.2 of the *Agreement on Agriculture*;

(e) upholds the Panel's ultimate conclusion that Korea's dual retail system for beef is inconsistent with Article III:4 of the GATT 1994;

(f) upholds the Panel's conclusion that Korea's dual retail system for beef is not justified under Article XX(d) of the GATT 1994; and

(g) finds it unnecessary to pass upon separately whether the ancillary sign requirement is consistent with Article III:4 or justified under Article XX(d) of the GATT 1994.

187. The Appellate Body recommends that the DSB request that Korea bring its measures found in this Report, and in the Panel Report as modified by this Report, to be inconsistent with Korea's obligations under the GATT 1994 and the *Agreement on Agriculture* into conformity with its obligations under those Agreements.

KOREA - MEASURES AFFECTING IMPORTS OF FRESH, CHILLED AND FROZEN BEEF

Report of the Panel

WT/DS161/R

TABLE OF CONTENTS

LIST OF ABBREVIATIONS OF PANEL AND APPELLATE BODY REPORTS REFERRED TO IN THE TEXT OF THE REPORT

Argentina – Textiles(AB) - Appellate Body report on Argentina - *Measures Affecting Imports of Footwear, Textiles, Apparel and Other Items*, adopted 22 April 1998, WT/DS56/AB/R;

Canada - FIRA - Panel report on *Canada - Administration of the Foreign Investment Review Act,* BISD 30S/140, adopted 7 February 1984;

Canada- Marketing Agencies (1988) - Panel report on *Canada - Import, Distribution and Sale of Certain Alcoholic Drinks by Provincial Marketing Agencies,* BISD 35S/137, adopted 22 March 1988;

Canada - Marketing Agencies (1992) - Panel report on *Canada - Import, Distribution and Sale of Certain Alcoholic Drinks by Provincial Marketing Agencies,* BISD 39S/27, adopted 18 February 1992;

Canada - Periodicals - Panel report on *Canada - Certain Measures Concerning Periodicals,*

WT/DS31/R, adopted 30 July 1997;

Canada - Dairy - Panel report on *Canada - Measures Affecting the Importation of Milk and Exportation of Dairy Products*, WT/DS103/R (US), WT/DS113/R (New Zealand), adopted 22 October 1999;

Canada - Dairy(AB) - Appellate Body report on *Canada - Measures Affecting the Importation of Milk and Exportation of Dairy Products*, WT/DS103/AB/R, adopted 22 October 1999;

EEC - Processed Fruits and Vegetables - Panel report on *EEC – Programme of Minimum Import Prices, Licences and Surety Deposits for Certain Processed Fruits and Vegetables,* BISD 25S/68, adopted 18 October 1978;

EEC - Beef - Panel report on *EEC - Imports of Beef from Canada,* BISD 28S/92, adopted 10 March 1981;

EEC- Imports from Hong Kong, - Panel report on *EEC – Quantitative Restrictions against Imports of Certain Products from Hong Kong*, BISD 30S/129, adopted 12 July 1983;

EEC - Oilseeds - Panel report on *EEC - Payments and Subsidies Paid to Processors and Producers of Oilseeds and Related Animal-Feed Proteins,* BISD 37S/86 (US), adopted 25 January 1990;

EEC - Parts and Components - Panel report on *EEC - Regulation on Imports of Parts and Components,* BISD 37S/132, adopted 16 May 1990;

EC - Bananas III – Panel report on *European Communities - Regime for the Importation, Sale and Distribution of Bananas,* WT/DS27/R(Ecuador, Guatemala, Honduras, Mexico, and United States), adopted 25 September 1997;

EC - Bananas III (AB) - Appellate Body Report on *European Communities - Regime for the Importation, Sale and Distribution of Bananas,* WT/DS27/AB/R, adopted 25 September 1997;

EC – Hormones (AB) – Appellate Body report on *European Communities – Measures Affecting Meat and Meat Products,* WT/DS26/AB/R-WT/DS48/AB/R, adopted 13 February 1998;

EC - Computer Equipment (AB) - Appellate Body report on *European Communities/United Kingdom/Ireland - Customs Classification of Certain Computer Equipment (AB),* WT/DS62/AB/R (US), WT/DS67/AB/R (US), WT/DS68/AB/R (US), adopted 22 June 1998;

EC - Poultry - Panel report on *European Communities - Importation of Certain Poultry Products,* WT/DS69/R (Brazil), adopted 23 July 1998;

EC – Poultry(AB) – Appellate Body report on *European Communities - Importation of Certain Poultry Products,* WT/DS69/AB/R, adopted 23 July 1998;

India - Quantitative Restrictions - Panel report on *India - Quantitative Restrictions on Imports of Agricultural, Textile and Industrial Products,* WT/DS90/R (US), adopted 22 September 1999;

Indonesia – Automobiles – Panel report on *Certain Measures Affecting the Automobile Industry,* WT/DS54 (EC); WT/DS55 (Japan), WT/DS59 (US), WT/DS64 (Japan), adopted 23 July 1998;

Italian Agricultural Machinery - Panel report on *Italy - Discrimination against Imported Agricultural Machinery,* BISD 7S/60, adopted 23 October 1958;

Japan - Agricultural Products - Panel report on *Japan - Restrictions on Imports of Certain Agricultural Products,* BISD 35S/163, adopted 2 February 1988;

Japan –Semi-conductors, Panel report on *Japan - Trade in Semi-conductors,* BISD 35S/116, adopted 4 May 1988;

Japan - Leather – Panel report on *Japanese Measures on Imports of Leather,* BISD 31S/94, adopted 15 May 1994;

Japan - Alcoholic Beverages - Panel report on *Japan - Taxes on Alcoholic Beverages.* WT/DS8/R (EC); WT/DS10/R (Canada); WT/DS11/R (US), adopted 1 November 1996;

Japan - Alcoholic Beverages (AB) - Appellate Body report on *Japan – Taxes on Alcoholic Beverages,* WT/DS8,10,11/AB/R, adopted on 1 November 1996;

Japan - Film – Panel report on *Japan - Measures Affecting Consumer Photographic Film and Paper,* WT/DS/44/R (US), adopted 22 June 1998;

Japan - Varietal Testing(AB) - Appellate Body report on *Japan - Measures Affecting Agricultural Products,* WT/DS76/AB/R, adopted 19 March 1999;

Korea - Beef - Panel report on *Republic of Korea - Restrictions on Imports of Beef,* BISD 36S/202 (Australia) 36S/268 (US), adopted on 7 November 1989;

Korea - Alcoholic Beverages (EC) - Panel report on *Korea - Taxes on Alcoholic Beverages,* WT/DS75/R (EC), adopted on 17 February 1999;

Korea - Alcoholic Beverages(US) - Panel report on *Korea - Taxes on Alcoholic Beverages,* WT/DS84/R (US), adopted on 17 February 1999;

Korea - Safeguards - Appellate Body report on *Korea - Definitive Safeguard Measure on Imports of Certain Dairy Products,* WT/DS/98/AB/R, adopted 12 January 2000;

Spain - Sale of Soybean Oil - Panel report on *Spain – Measures concerning the Domestic Sale of Soybean Oil,* L/5142, not adopted;

US - Hawaiian Regulations - Consultations on *United States - Hawaiian Regulations Affecting Imported Eggs*; L/411, 28 September 1955, no report;

US - Superfund - Panel report on *US – Taxes on Petroleum and Certain Imported Substances* (Canada, EEC, Mexico), BISD 34S/136, adopted 17 June 1987;

US - Sugar Head Note - Panel report on *United States - Restrictions on Imports of Sugar*, BISD 36S/331, adopted 22 June 1989;

US - Section 337 – Panel report on *United States - Section 337 of the Tariff Act of 1930,* BISD 36S/345, adopted 7 November 1989;

US - Malt Beverages - Panel report on *United States - Measures Affecting Alcoholic and Malt Beverages,* BISD 39S/206, adopted 19 June 1992;

US - Gasoline - Panel report on *United States - Standards for Reformulated and Conventional Gasoline,* WT/DS2/R (Venezuela); WT/DS4/R (Brazil), adopted 20 May 1996;

US – Gasoline (AB) – Appellate Body report on *United States - Standards for Reformulated and Conventional Gasoline,* WT/DS2/AB/R, adopted 20 May 1996;

US- Shirts and Blouses (AB) – Appellate Body report on *United States - Measure Affecting Imports of Woven Wool Shirts and Blouses,* WT/DS33/AB/R, adopted 23 March 1997;

US - Shrimp (AB) – Appellate Body report on *United States - Import Prohibition of Shrimp and Shrimp Products,* WT/DS58/AB/R, adopted 6 November 1998;

US-Section 301 - Panel report on *United States –Sections 301-310 of the Trade Act of 1974,* WT/DS152/R (EC), adopted 27 January 2000;

US-FISC (AB) – Appellate Body report on *United States – Tax Treatment for Foreign Sales Corporations,* WT/DS108/AB/R, adopted on 20 March 2000.

I. INTRODUCTION

1. On 1 February 1999, the United States requested consultations with the Republic of Korea ("Korea") pursuant to Article 4 of the Understanding on Rules and Procedures governing the Settlement of Disputes ("DSU"), Article XXII of the General Agreement on Tariffs and Trade 1994 (GATT 1994), Article 19 of the *Agreement on Agriculture* and Article 6 of the *Agreement on Import Licensing Procedures*, with respect *inter alia* to Korea's import measures on fresh, chilled, and frozen beef as well as its internal sale on the Korean market. Australia requested consultations with Korea on the same matter on 13 April 1999.

2. Consultations between the United States and Korea were held on 11 and 12 March 1999 and joined by Australia, Canada and New Zealand. Consultations between Australia and Korea were held 28 May 1999 and were joined by Canada, New Zealand and the United States. As the above-mentioned consultations did not result in a mutually satisfactory solution of the matter, the United States, in a communication dated 15 April 1999, requested the establishment of a panel with standard terms of reference as set out in Article 7 of the DSU (WT/DS161/5). Australia, in a communication dated 12 July 1999, requested the establishment of a panel with standard terms of reference as set out in Article 7.1 of the DSU (WT/DS169/5).

3. At its meeting on 25 May 1999 the Dispute Settlement Body (DSB) established a panel in accordance with the request made by the United States in document WT/DS161/5. At its meeting of 26 July 1999, the DSB agreed to Australia's request for the establishment of a panel (WT/DS/169/5) in the same matter. It also agreed, as provided for in Article 9 of the DSU in respect of multiple Complainants, that the Panel established on 26 May 1999 to examine the complaint by the United States will also examine Australia's complaint. Australia[1], Canada, New Zealand and the United States[2] reserved their third party rights to make a submission and to be heard by the Panel in accordance with Article 10 of the DSU

1. *Terms of Reference*

4. The following terms of reference applied to the work of the Panel:

"To examine, in the light of the relevant provisions of the covered agreements cited by the United States in document WT/DS161/5 and by Australia in document WT/DS/169/5, the matter referred to the DSB by the United States and Australia in those documents and to make such findings

1 In the case requested by the United States.

2 In the case requested by Australia.

as will assist the DSB in making the recommendations or in giving the rulings provided for in those agreements".

2. *Panel Composition*

5. The parties to the dispute agreed on 4 August 1999[3] to the following composition of the Panel:

Chairperson: Lars Anell

Members: Paul Demaret

Alan Matthews

6. The Panel met with the parties on 13 and 14 December 1999 and on 16 February 2000 and with third parties on 14 December 1999.

7. The Panel submitted its interim report to the parties of the dispute on 10 May 2000 and the final report on 15 June 2000.

II. FACTUAL ASPECTS

1. *Product Coverage of the Dispute*

8. The case before the Panel concerned measures maintained by Korea on imports of beef of the following tariff description[4]: 02.01-10: meat of bovine animals (fresh or chilled/carcasses and half-carcasses); 02.01-20: meat of bovine animals (fresh or chilled/cuts with bone in); 02.01-30: meat of bovine animals (fresh or chilled/boneless); 02.02-10: meat of bovine animals (frozen/carcasses and half-carcasses): 02.02-20: meat of bovine animals (frozen/cuts with bone in); 02.02-30: meat of bovine animals (frozen/boneless);

2. *Korea's Schedule of Concessions*

9. Korea's Schedule of tariff concessions (LX) provides for the entry of fresh, chilled and frozen beef with market access opportunities rising from 123,000 tonnes in 1995 to 225.000 tonnes in 2000. The bound tariff will be reduced from 44.5 per cent to 40 per cent in 2004. Korea's Schedule also provides that it shall "eliminate or bring into conformity with GATT provisions all remaining restrictions" on a range of specific products, including fresh, chilled and frozen bovine meat imports, from 1 January 2001.

---

3 Date of the formal agreement by the panellists to serve.

4 Legal Instruments Embodying the Results of the Uruguay Round of Multilateral Trade Negotiations Done at Marrakesh on 15 April 1994 - Schedule LX, Republic of Korea, pages 12147, 12150, 12215.

3. *Records of Understanding*[5]

10. Korea held consultations on beef with the United States, Australia and New Zealand, which resulted in the conclusion of separate bilateral "Records of Understanding" in 1990 and 1993. These Records were intended to implement the findings of the 1989 *Korea - Beef* panel (see paragraph 28). The Record of Understanding signed in March 1990 (L/6697) established base quota levels, which increased progressively over the period 1990-1992 to 66,000 metric tons. It also provided for the establishment of a "Simultaneous Buy/Sell" ("SBS") system to allow for an initial seven per cent of the quota to be entered by entities other than the Livestock Products Marketing Organization (LPMO)[6]. The Record of Understanding also provides that the SBS portion shall increase to 70 per cent by 2000. The three bilateral Records of Understanding signed in July 1993 (L/7270) between Korea on the one side, and Australia, New Zealand and the United States, respectively, on the other, specified quota amounts to be imported on a customs cleared basis for 1993-1995. These Records of Understanding also contained provisions intended to expand the scope of the SBS system. In the July 1993 Record of Understanding, Korea and the exporting countries agreed on the base amount of the beef quota covering the period '93-'95, the framework for the SBS system and the SBS mark-up. In that document, Korea also reaffirmed its commitment to eliminate its remaining restrictions or otherwise bring them into conformity with GATT provisions.

11. The Korea/United States 1 July 1993 Record of Understanding was modified in December of that year to the effect of extending the timetable for elimination of the quota to 31 December 2000. This timetable was ultimately made a part of Korea's WTO Schedule of Concessions. In the December 1993 Record of Understanding between Korea and the United States quota amounts, mark-up, and the SBS quota share were agreed upon for the period 1993 - 2000, as well as the annual tariff for the period 1995 to 2004. The December 1993 Record of Understanding also provides that all balance of payments restrictions on beef shall expire no later than December 2000, and that there shall be no quota, no mark-up, and no LPMO involvement in 2001.

4. *The Korean Regulatory Regime for Beef*

12. The Government of Korea operates a stabilization system for domestic beef producers pursuant to the *Act on Distribution and Price Stabilization of Agricultural and Fishery Products* which authorises measures to ensure the

---

5 The Records of Understanding are annexed.

6 The SBS System is defined in Section II of the July 1993 Record of Understanding between Korea and Australia as "the system through which suppliers of beef imported into the Republic of Korea conduct business directly with super-groups, end-users or customers." See also, Records of Understanding with the United States and with New Zealand. The *Management Guideline for Imported Beef* contains the same definition.

"smooth distribution of and maintenance of appropriate prices for agricultural and fishery products"[7] and the *Livestock Act,* under which the Minister of Agriculture and Forestry is required to establish and implement comprehensive livestock industry development plans and policies regarding: (i) the improvement and production of livestock breeds (ii) structural improvement of the livestock industry; (iii) balancing demand and supply of livestock and livestock products; (iv) stabilization of livestock and livestock product prices and enhancement of the livestock and livestock product distribution system; (v) stable supply of livestock feeds, treatment and utilisation of livestock excrement; livestock sanitation, etc.[8]

13. The import, distribution and sale of imported beef is regulated to give effect to the Government's stabilization policies. Article 25 of the *Livestock Act* provides that, in circumstances where it is deemed particularly necessary for consumer protection, the prevention of illegal distribution and the control of imported livestock products, the Minister of Agriculture and Forestry (MAF) retains certain powers in relation to the regulation and restriction of the quantity, timing, price, usage and sales methods for imported beef.[9] Until 1 October 1999, these requirements were elaborated through *the Regulations Concerning Sales of Imported Beef, Operational Guidelines for Beef Imported under the SBS System, Guidelines Concerning Registration and Operation of Specialized Imported Beef Stores* and *Imported Beef Dealer Designation and Product Supply Guidelines.* On 1 October 1999 they were replaced by the *Management Guideline for Imported Beef,* which contain the same essential measures as the former regulations.

5. *Measures Affecting the Importation, Distribution and Sale of Beef*

14. Import authority within the annual quota is divided between the *Livestock Products Marketing Organization* (LPMO) on the one hand, and the *Simultaneous Buy and Sell* (SBS) system on the other.

(i) Measures Applied to Beef Imported by the LPMO

15. The LPMO is a notified state trading agency for beef. The LPMO was established in 1988, and has, since its creation, been exclusively authorized by Korea to administer beef imports. In this role, it performs a variety of functions. The LPMO is the importer of a substantial share of the beef quota. The share imported by the LPMO has been progressively reduced and the LPMO currently imports 30 per cent of the beef quota. It also invites tenders and sells the imported beef at auction. In addition, LPMO exercises authority delegated from

---

[7] Act on Distribution and Price Stabilization of Agricultural and Fishery Products Article 1.

[8] *Livestock Act (revised 1999),* Article 3(1).

[9] *Ibid,* Article 25.

MAF to license imports made through the SBS system and to allocate quota share among the SBS quota holders. It imports its share of the annual quota through a tendering system.[10] The import, distribution and sale of beef imported by LPMO are regulated by the Government through the *Management Guideline for Imported Beef* mentioned above. Prior to this, the LPMO system was regulated through the *Regulations on Imported Beef* and the *Imported Beef Dealer Designation and Product Supply Guidelines.*

16. Article 3 of the *Management Guideline for Imported Beef* notes that beef is imported by the LPMO to stabilize demand and supply in the market. The objective of the LPMO is "to protect both producers and consumers through the stabilization of demand-supply and price of livestock products".[11]

17. The LPMO derives its authority to import from Article 53 of *the Foreign Trade Act*[12] and Article 24 of the *Livestock Act*. It imports beef at world market prices through a tender system and distributes it either by auction to wholesalers or directly to processors or the military. From 1988 to 1991, the LPMO was purchasing 100 per cent of the Korean beef import quota. Its share of the quota has been reduced over time. Currently the LPMO imports 30 per cent of the total beef import quota.

18. The LPMO determines an annual purchase and distribution plan for the coming year taking into account current and forecast levels of domestic beef demand, production and pricing. The LPMO sets a minimum acceptable auction price[13] for each cut and brand of imported beef on a daily basis,

(ii) The National Livestock Cooperatives Federation (NLCF)

19. The NLCF handles the storage and domestic auctions at the wholesale market on behalf of the LPMO. Under government regulations, the NLCF also been controls the discharge of beef on behalf of LPMO, including establishment and implementation of regional and purchaser-based sales plans and discretion to decide daily discharging volumes in consideration of price movements of domestic beef/cattle.[14]

20. Most beef imported by the LPMO, other than that consigned *inter alia* for processing and packaging, is in principle required to be traded on a livestock wholesale market or at an auction office in areas without a wholesale market.[15] Sales participants at an imported beef wholesale market may only supply im-

10 G/STR/N/4/KOR.

11 *L.P.M.O*, Foreword, page 1.

12 *Foreign Trade Act.*

13 Ibid, Article 11.1.

14 *Regulations Concerning Imported Beef*, Articles 4, 6(1), 6(2), 9(2).

15 *Ibid*, Article 5.

ported beef to specialized imported beef stores.[16] Imported beef is required, in principle, to be supplied on a cash payment basis.[17]

(iii) Measures Applied to Beef Imported under the SBS System

21. Since 1 October 1999, chapter 3 of the *Management Guideline for Imported Beef,* which regulates imports of beef under the SBS system, replaces those in the *Operational Guidelines for Imported Beef.* According to the 1993 Record of Understanding between the United States and Korea, the SBS system, is a system through which suppliers of beef imported into Korea carry out business directly with entities called "super-groups", end users, or customers. A super-group is defined as an organization or association of end users which has the right to import beef under the SBS system and, as appropriate, allocate SBS sub-shares among its affiliated end users. Twelve "super-groups" are currently entitled to import beef.[18] With the gradual increase of quota share, the number of super-groups has been increasing to meet the various usage of imported beef and market demand. Each super-group has a defined set of end users. To import beef through the SBS system an end user must be a member of a super-group.[19] An end-user can only belong to one super-group. Restrictions are imposed on cross-trading.[20]

22. Before the beginning of each fiscal year, the LPMO allocates to each super-group the annual quota that each may import under the SBS system.[21] Each super-group sets up quarterly purchase and sales plans for each end user or customer and report these to the LPMO by 15 January of each year.[22] End users and customers negotiate and contract with the exporter on cut, price, delivery, conditions of sale, etc, within the quarterly allocated amount;[23] Super-groups seek import approval on behalf of end users under a licensing system pursuant to Article 24 of the Livestock Act and administered by the LPMO.[24] Where the allocated amount is not purchased during the quarter, the super-group must withdraw the

---

[16] *Ibid,* Article 15.2.

[17] See also Annex 4.

[18] The super-groups are as follows: National Livestock Cooperatives Federation (NLCF); Korea Cold Storage Company (KCSC); Korea Tourist Supply Centre (KTSC); Korea Restaurant Supply Centre (KRSC); Korea Meat Industries Association (KMIA); Korea Super Chain stores Association (KOSCA); Korean Federation of Meat Purveyors (KFMP); Livestock Cooperative Trading and Marketing (LCTM): Korea Meat Packers Association (KMPA); Woo Joo Industrial Company Ltd; Korea Imported Meat Distributors Association (KIMDA); Korea Meat Processing Industry Cooperatives (KMPIC).

[19] *Management Guideline for Imported Beef,* Article 26.4.

[20] Idem.

[21] *Ibid,* Article 22.1.

[22] *Ibid,* Article 22.2.

[23] *Ibid,* Article 23.1.

[24] *Ibid,* Article 23.3.

shortfall and reallocate this to its end users or customers in the following quarter.[25] Quota allocation amongst end users of a super-group is done on forecast demand. When an end user does not meet its demand forecast, the resulting quota shortfall remains unused for the current period. Any reallocation of the shortfall takes effect the following period.

23. Each super-group must obtain information on the amount of any expected shortfall in its imports and report it to the LPMO President by 5 October of each year.[26] The LPMO must then reallocate this shortfall to other super-groups in the same proportion as the initial allocation. The regulations also impose record-keeping, reporting and labelling requirements on super-groups and their end-users which are administered by the LPMO.[27] 0

6. *Mark-ups*

24. The Korean government requires that a mark-up be applied to all SBS imports. The mark-up is imposed pursuant to Article 25 of the *Management Guideline for Imported Beef.* The mark-up calculation is based on the difference between the duty-paid CIF price of beef and the weighted average wholesale price for all imported boneless grain-fed beef cuts purchased and distributed by the LPMO. It is calculated on both a weekly and monthly basis.

25. The mark-up was phased out on 31 December 1999 in accordance with the terms of the December 1993 Record of Understanding between Korea and the United States. The maximum rate was 100 per cent in 1993, 60 per cent in 1996, 40 per cent in 1997, 20 per cent in 1998 and 10 per cent in 1999. The mark-up was paid into a fund, the stated purpose of which is to provide support to the domestic livestock industry pursuant to Article 34 of the *Livestock Act*.

7. *Measures Applied to the Retail Sale of Imported Beef*

26. The Government of Korea regulates retail outlets through the *Management Guidelines for Imported Beef* which came into effect on 1 October 1999 and prior to that date through the *Guidelines Concerning Registration and Operation of Specialized Imported Beef Stores.* The *Management Guideline for Imported Beef* specifies that imported beef (except for pre-packed imported beef) may only be sold in specialized imported-beef shops.[28] It also specifies that large-scale distributors (department stores, supermarkets, etc) must provide a separate sales area for imported beef.[29] Stores selling imported beef must display a "Spe-

---

25 *Ibid,* Article 22.4.

26 *Ibid,* Article 22.5.

27 Articles 27.3, 27.4, and 28.1 of the *Management Guideline for Imported Beef.*

28 *Management Guideline for Imported Beef,* Article 15.

29 *Ibid,* Article 9.5.

cialized Imported Beef Store" sign to distinguish them from domestic meat sellers.

8. Domestic Support Measures to the Korean Beef Industry

27. Korea notified its domestic support arrangements to the WTO Committee on Agriculture in 1995, 1996, 1997 and 1998.[30] In each year, the reported level of total domestic support (Current Total AMS) has been below its total AMS commitment level.[31] The bulk of the support has been directed to rice production. Over the four years notified by Korea, the reported domestic support level for beef has increased from 1.12 billion won in 1995, to 23.59 billion won in 1996, and 195.27 billion won in 1997.

9. Previous Dispute Settlement

28. In 1988, Australia, New Zealand and the United States requested GATT panel proceedings relating to Korea's import measures for beef which they claimed were inconsistent with Articles XI, II, and subsidiary, with X and XIII. Korea justified its import restrictions under Article XVIII:B. The panel found that *inter alia* that Korea's "import measures and restrictions, introduced in 1984/85 and amended in 1988, were not consistent with the provisions of Article XI and were not taken for balance-of-payments reasons. The panel did not find it necessary to examine the Korean measures under Articles II, X or XIII since any inconsistency with these Articles would normally disappear once the Article XI inconsistency had been eliminated. In the reports[32] of the panel circulated on 24 May 1989 the panel recommended that:

> Korea eliminate or otherwise bring into conformity with the provisions of the General Agreement the import measures on beef introduced in 1984/85 and amended in 1988; and,
>
> Korea hold consultations with Australia, New Zealand and the United States and other interested contracting parties to work out a timetable for the removal of import restrictions on beef justified since 1967 by Korea for balance-of-payments reasons.

10. Import Liberalization Programme

29. On 26 April 1994, in compliance with the results of the 1989 consultations with the BOP Committee and the Uruguay Round negotiations, Korea sub-

---

[30] *G/AG/N/KOR/7; G/AG/N/KOR/14; G/AG/N/KOR/18; G/AG/N/KOR/24.*

[31] *Legal Instruments Embodying the Results of the Uruguay Round of Multilateral Trade Negotiations Done at Marrakesh on 15 April 1994 - Schedule LX, Republic of Korea: Part IV - Agricultural Products: Commitments Limiting Subsidization,* page 13049 and supporting tables provided in G/AG/AGST/KOR.

[32] L/6504, 36S/202; L/6505, 36S/234; and L/6503, 36S/268.

mitted an import liberalization programme concerning 150 products, including beef, in which Korea notified that all the remaining restrictions on beef will be eliminated or brought into conformity with the provisions of the GATT from 1 January 2001.

III. PRELIMINARY REQUEST FOR RULINGS ON TERMS OF REFERENCE

30. **Korea** submitted that the Complainants' arguments that Korea has not fulfilled its commitments under the *Agreement on Agriculture* should be rejected. Korea noted that the request for the establishment of the Panel by the United States identifies the disputed measure as follows: "At the same time, Korea has increased the level of its domestic support for its cattle industry to the point that the total domestic support provided by Korea exceeds its Aggregate Measurement of Support (AMS) under the *Agreement on Agriculture*."[33] In the opinion of Korea, the disputed measures before the Panel are accordingly limited to the Korean measures of domestic support for its cattle industry. The data and calculation methods used in Korea's Schedule LX Part IV, or in broad terms Korea's Schedule LX by itself, are not mentioned as disputed measures. Accordingly, the arguments now raised in respect thereof are outside the terms of reference of the Panel.

31. The legal basis identified by both the United States and Australia in their requests for the establishment of the Panel is limited to Articles 3, 4, 6 and 7 of the *Agreement on Agriculture*[34]. Korea requests that the Panel limit its examination to these articles. The Panel, therefore, should not allow the Complainants to now bring arguments which are based mainly on Annex 3 of the *Agreement on Agriculture*, because Annex 3 was not identified as a legal basis on which the Complainants wished this dispute to be examined.

32. With regard to claims under Articles 3, 4, 6 and 7, the lack of specification on what precise claims would be raised under these Articles, leads, according to Korea, to the conclusion that none of these claims are properly before the Panel. At most, by reference to the measure identified, one could expect that the Complainants would raise claims that Korea may not have included all its domestic support measures to its cattle industry in its AMS calculations. Korea has been prejudiced in its right of defense due to the lack of proper identification and failure to present the problem clearly with regard to the claims relating to the

---

33 Request for the establishment of a panel by the United States, WT/DS161/5(16 April 1999); the request for the establishment of a panel by Australia (WT/DS169/5, 15 July 1999) contains nearly identical language and states: *"Korea has also increased the level of domestic support for its cattle industry in amounts which result in the total domestic support provided by Korea exceeding its Aggregate Measurement of Support (AMS) under the Agreement on Agriculture."*

34 Request for the establishment of a panel by the United States, WT/DS161/5 (16 April 1999); request for the establishment of a panel by Australia, WT/DS169/5, (15 July 1999).

Agreement on Agriculture in the request for the establishment of the Panel, because Korea was not in a position to understand what claims the Complainants actually intended to bring and actually brought before the Panel. Therefore, Korea could not adequately prepare its defense in this case from the moment the decision was taken to establish a panel. Furthermore, Korea argued that the Complainants, following the third party submission of New Zealand, started to borrow heavily from the claims of New Zealand and introduced new claims, which are clearly outside the terms of reference of the Panel.

33. **Australia** considered that the Panel is required by its terms of reference to consider whether Korea has met its obligations under Articles 3, 6 and 7 of the *Agreement on Agriculture*. In order to do so, the Panel must consider both Annex 3 of the *Agreement on Agriculture*, including Korea's calculation of its AMS on beef and its Total AMS, as well as Part IV of Korea's Schedule. Australia was, therefore, of the opinion that the Panel should reject outright the claims in paragraphs 30-32 because they have been raised without justification in Korea's second written submission, contrary to the rules of procedure proposed by the Panel and agreed to by all of the parties, including Korea. Specifically, in raising its claim at this time Korea is acting contrary to paragraph (e) of the rules of procedure for this Panel, which states that "any requests for preliminary rulings shall be included in a party's first written submission to the Panel. If the respondent requests any such ruling, the complaining parties shall submit their responses to such request prior to the first substantive meeting of the Panel at a time to be determined in light of the request. Exceptions to this procedure will be granted upon a showing of good cause."

34. Australia argued that Korea has advanced no reasons at all to justify raising these issues now, rather than at the beginning of these proceedings. The claims relating to the *Agreement on Agriculture* were included in Australia's request for establishment of a panel and were developed in Australia's first written submission. Korea had the opportunity in its first written submission to raise the issue of adequacy of the panel request, but it did not do so. Australia submitted that the Panel cannot act contrary to its own rules of procedure and contends that in the absence of any Korean claim or argument as to good cause, the Panel is not permitted to examine Korea's claims.

35. If the Panel decides to permit Korea to make its claim, Australia submitted that Korea has not met its burden of proof in showing a deficiency in Australia's request for a panel. Australia has identified the measure at issue and has listed the specific provisions of the *Agreement on Agriculture* alleged to have been violated. It does not have to do any more than that. As the Appellate Body noted in *EC-Bananas III,* there is a significant difference between the claims identified in the request for establishment of a panel, and the arguments supporting those claims which are set out in the submissions of the parties.[35]

[35] At para. 141.

36. Korea has advanced no legal argument in support of its claim, Australia continued, that in examining Korea's obligations under Article 6, the Panel is prevented from considering either Annex 3 or Part IV of Korea's Schedule. Korea has not mentioned or argued an inconsistency with Article 6.2 of the DSU. Korea has neither claimed prejudice, nor provided proof of it. Korea did not raise the *Korea - Safeguards* case or any other legal argument to support its claims in either of its written submissions. Australia, therefore, submitted that Korea has failed to meet its burden of proof and that its claims of a deficiency in Australia's panel request must, therefore, be rejected. It would be an abuse of due process to permit Korea to use the opening statement of the final meeting with the Panel to make good its failure to raise or argue this preliminary issue in its written submissions. Furthermore, as the Appellate Body in *Japan - Varietal Testing(AB)* made clear, the Panel is not entitled to make determinations or provide legal arguments on behalf of a party who has failed itself to make a *prima facie* claim.[36]

37. Australia argued that the key principle to emerge from *Korea – Safeguards (AB)* was that a request for establishment of a panel must be sufficiently specific so as not to prejudice the ability of a responding party to defend itself. However, the Appellate Body also made it clear that it is Korea that bears the burden of proof in claiming prejudice. Korea did not claim prejudice at the time the request for a panel was made, or in its first or second written submissions, or at the first Panel meeting, or in its responses to factual questions from the Panel relating to its calculations of domestic support.

38. There is no basis for Korea to claim that it did not understand the claims being made or that it was not accorded an opportunity to respond to these claims. Quite the contrary, Korea responded to Australia's claims regarding Article 6, and through Article 6, to Annex 3 and Part IV of its Schedule, in its first written submission. In that submission, Korea stated 'the AMS for cattle in 1997 did not exceed 10 per cent of the total value of cattle production and Korea's 1997 Current Total AMS did not exceed its reduction commitment level specified in Schedule LX. Korea cannot now be claiming that it did not understand the claims being made against it when it responded to these very same claims in its first written submission, and it did so without any apparent confusion as to the claims being made or the arguments being put.

39. In response to Korea's claim that Australia introduced new claims borrowed from the third party submission of New Zealand, Australia said that Korea was confusing claims with arguments. The Appellate Body had been very clear that Australia is not required to set out detailed arguments in its panel request. Australia raised no new claims in either its first or second written submissions which were not contained in its request for establishment of a panel. Furthermore, Australia included a range of arguments relating to Annex 3 in its first written submission. Nor did Australia "borrow" any new claims from New Zealand. New

---

[36] Paras. 118-131.

Zealand used arguments relating to Annex 3 in support of the claims already made by Australia and the United States that Korea's increased domestic support for beef had resulted in Korea's Total Aggregate Measure of Support for 1997 being over its permitted amount for that year. The most that could be said was that Australia supported the arguments of New Zealand in relation to Annex 3, but there is not prohibition in the DSU against that.

40. In case the Panel determines that it should consider the substance of Korea's claims, Australia submitted that a textual analysis of Article 6 makes it clear that if Article 6 is to have any meaning, the Panel must consider Annex 3 and Part IV of Korea's Schedule. Australia submitted that Annex 3 and Part IV of Korea's Schedule are so intrinsic to a panel's interpretation of Korea's obligations under Article 6 as to obviate any need to mention them specifically in a panel request. The fact that Korea has already responded to the substance of Australia's claims supports this view. It is not possible to make a determination about a Member's consistency with these obligations without reference to the formulations contained in Annex 3, because Annex 3 contains the methodology required to determine the AMS for specific products as well as the Total AMS. It is also not possible to decide whether Korea has met its obligations under these Articles without reference to the reduction commitments contained in its Schedule.

41. The Panel is required by its terms of reference to consider whether Korea has met its obligations under Articles 3, 6 and 7 of the *Agreement on Agriculture*. In order to do so, the Panel must consider both Annex 3 of the *Agreement on Agriculture*, including Korea's calculation of its AMS on beef and its Total AMS, as well as Part IV of Korea's Schedule.

42. The **United States** contended that Korea's arguments in paragraphs 30-32 are misguided. The scope of a panel's terms of reference has been considered in a number of Appellate Body reports. The beginning point is Article 7 of the *Understanding on Rules and Procedures Governing the Settlement of Disputes* (the *DSU*), which describes the standard terms of reference and directs that "[p]anels shall address the relevant provisions in any covered agreement or agreements cited by the parties to the dispute".

43. This issue has arisen most frequently in the context of arguments that the complaining party has not satisfactorily explained its claims as required by Article 6.2 of the DSU. The Appellate Body recently rejected an argument made by Korea in *Korea – Safeguards (AB)* that is similar to the one now made by Korea. There, the Appellate Body re-emphasized that "claims, not detailed arguments, are what need to be set out with sufficient clarity..." Indeed, in *EC – Bananas III (AB)*, the Appellate Body agreed with the panel's conclusion that "the listing of the articles to the agreements claimed to have been violated satisfied the *minimum* requirements of Article 6.2 of the DSU" in view of the circumstances of that case and, in particular, the lack of any demonstrated prejudice to the defending party.

44. The approach described above was adopted by the Appellate Body in at least three separate disputes: those relating to *EC – Bananas III(AB)*, *Korea –*

Safeguards (AB), and *EC - Computer Equipment(AB)*. In each instance, the Appellate Body examined the written panel request to determine whether the requirement contained in Article 6.2 for explication of the claim was satisfied and whether there was any indication that a defending Member had been prejudiced by lack of notice regarding the nature of the claim. In the cited cases, the Appellate Body found that no prejudice had been shown and the descriptions of the claims, thus, were adequate to satisfy the purpose of Article 6.2 of the DSU.

45. The US description of its claim regarding Korea's domestic support obligations under the *Agreement on Agriculture* is plainly set forth in its request for the establishment of a panel. In pertinent part, the US request states: " ... Korea has increased the level of domestic support for its cattle industry to the point that the total domestic support provided by Korea exceeds its Aggregate Measurement of Support (AMS) under the *Agreement on Agriculture*. The United States then concluded that it considered Korea's support measures to be inconsistent with Articles 3, 6 and 7 of the *Agreement*. The US claim, thus, plainly included a contention that Korea was not in compliance with its domestic support commitments as set forth in Articles 3, 6, and 7 of the *Agreement on Agriculture* and that this situation resulted from increases in the level of support provided to Korea's cattle industry. Korea has never claimed, and does not now allege, that it ever has been uncertain about or without adequate notice of the nature of the US claims regarding Korea's AMS obligations.

46. Apparently, Korea's argument is based on the fact that the United States did not expressly identify Annex 3 as one of the legal bases for its claims. However, even a cursory reading of Articles 6 and 7 of the *Agreement on Agriculture* reveals that the commitments there incorporated include a requirement that the applicable AMS be computed in conformity with the provisions of Annex 3. Korea could not possibly have been misled by the US panel request because the references in Article 6.1, for example, to "Total Aggregate Measurement of Support" and "Annual and Final Bound Commitment Levels" require consideration of the definitions set forth in Article 1 as well as the computation methodology contained in Annex 3. In fact, the definition of AMS set forth in Article 1 directs that AMS shall be "calculated in accordance with the provisions of Annex 3 of this *Agreement* ...."

47. Moreover, the United States continued, Annex 3 itself is entitled "Domestic Support: Calculation of Aggregate Measurement of Support" and contains provisions essential to the AMS computation. As a result, there is no question but that the Panel is compelled to consider Annex 3 in resolving the US claims under Article 6 of the Agreement. The United States specifically stated that its claim involved the calculation of the AMS under the *Agreement on Agriculture*. Annex 3 is so intrinsic to the calculation of the AMS that any analysis that ignores that provision could not possibly result in a construction of Article 6 which would be consistent with customary rules of interpretation under Article 3.2 of the DSU.

IV. MAIN ARGUMENTS[37]

A. *General*

48. The complaint examined by the Panel is related to Korea's measures governing the importation and marketing of fresh, chilled and frozen beef in Korea, falling within HS codes 0201-10, 0201-20, 0201-30, 0202-10, 0202-20 and 0202-30.

49. **Australia** requested the Panel to find that:

(a) the requirements imposed on the retail sale of imported beef operate as a quantitative restriction and discriminate against imported product contrary to Articles III and XI;

(b) the tendering process adopted by LPMO for the import of beef results in quantitative restrictions being applied to grass-fed beef, contrary to Articles II:1, III:4, XI:1 and XVII;

(c) the discharge procedures for LPMO beef restrict the distribution of imported beef into the market in a manner which constitutes a quantitative restriction, imposes non-tariff measures made effective through state trading enterprises and discriminates against imported beef in a manner contrary to Articles III, XI and XVII of GATT and Article 4.2 of the *Agreement on Agriculture*;

(d) restrictions on sales of beef imported by the LPMO, including cash payment and record-keeping requirements, discriminate against imported beef contrary to Article III:4;

(e) Korea applies a mark-up on beef imported under the SBS system which is not applied to domestic beef and is inconsistent with Korea's obligations under Article II or III;

(f) the SBS system applies limitations on the import and distribution of imported beef, and imposes labelling, reporting and record-keeping requirements, that discriminate against imported product contrary to Articles XI and III; and

(g) in 1997, Korea provided domestic support to its beef industry at levels which exceeded *de minimis* and which, therefore, were required to be included in its calculations of its Current Total Aggregate Measurement of Support (AMS). This resulted in Korea's Current Total AMS for 1997 being in excess of its reduction commitments for that year, contrary to Articles 3.6 and 7 of the *Agreement on Agriculture*.

---

[37] This section contains the main arguments by the parties as summarized and understood by the Panel. If not otherwise stated, the footnotes in this section are those of the parties. Note that Article numbers refer to the General Agreement on Tariffs and Trade 1994 if not otherwise stated.

50. Australia further requested the Panel to recommend to the DSB that Korea bring its measures affecting the import of fresh, chilled and frozen beef into conformity with its obligations under the GATT 1994 and the *Agreement on Agriculture*.

51. The **United States** requested the Panel to find that:

(a) Korea's requirement that imported beef be sold only in specialized imported beef stores and its laws and regulations restricting the resale and distribution of imported beef by SBS super-groups, as well as by retailers, customers, and end-users is inconsistent with its obligations under Article III:4;

(b) Korea's discretionary import regime, including, but not limited to, laws and regulations prohibiting the import of beef by any entity other than the super-groups and the LPMO, as well as the LPMO's establishment of minimum import prices and delay of both invitations to tender as well as quota allocations is inconsistent with its obligations under Article XI:1of GATT, Article 4.2 of the *Agreement on Agriculture*, and Articles 1 and 3 of the *Agreement on Import Licensing Procedures*;

(c) Korea's imposition of other duties or charges in the form of a markup not provided for in Schedule LX is inconsistent with its obligations under Article II:1; and

(d) Korea has failed to fulfill its reduction commitment for domestic support and the level of domestic support provided and is thus inconsistent with Korea's obligations under Articles 3, 6, and 7 of the *Agreement on Agriculture*.

52. The United States further requested the Panel to recommend that Korea bring its measures into conformity with its obligations under the GATT 1994, the *Agreement on Agriculture* and the *Agreement on Import Licensing Procedures.*

B. Claims to a "transitional period"

1. Remaining Restrictions

53. **Korea** stated that its Schedule of Concessions provides for a transition period until 1 January 2001 to eliminate or bring into conformity with the provisions of the GATT all remaining restrictions on beef. The claims raised by Australia and the United States are, therefore, inadmissible and contrary to Article II:1 of GATT 1994, Article 3:2 of the Understanding on Rules and Procedures governing the Settlement of Disputes (DSU) and Article 26 of the *Vienna Convention*. Korea, therefore, requested that the Panel rejects all arguments and claims made by Australia and the United States.

54. Korea submitted that the restrictions alleged by the Complainants were already in existence at the time of the conclusion of the Uruguay Round and hence constitute "remaining restrictions" within the meaning of Note 6 of Korea's

Schedule LX. The term "remaining restrictions" should be interpreted in accordance with its ordinary meaning pursuant to Article 31 of the Vienna Convention. The ordinary meaning of the words suggests that the "remaining restrictions" are otherwise not in conformity with the provisions of the GATT. There would be no need to provide that they should be eliminated or be brought into conformity with the provisions of the GATT by 1 January 2001 if they were. Indeed, if the remaining restrictions were in conformity, it would make no sense to provide that they should be eliminated or brought into conformity with GATT provisions. The only qualification is that they are "remaining" at the time of the conclusion of the Uruguay Round agreement.

55. Should the Panel, nevertheless, consider that the ordinary meaning and scope of the term "remaining restrictions" is not clear, then Korea submitted that the Panel, in accordance with the recent Appellate Body ruling in *Canada – Dairy (AB),* should refer to the preparatory work of the treaty in accordance with Article 32 of the Vienna Convention [supplementary means of interpretation]. In the view of Korea, the December 1993 Record of Understanding concluded with the United States constitutes the preparatory work of the Uruguay Round agreements, and makes it clear that the remaining restrictions cover all restrictions which were in existence for balance-of-payments reasons at the time of conclusion of the Uruguay Round. No specific measures were enumerated as constituting remaining restrictions in Note 6 of Korea's Schedule LX, but Korea considered that the language of Note 6 should be interpreted as Korea's commitment, in broad terms, to full liberalization of its beef import regime by the end of the year 2000. Therefore, even if any of the remaining restrictions are inconsistent with the provisions of the GATT, which Korea disputes, they would nevertheless be covered by the transitional period until 1 January, 2001.

56. Korea argued that the interpretation by Australia of the term "remaining restrictions" (see paragraph 83) in Note 6 of Korea's Schedule of Concessions contravenes the foregoing principles set forth by the Appellate Body (see paragraph 54). In the opinion of Korea, the interpretation advocated by Australia first of all contravenes Article 31 of the Vienna Convention which requires interpretation in accordance with the ordinary meaning to be given to the terms. Since Note 6 of Korea's Schedule refers to remaining *restrictions*, it is evident that more than one restriction was meant. Furthermore, Australia's interpretation of Note 6 as referring only to GATT inconsistent restrictions contained in the Schedule itself, in particular the quota, would deprive Note 6 of any *effet utile.* Indeed, Korea's Schedule LX Section I-B: Tariff Quota already explicitly provides for the quota to be eliminated by the end of the year 2000.

57. An interpretation in accordance with the ordinary meaning of the terms used in Note 6, Korea submitted, leads to the conclusion that all restrictions (limitations placed on actions) which existed at the end of the Uruguay Round and which were GATT inconsistent should be eliminated or brought into conformity with GATT by 1 January 2001. Indeed, if a cut-off date other than the conclusion of the Uruguay Round had been intended, it would have been so specified in Note 6. No other cut-off date is mentioned or implied by Note 6 and the Com-

plainants have provided no evidence from the negotiating history showing that another cut-off date was meant. Therefore, in accordance with the ordinary meaning of the term *"remaining,"* the restrictions at issue are those remaining at the time of conclusion of the Uruguay Round contained in Note 6. The phrase preceding the words "remaining restrictions," that reads "According to the results of the 1989 consultation with GATT/BOP Committee and the Uruguay Round multilateral trade negotiation" cannot be construed as implying that a 1989 cut-off date was meant. This phrase clarifies the negotiating background of the transitional period and grammatically does not qualify the term *"remaining restrictions"*. To interpret this phrase as implying a 1989 cut-off date would be inconsistent with the ordinary meaning of the phrase "and the Uruguay Round multilateral trade negotiation" and deprive it of any *effet utile*.

(i) Transitional Period

58. In **Korea**'s view, the operative consequence of Note 6 is that even if the Panel finds that certain "remaining restrictions" are inconsistent with GATT, no violation of Korea's obligations can be established at this point in time precisely for the reason that Korea still benefits from a transitional period until 1 January 2001. Hence, the claims brought by the United States and Australia with regard to the alleged GATT incompatibility of certain "remaining restrictions" are irrelevant at this point in time for all practical and legal purposes and, accordingly, Korea requests that the Panel dismiss these claims.

59. Korea objected to the Complainants' attempt to bring before the Panel and actively discuss, the issue of what the Korean measures on imported beef will exactly be on and after 1 January 2001. The possible future measures by Korea with regard to imported beef are outside the terms of reference of the Panel. Korea has still one year's time to review its current system and conform to the obligations contained in Note 6. For this reason, Korea also objected to the Complainants' attempt to prompt Korea to prematurely examine and decide which remaining restrictions are inconsistent with GATT and which remaining restrictions will be eliminated. Korea requests that the Panel limit its examination of the measures challenged within its terms of reference.

60. **The Complaining parties** submitted that the Appellate Body in *EC – Poultry(AB)* outlined the approach that should be taken in relation to the interpretation of a Member's obligations under the WTO Agreements. It found that Members' Schedules are annexed to the Marrakesh Protocol to the General Agreement on Tariffs and Trade 1994 and are integral parts of the GATT 1994. As such, they form part of the multilateral obligations under the WTO Agreement. The Appellate Body also noted that bilateral agreements are not "covered agreements" within the meaning of Articles 1 and 2 of the DSU. Nor are they part of the multilateral obligations accepted by Members pursuant to the WTO Agreement. The Appellate Body concluded that it is Members' Schedules which contain the relevant obligations of a Member under the WTO Agreement and it is the Schedules which form the legal basis for a dispute and which must be inter-

preted in accordance with "customary rules of interpretation of public international law" under Article 3:2 of the DSU. Consistent with Article 31 of the *Vienna Convention*, the term *remaining restrictions* in Note 6 must, therefore, firstly be interpreted according to its ordinary meaning in context and in light of the purpose of a Schedule and the commitments and obligations contained therein.

61. Referring to the text of Korea's note 6, **Australia** agreed with Korea, that the term *remaining restrictions* in the Note must be interpreted in light of the phrase "shall be removed or brought into conformity with GATT provisions". Australia agreed that it is only logically possible for the term *remaining restrictions* to refer to restrictions which are inconsistent with GATT provisions. In this respect, Australia agreed with Korea's statement in paragraph 54 that the ordinary meaning of the words suggests that the "remaining restrictions" are otherwise not in conformity with GATT provisions. Therefore, Note 6 only applies to those measures at issue in this dispute which are inconsistent with the provisions of the GATT. However, Korea also claims that, with the exception of the mark-up on SBS imports, none of the measures at issue in this dispute are in fact inconsistent with the provisions of the GATT.

62. Hence, Australia continued, Korea has claimed that the following measures are consistent with the GATT 1994 for reasons other than their coverage under Note 6:

- Dual retail system
- Discrimination against grass-fed beef
- Restrictions applied through the SBS system
- Quantitative restrictions arising from minimum prices for imports and withholding imported beef from the market
- Domestic support for agriculture

63. Australia further submitted that Korea appears to suggest that the consistency or otherwise of the remaining restrictions on imported beef is a unilateral determination for Korea to make *after* 1 January 2001 (see paragraph 80). Australia would be very concerned if Korea were suggesting that, having taken advantage of a transition period to remove remaining restrictions, it then reserves to itself the right to determine whether in fact any of these restrictions are inconsistent. Australia would also be very concerned if Korea were suggesting that Australia would be required, after 1 January 2001, to once again challenge the WTO consistency of Korean measures before a dispute settlement panel, should it disagree with Korea's determination of which remaining measures are inconsistent. Australia does not accept that Korea can claim on the one hand that Australia agreed to allow it a transition period to remove inconsistent restrictions and on the other hand reserve for itself the unilateral right to determine, *ex post facto*, whether the restrictions in question are in fact inconsistent.

64. Australia contended that Korea cannot have it both ways. Either Korea argues that the measures in this dispute are inconsistent, were agreed to be so at

the time of the signing of the Uruguay Round, are therefore covered by a transition period until 1 January 2001 and will be removed or brought into conformity on that date; or Korea submits that none of the measures are inconsistent, in which case they cannot, by definition, be covered by Note 6.

65. With respect to Australia's contention that Korea is trying to have it both ways (paragraph 64), **Korea** submitted that it has almost one full year left to examine and bring its remaining restrictions into conformity with its obligations. Korea considered that by bringing this dispute prematurely, the Complainants have improperly sought a ruling by the Panel on measures which are covered by the transitional period. Korea contended that it is not trying to maintain an "unspecified range of measures" during the transition period.

66. The **United States** was of the opinion that the disputed measures are not "remaining restrictions". Korea appears to claim that virtually all of the measures challenged by the United States in this dispute are "remaining restrictions" within the meaning of Note 6 to its Schedule and that such measures are, therefore, "grandfathered" at least for a transition period expiring on 31 December 2000. The United States considered that the reference to "remaining restrictions" relates only to balance-of-payments restrictions imposed prior to 1989. Therefore, the Panel does not even need to reach Korea's "grandfathered" argument since none of the challenged measures are included within the scope of the term "remaining restrictions."

67. Referring to an Appellate Body statement[38] and to Korea's Schedule[39], the United States submitted that the nature of a "remaining restriction" can only be determined in reference to a point in time or some other comparative reference. The words in Korea's Schedule, however, are ambiguous to the extent that they identify both the 1989 BOP Committee consultations and the Uruguay Round negotiations as possible reference points. Recourse to supplemental means of interpretation, consistent with Article 32 of the *Vienna Convention,* is, therefore, justified to that extent.[40] For this purpose, examination of the 1989 GATT/BOP Committee proceedings, as well as any pertinent Uruguay Round negotiations, is appropriate as each is mentioned in the quoted excerpt from Korea's Schedule. A review of those proceedings and negotiations also will reveal whether the parties

---

38 Appellate Body Report, *United States – Import Prohibition of Certain Shrimp and Shrimp Products* ("*United States - Shrimp*"), WT/DS58/AB/R, adopted 6 November 1998, DSR 1998:VII, 2755, para. 114.

39 "According to the results of the 1989 consultations with GATT/BOP Committee and the Uruguay Round multilateral trade negotiation, the remaining restrictions on the items marked as '*Note 6(a)', '*Note 6(b)', '*Note 6(c)', '*Note 6(d)', '*Note 6(e) in column 5 of Section I-A of part I of this Schedule shall be eliminated or brought into conformity with GATT provisions from dates specified as follows: ... Note 6(e): January 1, 2001".

40 Appellate Body Report, *Canada – Measures Affecting the Importation of Milk and the Exportation of Dairy Products* ("*Canada – Dairy*"), WT/DS103/AB/R, WT/DS113/AB/R and Corr. 1, adopted 27 October 1999, DSR1999:V, 2057, para. 132.

intended the term " remaining restrictions" to have a special meaning as provided in Article 31.4 of the *Vienna Convention*.

68. The United States contended that the more recent actions of the LPMO, including excessive delays in tendering for imports, withholding quota share from allocation, and failing to reallocate unused quota until late in the year are all questions of implementation that did not begin to occur until late in 1997. Thus, none of these "restrictions" could be encompassed within the scope of the term "remaining restrictions" appearing in Korea's schedule. Similarly, the national treatment violations that the United States has identified are not commonly referred to as "restrictions". In fact, the term "restriction" does not appear anywhere in the text of GATT Article III. Accordingly, Korea has no basis to assert that the term "remaining restrictions' encompasses any measure that would constitute a violation of Article III of the GATT.

(ii) BOP Committee Report

69. The **United States** submitted that an examination of the 1989 GATT panel report shows that the phrase "remaining restrictions" originated in the 1987 report of the Balance-of-Payments Committee.[41] As reflected in the panel report[42], the BOP Committee found that "the current situation and outlook for the balance of payments was such that import restrictions could no longer be justified under Article XVIII:B".[43] The Committee then concluded that "Korea would be able in the meantime to establish a timetable for the phasing-out of balance-of-payments restrictions and that Korea could consider alternative GATT justification for any remaining measures, thus obviating the need for such consultations".[44] The 1987 BOP Committee report, thus, establishes the missing temporal reference for the terms "remaining restrictions" contained in Korea 's Schedule. "Remaining restrictions", in the words of the Committee, are those measures that as balance-of-payments restrictions are to be phased-out since balance-of-payments restrictions are no longer justified. Any import restriction instituted by Korea after the Council's adoption of the BOP Committee report would necessarily be without balance-of-payments justification and, as a result, would not be a "remaining restriction".

70. Any doubt that the use of the term "remaining restrictions" was limited solely to GATT inconsistent quantitative restrictions existing at the time of the BOP Committee reports in 1987 and 1989, the United States continued, can be resolved through consideration of the BOP Committee's summary of its 23 October 1989 consultation with Korea.[45] After acknowledging Korea's commitment to

---

41 BOP/R/171.

42 *Korea - Beef*, para. 122.

43 BOP/R/ 171, para. 22.

44 *Ibid*, para. 23.

45 BOP/R/183/Add. 1, October 1989.

disinvoke Article XVIII:B, the Committee reported that "Korea was encouraged, in the light of established precedents, to develop, in consultation with other contracting parties, an orderly programme of liberalization which would phase-out *remaining restrictions* in a reasonably short time."[46] (emphasis added) Obviously, the BOP Committee's reference to remaining restrictions could only mean restrictions still existing at that time. Certainly the Committee's use of that term could not contemplate new measures that had not yet been introduced.

71. Any uncertainty regarding the meaning of the term, the United States continued, is also dispelled by the manner in which the term "restrictions" was used by Korean officials meeting with the BOP Committee during 1989. In a Korean written statement, dated 27 June 1989, submitted to the BOP Committee, the responsible Korean official stated:

> However, I do not foreclose the possibility of discussing disinvocation of Article XVIII:B, provided that the Balance-of-Payments Committee:
>
> > (1) recognizes Korea's need for and agrees to a grace period sufficiently long enough for further liberalization and phase-out of the *restrictions presently under BOP cover after its disinvocation,* (emphasis added)[47]

72. The exact nature of the measures maintained by Korea at the time of the loss of BOP coverage can be best determined by consulting the 1989 GATT panel report concluding the dispute between the United States, Australia, New Zealand and Korea concerning Korea's then existing import measures. The 1989 panel considered four major issues: (1) whether Korea's maintenance of various restrictions on imported beef were justified by its balance-of-payments situation; (2) whether Korea's 1985-1987 ban and, after 1987, its quota on imported beef were inconsistent with Article XI:1; (3) whether the LPMO's capture of quota rents through the imposition of an import surcharge, a so-called "mark-up", was a violation of Article II:4; and (4) whether the LPMO's state-conferred monopoly constituted a separate import restriction within the meaning of Article XI:1. Korea fails to identify anywhere in the panel report any discussion of the measures challenged in the current dispute. For example, the panel did not consider whether Korea's dual retail sales regime is consistent with Korea's international obligations since Korea did not institute its retail system until 1990 when the Guidelines Concerning Registration and Operation of Specialized Imported Beef Stores were first issued.

---

46 *Ibid*, para. 7.

47 BOP/R/183/Add.1.

73. Similarly, Korea cannot point to any discussion of the limitations imposed on participants in the SBS system, such as the prohibition on most cross-trading[48] and the use constraints established for imported beef. This is because the SBS system is a creature of the 1990 and 1993 Records of Understanding and, thus, is later in time than the GATT panel and the measures considered by that panel. The same situation exists regarding the various LPMO measures, including minimum acceptable bid or award prices at wholesale auctions, delay of tenders, and withholding of quota allocations. Once again, Korea introduced each of these measures after the GATT dispute and, therefore, such measures cannot constitute "remaining restrictions" as that term was used by the BOP Committee. According to the United States, the parties adopted the Committee's usage of the term in the Records of Understanding that they negotiated and the term ultimately was used with the same meaning in Korea's Schedule.

74. The United States submitted further that Korea's current measures such as the dual retail sale regime and limitations on cross-trading, which are shown below to be inconsistent with Article III:4, cannot be considered to be "restrictions" as that term is used in the GATT. Moreover, since the BOP Committee's discussion of "restrictions" was entirely in the context of which restrictions could no longer be justified under Article XVIII for balance-of-payments purposes, the term must be interpreted in light of its meaning in the GATT's balance-of-payments provisions. The GATT consistently uses the word "restriction" to refer *only* to quantitative restrictions on importation, not to any internal measures governed by Article III or to any price-based measure on importation governed by Article II. Article XVIII:9, in particular, permits certain contracting parties to "control the general level of [their] imports by *restricting the quantity or value of merchandise permitted to be imported*" for balance-of-payments reasons, as an exception to the prohibition on quantitative restrictions in Article XI. Nothing in Article XVIII:9 permits a contracting party to take measures inconsistent with Article II or Article III.

75. The Korean Schedule commitment at issue was negotiated against the background of Korea's obligations under Article XVIII. The only reading of "remaining restrictions" that is true to this context is one that includes *only* quantitative restrictions on importation and not measures regulated by Articles II and III. For instance, of the measures at issue in this case, the segregation of distribution channels for imported beef and the mark-up are clearly not "restrictions" and, therefore, by definition cannot be "remaining restrictions."

76. **Australia** submitted that, on the basis of the words "According to the results of the 1989 Consultation with GATT/BOP Committee and the Uruguay Round negotiations" in Note 6, the *remaining restrictions* must, in addition to being GATT-inconsistent, be quantitative in nature and have been applied for

---

[48] The term "cross trading" is intended to refer to commercial activity between and among the super-groups or between and among their customers and end-users.

BOP purposes. Korea applied a range of quantitative restrictions on a range of products for BOP purposes, which were required to be removed once Korea had disinvoked Article XVIII:B on 1 January 1990 in accordance with the BOP Committee conclusions of 1989.[49] As a result of the 1989 BOP Committee consultations, Korea began a programme of removing quantitative restrictions on a range of products, one of which was beef. The reference in Note 6 to the BOP consultations, therefore, limits the restrictions covered by a transition period to those maintained earlier for BOP purposes, all of which were quantitative in nature.

77. The 1989 BOP Committee conclusions also contain the timetable for removal of measures maintained for BOP purposes. Three phases each of three years (1989-1991, 1992-94, 1995-97) were agreed for the phase-out of restrictions. The final phase-out date for the removal of these quantitative measures on beef was originally agreed by the BOP committee to be 1 July 1997. In the context of the Uruguay Round, the phase-out date was extended until 1 January 2001 for the measures which had been maintained on beef. However, while the phase-out date for the quantitative restrictions maintained for BOP purposes, i.e. the quota, was extended in the course of the Uruguay Round negotiations, there was no extension of a transition period to any new measures, applied for whatever reason. In the opinion of Australia, Korea has produced no evidence to show otherwise.

78. The **United States** submitted that the dual retail system is not a "remaining restriction" as it did not exist at the time of the 1987 BOP Committee report or the adoption of the 1989 GATT panel reports[50] and could not be a measure taken for balance-of-payments purposes as it is not a "restriction". Likewise, Korea's argument that the current mark-up is a "remaining restriction" is difficult to comprehend. First, the 1989 panel ruled that the mark-up existing at the time of the dispute was not a violation of Article II:4 because it was imposed by an entity, the LPMO, which at the time possessed a monopoly on imports. Given the panel's ruling, there would have been no reason for treating the mark-up as a "remaining restriction" that was required to be eliminated due to any GATT inconsistency. Further, as indicated above, (paragraph 70) only quantitative restrictions were authorized measures for Article XVIII balance-of-payments purposes.

79. Korea's treatment of the current mark-up under the terms of the December 1993 Records of Understanding with the United States also belies Korea's contention that the mark-up was intended to be considered a "remaining restriction". As Korea concedes, Korea's Schedule provides for the elimination of all "remaining restrictions" by 1 January 2001. However, the December 1993 Record of

49 See BOP/R/183/Add.1, 27 October 1989, para. 12.

50 The dual retail regime was first introduced in January 1990, approximately two months after adoption of the GATT panel and BOP Committee reports.

Understanding requires that the mark-up be reduced to zero commencing on 1 January 2000. US exporters confirm that no mark-up has been imposed on imported beef in calendar year 2000. Korea has not explained why the mark-up has been eliminated already if it is a "remaining restriction" within the meaning of its Schedule and according to the terms of its Schedule is not required to be withdrawn until the beginning of 2001.

80. **Korea** submitted that 1 January 2001 is the deadline by which the phasing-out of remaining restrictions should be completed. It is up to Korea to decide which remaining restrictions should be eliminated or brought into conformity at which point in time during the transitional period. In response to the arguments in paragraph 79 with respect to the mark-up, Korea submitted further that it simply followed the agreed timetable for its elimination under the December 1993 Record of-Understanding with the United States and executed the Record of Understanding in good faith, notwithstanding the current dispute brought by the Complainants. This in no way contradicts Korea's position that it benefits from a transitional period under its Schedule LX.

81. Note 6 of Korea's Schedule of Concessions, Korea continued, is in full conformity with Article 4.2 of the *Agreement on Agriculture*, and more specifically with footnote 1 which makes it clear that Members may maintain import measures for balance-of-payments reasons. According to the 1989 BOP Committee report, Korea's import restrictions for balance-of-payments purposes were supposed to end by 31 December 1997. However, as Note 6 of Korea's Schedule of Concessions makes it plain, WTO Members, including the Complainants in this dispute, agreed during the Uruguay Round to defer elimination of such restrictions to 1 January 2001. Referring to the Appellate Body report on *Canada - Dairy*[51], Korea submitted that its Schedule of concessions is an integral part of the GATT. (See also arguments in paragraph 299 *et sequitur.*)

82. **Australia** submitted that to give the term *remaining restrictions* the broad meaning demanded by Korea, i.e. an unspecified list of any and all GATT-inconsistent restrictions existing at the time of the Uruguay Round, would be to undermine the binding nature of Schedule commitments and the certainty of Members in understanding the exact nature of the commitments which are agreed during trade negotiations. Australia also considered that Korea's proposed interpretation of Note 6 is contrary to the object and purpose of the GATT, which is "directed to the substantial reduction of tariffs and other barriers to trade and to the elimination of discriminatory treatment in international commerce".[52]

83. On this basis, Australia submitted that the *remaining restrictions* referred to in Note 6 can only be those contained in the Schedule itself, so that other Members can easily identify the restrictions to which the transition period applied. This would also be consistent with Members' understanding that the re-

---

[51] At para.s131 and 133.

[52] See Preamble to the GATT 1994.

strictions were only those previously maintained for BOP purposes. However, none of the measures at issue in this dispute are contained in Korea's Schedule and, therefore, cannot be covered by Note 6. Australia considered that this interpretation is both unambiguous and does not produce a result which is either manifestly absurd or unreasonable. Indeed, to come to any other conclusion would lead to a manifestly unreasonable result, since it would obligate all Members to agree to a transition period for an unlimited and unspecified range of restrictions until January 2001 as a result of bilateral arrangements to which they were not party and which were not notified to them. This would be contrary to the principles espoused in the *US - Sugar Head Note* case and would undermine the certainty provided by Members' Schedules about their commitments.

84. If the Panel considers that ambiguity exists as to the scope of measures covered by the transition period in Note 6, Australia submitted that none of the evidence adduced by Korea supports its claim that the measures in dispute are *remaining restrictions* within the meaning of Note 6. There is nothing in the preparatory work of the treaty, the circumstances of its conclusion, or the historical background, that supports Korea's interpretation of its commitments on beef. In fact, quite the reverse. The historical record proves that the term *remaining restrictions* has a much more limited application than claimed by Korea.

85. The notifications to the GATT referred to by Korea, Australia continued, do not provide any insight into the scope of restrictions for which Korea claims coverage through its Schedule. Korea's notification L/7449 of 29 April 1994, notes only that the "remaining restrictions" on the 150 items shall be eliminated or be brought into conformity with GATT provisions for the dates specified". There is no guidance on the range of restrictions applying to beef that are covered by this statement. It, therefore, adds nothing to the Schedule itself.

86. Australia also noted that the 1989 panel found that Korea was obliged to bring into conformity quantitative restrictions maintained on beef for balance of payments purposes. The panel's findings were limited to these quantitative restrictions and were based on the findings of the 1987 BOP consultations on Korea which found that there was no longer any justification for Korea to maintain import restrictions for BOP purposes. None of the measures at issue in the current dispute were adjudicated in the previous panel. Certainly, measures which violated the national treatment provisions of GATT were not maintained for BOP reasons, did not exist at the time of the earlier dispute and were not part of the negotiated outcome of that dispute.

(iii) The Records of Understanding

87. **Korea** emphasized its view that the December 1993 Record of Understanding concluded with the United States constitutes the preparatory work of the Uruguay Round agreements for the purposes of Article 32 of the *Vienna Convention* (see paragraph 55) and which was indeed consolidated into Korea's Schedule of Concessions, and makes it clear that the remaining restrictions cover all restrictions which were in existence for balance-of-payments reasons at the time of

the conclusion of the Uruguay Round. Note 6 of Korea's Schedule LX does not list specific measures as remaining restrictions, but should be interpreted as Korea's commitment, in broad terms, to full liberalization of its beef import regime by the end of the year 2000. Consequently, even if it were assumed, for the sake of argument, that any remaining restrictions are inconsistent with the provisions of the GATT, they would still be covered by the transitional period until 1 January 2001.

88. **Australia** disagreed with Korea's assertion that the restrictions at issue in this dispute have been implemented by Korea in accordance with the Records of Understanding concluded with interested parties following the 1989 GATT panel. Australia submitted that its Records of Understanding with Korea, signed in 1990 and 1993, are only relevant to the extent that they reflect the negotiated outcome of the 1989 panel and are not, therefore, works preparatory to the WTO Agreements. Australia's 1993 Records of Understanding with Korea expired in 1995 and was not renewed in the context of the Uruguay Round. Furthermore, the Records of Understanding were attempts to give effect to the findings of the panel in the 1989 case and must be read in that context.

89. Australia, therefore, did not accept that the existence of now-expired Records of Understanding can be held to represent Australia's agreement that the measures in dispute in this case are covered by the transition period in Note 6. The Record of Understanding to which Korea refers as being signed in December 1993 was a bilateral agreement between the United States and Korea. This agreement cannot be "read into" Korea's Schedule or even be used to interpret the intentions of Australia, or indeed those of any WTO Member, other than the parties involved. Australia cannot be held to have agreed to the terms of a bilateral agreement to which it was not a party and which was not notified to the then GATT CONTRACTING PARTIES, let alone to have agreed that the terms of that agreement were incorporated into Korea's Schedule without this being made specific in the Schedule itself. Korea has produced no evidence to support its claim that Australia should be bound by the terms of Korea's December 1993 Record of Understanding with the United States.

90. Schedules are multilateral in character, Australia continued, and subject to the basic principles of MFN. In Australia's view, the multilateral nature of Schedules would be undermined if bilateral arrangements, particularly those not notified to other Members, and which may contain elements both inconsistent with WTO rules and prejudicial to the interests of other Members, could diminish the commitments specified in a Member's Schedule, to the detriment of all other Members. In this respect, Australia takes issue with Korea's reliance on the findings of the Appellate Body in *Canada-Dairy* (see paragraph 54) to support its view that its December 1993 Records of Understanding with the United States should be interpreted to permit Korea a transition period for measures existing at the time of the Uruguay Round. While Australia does not disagree with the approach to interpretation, the facts of that case can be distinguished from the current situation. In *Canada - Dairy* the Appellate Body considered the failure of Canada and the United States to reach agreement on improvements to existing

conditions for cross-border trade of milk in the context of interpreting Canada's Schedule commitments and the intentions of the parties at the time the commitments were entered into. On this basis, the Appellate Body overturned the panel's interpretation of Canada's Schedule commitments, given that the panel's interpretation would have increased Canada's obligations in relation to that cross-border trade even though it was clear that the parties had not so agreed. This is a different proposition altogether from binding all other WTO Members to the terms of a bilateral agreement which, according to Korea, reduces Korea's Schedule commitments and permits it to act in a manner detrimental to the interests of all other WTO Members without their knowledge, let alone their agreement.

91. Australia further submitted that, to the extent that the Panel might consider any of Australia's Records of Understanding with Korea relevant to determining Australia's intentions, its Records of Understanding could only be relevant to the extent that they contain explicit reference to the measures at issue in this dispute. However, the Records of Understanding do not contain reference to any such measures except the mark-up on SBS imports. This is because the Records of Understanding were intended to give effect to the 1989 panel on quantitative restrictions maintained for balance of payment purposes as mentioned in paragraph 88. None of the measures in dispute in this case were, in the opinion of Australia, maintained for BOP reasons.

92. **Australia** and the **United States** contended that none of the measures challenged by the Complainants, with the exception of the SBS mark-up, are addressed anywhere in the various Records of Understanding. They are entirely silent regarding a dual retail sales regime and separate, and more onerous, requirements for the operation of specialized import stores. Indeed, the July 1993 Records of Understanding specifies that Korea shall not impose any unnecessary obstacles to trade. Thus, no provision in the Records of Understanding speaks to prohibitions on commercial transactions between end-users and customers for imported beef or limitations on the use of imported beef by those end-users and customers. Similarly, the Records of Understanding contain no reference to delays in LPMO tendering or delayed allocation of SBS quota sub-shares. All of those measures were imposed by Korea without prior consultation with the Complainants. There is no reference in any of the Records of Understanding to measures on retail sale, limits on grass-fed beef, manipulation of volumes and prices at wholesale, restrictions on end users and usage imposed through the SBS system, and other limitations on the wholesale sale of imported beef in either Korea's Schedule or in its Records of Understanding.

93. **Australia** added that Korea has no basis to argue that Australia "agreed" to these measures or agreed that they be covered by a transition period. Australia noted that the Records of Understanding specifically state that both parties reserve their GATT rights. Clearly, the parties agreed that disputes were to be resolved through the WTO dispute settlement mechanism. The fact that Australia has not previously opposed Korea's measures in no way indicates its acceptance that those measures fall within the scope of Note 6 in Korea's Schedule. Nor does it prejudice Australia's right to challenge these measures at any time in the WTO.

A breach of WTO obligations does not become valid because of a lack of challenge or because of the expiration of time.[53]

94. The **United States** was of the view that the history of the Records of Understanding entered into by the United States and Korea demonstrates that two contentions central to Korea's arguments in this case are factually untenable. First, the terms of the three Records of Understanding make it abundantly clear that the restrictions that Korea promised to eliminate in the Records of Understanding and then in its WTO Schedule are those associated with the 1989 BOPs report and dispute. Thus, any later-in-time measures imposed by Korea, namely those that are the subject of the present dispute, cannot be encompassed by the term "remaining restrictions" as that term was used, first, in the BOP Committee Report, then later, in the Records of Understanding, and still later, in Korea's WTO Schedule.

95. In response, **Korea** submitted that Section IV B2(e) of the July 1993 Record of Understanding makes it plain that the Complainants were well aware of the fact that a system of separation of sales outlets was in operation when the Record of Understanding was negotiated. The mentioned paragraph states that "Also beginning January 1, 1995, any butcher shops that are or become *registered dealers of imported beef* shall have the right to participate..." (emphasis added). In Section IV C6(a) of the same Record of Understanding, Korea continued, it is stated that "Beef imported...must be distributed and sold through *legal channels...*" (emphasis added). Korea submitted that it is clear from these excerpts that the negotiators were fully aware of the existence of the system of separation of sales outlets at the time of negotiating the Record of Understanding leading up to the Uruguay Round.

96. The **United States** submitted that Korea's contention that the term "remaining restrictions" encompasses most, if not all, of the measures challenged by the United States is refuted by language used in each of the three Records of Understanding negotiated between the United States and Korea. The Panel need only to consult Korea's notification of the 1990 and July 1993 Records of Understanding to satisfy itself that "remaining restrictions" could only have been intended to refer to the restrictions on market access for imported beef that Korea had in place in November 1989, when the BOP Committee and GATT panel reports were adopted. That the term "remaining restrictions" was used in the same manner, and with the same meaning, both in the BOP Committee Reports, and then in each of the Records of Understanding, is strong evidence that Korea and the United States intended the term, when incorporated in Korea's Schedule, to have the same meaning as when used in the Records of Understanding, and not a different meaning.

97. Each of the Records of Understanding contained references to "remaining restrictions" or "restrictions on beef" taken for balance-of- payment purposes.[54]

---

[53] *EEC- Imports from Hong Kong*, para. 28; *Japan - Leather*, para. 45.

Since there was no justification for continuing BOP restrictions, let alone introducing new BOP-based restrictions, after the finding of the 1987 BOP Committee, the reference to remaining BOP restrictions can mean only those BOP restrictions still in effect at the time the Committee report was issued in 1987, or at the very latest, the 1989 date of adoption of the Committee's report. Therefore, in the view of the United States, any measure introduced after that date was by necessity without BOP justification and could not constitute a "remaining restriction" for BOP purposes.

98. Korea in its communication of 4 July 1990, transmitting the 1990 Records of Understanding to the GATT Council, the United States continued, stated that Korea had held consultations with the three contracting parties to the 1989 dispute in accordance with the recommendations in the panel reports (L/6503, L/6504 and L/6505) adopted on November 7, 1989. More importantly, Korea reaffirmed in that communication its "undertaking to eliminate its remaining import restrictions on beef or otherwise bring them into conformity with GATT provisions." That the reference to "remaining restrictions" in Korea's WTO Schedule is intended to mean the same "restrictions" in place at the end of the 1989 dispute is made clear from consideration of the July and December Records of Understanding. The July 1993 Record of Understanding contained a reaffirmation by Korea of its commitment to eliminate its "remaining import restrictions on beef." Again, the discussion of these restrictions took place in the context of implementation of the recommendations of the GATT panel report. Thus, there can be no confusion about the nature of the commitment that Korea declared to undertake: it was the elimination of the GATT inconsistent import restrictions found by the 1989 panel.

99. The December 1993 Record of Understanding, unlike those that preceded it, was not limited to trade in beef, but also contained provisions relating to pork, poultry, dairy, and citrus. The purpose of the provisions governing beef were primarily to extend forward in time the terms of the July 1993 Record of Understanding. The December Record of Understanding provides for continuation of the beef quota through the year 2000, (ultimately made part of Korea's WTO Schedule of Concessions) as well as for increases in the quota, and identifies the relevant percentage of the quota to be assigned to the SBS system in each remaining year of the quota, together with the applicable maximum amount of the mark-up. In all other respects the July 1993 Record of Understanding was left

[54] In para. 2.1 of Korea's notification of the 1990 Record of Understanding to the Council, L/6697, Korea stated that it "reaffirms its undertaking to eliminate its remaining import restrictions on beef . . ." Article V of the July 1993 Record of Understanding with the United States reads as follows: "With regard to beef, the ROKG reaffirms its undertaking to eliminate is remaining import restrictions or otherwise bring them into conformity with GATT provisions as provided in the conclusion of the report on the GATT Balance of Payments Committee on consultations with the Republic of Korea adopted by the GATT Council on 7 November 1989." The December 1993 Record of Understanding simply states that "All balance-of-payments restrictions on beef shall expire no later than December 31, 2000."

unchanged.[55] Finally, the December Record of Understanding reiterated the same passage contained in the previous Record of Understanding and committed Korea to elimination of "*all balance-of-payments restrictions on beef*" and required that to be accomplished by "no later than December 31, 2000."

100. The United States noted that it did not participate in the formulation of the challenged measures. Korea's argument that the challenged measures were implemented at the request of the United States and other countries exporting beef to Korea cannot withstand scrutiny. The three Records of Understanding between the United States and Korea were all concluded after the adoption of the 1989 panel report. In the view of the United States, the Records of Understanding were intended to provide a transition for Korea from a situation in which imported beef was banned toward a liberalized market where commercial forces would determine the quantity of beef imported. An examination of the Records of Understanding reveals that Korea was not willing to accept a quick progression to an open market and an incremental approach was necessary.[56]

101. While the United States did press Korea to develop a market-oriented regime for imported beef and, in doing so, requested that Korea establish the SBS system as a bridge between the LPMO's monopoly control of imported beef and a market driven by commercial forces, the United States was by no means a partner in developing the specific regulatory provisions governing the operation of the SBS system. Likewise, the United States had no role in developing the LPMO's daily operating procedures, including the manner in which the LPMO conducts its wholesale auctions or the timing of its opening of tenders.[57] In fact, in quarterly meetings with Korea, the United States was forced repeatedly to seek Korea's implementation of the market liberalizing reforms that already had been negotiated.

(iv) Quarterly Bilateral Consultations

102. **Australia** submitted that Korea's claims regarding Australia's participation in bilateral quarterly consultations (see paragraph 105) in relation to the beef trade are of no relevance, and cannot be held as proof of Australia's agreement to the measures at issue in this dispute or to any transition period for Korea in rela-

55 More specifically, the last para. of the December 1993 Record of Understanding stipulates that "The current July 15, 1993 Record of Understanding (L/7270) shall continue to apply except as modified to incorporate the provisions of the new understanding."

56 Thus, the 1993 Record of Understanding provided for annual increases in the quota quantity, for a gradual increase in the number of super-groups participating through the SBS system, and for incremental increases in the proportion of the quota share dedicated to the SBS system, where customers and end-users could contract with foreign shippers relatively free from interference by the LPMO.

57 Although the July 1993 Records of Understanding specified when unused SBS quota would be reallocated among the various super-groups, the Records of Understanding did not direct either when or how allocation of quota increases would be made to new super-groups.

tion to these measures. If any relevance is to be ascribed to the bilateral quarterly consultations, it is the dissatisfaction of the Australian government with the range of measures adopted by Korea which Australia argued were not envisaged when the bilateral agreements were reached. Australia, in good faith, agreed to a transition period to permit Korea to move towards liberalization through the use of a time-limited quota. This cannot, however, be interpreted as an agreement by Australia to the measures challenged in this dispute. It is because Korea failed to adequately address Australia's concerns about these measures in a bilateral context that Australia now find itself before a WTO dispute settlement panel.

(v) Prior Panel Reports

103. The **United States** emphasized that regardless of the meaning given to the term "remaining restrictions" there is no legal basis for concluding that a Member may unilaterally limit or reduce its GATT 1994, or other WTO, obligations by providing in its Schedule for a supposed right to restrict imports. Thus, Korea's contention that it possesses the right to continue until 1 January 2001, all WTO inconsistent restrictions on imports of beef which were in place at the time of the conclusion of the Uruguay Round negotiations is entirely without foundation.

104. The United States referred to the *US – Sugar Head Note* case,[58] which considered whether import restrictions provided for in US Schedule XX were consistent with the obligations contained in Article XI:1. In finding that the US restrictions were inconsistent with the requirements of Article XI, the panel examined the issue in light of the wording of Article II. Based on the text of that Article, the panel found that Article II "permits contracting parties to qualify the obligation to exempt products from ordinary customs duties in excess of the levels specified in the Schedule, not however to qualify their obligations under other Articles of the General Agreement."[59] The panel concluded that " ... Article II gives contracting parties the possibility to incorporate into the legal framework of the General Agreement commitments additional to those already contained in the General Agreement and to qualify such additional commitments, not however to reduce their commitments under other provisions of that Agreement."[60] Korea's assertion that the Schedule LX reference to "remaining restrictions" exempts Korea from all of its obligations relating to beef under GATT 1994 is, therefore, untenable. In recent disputes involving *EC – Bananas III (AB)* and *EC – Poultry (AB),* the Appellate Body reiterated the legal conclusions reached by the *US - Sugar Head Note* panel.

105. Referring to the United States' arguments in paragraph 103, **Korea** replied that it does not contend that it may *"unilaterally"* exempt itself from specific GATT obligations. Korea merely referred to the existence of a transitional period

58 Page 331.
59 *Ibid*, para. 5.2.
60 *Id.*, para. 5.3.

in its Schedule of Concessions, which is based on multilateral negotiations and agreement between WTO Members in the Uruguay Round, explicitly referred to and confirmed by the language of Note 6. Second, none of the cases cited by the United States as legal authority dealt with the issue of whether a Schedule of Concessions can contain a transitional period and a phasing-in of GATT obligations. All the cited cases dealt with the issue of whether a provision in a Schedule of Concessions could allow GATT/WTO Members to violate certain GATT provisions on a permanent basis. Note 6 contains an obligation for Korea to eliminate or bring its remaining restrictions into conformity with GATT by 1 January 2001. The agreed transitional period has to be seen against the background of prior BOP restrictions, the previous GATT panel reports, the ensuing Records of Understanding and quarterly consultations which shape the transition to bring Korea's measures into conformity with GATT and the full liberalization of beef imports by 1 January 2001.

106. Hence, Korea continued, the issues contained in the cited panel and Appellate Body reports and Korea's Schedule of Concessions refer to two factually different situations: the former contains a prohibition to permanently deviate from the obligations of the GATT through agreements reflected in the Schedule of Concessions, whereas the latter contains a temporary provision which will expire on a set date. Korea, fully respecting its obligations under the GATT/WTO, did not diminish its obligations by indicating in its Schedule of Concessions that it will bring its measures into conformity within a defined transitional period. In other words, Korea did not add a right through its Schedule of Concessions: it accepted an unambiguous obligation to fully liberalize a previously protected market within a specified time period.

107. **Australia** and the **United States** also referred to the *EC – Poultry (AB)* in which the Appellate Body dismissed Brazil's claim that a concession contained in the European Communities' Schedule establishing a tariff-rate quota for poultry need not be administered consistently with Articles I and XIII. Brazil had argued that the terms of a bilateral agreement between the European Communities and Brazil following the *EEC - Oilseeds* dispute, accorded Brazil the entire tariff-rate quota for poultry. The Appellate Body, citing the *US Sugar Head Note* case, rejected Brazil's argument. In doing so, the Appellate Body emphasized the following finding from the *EC – Bananas III(AB)* dispute: "... a Member may yield rights but not diminish its obligations and ... [that principle] is equally valid for the market access concessions and commitments for agricultural products contained in the Schedules annexed to the GATT 1994."[61] The Appellate Body then observed that "a Member may yield or waive some of its own rights and grant benefits to other Members, but that it cannot unilaterally diminish its own obliga-

[61] Appellate Body Report, *European Communities – Measures Affecting the Importation of Certain Poultry Products* (" *EC – Poultry*"), WT/DS69/AB/R, adopted 23 July 1998, DSR 1998:V, 2031, para. 98.

tions."[62] These legal conclusions refute Korea's argument that it is entitled to continue WTO inconsistent measures relating to beef until the year 2001.

(vi) Article 26 of the Vienna Convention (good faith)

108. **Korea** submitted that by bringing the current dispute, the Complainants are denying the binding force of their agreement to Korea's Schedule of Concessions and are not acting in good faith. As such, they violate Article 26 of the Vienna Convention which stipulates the principle of *pacta sunt servanda* - a basic principle of public international law. The claims brought by the Complainants should necessarily fail for the reasons stated in paragraph 54 alone. But Korea also considered that none of the claims has any merit.

109. In response to Korea' arguments in paragraph 108, **Australia** contended that it is not clear to Australia that Article 26 of the *Vienna Convention* adds anything to the provisions of interpretation required to be applied by the Panel under Article 3:2 of the DSU, which explicitly incorporates the rules of interpretation of customary international law. Australia noted, however, that the Panel is limited by its terms of reference to consideration of the measures against the provisions of the WTO Agreements. Australia rejected Korean allegations of a lack of good faith on Australia's behalf and submitted that Korea has not met its burden of proof in making such a claim. Australia also rejected any links made by Korea between considerations of good faith and the admissibility of Australia's claims at this time. Korea's allegations, however, do highlight Australia's fundamental disagreement with Korea about its commitments rather than any lack of good faith.

110. To the extent that the notion of good faith has any relevance at all, Australia continued, it would only pertain to those measures that Korea concedes are GATT-inconsistent restrictions. Only then could Korea conceivably attempt to argue that the claims in this dispute have been brought prematurely. However, with the exception of its claims about the mark-up on SBS imports, Korea has made no such concession, indeed defending the GATT consistency of every other measure.

111. Australia noted that good faith is a matter requiring reciprocity. In the course of this dispute Korea has asserted that it alone has the right to unilaterally determine which of the remaining restrictions on imported beef it will remove on 1 January 2001. And although Korea has declared that it will remove or bring into conformity any remaining inconsistent restrictions, it has argued to the Panel the GATT-consistency of the majority of its measures. Australia is also concerned about reports it has received about measures proposed by Korea to limit the effect of the end of the quota on domestic beef. These measures include maintaining the dual retail system and increasing the level of financial support to domestic beef stores, the introduction of a mark-up on LPMO quota sales, the in-

---

62 *Id.*

troduction of country-of-origin labelling in restaurants as well as the banning of two current SBS groups, NLCF and LCTM, from the imported beef trade. Australia can but conclude that, if there is any question of good faith in this dispute, it does not rest with Australia.

112. The **United States** submitted that, contrary to Korea's claims in this regard, it has acted in good faith in this dispute. The United States has shown in paragraphs 100 *et sequitur* and 107 that the underlying basis for Korea's claims of bad faith are entirely groundless. Accordingly, Korea's request that the Panel find the US challenge to Korea's measures to be inadmissible must be rejected.

C. Claims under Article XI:1 of GATT

1. No Prohibitions or Restrictions...on the Importation of any Product

113. Referring to the text of Article XI:1[63], **Australia** argued that panels have interpreted the scope of Article XI:1 broadly, providing for a general ban on import or export restrictions or prohibitions. The panel in *Japan – Trade in Semiconductors* considered the wording of Article XI:1 to be comprehensive; it applies "to all measures instituted or maintained by a Member prohibiting or restricting the importation, exportation, or sale for export of products other than measures that take the form of duties, taxes or other charges.[64] Similarly, the panel in *India – Quantitative Restrictions* considered that the scope of the term "restriction" was also broad, as seen in its ordinary meaning which is "a limitation on action, a limiting condition or regulation".[65] The scope of the term "restriction" has most recently been defined by the Appellate Body as "a limitation on action, a limiting condition or regulation".[66] Restrictions applied on the entry of grass-fed beef through the tender process are, in the opinion of Australia, quantitative import restrictions within the meaning of Article XI:1. For a four-month period in 1999 all cuts of grass-fed beef, which is predominantly supplied by Australia, were arbitrarily excluded from the thirty per cent of the market controlled by the LPMO.

114. In some circumstances, Australia continued, a measure affecting imported product (for example, availability of end-points of sale) has the practical effect of

---

[63] "No prohibitions or restrictions other than duties, taxes or other charges, whether made effective through quotas, import or export licences or other measures, shall be instituted or maintained by any contracting party on the importation of any product of the territory of any other contracting party or on the exportation or sale for export of any product destined for the territory of any other contracting party."

[64] Para. 104.

[65] Panel Report, *India – Quantitative Restrictions on Imports of Agricultural, Textile and Industrial Products* ("*India – Quantitative Restrictions*"), WT/DS90/R, adopted 22 September 1999, as upheld by the Appellate Body Report DSR 1999:V, 1799, para. 5.128.

[66] *Ibid.*

restricting importation of the product itself, and is, therefore, covered by Article XI:1. This is supported by the fact that Article XI:1 uses the broad term "restrictions" on importation, rather than "laws, regulations or measures on importation". The reference to "whether made effective through quotas, import or export licences or other measures" indicates that the measure itself need not be directed at importation or apply at the point of import (such as import licences or quotas). It is sufficient that it has an effect on importation. Given that "restriction" has a broad scope, Article XI:1 applies to any measure which has the *practical* effect of restricting imports. Furthermore, restrictions at the point of distribution may have the practical effect of a quantitative restriction where they restrict the imported products end-points of sale.

115. Australia referred to the panel on *Canada – Alcoholic Drinks* which considered that limitations on the points of sale available to imported beer were restrictions within the meaning of Article XI.[67] Restrictions on distribution were within the meaning of "other measures" under Article XI:1, even though such measures might be examined also under Article III:4. Here, the restrictions, although related to distribution, were on importation. This was cited by the panel in *India – Quantitative Restrictions* which examined *inter alia* an Indian measure in which import licences were available only to "actual users". The panel considered that the "actual user" condition was a restriction on imports because it precluded imports of products for resale by intermediaries, i.e. distribution to consumers who are unable to import directly for their own immediate use is restricted. It operated as a restriction on imports within the meaning of Article XI.[68]

116. In addition to maintaining a quota, the **United States** argued, Korea maintains quantitative restrictions consisting of import licensing requirements ("import recommendations") and sales and distribution constraints on imported beef. These restrictions are set forth in the Livestock Industry Act, the Final Livestock Act, as well as MAF's implementing Guidelines and Regulations. Korea also identified several of the restrictions that are the subject of this dispute in its 21 November 1996 reply to the questionnaire on import licensing procedures from the Committee on Import Licensing Procedures.[69] Measures associated with the administration of the beef quota were also notified to the Committee on Agriculture.[70] These restrictions constitute continuing violations of one of the most fundamental rules of the world trading system, i.e. Article XI:1.

117. The United States submitted that the measures that are the subject of this dispute are "restrictions other than duties, taxes or charges" as defined in Article XI:1. Under the WTO, the panel in *EC – Bananas III* acknowledged that "Past GATT panel reports support giving the term 'restriction' [in Article XI:1] an ex-

---

67 Para. 4.24.

68 Para. 5.141-5.143.

69 See G/LIC/N/3/KOR/1.

70 See G/AG/N/KOR/1, 31 May 1995.

pansive interpretation.[71] Referring to the GATT 1950 working party report on a "Notification by Haiti under Article XVIII"[72], to the 1950 report on "The Use of Quantitative Restrictions for Protective and other Commercial Purposes" which was approved unanimously by the CONTRACTING PARTIES under Article XXV[73] and which refers to import licensing as an import restriction[74], to the 1978 panel in *EEC –Processed Fruits and Vegetables* which found that a non-automatic licensing system denying licences for imports below certain minimum prices was a "restriction" within the meaning of Article XI,[75] to the panel in *Japan –Semi-Conductors* which found that "this wording [of Article XI:1] was comprehensive; it applied to all measures instituted or maintained by a contracting party prohibiting or restricting the importation, exportation or sale for export of products other than measures that take the form of duties, taxes or other charges[76], as well as to the panel on *India – Quantitative Restrictions,*[77] which concluded that a non-automatic licensing system in India operates as a restriction on imports within the meaning of Article XI:1, the United States contended that Korea's import "recommendation" system is, like India's licensing regime, a discretionary system and as such an import restriction that is inconsistent with Korea's obligations under Article XI:1.

2. *Measures Imposed on Retail Sale of Imported Beef*

118. In the present case, **Australia** argued, Korea restricts the sale of imported beef to specialized imported beef stores. This prevents domestic butcher shops from purchasing imported beef and limits the end points of sale for imported beef. The sale of imported beef is limited to only 5,000 stores, compared with the other 48,000 outlets which would be available if the restriction did not apply. While the restriction is related to the distribution of imported beef, it has the effect of a restriction on the importation of beef within the meaning of Article XI:1.

119. **Korea** submitted that Australia's argument concerning separate retail stores for imported and domestic beef (see in particular paragraphs 114, 115 and 118) is fundamentally flawed in several respects. The separate sales outlets system, which is designed to prevent the fraudulent practice of passing off imported beef as domestic beef, applies the same restrictions both to stores selling domestic beef and to specialized stores selling imported beef. Domestic beef stores are

---

71 Para. 7.154, citing panel report on *Japan - Semiconductors*, paras. 104-105; panel report on *EEC - Processed Fruits and Vegetables*, para. 4.9.

72 BISD Vol. I, page 46, Article XVIII:12. GATT/CP.5/25, adopted on 27 November 1950, BISD Vol. II/87.

73 GATT/CP.5/33, adopted on 3 April 1950, republished as "The Use of Quantitative Restrictions for Protective and other Commercial Purposes," Sales No. GATT/1950-3.

74 *Id.*, page 7, paras. 5-7.

75 Para. 4.9.

76 Para. 104.

77 Appellate Body Report, *India – Quantitative Restrictions*, *supra*, footnote 65, para. 5.19-5.130.

equally prohibited from selling imported beef. The separate sales outlets system does not, therefore, disadvantage imported product and cannot be considered a restriction on the importation of beef. More importantly, there are no restrictions relating to the number of imported beef stores which may operate at any given time, or with respect to their geographic location. Regarding the Complainants' arguments in, for instance paragraphs 118 and 175 with respect to the small number of imported-beef shops, Korea admitted that the number of imported beef stores is at the present time smaller than the number of domestic beef stores. However, this is a consequence the quota on beef products. The supply of imported beef is, therefore, insufficient to support further imported beef stores at the present time. Following the liberalization of Korea's beef sector on 1 January 2001, imported and domestic beef stores and beef product will compete freely in the market, and the number of either domestic or imported beef stores will be determined in accordance with market demand. The separate sales outlets system is the result of purely internal anti-fraud measures and is in no way related to the importation of products. Therefore, Article XI:1 does not apply to this measure. Since the same restrictions are applied to both domestic and imported beef stores, it is meaningless to refer to a "restriction on importation" within the meaning of Article XI:1.

120. The separate sales outlets system applied by Korea, Korea continued, bears no resemblance to the type of "restrictions" examined by the panels in *Canada - Marketing Agencies* and *India - Quantitative Restrictions,* cited by Australia. In the *Canada - Marketing Agencies* case, the limitation on the points of sale available to imported beer applied solely to imported product, while domestic product was not similarly constrained In the present case, as the same rule applies to both domestic and imported beef stores, there can be no claim that a limitation on the points of sale is being applied to the imported product compared with domestic product.

121. Similarly, the restriction at issue in *India - Quantitative Restrictions,* the *"actual user"* condition, precluded imports of products for sale by intermediaries while no such restriction applied to domestic product. The measure thereby restricted the importation of the relevant products by foreclosing an avenue of distribution solely for imported products, restricting the points of distribution compared with domestic product. While Korea does maintain a quota on beef, no restrictions of any kind are applied at the retail level with respect to the number of imported beef stores, their location, or any other restriction.

3. LPMO Tendering Opportunities

122. **Australia** submitted that the restrictions applied on the entry of grass-fed beef through the LPMO tender processes were quantitative restrictions within the meaning of Article XI:1. The LPMO has used its tender processes to exclude grass-fed beef from the market: in the period from June to September 1999, the LPMO held three tenders from which grass-fed beef was excluded. Although Korea claimed that this exclusion was on the basis of reduced demand, its own

figures showed that sales of grass-fed beef had increased by over three times sales in the same period in 1998 (when the LPMO did purchase grass-fed beef)[78]. Prior to the exclusion of grass-fed beef in the 1999 tenders, grass-fed beef had generally secured approximately 50 per cent of each tender.

123. **Korea** submitted that the complaints raised by Australia with respect to grass-fed beef have no basis under Article XI:1. All tenders are open to all supplying countries and perfectly origin neutral. Australian exporters are free to participate both in tenders for grass-fed and grain-fed beef. The distinction between grass-fed and grain-fed beef does not by itself constitute discriminatory treatment or an infringement of MFN principles. As long as Korea does not discriminate on the basis of origin of the products obtained, in violation of the MFN principle, Korea is not obliged to affect its purchases of beef according to sub-groupings of various beef types. The LPMO consistently purchases its full quota amount, according to an open bidding procedure and according to origin-neutral criteria. It cannot, therefore, be claimed that Korea applies quantitative restrictions with respect to beef (beyond that resulting from the quota). Australia has not adduced any evidence that Australian products have been discriminated against based on their origin. On the contrary, total purchases from Australia (by the LPMO) in the first six months of 1999 represented a 44 per cent share of all purchases which is much higher than their previous shares of 33.3 per cent in 1997 and of 30 per cent in 1998. These data do not suggest any *de facto* discrimination of Australian products. Hence, Korea submitted that the claims of Australia with respect to this issue are unfounded and the question of import restrictions contrary to Article XI:1 does not arise. CF paragraph 324.

(Cf also paragraphs 287-289 and 346.)

124. **Australia** and the **United States** submitted that panels have found that restrictions on points of sale and distribution are quantitative restrictions within the meaning of Article XI:1. Therefore, measures which restrict the *number* of points of import will also fall within Article XI:1. In *India – Quantitative Restrictions*, the panel found that an "Actual User" condition which denied a licence for imports by intermediaries constituted an import restriction within the meaning of Article XI. In considering the scope of the prohibition under Article XI:1, the panel drew on earlier panel reports, noting that a minimum import price system had been considered to be a restriction within the meaning of Article XI:1, as had limitations on points of sale available to imported beer because they had imposed "limitation on action, a limiting condition or regulation". The panel found that, applied to the "Actual User" condition, they led to the conclusion that it is a restriction on imports because it precludes imports of products for resale by intermediaries, i.e. distribution to consumers, who are unable to import directly for their own immediate use. Based on the foregoing, the Complainants argued, the procedures of the LPMO, itself a state-trading enterprise, restrict imports by *inter*

78 122,000 MTs in May/June 1998 compared with 372,000 MTs in May/June 1999.

alia withholding quota allocations and delaying any invitations to tender, and, thus, are inconsistent with Article XI:1.

125. Referring to the arguments by the Complaining parties that some of Korea's measures on beef are a violation of both Article. III:4 and Article XI, **Korea** was of the view that there is a clear dividing line between the two provisions. The former deals with internal measures, that is measures applicable to products after they have been cleared through customs, whereas the latter deals with border measures, namely QRs. Hence, it is logically impossible for a domestic measure to be 'caught' simultaneously by the two provisions. For a violation of Article XI to be established, the Complaining parties need to show that a government-induced QR restricts imports of foreign products independently of the manner in which domestic like products are treated. With respect to the argument by the Complainants that the LPMO delayed invitations to tender, Korea noted that the LPMO has consistently filled its quota share, even during the height of the crisis in 1997 and 1998. In addition, Korea contended that the Complainants' assertion that Korea delayed quota allocations to super-groups is inaccurate. At the beginning of 1999, Korea explained, part of the quota was reserved for three new super-groups which started participating in the SBS system. The quota was allocated by 14 June 1999, i.e. once the quantities required by these super-groups were established. None of the super-groups had exhausted their initial quota by that time and, according to Korea, no negative effects on beef imports resulted from this circumstance.

4. *Measures with Respect to the Discharge of Imported Beef in the Wholesale Market*

126. **Australia** claimed that both the LPMO and the NLCF, pursuant to their obligations under the *Regulations Concerning the Sale of Imported Beef*, have acted to withhold beef imported by the LPMO from the wholesale market in order to stabilize demand and supply for domestic beef. The limitations are applied through the LPMO monthly sales plan, minimum wholesale prices and the daily discharge practices of the NLCF. The result of the discharge system has been to artificially constrict the supply of imported beef and constrain imports to the extent that in 1998 and the first half of 1999 there was substantial under-filling of the LPMO beef quota. The cumulative effect of these pricing and distribution measures has been a significant increase in LPMO stocks of imported beef during the last two years.[79] In turn, these rising stock levels have led to delayed tenders

[79] In October 1997, the LPMO had an estimated 28,000 tonnes of imported beef in stock. By the end of 1998 LPMO had accrued stocks of 67,934 tonnes of imported beef, more than the LPMO's entire quota allocation for 1999. As at July 1999, these stocks had fallen only slightly to 61,524 tonnes, notwithstanding rising demand in the market for imported beef.

and reduced imports by the LPMO.[80] Shipping delays have also been necessary in relation to the 1999 quota, with delivery dates extending into 2000.

127. **Australia** and the **United States** submitted that the LPMO sets a minimum acceptable auction price on a daily basis for each cut and brand of beef and that the NLCF periodically withholds imported product from the market. Australia produced charts showing demand, sales and acceptable bid prices for a range of brands and cuts of beef which, Australia submitted, proved the operation of a minimum price. Whilst auction participants do not know this price, the previous day's acceptable price is, according to the Complainants, a good guide. It is well understood in the trade that bids below the minimum price will not be accepted. Such measures are taken to stabilize the price of domestic beef, with prices being set for imports that are contingent on the price of competing domestic product. The price of imported beef in the wholesale market is, therefore, decided by reference to the price of its domestic competition. A press release issued by the MAF on 22 July 1999, reflects this policy.[81] The Complainants argued that the minimum price has been set at levels which have considerably dampened demand for imported beef but which have ensured that imported beef prices have stayed sufficiently high so that domestic product could remain competitive. The minimum price has generally been too high to attract the interest of end users and as a result distribution of imported beef has been considerably less than stocks actually held. These measures have the effect of quantitative restrictions on imported beef contrary to Article XI:1. **Australia** claimed that these measures are also contrary to Article 4.2 of the *Agreement on Agriculture*.

128. **Australia** did not accept that minimum pricing was the result of Korea's financial crisis in late 1997/early 1998 or of losses incurred by the LPMO during that period arising from the currency crisis. Australia's calculations, based on data provided by the LPMO relating to import prices, shipping dates and exchange rate fluctuations, show that there were several months in 1998 where the LPMO did not sustain losses resulting from the difference between the import price and the minimum wholesale price. Except for beef purchased in Korea's final tender in 1997, none of Korea's 1997 purchases of beef were affected by the currency crisis. The currency crisis hit Korea in November 1997, reached its peak in December 1997 and January 1998 and began to improve by July 1998. However, the last tender for beef in 1997 was held on 21 October 1997 and was for a quantity of 9361 tonnes. While most of this last tender purchase would have arrived in Korea during the currency crisis, all other 1997 tenders were purchased and customs cleared by the time the currency crisis hit. Furthermore, no more

[80] In 1998 40,237 tonnes (53.8 per cent), of a total 1998 quota of 74,800 tonnes, was not permitted to enter Korea until 1999. As a consequence, 1999 imports have been affected. As at 22 October 1999, the LPMO will have purchased 35,099 tonnes out of a total quota for 1999 of 61,800 tonnes i.e. 56.8 per cent of its annual quota amount.

[81] "MAF to raise unlimited supply of imported beef to stabilize extraordinary cattle prices", Ministry of Agriculture and Forestry press release, 22 July 1999.

imported beef entered Korea until July 1998, when the exchange rate was recovering. Australia, therefore, submitted that LPMO had stocks on hand which were purchased at pre-currency crisis levels and which entered Korea before the currency crisis hit. Korea would have been able to sell, without loss, from these stocks. Australia hence argued that the only explanation for the high minimum prices of imported beef at that time was that LPMO was acting to protect the competitiveness of domestic beef *vis-ä-vis* imported beef.

129. Australia also noted that minimum prices have continued to be imposed throughout 1999, regardless of the recovery in the Korean economy, stabilization of exchange rates and rising levels of demand for beef. The cumulative effect of the pricing and distribution measures has been to significantly increase LPMO stocks of imported beef, leading directly to tender and shipment delays in 1998 and 1999, causing imports to fall to amounts considerably less than the LPMO quota share in those years. The persistence of minimum pricing in 1999 will also have an impact on LPMO imports for 2000, given that significant amounts purchased in 1999 are not actually permitted to enter Korea until late 2000. (See also paragraphs 205-206 below.)

130. **Korea** responded that Korea has never established, nor employed, minimum import prices. The LPMO initiates international tenders, and the tenders are awarded on a purely commercial basis, in ascending order from the lowest bid received. All participants in the tender process therefore compete on the basis of price, and are awarded purely on the basis of the competitiveness of the offers submitted. The procedures employed by the LPMO, therefore, bear no resemblance to a system of minimum import prices. With respect to imports effected through the SBS system, contracts are negotiated and concluded between members and suppliers on an entirely commercial basis, without any government interference or scrutiny with respect to price.

131. The LPMO will, however, as a trading entity operating under commercial considerations, seek to ensure that the imported beef product is not sold at a loss at the wholesale auction. For this reason, while no rigid minimum price is set, basic target prices are set for the sales at wholesale auction. Target prices are established by the LPMO and are used by the NLCF as a guideline during wholesale auctions to avoid the sale of imported beef below a certain price level. However, these target prices are not inflexible and the establishment of target prices does not mean that bids falling below the target price will never be accepted. Despite the severe market situation prevailing in 1998, Korea continued to exert its best efforts to sell the maximum amount of imported beef possible. To this end, Korea resorted to selling below the established target price. The target prices are closely linked to import prices (c.i.f. plus tariff plus sales cost). During the financial crisis, Korea argued, the LPMO would have made losses on the imports of beef and that therefore it was justified in maintaining the target price at a level preventing losses on sales of imported beef (see Annex 4).

132. **The Complaining parties** responded that the LPMO had not sold imported beef below the minimum price during the financial crisis and as a conse-

quence, stocks of imported beef rose rapidly. Australia contended that if the target price is not reached, the beef is not sold. The LPMO did not make any attempt to run down its stocks during either 1998 or 1999, which would possibly have been the most commercially viable option. Instead, LPMO continued to withhold imported beef from the market by setting an artificially high minimum price, based on domestic beef prices. As a result, stocks of imported beef rose to nearly 61,000 tonnes by mid-1999." They added, amongst other things, that the high level the LPMO sales costs may explain Korea's assessment of the LPMO's losses.[82]

133. **Australia** and the **United States** contended that various discharge procedures adopted by the LPMO represent "restrictions" which fall within the purview of Article XI:1. They referred to the *ad note* to Articles XI, XII, XIII, XIV and XVIII, which states that the term 'import restrictions' in these Articles covers restrictions made effective through state trading operations. They also referred to the panel in *Japan - Agricultural Products* which firmly rejected Japan's argument that Article XI:1 did not apply to import restrictions made effective through state trading. Likewise, in the 1988 panel report on *Canada - Marketing Agencies (1988)*, the panel observed that the *ad note* provided that throughout these Articles "the terms 'import restrictions' and 'export restrictions' include restrictions made effective though state-trading operations".

134. The **United States** also referred to the Haitian import restrictions mentioned above (paragraph 117) which were maintained through a tobacco monopoly, as well as to the working party on the *Italian Restrictions Affecting Imports from the United States and Certain Other Contracting Parties*, which states that "Insofar as the State-trading operation had the effect of restricting imports, the Italian authorities fully recognized that, by virtue of the interpretative notes *ad* Articles XI, XII, etc. in Annex I to the General Agreement, it constituted an import restriction within the purview of Article XI."[83] Furthermore, in the 1989 panel report on the US complaint concerning *Korea - Beef*, that panel found that the Korean import restrictions, administered through a state trading entity, violated Article XI.[84]

135. **Australia** submitted that Members should not be able to avoid their obligations by establishing state trading enterprises to carry out functions which have the effect of influencing the level of imports beyond an established concession such as a tariff or a quota. The issue is not whether the state trading operation is a monopoly but the effect on trade.[85] The panel in *Japan - Film* acknowledged "a

---

[82] The United States contended that the 32- 40 per cent sales costs of the LPMO are in striking contrast with the 2-3 per cent cost that the super-groups are allowed to charge by the MAF.

[83] Report of the working party under Article XXII:2 on *Italian Restrictions Affecting Imports from the United States and Certain other Contracting Parties*, L/1468, adopted on 16 May 1961, BISD 10S/117, 119, para. 7.

[84] Paras. 113, 115.

[85] See *Korea - Beef*, para. 115.

risk that WTO obligations could be evaded through a Member's delegation of quasi-governmental authority to private bodies." The value of concessions would be undermined if governments, through the activities of state trading enterprises, whether or not they are monopolies, could avoid the requirements of Article XI:1. In the case of the release of beef imported and distributed under the LPMO system, Australia continued, it is artificial to make a distinction between restrictions imposed by import monopolies and those carried out by state trading enterprises that have as their stated objective the stabilization of domestic beef and cattle prices. It is with this purpose in mind that the LPMO has established monthly sales plans and minimum wholesale prices for imported beef and the NLCF has withheld daily discharge volumes of imported beef onto the wholesale market. The effect has been a rise in stocks of imported beef, restricting, in the view of Australia, the LPMO's imports beyond the limits imposed by the quota.

136. The **United States** submitted that in its notification to the Committee on State Trading Enterprises, Korea identifies the LPMO as the entity appointed by MAF to administer the import regime for beef.[86] Moreover, MAF has delegated extensive powers to the LPMO to administer Korea's licensing regime for imported beef while retaining control over the LPMO's functions in this regard. The LPMO not only possesses the exclusive right to import a substantial portion of the beef quota, but also exercises considerable control over the use of the remaining portion of the quota through its authority to allocate quota shares to the SBS super-groups and to approve their import requests.[87] In this latter role, the LPMO not only delayed the initiation of tenders for imports until approximately mid-year in 1998, it also severely limited the invitation of tendering in 1999, so that as of June 1999, less than 9,451 metric tonnes had been imported by the LPMO out of a 1999 quota share of 61,800 metric tonnes. In addition, the LPMO has withheld allocation of quota share to the super-groups and placed pressure on them to reduce the quantity of imported beef for which they seek import approvals.

137. **Korea** submitted that the arguments advanced by the Complainants with respect to the discharge procedures of the LPMO in no way establish a violation of Korea's obligations under Article XI:1. Korea stressed that it is under no obligation to actively take steps to import its entire quota amount, regardless of the prevailing market conditions. Despite this, Korea has consistently exerted its best efforts to ensure that the quota is fully absorbed, even under the very difficult circumstances surrounding the financial crisis. The LPMO has without fail purchased its entire quota amount on an annual basis.

138. The severe financial crisis affecting Korea in 1998, from which Korea is still in the process of recovery, resulted in a substantial negative impact on Korean demand for beef and the Korean beef market. Slumping demand in Korea, as

86 See G/STR/N/4/KOR, 10 December 1998.

87 See page 7 of G/STR/N/4/KOR, 10 December 1998.

well as currency fluctuations which lessened the price differential between imported and domestic beef, had a depressing effect on demand for imported product. Under these exceptional circumstances, the LPMO, operating on the basis of commercial considerations, was forced to temporarily delay the initiation of tenders for imports between the end of October 1997 and end of May 1998. Korea argued that the LPMO did not call for tenders during this period because of stagnant beef sales due to decreased demand. Korea added that the reason for the release volumes being less than domestic demand is that bid prices for the bulk of imported beef were lower than the minimum auction prices. The developments which necessitated this move were entirely market-driven and outside the control of the LPMO. In addition, the LPMO accelerated the beef-purchasing schedule to fill its quota share despite enormous losses amounting to 37.4 billion won in 1998. In view of the fact that the LPMO fully absorbed the 1998 quota, the actions undertaken by the LPMO can in no way constitute a restriction on imports in violation of Article XI:1.

139. The additional allegation advanced by the United States (paragraph 136) that Korea *"withheld allocation of quota share to the super-groups"* is factually inaccurate. Korea explained that the LPMO allocates the quota share for itself and for each SBS super-group for every fiscal year. Korea does not intervene in the quota allocation process, however, as the total quota amount and the share for the SBS super-groups are pre-determined in accordance with the Uruguay Round commitments and the Records of Understanding.[88] In 1999, in order to allocate quotas to any newly designated super-groups, 32,000 tonnes out of the entire 206,000 tonnes of quotas were reserved, a quantity which was allocated to the existing and new super-groups in April 1999. Therefore, contrary to the assertions of the United States, the LPMO did not restrict imports in violation of Article XI:1 by withholding the allocation of quota share to the super-groups.

140. **Australia** and the **United States** replied that Korea's own data shows that the LPMO did not make losses consistently throughout 1998. Furthermore, minimum prices for imports in the wholesale market continue to be applied, despite the recovery in the economy and improvements in exchange rates. In any event, Australia has shown that minimum prices for imports and manipulation of volumes permitted to be sold have resulted in additional quantitative restrictions being applied to imported beef. These restrictions have led directly to the substantial under-filling of the LPMO quota in 1998 and 1999 and will also affect the quota fill for 2000.[89]

141. **Australia** added that it did not take issue with the severity of the financial crisis in Korea in 1997/1998 Australia, like many other countries, was quick to offer extensive financial assistance to Korea during this period. However, Austra-

[88] LPMO Public Notice No. 217.

[89] Tables submitted by Australia shows that the LPMO quota was under-filled on customs cleared basis by 8,234 tonnes in 1997, by 47,839 tonnes in 1998 and by 39,479 tonnes in 1999.

lia submitted that the economic crisis is irrelevant to the issues in dispute in this case, i.e. the measures taken by Korea which discriminate against imported beef and limit the benefit of the quota conferred by its Schedule. The majority of the measures at issue predate the financial crisis. They form part of the regulatory framework for imported beef which has as its fundamental policy goal the protection of domestic beef. That some of these measures may have had an even greater impact on imported beef at a time of economic upheaval in Korea is immaterial, except to the extent that they highlight the deleterious effect of the measures on the competitiveness of imported beef in times of economic downturn. Australia submitted that it is not acceptable that imported beef should have been made to bear the brunt of the financial crisis in order to protect domestic beef from the full impact of the downturn.

5. *Measures Applied through the SBS Regime*

142. **Australia** submitted that restriction of imports under the SBS system to specific super-groups and end users also falls within the scope of Article XI:1. The system imposes limitations on action, limiting conditions or regulations. The effect of these restrictions is to exclude from the SBS system any user or potential user which is either not a member of an SBS super group or not a defined user under the regulations. The restrictions imposed through the SBS system thus have the effect of quantitative restrictions contrary to Article XI:1. The effect of the measures which limit the range of end-users, restrict end-users to membership of only one super group and forbid cross trading is to limit the amount of beef that could otherwise enter the market under the existing quota. Australia considered that it has adduced proof that the system of end-user and usage restrictions as well as the system of quota and sub-quota allocation operate to restrict the opportunities provided by the quota contrary to Article XI:1. In the opinion of Australia, Korea has not rebutted these claims, except by reference to the financial crisis (see paragraph 138) which, in the view of Australia, is not pertinent to these measures. The measures at issue predate the financial crisis, exist in addition to the quota and limit the quota opportunity Korea is obliged to provide. According to Australia, the super-groups themselves have noted the limiting effects of the measures and requested the Korean government to remove them.

143. The **United States** argued that Articles 5 and 6 of the *Operational Guidelines for Imported Beef Under the SBS System*, which exclude all wholesalers, retailers, and end-users, other than a small number of super-groups, from eligibility for import licences is also a "restriction" on imports within the meaning of Article XI.[90] GATT panels[91] have found that a denial of licences for imports be-

---

90 This restriction is also contained in the October 1999 Guidelines for Handling Imported Beef. See Articles 2 and 19.

91 *EEC - Processed Fruits and Vegetables*, para. 4.9. *Canada - Marketing Agencies*, paras. 5.28-5.31

low certain minimum import prices constitutes an import restriction within the meaning of Article XI:1. For the same reasons, Korea's confinement of import approvals to super-groups is an Article XI:1 restriction on imported beef because Korea's measure precludes beef from being licensed for import by any other participants in the marketing and distribution of imported beef, and thereby diminishes import opportunities for beef in the same manner that a minimum price requirement does. Therefore, Korea's limitations on the eligibility to import also constitutes a "restriction" that violates Article XI:1.

144. In conclusion, the United States submitted, the restrictions that Korea imposes on importation of beef (i.e. granting import licences only on a discretionary basis, confining import licences to super-groups, prohibiting and penalizing any cross-trading in imported beef between and among the super-groups and their customers and end-users) the LPMO's delay in both inviting tenders from foreign beef exporters and in allocating quota share to the super-groups, and LPMO's establishment of minimum bid prices for imports at auction, each constitute a quantitative restriction within the meaning of Article XI:1 as construed in the various panel reports referred to. Therefore, such measures are inconsistent with Korea's WTO obligations. *Any* restriction on imports other than duties, taxes or other charges violates Article XI:1; the fact that Korea's import regime *combines* several separate restrictions on imported beef underlines the flagrant character of the violation in this case.

145. **Australia** submitted that the allocation by super-groups to their end-users is done on the basis of forecast demand and not actual demand of end-users. Where an end-user fails to meet its demand forecast, the resulting quota shortfall remains unused for the current period. Any reallocation of the shortfall only takes effect the following period and there is no guarantee that all of the surplus will be taken up. The system gives rise to a possible situation where end-users, who want to import more beef, are restricted at the same time as the quotas of other end-users go unfilled. Australia considered that this lack of flexibility operates as a quantitative restriction on imported beef. The same applies, Australia continued, to the allocation of the quota to super-groups. While any shortfall may be reallocated to other super-groups later in the quota allocation, this is not done on the basis of individual demand, but in the same ratio as the initial allocation. There is no guarantee, therefore, that the full reallocation will be taken up. Moreover, reallocation so late in the season also prevents any shortfall from being taken up.[92] The system of fixed quotas for super-groups and end-users and the preven-

[92] In 1998, 112,200 tonnes was allocated among the SBS super-groups (60 per cent of Korea's minimum access requirement). Of this amount, only 69,933 tonnes or 62.3 per cent was actually taken up. Among the various super-groups, KMPA, LCTM and KMIA used up 99.8 per cent, 99.3 per cent and 97.0 per cent of their allocations, respectively. However, KTSC, KFMP and KRSC used up only 33.0 per cent, 26.0 per cent and 14.8 per cent of their allocation. This suggests that super-groups with excess demand were prevented from purchasing additional imports whilst other super-groups had unused quotas.

tion of cross-trading between super-groups and end-users, therefore, constitutes, according to Australia, a quantitative restriction on imports of beef.

6. *Burden and Standard of Proof*

146. **Korea** considered that Australia and the United States have failed to establish a *prima facie* case that any of the measures at issue violate Article XI:1. Indeed, no such violation exists as the targeted Korean measures merely implement a legally valid quota on beef, in full compliance with its commitments under the GATT 1994. A quota is, by definition, a quantitative restriction. In addition, in order to effectively enforce the quota, it is necessary to use various measures such as import licences, allocation of quota shares etc. The undisputed fact in this case, Korea argued, is that Korea currently maintains a legally valid quota on imports of beef. Therefore, the quantitative restriction on beef falls outside the scope of Article XI:1. In addition, since a quota cannot be enforced without implementing measures, these must also fall outside Article XI:1, provided that they do not, in and of themselves, create an additional, separate quantitative restriction which acts to intensify the quota effect by further limiting imports. Against this background, an examination is required as to what the Complainants must prove in order to establish a violation of Article XI:1.

147. First, since Korea is under no obligation to allow imports of beef above the quota level, a restriction (other than duties, taxes or charges) on importation for the purposes of Article XI:1 must in this context be taken to mean a separate, identifiable restriction which limits imports below the quota level. Korea is not required, under the GATT, to guarantee that the level of imports will in all cases reach the maximum quota level. Whether or not the quota is filled will depend on market factors, such as the competitiveness of the industries exporting to Korea, consumer preferences, patterns of consumption and fluctuations of currencies etc. The mere fact that a quota is not fully utilized does not, therefore, establish a violation of Article XI:1. On the other hand, if the quota is filled, this must be considered as a strong indication that Korea does not make effective additional restrictions to further constrain imports in violation of Article XI:1.

148. Furthermore, Korea added, Article XI:1 refers to prohibitions or restrictions which are "made effective" through quotas, import and export licences or other measures. The words "made effective" in this sentence indicates the results-oriented nature of this provision. Therefore, the Complainants must establish that a separately identifiable prohibition or restriction on imports exists and that such a restriction is actually having the effect of limiting imports to a level below the quota level. Since non-fulfilment of the quota can be due to a multitude of market factors which have nothing to do with any restrictive measures maintained by Korea, the provisions of Article XI:1 in the context of this case require that the Complainants establish a clear causal relationship between the measures, separately identifiable, which are alleged to be restrictions on imports on the one hand, and the non-fulfilment of the full quota amount on the other hand.

149. On the one hand, Korea continued, Article XI:1 is formulated broadly to apply to "measures" other than duties, taxes or charges which prohibit or restrict importation. On the other hand, the requirement to demonstrate a clear causal link and that restrictions are manifestly having their desired effect stems from the need to balance the sovereign rights of Members under this provision. If any measure maintained by a Member could be attacked merely by reference to allegations that such a measure could, theoretically, result in restrictions on the importation of goods, this would result in undue interference in the sovereign rights of Members.

150. Korea noted, as shown in paragraphs 146-149 above, that the quota maintained by Korea is legal (and thereby the measures implementing the quota, subject to the limitations outlined above). Moreover, the quota and the measures which serve to implement this quantitative restriction can not be considered as being based on an exception to GATT rules. The burden of proof does not, therefore, lie with Korea to establish the conformity of any targeted measures under Article XI:1. Nor are the targeted measures to be subject to a stricter necessity test, such as under the general exceptions to GATT obligations detailed under Article XX. On the contrary, the burden of proof for establishing each of the elements outlined above lies with the Complainants. With respect to burden of proof issues, GATT/WTO panels have consistently followed the approach of various international tribunals, and the vast majority of developed legal systems, in requiring that the party making an allegation bears the burden of proving that allegation. Only when a *prima facie* case has been established does the burden shift to the other party. In this regard, Korea referred to the Appellate Body report on *US –Shirts and Blouses (AB)* which provides:

> "... the issue in this case is which party has the burden of demonstrating that there has, or has not been, an infringement of the obligation [...]. In addressing this issue, we find it difficult, indeed, to see how any system of judicial settlement could work if it incorporated the proposition that the mere assertion of a claim might amount to proof. It is, thus, hardly surprising that various international tribunals, including the International Court of Justice, have generally and consistently accepted and applied the rule that the party who asserts a fact, whether the claimant or the respondent, is responsible for providing proof thereof."[93]

151. In the opinion of Korea, the Complainants' fall short of meeting this burden of proof. Each of the Complainants' allegations are mere unsubstantiated assertions and based on inaccurate characterizations of the measures and systems mentioned.

---

[93] See Appellate Body Report, *United States – Measure Affecting Imports of Woven Wool Shirts and Blouses from India ("US – Shirts and Blouses")*, WT/DS33/AB/R and Corr. 1, adopted 23 May 1997, DSR 1997:I, 323, at 335.

152. However, even if it were conceded, for the sake of argument, that any of the measures and systems criticized by the Complainants had any restrictive effect whatsoever, their arguments must be rejected because they have failed to provide *prima facie* evidence (i) establishing that a separately identifiable restriction or prohibition exists beyond the implementation of the quota itself; (ii) that such restriction has intensified the effect of the quota by restricting imports to a level below the quota level; and (iii) that any non-fulfilment of the quota has been actually caused by restrictive measures or systems (as opposed to other factors) and that the restrictions have thereby been "made effective" within the meaning of Article XI:1.

153. In the view of Korea, the Complainants do not properly explain how any of the alleged restrictions constitute restrictions in addition to those imposed for the purposes of implementing the legally valid quota. In support of their argument concerning the nature of a "restriction" on importation in the context of Article XI:1, the Complainants cite cases which, without exception, dealt with a situation where there was no legal quota in place and are, therefore, not relevant. In such a situation, measures which constitute quantitative restrictions must be evaluated differently than in the present case. This failure must lead to the conclusion that the Complainants have not identified any separate "restriction" within the meaning of Article XI:1 in addition to the quota.

154. Furthermore, the Complainants have failed to establish, in the opinion of Korea, a causal link between any alleged restrictions on importation on the one hand, and reduced imports below the quota level on the other hand. There has, therefore, been no showing that any alleged restrictions (beyond the legal quota) were "made effective" through, quotas, import and export licences or other measures. Specifically, in their arguments concerning the decrease in imports, particularly in 1998 (see, for instance, paragraph 136 and footnote 92), the Complainants virtually ignore the effects of the severe and widespread financial crisis in Korea and much of Asia. While this crisis commanded the focus of the world's financial media and trading partners, it is barely mentioned by the Complainants', much less analyzed in terms of breaking the causal link between any alleged restrictions and decreased imports from these countries. Korea considered that none of the measures cited by the Complainants constitute restrictions on importation contrary to Article XI:1. Korea requested the Panel to reject the Complainants' claims under Article XI:1 in view of the lack of evidence with regard to the factors required to establish a *prima facie* case of violation of Article XI:1.

155. **Australia** replied that it has proven each of its claims through factual evidence and legal argument and has made a *prima facie* case in relation to each of the measures. The burden of proof, therefore, transfers to Korea to disprove Australia's *prima facie* case. Korea has made several assertions about Australia's failure to meet its burden of proof but has not adduced either alternative factual evidence or persuasive legal arguments, including by reference to the findings of previous panels and the Appellate Body, to substantiate its assertions. Australia submitted that Korea has not disproved Australia's *prima facie* case. Australia further considered that Korea's specific claims about Australia's burden of proof

under Articles III (see paragraphs 226-229) and XI are legally incorrect. Australia was of the view that it has shown that the exclusion of imported beef from the existing retail infrastructure for domestic beef has the effect of a quantitative restriction on imported beef additional to the current quota. Australia has also argued that a number of other measures are inconsistent with Article XI:1. Australia rejected Korea's attempt to expand the burden of proof under Article XI:1 to include proof of injury (see paragraphs 232-233). Australia contended that Article XI:1 only requires Australia to prove that there are prohibitions or restrictions in place on imports. Australia is not required to prove the trade effect of these measures by reference to the effect of that measure on another existing quantitative restriction. A plain reading of Article XI:1 indicates that Australia needs to prove the existence of prohibitions or restrictions made effective through quotas, import or export licences or other measures. Australia considered that it has proven that a range of measures, additional to the current quota, which meet the requirements of Article XI:1. The existence of a quota does not permit Korea to impose additional quantitative restrictions.

156. When the quota is taken into account, Korea submitted, none of the measures complained of constitute restrictions contrary to Article XI:1 in addition to the quota legally maintained by Korea. The undisputed fact in this case is that, with the exception of the extraordinary conditions prevailing in 1998, Korea has consistently and fully absorbed the applicable annual quota amount for imported beef. In Korea's view, this fact is irreconcilable with the Complainants' allegation that the Korean import regime for beef involves additional restrictions beyond the legal quota, in violation of Article XI:1 . Nearly all of the measures which the Complainants allege to be inconsistent with this provision are inherent to the basic architecture of the Korean beef import regime. If the Korean beef import regime inherently involves restrictions on the importation of beef in addition to the quota, then it would logically be expected that Korea would consistently have failed to absorb the full quota since the inception of the import regime. This is not the case, which, in Korea's view, is a conclusive indication that the Korean beef import regime does not restrict the importation of beef in addition to, or beyond, the quota level.

157. The **Complainants** submitted that previous GATT panel reports have concluded that a showing of "trade effects" is not a requisite element of a violation under Article XI:1, as proposed by Korea. Thus, the panel in *EEC - Oilseeds*[94] observed that the "CONTRACTING PARTIES have consistently interpreted the basic provisions of the General Agreement on restrictive trade measures as provisions establishing conditions of competition. Thus, they decided that an import quota constitutes an import restriction within the meaning of Article XI:1 whether or not it actually impeded imports." Similarly, the 1984 Report of the panel on *Japan - Leather* found that restrictions on imports of leather consti-

[94] Para. 150, referring to *Japan - Leather*.

tuted a *prima facie* case of nullification and impairment. The panel concluded that " ... the existence of a quantitative restriction should be presumed to cause nullification or impairment not only because of any effect it had had on the volume of trade but also for other reasons e.g. it would lead to increased transaction costs and would create uncertainties which could affect investment plans".[95] The Complainants, therefore, are not required to show actual trade impact. (See also paragraphs 232-235)

158. The key principles underpinning the rejection of a trade effects test, **Australia** argued, and the interpretive approach to Articles III and XI, were recently reiterated by the panel in *US-Section 301* The panel noted the importance, when determining whether a measure is in violation of the covered agreements, of taking into consideration the chilling effect on economic activity of a particular measure.[96] The panel noted the findings in *US - Superfund* which reached its findings through consideration of the effect of measures on the relative competitive opportunities between imported and domestic products. The panel in that case stated that: "Both Articles [GATT Articles III and XI] are not only to protect current trade but also to create the predictability needed to plan future trade." (See also paragraphs 232-233.)

159. Australia submitted further that the range of restrictions applied by Korea to imported beef, including separation of retail sale, imposition of minimum prices, discrimination against grass-fed beef, end-user and usage limits and other distribution restrictions, as well as reporting, record-keeping and labelling requirements, have a negative impact on economic activity and investment in the imported beef trade. They will continue to do so for as long as they are maintained by the Korean government. (See also paragraphs 201, 232 and 233.)

160. The **United States** submitted that claims under Articles III:4 and XI:1 do not require a showing of economic harm. In the view of the United States, any proposition that the burden of proof is increased beyond what it would otherwise be in circumstances when a quota exists is contrary to GATT jurisprudence because its adoption would reward Members who maintain trade distorting practices. The United States considered that there is no minimum impact requirement under Article XI:1. However, if there were such a requirement, it is clear that the minimum auction prices set by the NLCF and the LPMO and the six month interruption in tender invitations are two examples of measures that had identifiable adverse effects on quota fill and, thus, on US beef exports to Korea. (See also paragraphs 234-235.)

161. Without prejudice to the fact that no showing of trade damage is required for a finding of violation of Article XI:1, the United States noted the following information for the Panel. Korea's claim that its measure mandating the separate retail sale of imported beef does not have an adverse effect on the number of out-

95 Paras. 47-48, 53, 55.

96 See analysis from paras. 7.71-7.86.

lets selling imported beef and, thereby, on beef imports, disregards the limited number of special imported beef stores when compared to the total number of retail beef outlets in Korea. Korea also ignores the effect that the dual retail regime has had in disproportionately concentrating imported beef sales in the restaurant sector. Moreover, the decline in the last three years in the number of specialized imported beef stores suggests that the additional costs of maintaining stores to sell only imported beef is taking its toll even as that situation was aggravated by the financial crisis of 1998. No doubt, the situation of the imported beef stores was also aggravated by the LPMO's refusal to tender and the maintenance of high minimum bid prices for imported beef.

162. It is clear from the foregoing, the United States continued, that without the existing restrictions on the retail sale of imported beef and Korea's other trade restricting measures, a far larger distribution base could have been established for imported beef in anticipation of the end of the quota next year. Korea's policies have precluded the pursuit of such marketing strategies, and have enabled the Korean beef industry to keep a stranglehold on retail distribution, especially on the traditional butcher shops that account for approximately 90 per cent of all retail outlets for beef. If any proof of trade effects were necessary, the rapid decline in the volume of imported beef in 1998 and the decrease in the number of imported beef stores would be sufficient.

163. However, the issue that this Panel must consider is the denial of competitive opportunity to imported beef. The amount of damage done by Korea's discriminatory treatment of imported beef need not be quantified; nor need this Panel quantify the effect of Korea's violations of Article XI:1. Indeed, the loss of potential competitive opportunities is sufficient to establish that a measure is inconsistent with either Article III:4 or XI:1. Nonetheless, in this dispute, the United States has shown not only that Korea's measures relating to imported beef may result in competitive disadvantages, but that Korea's measures have actually had that effect.

164. **Korea** responded that the legal and factual circumstances pertaining to the Korean beef market must be fully examined in order for the Panel to reach a correct interpretation of Article III:4 and Article XI:1. Throughout these proceedings, the Complainants have in effect argued that the analysis of, in particular, Article III:4 and Article XI:1, can and should be separated from the analysis of the legal quota maintained by Korea. Korea submitted that this cannot be done. Korea also noted that it shares the concerns expressed by Canada in its third party submission with respect to the Complainants' erroneous application of Article XI:1 in the context of this case. None of the case law cited by the Complainants with respect to these two provisions have dealt with the specific legal and factual circumstances which are present in the current dispute.

165. In a case where a legal quota is maintained by a Member, Korea continued, the term "restriction" in Article XI:1 cannot be interpreted in the same way as was done in the cases cited by the Complainants. In the present case, Korea maintains a legal quota on beef and Korea has acquired a negotiated right not to

permit market access for imported beef above the agreed quota level. In addition, the quota has consistently been fully absorbed with the exception of the crisis year. Under these circumstances, it is completely nonsensical for the Complainants to argue that the cited Korean measures restrict imports within the meaning of Article XI:1 because the maximum of their entitlement with respect to market access has been utilized.

166. Korea submitted that this is the reason why panels have not required a showing of actual trade effects in cases where no legal quota was applied. In these cases, a GATT-inconsistent quantitative restriction would virtually always have potential, if not actual, trade effects and therefore there is a restriction within the meaning of Article XI:1 since it is a restriction in relation to an otherwise limitless entitlement negotiated under the GATT. It is on this basis that the presumption of nullification or impairment has been made. On the other hand, where a legal quota exists and is being filled, this must be taken as overwhelming, if not conclusive, proof that no restriction within the meaning of Article XI:1 can be alleged. If the quota is being filled, it is clear that it cannot be claimed that actual competitive opportunities have been lost since there is no entitlement to further market access. Equally, however, it is impossible to claim a loss of even potential competitive opportunities when the quota is being filled for precisely the same reason. In the opinion of Korea, this is a crucial difference between the present case and the cases cited by the Complainants.

167. Therefore, Korea argued, the Complainants' claims that any of the alleged measures constitute restrictions on importation within the meaning of Article XI:1 must be rejected. Contrary to the Complainants' assertions, they have not established a *prima facie* case that Korea maintains any separately identifiable restrictions in addition to the quota. In addition, the measures have conclusively been shown to permit market access for beef in Korea up to the quota level to which Korea is committed. Since virtually all the measures complained of were in force both during the years when the quota was filled, and in the exceptional year 1998 when it was not, it cannot logically be argued that it is these measures that are responsible for the exceptional drop in imports in 1998 and it is, therefore, impossible to claim that these measures restrict imports beyond the quota. Hence, the Complainants' arguments under Article XI:1 with respect to, among others, the separation of sales outlets, the operation of the SBS system including quota allocations, the alleged restrictions on cross-trading in the SBS system, and the operating and auctioning procedures of the LPMO, must conclusively be rejected.

D. Claims under Article III:4 of GATT

1. "Like product"

168. **Australia** and the **United States** submitted that there are four requisite elements to any finding that a measure is inconsistent with Article III:4: (i) a law, regulation or requirement must be involved; (ii) the law, regulation or require-

ment must affect the internal sale, purchase, transportation, distribution, or use of the product; (iii) the imported product must be like the domestic product; and (iv) the imported product is accorded less favorable treatment than the like domestic product.[97] Article III:4 not only covers laws, regulations and requirements expressly stated to apply to internal sale or purchase, but also those which *affect* conditions of sale or purchase.[98]

169. The **Complainants** submitted that an examination of the properties and characteristics, end-uses, consumer tastes as well as habits and tariff classification show that Korean beef and imported beef are "like products". In terms of physical characteristics (such as appearance and taste) and end-uses, Korean beef and imported beef is very similar if not identical. Indeed, Korea has justified separate distribution of imported beef on the basis of a perceived need to prevent cheaper imported beef from being fraudulently sold as more expensive Korean beef, because consumers are not able to tell the difference. The Complainants considered that imported and domestic beef are "like products" for the purposes of Article III:4.

170. **Korea** has not contested that imported and Korean beef are like products

2. *Measures with Respect to Retail Sale of Imported Beef*

171. **Australia** submitted, that the purpose of Article III "is to ensure that internal measures 'not be applied to imported or domestic products so as to afford protection to domestic production". Toward this end, Article III and various panel and Appellate Body reports[99] indicate that treatment no less favourable requires *equality of competitive conditions* for imported products in respect of laws, regulations and requirements affecting internal sale.[100] Where a benefit is

---

[97] See Panel Report, *United States – Standards for Reformulated and Conventional Gasoline*, ("*United States – Gasoline*"), WT/DS2/R, adopted 20 May 1996, DSR 1996:I, 29, para. 6.5. There is no requirement under Article III:4 that the regulation affords protection to a domestic industry. The Appellate Body in *European Communities – Regime for the Importation, Sale and Distribution of Bananas* ("*EC – Bananas III*"), WT/DS27/AB/R, adopted 25 September 1997, DSR 1997:II, 591, found that unlike Article III:2 which refers to Article III:1 by specific reference, Article III:1 does not comprise a part of the context of Article III:4. Therefore, the Appellate Body concluded that "a determination of whether there is a violation of Article III:4 does not require a separate consideration of whether a measure 'afford[s] protection to domestic production." See para. 216.

[98] L/833, adopted 23 October 1958, 7S/60, 64 paras. 11-13. See also Appellate Body Report, *Japan - Alcoholic Beverages* ("*Japan – Alcoholic Beverages*"), WT/DS8/AB/R, WT/DS10/AB/R, WT/DS11/AB/R, adopted 1 November 1996, DSR 1996:I, 97, at 109; *US - Section 337*, para. 5.13; *United States - Gasoline, supra*, footnote 97, para. 6.10.

[99] *US - Section 337(AB)*, paras. 5.11 and 5.13. Panel Report, *United States – Gasoline, supra*, footnote 97, para. 6.10. Appellate Body Report, *Japan - Alcoholic Beverages, supra*, footnote 98, at 109. Panel Report, *Japan – Measures Affecting Consumer Photographic Film and Paper* ("*Japan – Film*"), WT/DS44/R, adopted 22 April 1998, DSR 1998:IV, 1179, para. 10.379.

[100] Appellate Body Report, *Japan – Alcoholic Beverages II, supra*, footnote 98, at 109; *Italian Agricultural Machinery*, paras. 11-13; *Canada - FIRA* , paras. 5.7-5.11; *Canada - Marketing Agencies (1992)*, para. 5.5; and *US - Malt Beverages*, paras. 5.30-5.33.

conferred on domestic products, this must also be extended to imported products. Conversely, where a charge or requirement is imposed, this must cover both imported and domestic products.

172. **Australia** submitted that the panel report in *US - Section 337* emphasised that Article III:4 is concerned with the effective equality of opportunities in the application of laws, regulations and requirements. The application of formally identical legal provisions, may, in some cases have the practical effect of according less favourable treatment to imported products.[101] The *application* of the separate system results in imported beef having significantly fewer sales outlets, and therefore notably fewer sales and marketing opportunities, than domestic beef. Imported beef, Australia argued, is therefore subject to a competitive disadvantage *vis-à-vis* domestic beef.[102] The requirement to establish separate sales establishments for imported beef, and the associated costs of doing so, have limited the competitive opportunities available to imported beef compared to those afforded to domestic beef. Put simply, the regulation separating the sale of imported beef from that of domestic beef denies to imported beef the opportunity to be sold in over 40,000 existing meat retail outlets through which the majority of beef in Korea is sold. Imported beef has been completely excluded from this retail infrastructure. The system imposes additional costs on the sale of imported beef by requiring that any existing meat retailer seek permission for, and open, new premises. The costs associated with the establishment of separate establishments reduces the competitive opportunities afforded to imported beef. The fact that all imported beef stores must carry a sign identifying them as such exacerbates the discrimination against imported beef.

173. Australia was of the view that the limitation on end points of sale and the separate display requirements in larger outlets discriminates against imported beef because it also has the effect of emphasising any perception of quality differences between domestic and imported product. There is a Korean perception that local Hanwoo beef is superior to imported product which is not based on an objective evaluation of quality.[103] This perception is exacerbated by the separation of domestic and imported beef, either in separate shops or in separate cabinets and have a negative effect on the marketability of imported beef. The limited availability of imported beef relative to domestic beef aggravates this problem. This has the further effect of forcing lower prices for imported beef, to compensate for perceived differences in quality (see also the panel report in the *US - Gasoline* case.)

[101] Para. 5.11.

[102] See also *Canada - Marketing Agencies (1992)*, para. 5.5-5.6.

[103] [In [the][a] sensory analysis conducted in 1995, 688 Korean consumers were asked to taste beef samples from Korea, Australia, USA and New Zealand. The consumers identified three groups of beef on the basis of eating quality, not country of origin. "Sensory Analysis of Beef by Korean Consumers" op. cit pages 74-79. Nonetheless, the survey also identified a consumer preference for eating beef identified as Korean. Ibid, page 88.

174. Australia did not accept Korea's claim that the separate retail sale of imported beef arises merely because of the existence of a quota. Nor does Australia agree with Korea's subsequent claim that the burden of proof in relation to Article III, in situations where a legal quota exists, requires Australia to prove that the internal measure has affected the filling of the quota. Australia rejects this claim on the basis that it would remove Korea's national treatment obligations under which Korea is required to provide equality of competitive opportunities for imported products once they have come across the border.

175. The **United States** submitted that Korea's restrictions on the sale, distribution and use that apply exclusively to imported beef draw an impermissible distinction based on the origin of the beef. This distinction, which results in a Korean-imposed handicap on the competitiveness of imported beef, is inconsistent with both the intent and letter of Article III:4. A succession of panels has concluded that the intent of Article III:4 is "to provide equal conditions of competition once goods had been cleared through the customs".[104] The Korean laws and regulations preclude such equal conditions of competition. By requiring imported beef to be sold in stores that cannot sell Korean beef, Korea denies imported beef the opportunity to sell in the vast majority of meat stores. Imported beef may be sold in approximately 5,000 stores, whereas there are approximately 45,000 stores where Korean beef may be sold. This disparity of opportunity cannot be ignored or minimized. The result is that imported beef is excluded from thousands of stores where Korean consumers shop for meat.

176. Korea's restrictions on the sale, distribution, and use of imported beef, the United States continued, are equally inconsistent with the requirements of Article III:4. Korea imposes these restrictions only on imported beef. Korean beef confronts no similar limitations on its distribution, use, and sale. Korean beef when sold to certain classes of customers the United States continued, is not confined to specific uses by those purchasers. There are no restraints on the resale of Korean beef akin to those imposed on imports. Whereas cross-trading of imported beef is forbidden, Korean beef may be freely sold without constraints by traders and distributors. This differentiation in distribution and sales opportunities denies imported beef the more favorable treatment accorded to the domestic product and, thus, is inconsistent with Korea's obligations under Article III:4.

177. The United States further contended that the information submitted by Korea shows that the number of imported beef stores declined between 1994 and 1998 from 6,088 to 5,498 stores; a decline of approximately 10 per cent. During this same period the volume of imported beef permitted under the quota increased from 106,000 to 187,000 metric tonnes. In recent years, there is, thus, no evidentiary support for Korea's assertion that the number of imported beef stores is a function of the quota quantity.

---

[104] *Italian Agricultural Machinery*, paras. 11-13; *US - Section 337,* paras. 5.11-5.13 *Canada - FIRA* , para. 6.6.

178. In very similar circumstances, United States continued, other panels have found that the exclusion of imported products from particular channels of distribution constituted discrimination, resulting in less favorable treatment for imports. In the 1992 panel report on *Canada - Marketing Agencies (1992),*[105] the panel examined restrictions imposed by provincial liquor authorities on access for imported beer to points of sale. The panel concluded that by excluding imported beer from points of sale where domestic beer could be sold, imported beer was denied certain competitive opportunities enjoyed by domestic beer. A similar result was reached in the panel on *US - Malt Beverages,* where the panel concluded that a state exemption of domestic wine from a prohibition on the sale of wine resulted in less favorable treatment for imports where imported wine was banned. Korea's requirement that imported beef be sold in separate sales facilities denies competitive opportunities to imported beef. Like Canada's previous exclusion of imported beer from certain points of sale, Korea's exclusion of imported beef from most beef sales sites, constitutes a measure that is inconsistent with the obligations for national treatment under Article III:4.

179. According to **Korea**, the Complainants have not been able to identify which "law, regulation, or requirement" led to discriminatory results as concerns the separate sales outlets. Korea emphasized that the same regulation applies to domestic beef stores and, therefore, Korea's system of separating sales outlets treats both imported and domestic beef on equal footing. Hence, Korea can only surmise that what the Complainants argue is a case of *de facto* discrimination. Korea submitted that under these circumstances, what matters is determining which precise fact causes the less favourable treatment. There is no discrimination between domestic and imported beef stores as to the opening and operation of the stores. Nor are there any additional costs or requirements involved in setting up an imported beef store as compared with a domestic store. An owner of a domestic beef store may change his store to one selling imported beef by submitting a notification to the authority and changing the sign. Likewise, an owner of an imported beef store may also change his store to one selling domestic beef by notifying the authority and changing the sign. The decision on whether to sell either domestic beef or imported beef depends entirely on the owner himself. It is, therefore, entirely baseless to imply that the number of imported beef stores in operation compared with that of domestic beef stores can constitute evidence, much less proof, of discrimination against imported beef.

---

105 Para. 5.5: The panel recalled:

... that the CONTRACTING PARTIES had decided in a number of previous cases that the requirement of Article III:4 to accord imported products treatment no less favorable than that accorded to domestic products was a requirement to accord imported products competitive opportunities no less favourable than those accorded to domestic products. The Panel found that, by allowing the access of domestic bear to points of sale not available to imported beef, Canada accorded domestic beer competitive opportunities denied to imported beer.

180. **The Complaining parties** responded that the distinction between *de facto* and *de jure* discrimination being applied by Korea was a distraction from the question of equality of competitive conditions. The application of the separate system, applied by law under Article 15 of the *Management Guideline for Imported Beef*, results in imported beef having significantly fewer sales outlets than Korean beef, and therefore significantly fewer sales and marketing opportunities, than Korean beef.

181. **Korea** submitted that the standard of review with respect to *de jure* or *de facto* discrimination cannot be the same. A careful delineation of what the Complainants need to prove in this respect is required, after which a clear, uninterrupted causal link between the regulatory intervention by Korea and the alleged discrimination must be established. As concerns less favourable treatment, Korea considered that the Complainants' argument in this respect falls far short of the threshold required to discharge their burden of proof. The number of sales outlets selling imported beef is smaller than the number of sales outlets selling domestic beef simply because there is a legal quota in place which limits the overall quantity of imported beef sold in Korea. Presumably, the number of sales outlets will be much higher once the quota is removed by 1 January 2001. This is one more reason why Korea suggests that the Complainants' claim is at this stage inadmissible: the picture of the beef market in Korea is right now skewed because of the existence of the quota. The decision to open either type of outlet, Korea continued, rests entirely with private operators. In presence of the legal quota, more private operators tend to opt for sales outlets selling domestic beef. However, the regulatory requirements do not prejudge decisions by the private operators. It is the existence of the quota that has influenced these decisions so far. Korea submitted that in the absence of an element of causality between the regulatory intervention and the decision of private operators to opt for either type of outlet, it is not possible for the Complainants to discharge their burden of proof under Article III:4. Such actions by private parties are not attributable to Korea; the *Japan - Film* case lends full support to this proposition.

182. Referring to the Complainants arguments in paragraphs 177-178 concerning separate sales outlets for imported beef, Korea submitted that the US and Australian claims in this respect must be rejected. The separation of stores under Korean law selling imported and domestic beef does not contravene Article III:4 to the extent that the relevant legislation imposes identical regulatory requirements as far as the opening and the functioning of such stores is concerned. GATT, and more recently WTO, panels have made it clear that the purpose of Article III is to ensure that WTO Members do not add to the consolidated border protection through internal measures [106].

[106] For a recent expression of this interpretation of Article III, see the Panel Report, *Japan - Alcoholic Beverages* ("*Japan – Alcoholic Beverages*"), WT/DS8/R, WT/DS10/R, WT/DS11/R, adopted 1 November 1996, DSR 1996:I, 125, upheld in this respect by the Appellate Body.

183. Korea submitted further that the Complainants' arguments with respect to separation of sales outlets rest on the assertion that if imported beef cannot be sold in certain domestic stores, this will *per se* result in less favourable treatment. The fundamental aspect overlooked by the Complainants, however, is that the treatment afforded imported beef is inherently neutral because the same restriction applies to stores selling domestic beef. This is not comparable to the measures examined in *Canada - Marketing Agencies (1992)*. In that case, the restriction on points of sale was exclusively applied to imported product. Likewise, in *US - Malt Beverages*, the measure at issue prohibited the sale of imported wine in circumstances where domestic wine was specifically exempted. It is obvious that in such circumstances, less favourable treatment for the imported product will result. These cases in no way approximate the present Korean situation, as there is no question of allowing special privileges or rules for domestic stores or product which do not equally apply to stores selling imported product. The Complainants' referral to the above-mentioned cases in the context of this dispute is, therefore, misleading.

184. Apart from the limitations inherent in the current legal quota system in terms of available quantities of imported beef, the stores selling imported beef are not subject to any less favourable treatment than that which applies to selling domestic beef. The imported beef stores and domestic beef stores operate under equal conditions in all fundamental aspects of business operations such as retail pricing, operating hours, advertisement as well as with regard to safety inspections involving marking of origin, grading, price display, and taxes. Korea thus contended that the Complainants' claim regarding separation of sales outlets must be rejected. The separation of stores under Korean law selling imported and domestic beef does not contravene Article III:4 to the extent that the relevant legislation imposes identical regulatory requirements as far as the opening and functioning of such stores is concerned.

185. Referring to the text of Article III:1[107], Korea argued that the logical conclusion with respect to the scope of Article III is to ensure that the only form of permissible protection in the GATT/WTO system is that of legalized (i.e. negotiated and agreed upon) border protection. What is prohibited under Article III:4 is discriminatory treatment between domestic and imported like products which affords less favourable treatment to imported products than that accorded to like products of national origin. Korea was of the opinion that the 1989 panel report on *US - Section 337* perfectly captures this point:

> "... The words 'treatment no less favourable' in paragraph 4 call for effective equality of opportunities for imported products in respect of the ap-

---

107 "The contracting parties recognize that internal taxes and other internal charges, and laws, regulations and requirements affecting the internal sale, offering for sale, purchase, transportation, distribution or use of products, and internal quantitative regulations requiring the mixture, processing or use of products in specified amounts or proportions, should not be applied to imported or domestic products so as to afford protection to domestic production".

plication of laws, regulations and requirements affecting the internal sale, purchase, transportation, distribution or use of products. This clearly sets a minimum permissible standard as a basis. On the one hand, contracting parties may apply to imported products different formal legal requirements if doing so would accord imported products more favourable treatment. On the other hand, it also has to be recognized that there may be cases where application of formally identical legal provisions would in practice accord less favourable treatment to imported products and a contracting party might thus have to apply different legal provisions to imported products to ensure that the treatment accorded to them is in fact no less favourable. For these reasons, the mere fact that imported products are subject under Section 337 to legal provisions that are different from those applying to products of national origin is in itself not conclusive in establishing inconsistency with Article III:4. In such cases, it has to be assessed whether or not such differences in the legal provisions applicable do or do not accord to imported products less favourable treatment."[108]

186. Korea also noted that Article XVII of GATS (which was enacted after the mentioned jurisprudence and has arguably been influenced by it) makes this point clear in its second paragraph concerning the national treatment obligation.

187. The **United States** considered that Article III:4 has been interpreted consistently by GATT/WTO panels as "establishing the obligation to accord imported products competitive opportunities no less favorable than those accorded domestic products."[109] The United States contended that the MAF regulations deny such opportunities to US beef. The requirement for separate retail marketing channels for imported beef and the imposition of restrictions on the distribution and sale of imported beef, put imported beef at a competitive disadvantage to Korean beef. In similar circumstances, the panel in *US - Section 337*[110] concluded with respect to Article III:4 that: "Given that the underlying objective is to guarantee equality of treatment, it is incumbent on the contracting party applying differential treatment to show that, in spite of such differences, the no less favourable treatment standard of Article III is met." Korea cannot fulfill this burden and, as a consequence, these measures violate the national treatment provisions .

188. **Australia** responded that the requirement to sell imported and domestic beef in separate stores is a matter of government regulation, not a private undertaking. The Korean government requires an existing domestic beef seller to open new and separate premises and undergo new licensing procedures if it wishes to

---

108 See para. 5.11.

109 See, e.g. *US - Section 337*, para. 5.11; *Canada - Marketing Agencies (1992)* at 75 and the panel report in the same styled case in *Canada - Marketing Agencies (1988)*, at 90; *Italian Agricultural Machinery*, paras. 11-13 ("the intention of the drafters of the Agreement was clearly to treat the imported products in the same way as the like products once they have been cleared through customs.")

110 Para. 5.11.

sell imported beef. The regulation also removes from the retailer the power to sell the like products in the same store if they so desire. Australia emphasised that when Korea introduced the dual retail system, imported and domestic beef were not on the same competitive footing. When the regulation was introduced in 1990, there was an existing infrastructure for the sale of beef. However, given the longstanding import restrictions that existed on foreign beef until 1988, the majority of beef sold in Korea at that time was domestic beef. The introduction of separate requirements, therefore, removed imported beef from the existing retail infrastructure, including the small butcher shops through which the majority of beef was, and continues to be, sold in Korea.

189. In response to the US arguments in paragraph 177, **Korea** submitted that the figures contained in the table referred to by the United States (see footnote 111) show that the number of stores steadily grew during the period of 1994-1996, with a slight decrease in 1997. It was only in 1998 that the number of stores decreased substantially. Furthermore, Korea considered that, for the purpose of determining the effect of the system of separation of sales outlets on the number of stores, the relevant figure is the quantity of beef available for sale at the retail level, not the quota amount. Korea has provided such figures. The figures show that in 1998 there was a substantial decrease in the volume of beef sold at the retail level. If there is anything that can be derived from these figures, it is that the decrease in beef consumption in Korea during the period from late 1997 to 1998 was due to the financial crisis.

190. Korea considered that it has conclusively refuted the claims regarding price comparisons as unfounded. First, it is common knowledge in Korea that imported beef is generally cheaper than its domestic counterpart. Second, imported beef stores have precisely the same tools at their disposal as domestic beef stores to market, advertise and promote their products and indicate any competitive advantages such as price. In addition, consumers will compare prices between domestic and imported beef stores in precisely the same way as they compare prices between different domestic outlets selling beef, by shopping around. Finally, Korea argued that the Complainants must show how the system of separation of sales outlets results in "less favorable treatment" in the presence of undisputed evidence suggesting that for years the quota has been fully absorbed through a system of separation of sales outlets which remained virtually unchanged for a period of nine years.

191. Referring to the United States arguments in paragraph 175 above, Korea submitted that the fact that there are more stores selling domestic rather than imported beef does not constitute discrimination and does not engage the responsibility of Korea. To penalize Korea in this respect would amount to penalizing the legal beef QR since the limited volume of imported beef circulating in the Korean market (a government choice which is perfectly consistent with Korea's WTO obligations) explains the number of stores selling imported beef in the Korean market. Korea further submitted that the two cases referred to by the United States in paragraph 178 are irrelevant to this case since they both deal with issues of regulatory diversity: in both cases, there was a regulatory requirement which

distinguished between domestic and imported products. In the Canadian case, imported beer had no access to some points of sale. In the US case, domestic wine was exempted from a prohibition on the sale of wine. This is not the case here. Imported beef can be sold anywhere in Korea. There are no differential regulatory requirements applied to imported beef. It all depends on the decision of private operators to opt for a store selling either domestic or imported beef.

192. Moreover, historically the number of stores has proven not to be a problem when it comes to absorbing the QR, in place for almost ten years now. It is the negotiated outcome of a previous dispute settlement between the present Complainants and Korea and part of Korea's commitments under the Uruguay Round agreements. The number of stores selling imported beef has evolved freely over the years since the introduction of the QR, as shown in the data below.[111] Until 1997, the QR was fully used, 1998 being the first year in which the QR was not absorbed. The reason for this has nothing to do with the number of stores selling imported beef but rather with the well-known financial crisis that hit Korea in 1997 which led to a sizeable reduction of the demand in the market: overall beef consumption dropped by 4.5 per cent.

193. Imported beef obviously could not escape the reduction in demand, Korea continued, particularly since domestic beef prices collapsed to historical lows. The wholesale price difference between imported and domestic beef narrowed from 1.74 in 1995 to 1.39 in 1998. In addition, the price of the feed, which relies heavily on the price of imported raw materials, became untenably high and forced farmers to release their cattle irrespective of the falling prices. Another significant factor is that in view of the severe economic recession, demand in the restaurant sector which used to consume about 44.3 per cent of the total imported beef amount plummeted. Korea concluded that the number of stores which operate under identical regulatory conditions is irrelevant when it comes to explaining the reasons why the beef quota was not filled in 1998.

194. **Australia** responded that while quota levels have been rising, the number of imported beef stores have been falling, indicating that it was not the existence of a quota that was the cause of the relatively small number of imported beef stores. Australia stated that it was surprising that the number of imported beef outlets had not grown significantly in the early 1990s, given that the market had known that imported beef quotas would grow steadily until 2000 and that the quota would be removed from 1 January 2001. The additional costs associated with establishing an imported beef shop, the limited range of products that may be sold and the uncertainty of price and availability of imported beef have all mitigated against the growth of imported-beef shops over the past decade.

[111] Number of foreign beef stores:

Year	1990	1991	1992	1993	1994	1995	1996	1997	1998
Number	2,193	4,178	4,472	4,838	6,088	7,713	7,569	7,026	5,498

Source: MAF

195. **Korea** submitted that the US and Australian arguments, if accepted, would amount to constructing the WTO as an instrument advocating de-regulation. This, in the view of Korea, is not the function of the WTO, which is simply an instrument outlawing discrimination between domestic and imported products. It does not put into question the regulatory function of Members to the extent that this has not been transferred at the international level. Under Article III, WTO Members only transferred to the international level their discretion to discriminate between domestic and imported products. They retain full authority to regulate as long as imported products are not treated less favourably than domestic ones.

196. In the present case, Korea considered that it regulated in a non-discriminatory manner: under identical conditions, traders are free to choose whether they will open a store selling domestic or imported beef. What counts, however, from a legal perspective is that whatever store they choose to open they will face an identical regulatory burden (or lack of it). Consequently, the Korean legislation affecting sale, offer for sale, etc. of beef does not reserve less favourable treatment for imported products and thus does not constitute a violation of Article III:4. Article XX is the best proof that this is the case. WTO Members can continue to pursue their regulatory objectives to the extent that their actions are not in conflict with their GATT/WTO obligations.

197. **Australia** responded that it was not claiming that Korea must de-regulate - only that its internal regulations for imported beef meet the requirements of Article III:4 - that is, that they provide for equality of competitive opportunities for imported beef *vis-à-vis* domestic beef.

198. Referring to the panel on *US - Hawaiian Regulations*[112] as well as to the 1956 working party report on *"Certificates of Origin, Marks of Origin, Consular Formalities"*[113], Australia remarked that the requirement to display the sign "Specialized Imported Beef Store" clearly goes beyond the indication of origin on products. GATT history indicates that a restriction of this type is contrary to Article III:4. This sign also has the effect of emphasising any negative perceptions about the quality of imported beef.

199. **Korea** responded that a specialized store must install a signboard indicating that it is a "specialized store of imported beef", as provided in Article 9 of the Management Guideline for Imported Beef. All stores in Korea choose their own trade name to promote their business by putting up a signboard. Hence, installing a signboard itself does not impose any additional financial burden on the person who intends to open a specialized store. The only trivial difference would be that the government has made it an obligation for stores selling imported beef. This requirement is inspired by the need to adequately inform the consumers that the store sells imported beef, thus preventing fraudulent practices.

---

[112] L/411/add.1; SR.10/13, 1955.

[113] Para. 13.

200. The allegations made by the Complainants that such signboards may have negative promotional effects cannot be taken seriously. The effect of the indication on a signboard depends entirely on the consumer's perception of domestic and imported beef, and there is no allegation made by the Complainants that Korea has restricted in any way the promotion or advertising of imported beef in Korea. The perception of the signboard can be highly positive if Korean consumers consider imported beef to be inexpensive and of high quality. Thus, Korea considers that the requirement to install a signboard to indicate a specialized store selling imported beef cannot be deemed as being by definition less favourable treatment in circumstances where advertisements and promotion of imported beef (such as its price, quality, etc.) are freely allowed.

201. In **Australia**'s view, it is irrelevant to the issue of equality of competitive opportunities that packaged imported beef is permitted to be sold in domestic beef stores, particularly given the declining importance of such sales.[114] Australia furthermore submitted that the separation of retail sale should be seen as an effort to protect domestic beef from the impact of import competition. Korea has pursued a policy of systematic separation of the market as a means of creating a permanent distinction in the minds of traders and consumers between domestic and imported beef, despite the fact that they are like and competitive products. In doing so it sends misleading signals to the market that ultimately distorts the competitive relationship between imported and domestic beef.

202. As imported and domestic beef are "like products" for the purposes of Articles III, **Australia** argued, there is no justification for the further differentiation applied to imported product between grass-fed and grain-fed product, particularly since no such distinction is applied to domestic product. Nor does Korea's tariff schedule contain such a distinction. Nor is making a distinction between grass-fed and grain-fed beef a reliable indicator of quality, which is more accurately measured on the basis of such indicators as marbling, texture, meat

114 The sale of imported packaged beef as a proportion of total imported beef sales since 1991 is as follows:

Year	Total Packaged Sales	Total Sales	% of total sales
1990	41,587	82,064	51
1991	55,802	124,741	45
1992	52,240	127,314	41
1993	36,988	103,373	36
1994	26,556	122,537	22
1995	27,203	146,495	19
1996	15,801	149,204	11
1997	14,612	134,225	11
1998	10,501	85,416	12
1999*	7,341	130,000	7

***As at 30 November.**

Source: MAF, LPMO Yearbooks, NLCF.

colour, fat colour and maturing level. Indeed, these are the indicators applied by Korea to domestic beef to grade quality.

203. While applied through the tender system, Australia contended, the separation of grass-fed and grain-fed beef is a law, regulation or requirement affecting internal sale. In particular, the association of a quality differential between grass-fed (general beef) and grain-fed (high quality beef), has a negative impact on the internal sale of grass-fed beef among consumers who have been encouraged to associate grass-fed beef with a product of lesser quality than grain-fed beef.

204. The distinction between grass-fed and grain-fed, Australia continued, and the association by the Korean government and the LPMO of relative differences in quality between them, is a distinction applied only to imported beef. This distinction has allowed the LPMO to exclude grass-fed beef, the majority of which is supplied by Australia, from the tender on three occasions in 1999. No similar limitations are applied to sales of domestic beef because no such grass/grain-fed distinction exists for domestic beef. Less favourable treatment is also accorded to imported grass-fed beef because of the association drawn between grass-fed beef and beef of "general" or lesser quality. This has created an arbitrary distinction in the minds of consumers that has adversely affected imports, sales and prices of grass-fed beef in both the LPMO and SBS systems.

3. *LPMO Tendering Opportunities*

(For arguments under this section see paragraphs 122-125. Cf. also paragraphs 287-292 and 346.)

4. *Measures with Respect to the Discharge of Imported Beef in the Wholesale Market*

205. **Australia** submitted that pricing of imported product in order to protect and stabilise domestic prices is contrary to Article III:4. The sale of imported beef in Korea is, according to Australia, manipulated by the LPMO and the NLCF with the aim of protecting the competitiveness of domestic product. These organizations have both taken measures to raise the price of imported beef which is decided by reference to the price of its domestic competition. This results in less favourable treatment for imported beef contrary to Article III:4. In establishing a case that minimum prices are applied to imports, Australia argued, it is not necessary to point to an officially published minimum price for imported beef. Minimum pricing can also be established from an analysis of the discharge procedures operated by the LPMO and the NLCF in accordance with the *Regulations Concerning Sales of Imported Beef* and an assessment of whether this measure, in its application, has the effect of a minimum price for imported beef, contrary to Article III:4.

206. Referring to price charts for imported beef, which indicate the maintenance of daily minimum prices for imported beef, as well as to the acknowledgement in the MAF press release of 22 July 1999 and the Yonhap News article

relating to reductions in the minimum price, Australia argued that these reinforce the view that there is a minimum wholesale price for imported beef which is manipulated in relation to the state of domestic cattle and beef prices. In *Canada - Marketing Agencies,* the panel concluded that the maintenance by an import and sales monopoly of a minimum price for an imported product at a level at which a directly competing, higher- priced domestic product was supplied, was inconsistent with Article III:4. While the panel in that case was considering the practices of import and sales monopolies, the critical principle to emerge from its analysis, according to Australia, is that the setting of minimum prices for imports in relation to the price of competing domestic product, rather than by suppliers' prices, would be contrary to Article III:4. Australia claimed that the discharge system for LPMO beef does precisely this by making decisions on prices of imported beef on the basis of the price of domestic product. (See also paragraph 128 above)

207. **Korea** contended that the price of imported beef is decided by reference to the price of its domestic competition which would seem to be evidence of normal commercial behaviour rather than constituting treatment less favorable within the meaning of Article III:4. Any commercial enterprise will normally set its prices by reference to the prices of competing products. (See also paragraphs 130 and 131 above.)

208. Referring to the 1984 panel report in *Canada - FIRA* [115]and to the 1992 panel report in *US - Malt Beverages*[116], **Australia** contended that in relation to the wholesale requirement for imported beef under the LPMO system, less favourable treatment arises since beef imported by LPMO must be sold through a wholesale market (all of which are run by NLCF), or processed and packaged, i.e. producers of imported beef are denied the opportunity to choose their preferred method of marketing. No such limitation on marketing is applied to domestic producers. Moreover, the obligation to purchase LPMO beef through a wholesale market also imposes an additional distribution level for imported beef which gives rise to additional transaction and distribution costs (eg. middle-men charges) to which producers of domestic beef are not subject.

209. The **United States** was of the opinion that, consistent with Article 31 of the *Vienna Convention*, the terms "laws, regulations and restrictions" under Article III:4 are to be given their ordinary meaning in their context and in the light of the treaty's object and purpose.[117] Korea's laws, regulations, and guidelines relating to the importation, sale and distribution of imported beef clearly are encom-

[115] Para. 5.10.

[116] Paras. 5.30-5.33.

[117] The Appellate Body has declared that the *Vienna Convention* "has attained the status of a rule of customary or general international law. As such, it forms part of the 'customary rules of interpretation of public international law' which the Appellate Body has been directed, by Article 3(2) of the DSU, to apply in seeking to clarify the provisions of the *General Agreement* ..." (footnotes omitted) Appellate Body Report, *United States – Standards for Reformulated and Conventional Gasoline*, ("*United States – Gasoline*"), WT/DS2/AB/R, adopted 20 May 1996, DSR 1996:I, 3, at 16.

passed in the ordinary meaning of those terms, as used in Article III:4. The titles that Korea has given to the various legal documents restricting activities regarding the importation and distribution of imported beef also reinforces their categorization as "laws, regulations and requirements. The United States submitted that Korea's restrictions, therefore, constitute "laws, regulations and restrictions affecting the internal sale, " of imported beef within the meaning of Article III:4. This is confirmed by consideration of how other panels have construed the term "affecting" for purposes of Article III:4.[118] Korea's laws and regulations adversely modify conditions of competition. Therefore, these measures constitute laws or regulations *affecting* their internal sale, purchase, distribution and use for purposes of Article III:4.

210. Furthermore, the United States continued, Korea's laws, regulations and guidelines specifically govern and confine the precise manner in which imported beef is sold in Korea, as well as its distribution and use. Korea restricts the sale of imported beef to specialized stores. In addition, Korea imposes tight limitations on the use of imported beef by end-users and customers, confining its use to designated purposes within each customer/end-user class. In addition, Korea severely circumscribes the distribution channels for imported beef. Cross-trading among super-groups or the members of super-groups is prohibited, and violations are punished with loss of quota sub-share and exclusion from further participation in the SBS system.

211. Referring in particular to the United States' arguments in paragraph 209-210, **Korea** responded that the LPMO and the twelve super-groups buy the quota amount and then distribute the products. This system is in place as a result of the US insistence to establish a system more responsive to market needs. The Records of Understanding is the best evidence of this statement. Subsequently, Korea agreed during the Uruguay Round to remove all remaining restrictions by 1 January 2001. Hence, the claim by the United States in this respect is illegitimately invoked at this point in time, since Korea can lawfully maintain the existing system until the end of 2000. Moreover, the US claim suffers from a number of inaccuracies: First, it is not true that super-groups do not trade with each other. Following government intervention to this effect, any super-group which has exhausted its share can request reallocation of the quota. In 1998, there was a request for reallocation of the quota three times and the requests were granted. Consequently, the US allegation in this respect must be rejected.

212. Second, it is not true, Korea submitted, that stores selling imported beef cannot cross-trade. Indeed, the opposite is true. Stores belonging to different super-groups can, and often do, cross-trade. The LPMO/super-group structure is there to administer the QR. Korea has to ensure somehow that the QR will be properly administered. In a demonstration of good faith, Korea did not establish the system in a unilateral manner but after consultations with interested parties,

[118] *Italian Agricultural Machinery*, paras. 11-13; *US - Section 337* para. 5.11.

i.e. the United States. Korea explained that paragraph 14.5.5 of the former Imported Beef Sales Regulations prohibited the specialized stores from reselling or supplying imported beef to other specialized stores or domestic butchers. The revised Management Guideline for Imported Beef, however, prohibit only the resale of imported beef by a specialized store to their counterparts selling domestic beef. Therefore, cross-trading between specialized stores is allowed. A comparable structure does not exist with respect to domestic beef because there is nothing like a QR for domestic beef. Korea did not take this measure in the context of Article XX(g). Only in that case would it have to ensure a comparable system for domestic products. Hence, in Korea's view, it is impossible to establish a violation of Article III:4.

5. *Other Measures Applying to Imported Beef*

213. **Australia** argued that the requirement for cash-only sales, which is not applied to domestic beef, discriminates against imported product by restricting the marketing possibilities and therefore the competitive opportunities available to imported beef *vis-à-vis* domestic beef.[119] The availability of credit is a factor in encouraging sales. As such, a requirement that imported beef be sold on a cash payment basis affords it less favourable treatment as no such requirement applies to domestic beef. While the regulations give rise to the possibility of credit sales of imported beef, it is subject to administrative discretion as to duration, limits and availability ("when deemed inevitable"). There is no requirement that this discretion be exercised to permit credit sales in individual cases. In judging whether a measure is contrary to Article III:4, it is not relevant whether it applies across-the-board or on an *ad hoc* basis.[120]

214. **Korea** responded that the LPMO's sales of imported beef through the wholesale market shall in principle be on a cash basis. This requirement, however, is also applied to the NLCF sales of domestic beef to domestic beef stores. Both imported and domestic beef stores sell their products mostly on a cash basis except where a credit relationship is formed between the traders or when the trader has secured a mortgage bond.

215. **Australia** retorted that purchasers of domestic product are not limited to the NLCF markets to purchase their beef. On the other hand, beef imported by the LPMO is only permitted to be sold through these wholesale markets, unless processed and packaged.[121]

---

[119] *Management Guideline for Imported Beef*, Article 13; *Regulations Concerning Sales of Imported Beef*, Article 11.
[120] *Canada - FIRA* , para. 5.5; *United States - Gasoline, supra*, footnote 97, para. 6.14, citing *US - Section 337.*
[121] Article 15.2, *Management Guideline for Imported Beef.*

6. *Measures Applied through the SBS Regime*

216. **Australia** submitted that the SBS system restricts the marketing of imported beef by limiting the range of end-users eligible to make purchases through the system. Korea imposes no such controls on domestic beef. Purchasers of domestic beef are not required to join an industry association to purchase beef. They, therefore, do not have to meet the additional costs associated with such membership. Furthermore, the fact that an end-user may only import through the super-group to which it belongs, is only entitled to membership of one super-group, may only use imported beef for the uses permitted for that super-group and is forbidden from cross-trading, impose restrictions on the distribution of imported beef that are not applied to its domestic competition. The SBS system also excludes any user or potential user which is not a defined end user or customer under the regulations. No such restrictions exist on 'users' of domestic beef. For these reasons, the restrictions on end-users in the SBS system are contrary to Article III:4. The effect of these restrictions, both individually and cumulatively, Australia claimed, is to restrict the competitive opportunities available for imported beef.

217. Australia noted that previous panels have found inequality of competitive conditions when the possibility of purchasing imported product directly from a foreign producer is excluded,[122] or when imported products have to be sold only through in-state wholesalers.[123] or when requirements result in imported product having access to fewer points of sale.[124] Logically, requirements that result in imported product having access to fewer end-users than domestic beef would, therefore, also fall within the ambit of Article III:4 (For arguments by Korea and the United States see also paragraphs 209-211.)

218. Australia also considered that the requirement of super-group membership imposes additional costs on the purchase of beef, such as membership fees, and other expenses related to the operation of the super-group as a "middleman" for imported beef purchases by end users, additional costs that are not imposed on domestic beef. In the case of NLCF, there is further discrimination against imported beef arising from the operation of Article 21 of the NLCF's *SBS Operation Guidelines.* Australia noted that Article 21 states that the NLCF may adjust prices of imported beef "considering the domestic livestock product price trends and the wholesale market prices". Given that NLCF beef may be priced other than according to commercial considerations (i.e. to protect domestic beef production), beef imported through the NLCF super-group is subject to less favourable treatment than domestic beef.

219. **Korea** submitted that, as concerns the claim that the system constitutes a violation of Article III:4, since contrary to what is the case with respect to domes-

---

122 *Canada - FIRA* , para. 5.10.

123 *US - Malt Beverages,* paras. 5.30-5.33.

124 *Canada - Marketing Agencies(II),* para. 5.6.

tic beef, imported beef has to be sold through specialized organizations; and the claim that the system constitutes a violation of Article III:4, because end-users or customers cannot belong to more than one super-group; and that the system constitutes a violation of Article III:4, since it distinguishes between grain- and grass-fed beef only with respect to imported beef, Korea considered that these claims are inadmissible, since it is impossible to establish comparability between domestic and imported beef in these respects: there is no quota for domestic beef. Korea further noted that there are no costs or other requirements associated with becoming an SBS member.

220. **Australia** and the **United States** submitted that the SBS system imposes labelling, reporting and record-keeping requirements, that discriminate against imported product contrary to Article III. The effect of these restrictions is to limit the amount of imported beef which might be imported in the absence of such restrictions.[125] The *Management Guideline for Imported Beef* and the *Operational Guidelines for Beef Imported under the SBS System* are, in the opinion of Australia, laws, regulations and requirements which directly govern the internal sale, offering for sale, purchase, transportation, distribution or use of domestic or imported beef. The requirement to report all monthly sales and importation to the LPMO President and the obligation to record all purchases and sales and retain such records for at least two years imposes compliance costs on end users and super-groups in terms of time and expense, which in turn has an impact on prices for imported beef. No similar requirements apply to distributors of domestic beef, hence according domestic product more favourable treatment.

221. **Australia** contended that the supervisory powers of the LPMO have been used to apply restrictive labelling requirements on imported beef. These conditions were agreed between the LPMO and the super-groups and require imported cartons to be labelled with a 10 cm x 5 cm label exclusively in the Korean language showing commodity name, contract number and importer's name. The new requirements apply to all imported product contracted from 1 October 1999 and is compulsory.[126] This labelling requirement has been applied in addition to the existing Korean country of origin labelling requirements that apply to both domestic and imported product.[127]

222. Australia considered that the new and additional labelling requirement for imported beef is inconsistent with Korea's obligations under Article III:4 . The requirement leads to less favourable treatment for imported product than for like

[125] For example, in 1998, a quota of 112 200 tonnes of imported beef was allocated among the SBS super-groups (60 per cent of Korea's total quota amount). Of this, only 69 933 tonnes or 62.3 per cent was actually taken up but Korea was not prepared at that time to eliminate restrictions on end users in order to encourage uptake of the full quota amount.

[126] Note from KMIA to Supplier's Agents informing them of Buyer Identification Label requested in relation to the Strengthening of Imported Beef Inspection.

[127] Agricultural Product Country of Origin Labeling Guidelines, Ministry of Agriculture and Forestry Notice 1997-79 of 5 January 1998.

product of national origin and affects the internal sale of the imported product. The requirement imposes an unnecessary, impractical and expensive measure imposed only on imported product, thereby artificially reducing the competitive ability of the imported product. The measure is unnecessary because current labelling of Australian product clearly identifies the origin and product. It is, therefore, unclear what benefit the new requirement adds. The measure is impractical because the contract number and super-group may be unknown at the time the product is packed by the producer. The measure, therefore, requires re-labelling either prior to shipment or in Korea. Whether re-labelled in Korea or Australia, there will be additional costs for the re-labelling, which will serve to make the imported product less competitive, regardless of whether the cost is borne by the super-group or the Australian exporter.

223. **Korea** responded that stores selling imported beef are no longer required to keep records of sales under the *Management Guideline for Imported Beef*. The former Guidelines on Notification and Operation of specialized store 5(d) specified that the "Specialized Store" shall keep the records related to the supply of imported beef for not less than 2 years. This was to maximize protection against deceptive sale practices by ascertaining through records that no imported beef was sold as domestic Hanwoo beef. However this obligation has been eliminated. As concerns labelling, Korea continued, all imported livestock products including beef are required to be marked with, among other things, the name of the product, importer, the address of the importer, production date, and shelf life. These are necessary to facilitate the importation of these products and are also used for custom clearance purposes as well as distribution. The domestic beef traders must also mark the name of the products, producer, shelf life, and the production date. These requirements aim to protect public health and to establish sound distribution processes. There is no discrimination between imported beef and domestic beef.

224. **Australia** rejected Korea's claims with respect to record-keeping, reporting and labelling that these measures are now no longer in place or apply equally to domestic beef. In the opinion of Australia, Korea has not rebutted Australia's claims that limitations on end-users and usage unreasonably restrict and discriminate against imported beef. Australia acknowledges the apparent abolition of some cross trading prohibitions since December 1999[128], but notes that access to imported beef is still dependent on SBS membership, end-users are still limited to membership of only one type of super-group and restrictions on usage remain. Quota allocation processes within this restrictive framework also have a negative effect on commercial trade of imported product. The largest proportion of the quota continues to be awarded to the state trading agencies LPMO and NLCF or their affiliates, all of which are dominated by domestic producers. There are also

128 "Guideline for Handling Imported Beef", 3 December 1999, Article 26(1).

supervisory powers exercised by law over the super-groups with consequent obligations imposed in terms of reporting, record-keeping and labelling.

225. Australia further submitted that it makes no sense for Korea to claim that treatment of domestic and imported beef in the SBS system is permitted to be discriminatory because there is no quota for domestic beef. Korea does not substantiate its claim that super-groups can trade with each other. Government reallocation of quota amounts is not the same thing as commercial trade between super-groups. In relation to the use of super-groups themselves as the sole channel for import, it is not sufficient for Korea to argue that this provides effective economies of scale and that small-scale retailers prefer to use super-groups. This is a commercial proposition and, if true, need not be enforced through compulsory regulation

7. *Burden and Standard of Proof*

226. **Korea** considered that it was up to the Complainants to show that the Korean measure at hand amount to a violation of Article III:4. Korea was of the view that the Appellate Body report on *US Shirts and Blouses (AB)* confirms this:

> "... the issue in this case is which party has the burden of demonstrating that there has, or has not been, an infringement of the obligation assumed under ... . In addressing this issue, we find it difficult, indeed, to see how any system of judicial settlement could work if it incorporated the proposition that the mere assertion of a claim might amount to proof. It is, thus, hardly surprising that various international tribunals, including the International Court of Justice, have generally and consistently accepted and applied the rule that the party who asserts a fact, whether the claimant or the respondent, is responsible for providing proof thereof."[129]

227. The burden of proof would shift to Korea only if the Complainants "adduce evidence sufficient to raise a presumption that what is claimed is true".[130] Korea was of the opinion that the Complainants have not done so in this case. Korea submitted that its quantitative restriction (QR) on imports of beef has an impact on trade in beef between the Complainants and Korea, since it restricts the amount of foreign beef into the Korean market to the level permitted under the QR. The resulting injury cannot, however, be challenged under WTO law, since the QR is legal and indeed is not challenged in the present dispute. The Complainants, in order to discharge their burden of proof, need to demonstrate how the system of separation of stores selling beef prejudices their rights under the GATT *independently* of the injury resulting from the very existence of the Korean quota.

---

[129] Appellate Body Report, *US - Shirts and Blouses, supra*, footnote 93, at 334-335.
[130] Ibid.,at 335.

228. Theoretically, Korea argued, two situations could be imagined: the first is where the QR has been fully absorbed. In such a scenario, the Complainants would have to demonstrate that the WTO law has been violated and that, consequently, their rights under the WTO Agreement are prejudiced, i.e. the Complainants would have to demonstrate that the Korean QR would not only have to be fully filled but to be filled in a particular manner. Korea considered that this would be absurd, firstly because when a QR is negotiated there is no obligation to import the full amount. Rather, it gives the right to the importing Member not to import beyond the set threshold. Even if there were an obligation to fully absorb the QR, it would be an obligation of result and not an obligation of conduct (cf. paragraph 232). This would mean that the QR must be absorbed independently of the means used. If nothing has been negotiated relating to the manner in which the QR must be absorbed, it is not up to the international adjudicating body to add to the existing obligations. As the Appellate Body has reminded us, echoing the standing jurisprudence of the International Court of Justice, no presumptions limiting the scope of national sovereignty is permissible in the realm of public international law. Hence, Korea argued, the only possible conclusion in this respect is that in case the QR is absorbed, the claim that the WTO Agreement has been violated, and as a result the Complainants' rights have been prejudiced, has to be rejected.

229. The second situation is where the QR has not been not fully absorbed. In this case, Korea submitted, the Complainants would have to show that the Korean regulation imposing on traders the obligation to sell domestic respectively imported beef in separate stores is the very reason why the QR has not been absorbed. The Complainants would find themselves in an awkward position since the same number of stores in some years suffices and in some years does not suffice to ensure that the QR is fully absorbed. Hence the causal link between the number of outlets and the absorption of the QR cannot be established.

230. **Australia** did not agree with Korea's interpretation of what is required to prove an inconsistency under Articles III and XI:1 when a quota exists. If Korea's argument that its measures are permitted because of the existence of a quota were to prevail, it would be manifest to a finding that any and all measures taken with the existence of a quota are *ipso facto* WTO consistent. This interpretation would render Articles III, XI and XIII redundant, contrary to the rules of interpretation contained in the *Vienna Convention.* Australia considered that Korea is wrong in its assertion of Australia's burden of proof in relation to Article III:4. Australia submitted that it is not required to demonstrate that the measures claimed to be inconsistent with Article III:4 prejudice Australia's rights in relation to the filling or otherwise of an existing quota. The existence and/or filling of the quota is immaterial to a finding of consistency in relation to Article III. To find otherwise would be to limit the operation of the national treatment provision in instances where a quota exists. Neither Article III itself, nor any other provision of the GATT 1994, explicitly makes such an allowance, nor implicitly permits such an interpretation.

231. **Korea** contended, as stated in paragraphs 164-167, that the injury resulting from the very existence of the quota to US and Australian beef exporters should not be attributed to the Korean regulation requiring that, in principle, foreign and domestic beef should be sold through separate stores. The Complainants must show injury resulting from this regulatory requirement independent of the protection afforded to domestic production through the negotiation and conclusion of the quota for beef currently legitimately applied by Korea.

232. **Australia** submitted that Korea is attempting to read a trade effects test into Article III. The Appellate body has rejected such a test. The essence of Article III:4 is equality of competitive conditions. Australia submitted that the competitive opportunities afforded to domestic beef have been denied to imported product and that Korea is therefore in breach of its obligations under Article III . The existence or filling of a quota has absolutely no bearing on this fact. No trade effects, or proof of injury test, Australia continued, can be read into either Article III or XI. Previous panels have been explicit on this point, in relation to both Articles. In making out a case with respect to Article III:4 Australia considered that it is not required to show actual proof of injury, as claimed by Korea. In particular, Australia is not required to show injury through under-filling of the quota. Australia rejected Korea's claim (see paragraph 228) that Article III is an obligation of result rather than conduct. The Korean argument in this case seeks to insert a trade effects test into Article III. If the Panel were to accept Korea's argument, the national treatment provision would not apply in cases where a quota exists. This is clearly not the aim of Article III which requires non-discrimination once goods have come across the border. Australia is required to show inequality in competitive conditions. Australia has so shown, and Korea has not provided evidence to rebut this.

233. The panel in *Korea - Alcoholic Beverages*, endorsed by the Appellate Body, Australia continued, was explicit in its finding that "a focus on the quantitative extent of competition instead of the nature of it, could result in a type of trade effects test being written into Article III cases". The panel stated that, if a particular degree of competition had to be shown in quantitative terms, that would be similar to requiring proof that a tax measure has a particular impact on trade. It considered such an approach akin to a "type of trade effects test" and rejected the argument.[131] The Appellate Body had previously found against inserting a trade effects test into Article III in *Japan - Alcoholic Beverages*. The Appellate Body found that "it is irrelevant that the trade effects of the tax differential between imported and domestic products, as reflected in the volumes of imports, are insignificant or even non-existent; Article III protects *expectations*, not of any particular trade volume, but rather of the equal competitive relation-

---

[131] See Panel Report, *Korea – Taxes on Alcoholic Beverages*, ("*Korea – Alcoholic Beverages*"), WT/DS75/R, WT/DS84/R, adopted 17 February 1999, DSR 1999:I, 44, para. 10.42; and Appellate Body Report, *Korea – Taxes on Alcoholic Beverages* ("*Korea – Alcoholic Beverages*"), WT/DS75/AB/R, WT/DS84/AB/R, adopted 17 February 1999, DSR 1999:I, 3, paras.129-131.

ship between imported and domestic products".[132] (Emphasis added.) (See also paragraphs 157-159 above).

234. While the **United States** submitted that its competitive opportunities in the Korean market have been prejudiced by the Korean requirement that imported beef be segregated for sale, as well as by the other limitations imposed only on imported beef, proof of actual trade damage is no more required by Article III:4 than by Article XI. Korea fails to point to any textual support for the existence of the alleged requirement. For the last 50 years, since the *Brazilian Internal Taxes* case,[133] Article III has been interpreted as requiring *no* trade impact of the measures in question. Indeed, the GATT expressly rejected an injury test of the sort argued by Korea, when the GATT 1947 Council expressly rejected the mistaken panel report of 1981 on *Spain –Sale of Soybean Oil.*

235. Furthermore, the United States continued, GATT panels have consistently concluded that the pertinent criterion under Article III:4 is whether Members "provide equal conditions of competition" once goods are cleared through customs. (The relevant cases are cited in footnote 97.) The panel in the *US - Section 337* dispute, for example, clearly rejected the position that Korea espouses. The panel concluded that:

> "Article III would not serve this purpose if the United States interpretation [referring to the US defense advanced in the *Section 337* dispute] were adopted, since a law, regulation or requirement could then only be challenged in GATT after the event as a means of rectifying less favourable treatment of imported products rather than as a means of forestalling it ... [The panel] noted that this approach is in accordance with previous practice of the CONTRACTING PARTIES in applying Article III, which has been to base their decisions on the distinctions made by the laws, regulations or requirements themselves and on their *potential* impact, rather than on the *actual* consequences for specific imported products." [emphasis added; footnotes omitted][134]

See also arguments in paragraphs 157-158 and 160 -163.

236. **Korea** reiterated that the Complainants have not met their burden of proof with respect to any of the claims raised under Article III and Article XI. Korea emphasized that the injury resulting from the existence of the QR itself cannot be challenged under WTO law because the legality of the QR is not in dispute. Korea argued that the Complainants have failed to establish a *prima facie* case that their rights have been prejudiced independently of the injury resulting from the legal QR.

132 Appellate Body Report, *Japan - Alcoholic Beverages*, *supra*, footnote 98 at 110.

133 Working party on Brazilian Internal Taxes, Vol. II, pages 184-185, para. 13-16.

134 Para. 5.13.

E. *Claims under Article XX(d) of GATT*

237. **Korea** explained that the "specialized store" system for imported beef was established in order to protect consumers from widespread deceptive practices of selling imported beef as domestic products. The majority of beef stores in Korea are operated in the form of small-scale butcher shops where all meat is stored in one huge freezer and sold in slices. It is extremely difficult for consumers to distinguish domestic beef from imported beef at sight, nor is there any practical technique developed for easy distinction between the two. Under such circumstances, the considerable price difference between the imported and the domestic beef would easily raise the incentives for the owners of the butcher shops to engage in fraudulent practices, which the Korean Government found were extremely difficult to detect and sanction.[135] Thus, the system of separate sales outlets was introduced as the only practical solution to effectively deal with the problem of widespread fraudulent sales practices. Government intervention is limited to imposing identical regulatory requirements for both categories of stores in full compliance with Article III:4. Indeed, the same restrictions apply to domestic beef stores (they cannot sell imported beef), as to imported beef stores (they cannot sell domestic beef).

238. Korea submitted that, were the Panel to reject its arguments presented in the context of Article III:4 above and rule that sales of domestic and imported beef through separate stores constitute discriminatory treatment against imported goods, and thus a possible violation of Article III:4 is established, its legislation is justifiable through recourse to Article XX(d). Referring to the text of Article XX(d)[136], Korea argued that sales of domestic and imported beef through separate stores is necessary to counteract fraudulent practices. Except for the exceptional circumstances surrounding the financial crisis in 1997, the price of domestic beef is substantially higher than that for imported beef. Beef is sold either prepackaged or fresh. With respect to the first category, it is easy to impose labeling requirements indicating the origin of the beef; with respect to the latter it is impossible. Moreover, traders have a strong incentive to sell all beef as domestic beef since by doing so they can profit from the higher sales price. Such are the fraudulent practices that the Korean regulation aims at counteracting. Korea

---

[135] According to Korea, a Marketing Association confirmed, in the late 1980's that 28 per cent of imported beef transacted at general butcher shops had been faked and sold as Hanwoo. In 1990, the Report of the Proceedings of the National Assembly's Committee on Agriculture, Forestry and Fisheries found that fraudulent beef sales had taken place in 604 cases.

[136] "Subject to the requirement that such measures are not applied in a manner which would constitute a means of arbitrary or unjustifiable discrimination between countries where the same conditions prevail, or a disguised restriction on international trade, nothing in this Agreement shall be construed to prevent the adoption or enforcement by any contracting party of measures:

> (d) necessary to secure compliance with laws or regulations which are not inconsistent with the provisions of this Agreement, including those relating to customs enforcement, the enforcement of monopolies operated under para. 4 of Article II and Article XVII, the protection of patents, trade marks and copyrights, and the prevention of deceptive practices."

submitted that Article XX(d) provides the appropriate legal framework to justify the regulation regarding separation of stores selling beef.

239. Korea contended that the leading GATT[137] case in the area of Article XX(d) is the *US - Section 337*, which report essentially made two points: on the one hand it interpreted what kind of measures are deemed to be necessary for the achievement of a regulatory objective at the national level, and on the other that the level of enforcement sought by the national regulatory objective cannot be put into question by a panel. The Appellate Body report on *US – Shrimp(AB)* where the Appellate Body, contrary to what used to be the case before, recognized the sovereign right of the United States to pursue its own environmental policy, made this point clear.

240. Regulatory diversity, Korea continued, to the extent that it is applied in a non-discriminatory manner, is not put into question in the WTO system. The WTO, and Article XX more specifically, support a pure necessity test whereby the adjudicating bodies put into question neither the invocation of the national regulatory objective sought, nor the desirable level of enforcement; they can only put into question the means used to reach the objective sought. Hence, the question that panels must answer when reviewing the compatibility of a national legislation with Article XX is whether the national mechanisms aimed at realizing the said objective are applied in a non-discriminatory manner and whether the option sought is necessary.

241. Korea noted that the term "necessary" in Article XX has traditionally been interpreted as meaning that WTO Members must always, when intervening either in the context of Article XX(b) or Article XX(d), use the least restrictive among the available options. Korea considered that this interpretation is at best not very helpful since national authorities are not always in a position to know *ex ante* whether the least restrictive option can guarantee the level of enforcement sought. Referring to the panel report on *US - Section 337* [138], Korea submitted that, although it is difficult to quantify legal inconsistency, the panel most likely had in mind that in case various options are reasonably available to a domestic authority and all of them are inconsistent with the WTO obligations of the Member concerned, the latter must choose the one that causes the least burden possible to non discriminatory trade flows.

---

137 According to Appellate Body Report, *Japan - Alcoholic Beverages*, *supra*, footnote 98, the GATT panel reports provide very meaningful guidance on the interpretation of the relevant provision and should be taken into account by subsequent panels dealing with the same issue.

138 "It was clear to the Panel that a contracting party cannot justify a measure inconsistent with another GATT provision as 'necessary' in terms of Article XX(d) if an alternative measure which it could reasonably be expected to employ and which is not inconsistent with other GATT provisions is available to it. By the same token, in cases where a measure consistent with other GATT provisions is not reasonably available, a contracting party is bound to use, among the measures reasonably available to it, that which entails the least degree of inconsistency with other GATT provisions."

242. Korea noted that so far GATT/WTO case law has not explored the link between regulatory diversity, on the one hand, and the necessity requirement, on the other. Korea submitted that there is a correlation between the two in the sense that were a regulatory objective to be sought in a very strict manner, the choice of instruments would consequently be influenced. Since the *level* of protection sought cannot be put into question, the choice of *instrument* will have to be appreciated in the same context.

243. Korea furthermore noted that the judgement by the adjudicating body whether the instrument chosen is the necessary instrument will be done by reference to the instruments "reasonably available" to the Member at hand. This term provides the link to local circumstances. The situation (financial, health, environment, education, etc.) is not the same throughout the globe. There is nothing objective about setting regulatory targets and pursuing them. This is precisely the reality captured by the term 'reasonably available' in the cited panel report. Second, such regulatory choices are the outcome of a democratic process, reflecting the sovereign will of the electorate. To the extent that they do not constitute a clear-cut case of violation of international obligations, they should not be light-heartedly overturned.

244. Korea explained that the Korean Government allows stores selling domestic beef to also sell pre-packed imported beef since in this case the risk of fraudulent practices is reduced. With respect to sales of fresh beef, however, the situation is not the same. The Korean Government found it impossible to come up with any other means that would enable it to reach the objective sought. Continuous policing of the shops is not an option in view of the substantial costs involved, since only an around the clock policing of all shops selling beef could help reach this objective (see also paragraph 249).

245. On the other hand, compulsory pre-packaging for all imported beef is not an option either. since such a requirement could easily amount to a violation of Article III.4, constituting a *de jure* discriminatory treatment against imported products, thus affording protection to domestic production. Hence, the measure would have to be justified under Article XX(d). Such a measure however, is far more restrictive than the option chosen in this case, since it would impose considerable adjustment costs to foreign producers and at the same time place the imported product at a disadvantage. Whereas domestic beef would be sold either fresh or pre-packaged, imported beef would be sold only in pre-packaged form. Hence, consumers would be in a position to choose from a much wider range of domestic products. The Korean policy choice is aimed at guaranteeing that no such competitive disadvantage would result for imported beef and that the whole regulatory framework would be drafted in such a manner so as to ensure that it will strictly serve its assigned purpose.

246. Hence, Korea continued, the most feasible idea was to establish a dual distribution system whereby, under identical conditions, private operators can set up a retail store for sales of either domestic or imported beef. In such a manner, without imposing any additional burden on sales of imported beef, the Korean

Government can be sure that the risk of fraudulent practices is significantly and effectively reduced since the Government can better guarantee, by supervising the distribution channel, that stores selling imported beef will only be buying imported beef whereas stores selling domestic beef will only be buying domestic beef.

247. To complement the system, Korea continued, the Government requests that stores selling imported beef indicate that they sell such beef. The sign should inform consumers that imported beef is being sold and accordingly they should expect to get cheaper prices than for domestic beef which has been traditionally more expensive. Without this regulatory requirement, these stores would have the incentive to 'cheat'. Stores selling domestic beef do not have such an incentive since they already paid a high price to buy the expensive domestic beef. But for the existence of the sign requirement, therefore, only one category of stores has an incentive to cheat and has recourse to fraudulent practices.

248. As the Appellate Body in its report on *US – Shrimp(AB)* made it plain, once a national legislation has passed the test of a particular sub-paragraph of Article XX, it must also be found to comply with the chapeau of that Article, in the sense that it must be applied in an even-handed manner. Korea submitted that its measures indeed comply with the requirement of even-handedness. Not only identical requirements apply for the opening of stores selling imported and domestic beef, but the Korean government ensures that this is the case in practice. Indeed, there has never been a claim that the Korean Government does not follow the letter of its legislation and the Complainants have not claimed that such is the case.

249. Korea did consider other alternatives to prevent these fraudulent deceptive practices such as more strict country of origin marking requirement and mandatory pre-packing requirement for all beef. However, these alternatives were not adopted. A labeling requirement, no matter how strictly enforced, could not do the trick since consumers, in general, demand that they be able to purchase fresh slices cut from unpacked chunks. The nature of the products and the commonplace retailing practice prevalent in Korea do not allow for any other method but separation of sales outlets system to distinguish the two products. Moreover, it would be virtually impossible for the law enforcement agency to gather sufficient evidence in the absence of the system of separation of sales outlets, since the stores would have at their disposal the packages, boxes, and other items used for both imported and domestic beef.

250. With respect to the "secure compliance with laws or regulations which are not inconsistent with the provisions of this Agreement" element of Article XX(d), Korea submitted that the law sought to be enforced through the system of separation of outlets is the "*Unfair Competition Prevention and Business Secret Protection Act.*" The *Unfair Competition Act* purports to address anti-competitive acts (fraudulent practices). The purpose of the Act, as stated in Article 1, is to "maintain the order of sound transactions by preventing unfair competitive acts." In

paragraph 1 of Article 2 of the Act, the term "unfair competitive acts" is defined as follows:

> "(1) Act misleading the public to understand the place of origin of any goods either by falsely marking that place on any commercial document or communication, in said goods or any advertisement thereof or in any manner of misleading the general public, or by selling, distributing, importing or exporting goods bearing such mark;
>
> (2) Act making a mark misleading people to understand as if any goods were produced or processed in an area other than that where said goods are produced, manufactured or processed, on any commercial document or communication, in said goods or any advertisement thereof, or in any manner of misleading the general public, or act selling, distributing, importing or exporting goods bearing such mark."

251. Korea was, furthermore, of the opinion that the system of separation of sales outlets is in full conformity with Article XX(d). Korea reiterated that on the one hand, the system as such, if found to be discriminatory by the Panel, is justified through recourse to Article XX(d) as the necessary means to enforce the Unfair Competition Act; and that on the other, the only observable regulatory diversity between sales outlets selling domestic and imported beef, the sign requirement, is justified through recourse to Article XX(d) since it is necessary to enforce the Act which is aimed at combating fraudulent practices.

252. Its objective, Korea continued, is to avoid fraudulent practices (what has been translated as "*unfair competitive acts*" in Articles 1 and 2 of the Act) in the context of beef sales. To this end the Unfair Competition Act was enacted. The "prevention of deceptive practices" is specifically mentioned in Article XX(d) as one of the area where GATT-inconsistency is presumed to be established. Furthermore, Article IX(6) of GATT provides that "*The Contracting Parties shall co-operate with each other with a view to preventing the use of trade names in such manner as to misrepresent the true origin of the product.*"

253. Korea pointed out that the enforcement of the obligation sought under the Act is the prevention of sales of "falsely marked" goods. Within the framework of this Act, the term "marking" covers all incidents of representations related to the country of origin of the product being sold. Hence, the term includes all representations made by a butcher shop as it relates to the country of origin of the beef sold, including, but not limited to, the sign posted in front of a "chunk" of beef as well as all verbal representations made by the shop operator. Korea noted that the marking of the place of origin is normally done through labeling on the product itself. In the case of beef sold in Korea, however, some are packaged along with proper labeling and others are sold un-packaged in "chunks." With respect to packaged beef a workable country of origin mechanism is in place and, therefore, there is no need for these products to be sold separately. However, the majority of imported beef is sold un-packaged and in these situations the "normal" way of marking is not practicable and an alternative was therefore necessary in the form of separation of sales outlets combined with the sign requirement.

254. The separation of sales outlets, Korea continued, does not have a mere indirect incidence on Korea's stated objective of eliminating fraudulent practices. On the contrary, there is an uninterrupted causal link between the measure and the objective sought. Korea noted that it carefully considered which traders have an incentive to cheat in view of the price differential between imported and domestic beef. This is only the case with respect to traders who purchase imported beef and then sell it as domestic beef. Traders that purchase imported beef and sell it as such do not profit from fraudulent practices.

255. However, if Korea only checks the supplies without checking whether what is sold corresponds with what is purchased, the risk for fraudulent practices remains. This is why Korea came up with the requirement to on the one hand separate sales outlets, and on the other require only those that sell imported beef to signal the origin of the beef sold. Korea is of the opinion that it's intervention is the least restrictive to achieve the stated objective, because, by virtue of the separation of outlets, Korea will have to examine only supplies to outlets selling domestic beef (since only such outlets have an incentive to cheat). On the other hand, by imposing the signalling requirement to outlets selling imported beef, the incentive to cheat is removed, since they would incur losses if they purchased domestic beef. It is therefore obvious, Korea argued, that the separation of outlets does not simply share the same objectives with the Korean *Unfair Competition Act*. It is the enforcement mechanism of the said Act.

256. Korea further explained that when beef imports into Korea resumed in August 1988, imported beef was permitted to be sold in butcher shops together with domestic beef (hereafter referred to as the "simultaneous sales system"). In response to deceptive practices, the Korean Government introduced in March 1989 the specialized sales outlets system for imported beef, in addition to the simultaneous sales system but the deceptive practices still continued. As the magnitude of the fraudulent behaviour was being uncovered and publicized, this controversy evolved into a major social issue.[139] Accordingly, with a view to preventing such deceptive practices, the Korean Government decided in 1990 to eliminate the simultaneous sales system, which was found to be the major source of deceptive sales practices, thereby integrating the imported beef sales into one system - the specialized sales outlets system for imported beef - which has remained virtually unchanged.

257. In response to Australia's argument that no measures are in place to prevent the fraudulent substitution of different grades of domestic beef, Korea noted that this argument fails to take into account that it is relatively easy to distinguish by sight between lower and higher grades of domestic beef. As concerns the prevention of fraudulent substitution in restaurants, Korea submitted that a restaurant is a service industry selling the skill of the chef, ambience of the venue and convenience of location as well as quality of food. The price of beef is a mere frac-

---

139 Refer to articles from the Korea Herald, Chosun Daily and the Dong-A Daily.

tion of what one pays at a restaurant. No solid argument can result from comparing a beef store with a restaurant. Besides, restaurants do not usually indicate whether they are using imported or domestic beef as ingredients in their prepared meals.[140] Hence the type of fraud found in beef stores is not committed. In conclusion, the separation of sales outlets can also be fully justified under Article XX(d).

258. The separation of sales outlets system, Korea continued is not necessary in the case of meat from domestic dairy cows since Korea has already developed a reliable testing method for distinguishing meat from domestic dairy cows from domestic beef, "Hanwoo." Furthermore, in Korea's view, the amount of dairy cow meat sold at the retail level is quite negligible and does not warrant any special consideration.[141]

259. New Zealand's suggestion that audit trails could be used as the means to prevent deception, Korea continued, ignores Korea's underdeveloped distribution system. Audit trails are not a feasible option at the present time. In addition, few merchants in practice maintain comprehensive and accurate book records. New Zealand also argues that deceptive practices can be prevented by imposing stricter penalties. Article 18(3) of the *Unfair Competition Act* provides that a person "*who commits an unfair competitive act may be subject to imprisonment for a period of up to three years or a maximum fine of thirty million won.*" These penalties are not to be regarded lightly. Korea, therefore, sees no merit in the argument that even stricter penalties would have any measurable impact on the situation. The problem is not the level of penalties but rather the fact that the penalties are in practice not effective due to the difficulties of investigating and gathering sufficient evidence to apply the laws.

260. In view of the foregoing, Korea submitted that it has met the "necessity" requirement of Article XX(d) since the system of separation of sales outlets provide for a least restrictive method of complying with the *Unfair Competition Act*. Under this system, the Korean Government, without imposing any additional burden on sales of imported beef, can ensure that the risk for fraudulent practices is significantly and effectively reduced.

261. **Australia** and the **United States**, addressing Korea's claim that the separate retail sale of imported beef can be justified under Article XX(d), submitted that the burden of proof in making this claim rests with Korea. The Complainants

---

[140] Korea also stated that an important portion of imported beef (about 45 per cent) is also sold in the restaurant sector. Cf. paragraph 193.

[141] According to Korea, beef imported in 1990 amounted to 84,000 MT in excess of the 58,000 MT quota for that year while according to MAF statistics, Korean beef production amounted to 95,000 MT of which about 42 per cent came from dairy cattle. In 1991, imports of beef amounted to 124,000 MT and domestic beef amounted to 98,000 MT, of which 42 per cent came from dairy cattle. In 1998, total consumption in Korea amounted to 345,000 MT of which 91,000 MT was imported, and about 254,000 MT came from domestic production. According to statistics by the NLCF, dairy cattle represented, in 1998, 18.25 per cent of total Korean slaughter (head).

considered that Korea has failed to discharge this burden. First, Korea has not shown which law or regulation, otherwise consistent with GATT 1994, that it is seeking compliance with. Secondly, Korea has not demonstrated that the measures actually secure compliance with these laws or regulations. Thirdly, Korea has failed to show that the measures are necessary to secure compliance. And finally, Korea has not proven that the measures meet the requirements of the chapeau of Article XX.

262. A measure cannot be said to be *necessary* to ensure the prevention of deceptive practices, **Australia** continued, unless it actually goes some way towards achieving that end *in effect*. In consultations with Australia on 28 May 1999, Korea conceded that it was difficult to quantify the number of specialized beef shops. When asked how it enforced its retail requirements if it did not know where the stores were, Korea stated that the central Government did not administer the enforcement of regulations. This was the responsibility of municipal governments which are under no obligation to report to the central Government. Furthermore, Korea admits that it is unable to enforce the requirements in supermarkets, where beef is required to be sold in separate display cabinets. Australia submitted that a measure cannot be necessary where it cannot be enforced and that there is no basis to Korea's claim that the regulation "strictly serve its assigned purpose" (see paragraph 245). The Korean measures are also not "necessary" where there are alternative measures reasonably available which prevent fraudulent substitution of imported and domestic beef and which are less trade restrictive. Korea admits that no regulations exist to prevent substitutions in restaurants. Restaurants are able to sell both domestic and imported beef. Separate distribution arrangements do not exist for imported and domestic pork or chicken. Nor, as detailed by the United States in paragraph 273, are separate distribution arrangements in place for a range of other products for which Korea claims there is a danger of substitution between like imported and domestic products. Finally, there are no measures in place to prevent the fraudulent substitution of different grades of domestic beef, even though this is reported to be a significant problem.

263. Australia considered that it was pertinent that while record-keeping requirements were imposed on imported beef stores, similar record-keeping requirements are not imposed on domestic beef stores. Australia questioned how Korea could ascertain the sources of supply for domestic-beef shops, and hence the existence of fraud, when no records are kept and when, as Korea argues, it is physically impossible to tell the difference between imported and domestic beef. Australia argued that it was difficult to understand how Korea is able to state with any certainty that the fraudulent sale of imported beef as domestic beef is a persistent problem when it is unable to prove the existence of fraud in the first place.

264. Australia submitted that Korea's claim that separation of domestic and imported product is only required for beef, and not for other products, because of the existence of a large number of tests to prove the physical difference between all other imported products and their domestic equivalents, were not convincing. Australia questioned why Korea did not separate the retail sale of these products

before such tests existed, why beef was not separated in restaurants and why different types of domestic beef were not sold separately prior to the apparent discovery of DNA testing in 1998. Australia also submitted that, on the basis of advice from Australia's peak scientific research organization, it had serious doubts about the accuracy of DNA testing for cattle to classify individual beasts into a particular breed

265. Australia referred to *US - Malt Beverages*, in which case the panel found that the United States had failed to meet its burden of proving that wholesaler and common carrier requirements in various states were the only reasonable measure available to secure enforcement of state excise laws. The fact that not all fifty states maintained these measures indicated that *alternative* measures for the enforcement of state excise laws existed.[142] Australia also submitted that in cases where there is no discernible difference in the product, i.e. if the products are identical in physical characteristics and have the same end uses, it is not necessary to put measures in place to distinguish between the products. These products are directly competitive and should be permitted to compete against each other in the market place on the basis of a variety of factors such as price, quality, consumer preferences etc.

266. Australia also submitted that Korea had failed to show a link between the dual retail system, including the signage requirements, and the enforcement of the prohibition against "falsely marking the place of origin of a product" in the Korean *Unfair Competition Act*. It was not clear how the dual retail system is related to the enforcement of laws relating to false marking of origin or how such a system was necessary to secure compliance with these laws.

267. Since the price differential between domestic and imported beef is largely a result of actions by the Korean government through the delivery of substantial market price support and protection of domestic beef from market driven competition, Australia also submitted that by maintaining separate retail sales, Korea is actually exacerbating the price differential between domestic and imported beef, and therefore increasing the likelihood of fraud. Australia did not agree with Korea's argument that the separate retail arrangements do not impose an additional burden on imported beef (see paragraph 246). The regulations prohibit the sale of imported beef from the majority of beef retail establishments in the country and impose additional compliance costs in relation to setting up new premises, or separate areas in supermarkets, as well as signage requirements. These are not insignificant and seriously affect the competitive opportunities afforded to imported beef.

268. The **United States** considered that Korea has not satisfied any of the requirements cited in paragraph 261 for the application of Article XX(d). Korea has not even specifically identified which of its laws or regulations are intended to be advanced through segregation of imported beef at the retail level. Further-

[142] Paras. 5.43 and 5.52.

more, Korea has not shown the retail sale restriction to be necessary to secure compliance with any of its laws, including those relating to the prevention of deceptive practices. Without a reasonable showing that fraud is a real, and not an imagined, issue and that other measures would be inadequate to secure compliance with Korea's laws, Korea cannot demonstrate such measures to be necessary. Korea, therefore, cannot avail itself of Article XX(d) to insulate GATT inconsistent measures from challenge.

269. Korea has not met its burden of showing the requisite elements for Article XX(d) to apply, continued the United States. First and most fundamentally, the retail restrictions are not measures which fall within the scope of subparagraph (d) of Article XX. The panel in *EEC - Parts and Components* found that Article XX(d) covers only measures necessary to the enforcement of obligations under laws or regulations consistent with the General Agreement. In the opinion of the United States, the regulations relating to separate retail distribution channels do not serve to enforce any Korean laws relating to fair trading or deceptive practices. At best, the segregated distribution of imports serves the same objectives as these unfair competition statutes, but this is far from being *necessary to the enforcement of* such laws.

270. The proof necessary to meet the requirement of Article XX(d) in this regard was addressed by a panel in *Canada - Periodicals*. In that dispute, Canada asserted that a prohibition on imported magazines containing domestic advertising was required to secure compliance with a tax measure that limited deductions to expenses incurred in advertising in domestic magazines. The panel concluded that although the ban on imported magazines might have the incidental consequence of ensuring that the tax deduction was not abused, and, therefore, the ban might have a common objective with the tax measure, that alone was insufficient to establish that the import ban was meant to secure compliance with tax legislation. The panel observed that any other construction of the requirement in Article XX(d) that the measure "secure compliance with laws and regulations" would lead to a situation where "[w]henever the objective of a law consistent with the General Agreement cannot be attained by enforcing the obligations under that law, the imposition of further obligations inconsistent with the General Agreement could then be justified under Article XX(d) on grounds that this secures compliance with the objective of that law".

271. The United States further submitted that the situation in the present matter, for the purposes of the application of Article XX(d), is the same as that before the panels in the *Canada – Periodicals* and in the *EEC - Parts and Components* disputes. Although Korea argues that the segregated sale of imported beef is meant to secure compliance with the provisions of the *Unfair Competition Act*, Korea has not shown how the retail restrictions do that. At most, the segregation of retail sales outlets may reduce the opportunities to misrepresent the identity of beef, but Korea has not shown that even this is achieved by the retail measures. The most that can be said is that the measures segregating the retail sale of imported and domestic beef may possess, in part, a common objective with the *Unfair Competition Act*.

272. Even if the Panel were to conclude, the United States continued, that the retail restrictions are "to secure compliance" with Korea's fair trading laws, Korea has not demonstrated that they are "necessary" for this purpose. Allegations concerning fraudulent practices do not relate to current activity, but instead are dependent on concerns regarding fraud allegedly occurring at the time that the dual regime was implemented in 1990. Korea has not indicated that any information exists that suggests that any fraudulent conduct persists, or that any fraud that does exist is at such levels as to warrant the draconian measures that Korea has instituted.

273. In addition, the United States submitted, there are a range of alternative measures that would make the maintenance of separate retail channels unnecessary in the event that any fraud is sufficiently prevalent to justify Korea's measures. That this is the case is evident from the fact that Korea has not elected to replicate the separate retail store requirement in other areas in which fraud of the same alleged nature is evidently occurring. In a Korean Fair Trade Commission announcement appearing on 19 August, 1999 in the Korean Economic Daily, it was reported that an investigation of 21 importing agencies involving 61 agricultural products, including oranges and milk, was underway. Yet, no product other than beef is subject to a requirement that separate stores be maintained. Korea has alleged fraud in connection with imported products as varied as sesame seeds, pork, rice and garlic, all of which are said to be less expensive than their Korean counterparts and subject to misrepresentation as Korean products. But no separate stores have been required for the sale of such products, indicating that Korea has found alternative ways of addressing any fraud.

274. In the case of these other products, Korea has relied on investigations and prosecutions to address instances of fraud that appear to be, if anything, much more widespread than any involving imported beef. Korea has not indicated why such measures are not equally effective in the case of beef for any fraud that might exist. Indeed, if Article XX(d) permitted Members to discriminate against imported products whenever they are sold at a lower price than a domestic counterpart, Article III:4 would no longer provide any meaningful national treatment protection.

275. The United States submitted that while Korea claims that this Panel should not interfere with the allegedly democratic process that led to the institution of the dual retail sale regime, the United States noted that the regulations prohibiting sale of imported beef in Korean beef stores were issued in January 1990 without benefit of legislative authority. Thus, the regulations were simply the result of administrative action. This oversight was not corrected until the enactment of the Revised Livestock Act in 1999, approximately nine years after the regulations were first promulgated.

276. Replying to the US arguments in paragraph 273, **Korea** explained that with the exception of rice and potato flakes, all products mentioned by the United States in its statement contain certain physical characteristics which would allow Korean experts to distinguish the imported products from those of domestic ori-

gin. With respect to rice, the standard retail practice is to sell in its original packaging (i.e. unlike beef, rice retailing does not entail displaying portions outside of its original packaging). As for potato flakes, garlic and safflower seed, the imported volume and the total consumption simply do not warrant any special treatment. Furthermore, for products such as sesame seed, garlic and safflower seed, Korea has already developed a technical means of differentiating imported from domestically grown products. Beef is different from all the products mentioned by the United States in that it is hardly distinguishable by sight, nor is there technology to distinguish imported beef from domestic beef. Moreover, the import volume and the proportion it represents of general food consumption is too large to consider the issue of consumer protection lightly.[143]

277. With reference to the US assertion that, because Korea does not maintain separate sales outlets for a wide range of other products where fraudulent practices allegedly occur, the Korean measure with respect to beef cannot be "necessary" within the meaning of Article XX(d), Korea referred to the Appellate Body reports in the *US – Shrimp (AB)* and *US – Gasoline (AB)* cases that the analysis of a measure under Article XX must be made strictly on a case-by-case basis. The Panel is not called upon in this case to examine any measure as it relates to any product other than beef. Indeed, to do so would clearly fall outside the terms of reference of the Panel. It is therefore irrelevant what measures are or are not applied to other products. To draw any valid conclusions with respect to regulatory measures affecting these other products, and their relation to Article XX, the same comprehensive assessment would need to be made for each product on a case-by-case basis. Since this would fall outside the terms of reference of the Panel, it is clear that any consideration of other products, and measures affecting those products, must be disregarded entirely.

278. **Australia** submitted that ultimate availability of the Article XX exception is subject to the compliance by the invoking Member with the requirements of the chapeau.[144] Notwithstanding that a measure falls within the list of exceptions, it must still satisfy the requirement that it was "not applied in a manner which would constitute a means of arbitrary or unjustifiable discrimination between countries where the same conditions prevail, or a disguised restriction on international trade." The Appellate Body in *US – Gasoline(AB)* stated that "the chapeau by its express terms addresses, not so much the questioned measure or its specific contents as such, but rather the manner in which that measure is applied".[145] The Appellate Body in *US – Shrimp (AB)* also emphasised the *application* of a measure for Article XX.

279. The policy goal of a measure at issue, Australia continued, cannot provide its justification under the chapeau of Article XX. The legitimacy of the declared

143 Imported beef sold in retail shops range between 10 – 11 per cent of Korean beef consumption. Total beef imported amounted to 26 per cent of beef consumption in 1998.

144 Appellate Body Report, *United States - Shrimp*, *supra*, footnote 38, para. 157.

145 Appellate Body Report, *United States – Gasoline*, *supra*, footnote 117, at 20.

policy objective of the measure, the relationship of that objective with the measure itself, and its general design and structure, are examined under paragraphs (a)-(j). If the measure is not held provisionally justified under an exception, it cannot be ultimately justified under the chapeau. On the other hand, it does not follow from the fact that a measure falls within the terms of an exception that the measure will also comply with the requirements of the chapeau.[146]

280. The terms "arbitrary or unjustifiable discrimination" and "disguised restriction on international trade" can be read side-by-side. The fundamental theme is to be found in the purpose and object of avoiding abuse or illegitimate use of the exceptions to substantive rules available in Article XX.[147] Australia submitted that the potential for deceptive practices arises out of Korean government measures which create or exacerbate the price differential between domestic and imported beef, i.e. domestic price support, and lack of competition arising from separate retail sale. In the opinion of Australia, Article XX is not intended to justify such measures. Furthermore, the retail separation of imported and domestic beef constitutes "arbitrary or unjustifiable discrimination" and a "disguised restriction on international trade" in the context of Article XX because it affords protection to domestic production, is applied only to imported beef, and not to other imports, and is applied only between imported and domestic beef while not being applied to different types of domestic beef, where large price differentials also prevail.

281. Australia argued that Korea must have known that separating only imported and domestic beef sales, while imposing no equivalent separation requirements on different types of domestic beef, would have a disproportionate effect on imported product. In not dealing with the same apparent problem in the same way, Korea has arbitrarily and unjustifiably discriminated against imported beef. It has done so to protect domestic beef from the full impact of import competition, contrary to the chapeau of Article XX

282. The **United States** submitted that Korea has not satisfied the requirements of the chapeau as it appears that Korea has eschewed the application of the same requirement for separate stores to address a problem involving fraud related exclusively to Korean beef. Press reports indicate that some of the worst cases of fraud involve retailers mis-labelling and selling meat from Korean dairy cows as Hanwoo beef. Estimates indicate that almost 50 per cent of the Korean beef sampled in 1998 was mis-identified as being Hanwoo, when it was a much inferior grade from dairy cows. Furthermore, contrary to Korea's assertion that dairy beef sales are negligible, meat from dairy animals constitute approximately 10 to 15 per cent of total beef consumption. By not requiring separate stores for the sale of beef from Korean dairy cows, Korea has elected to apply one set of measures to address an alleged problem of fraud with respect to imports, while rejecting the

---

[146] Appellate Body Report, *US – Shrimp, supra*, footnote 38, para. 149.

[147] Apellate Body Report, *United States – Gasoline*, *supra*, footnote 117, at 21.

same approach for fraud affecting a domestic product. Such action is unjustifiable discrimination within the meaning of the chapeau of Article XX. Moreover, within the context of the chapeau of Article XX it makes no difference whether the unjustifiable discrimination is prescribed by the measure or the result of its application.[148]

283. Indeed, in the *US - Gasoline* case *(AB)*[149], the Appellate Body described the showing that must be made by a Member wishing to avail itself of the protection of Article XX: "In order that the justifying protection of Article XX may be extended to it, the measure at issue must not only come under one or another of the particular exceptions - paragraphs (a) to (j) - listed under Article XX; it must also satisfy the requirement imposed by the opening clauses of Article XX. The analysis is, in other words, two-tiered: first, provisional justification by reason of characterization of the measure under XX(g); second further appraisal of the same measure under the introductory clauses of Article XX."[150]

284. The United States referred to the *US – Gasoline (AB)* case, in which the Appellate Body stated that the purpose and object of the introductory clauses of Article XX is generally the prevention of abuse of the Article XX exceptions:

> ... The chapeau is animated by the principle that while the exceptions of Article XX may be invoked as a matter of legal right, they should not be so applied as to frustrate or defeat the legal obligations of the holder of the right under the substantive rules of the *General Agreement*. If those exceptions are not to be abused or misused, in other words, the measures falling within the particular exceptions must be applied reasonably, with due regard both to the legal duties of the party claiming the exception and the legal rights of the other parties concerned.[151]

285. In the opinion of the United States, Korea has failed to satisfy either the requirements of paragraph (d) of Article XX or the criteria contained in the chapeau. Therefore, Korea's reliance on Article XX to insulate its dual retail sale regime from challenge under Article III:4 must fail. Any other result would constitute an abuse of the exception contained in Article XX (d).

286. **Korea** rejected the argument advanced by the United States that it is inconsistent for Korea not to impose the same measure with respect to meat from Korean dairy cows. Korea argued that the separation of sales outlets is not neces-

148 In Appellate Body Report, *United States – Shrimp, supra*, footnote 38, para. 160, the Appellate Body made the following observation: "We note, preliminarily, that the application of a measure may be characterized as amounting to an abuse or misuse of an exception of Article XX not only when the detailed operating provisions of the measure prescribe the arbitrary or unjustifiable activity, but also when a measure, otherwise fair and just on its face, is actually applied in an arbitrary and unjustifiable manner."

149 See above.

150 See also Appellate Body Report, *United States – Shrimp, supra*, footnote 38, para. 118.

151 Appellate Body Report, *United States – Gasoline, supra*, footnote 117, at 20; Appellate Body Report, *United States - Shrimp, supra*, footnote 38, para. 118.

sary in the case of meat from dairy cows since Korea has already developed a reliable testing method for distinguishing between meat from dairy cows from domestic beef, "Hanwoo." Furthermore, the amount of dairy cow meat sold at retail level is quite negligible and does not warrant special consideration. Korea, therefore, argued that the system of separation of sales outlets and the accompanying requirement to indicate the origin of beef imposed only on imported beef are in full conformity with the requirements contained in the chapeau of Article XX. Korea reiterated its contention that the system of separation of sales outlets is in full compliance with Article XX(d) of GATT. Korea further noted that, were the Panel to reject Korea's arguments in this respect, the separation of sales outlets is a "remaining restriction" within the meaning of Note 6 in Korea's Schedule of Concessions.

F. Claims under Article II of GATT

1. LPMO Tendering Opportunities

(See also paragraphs 122-125.)

287. **Australia** submitted that the tendering process adopted by the LPMO for the import of beef results in quantitative restrictions being applied to grass-fed beef, contrary to Article II. Furthermore, LPMO imposes a quality distinction between grass-fed and grain-fed beef which further discriminates against grass-fed product and limits the sales of high quality grass-fed beef in the Korean market. The Korean tender mix system has the effect of imposing limits on the volume of the grass-fed beef that Australia is permitted to export to Korea. This is less favourable treatment of Australia than that provided for in Korea's Schedule contrary to Article II. Australia noted that Korea's Schedule of Concessions includes tariff bindings on all beef imported within the tariff quota of 43.6 per cent, reducing to 41.6 per cent by 2000. The tariff currently applied to imports of beef is 42 per cent. Korea has made no qualification in its schedules under column 7 "other terms and conditions" and no reference to either grain-fed or grass-fed beef.

288. In allocating the LPMO quota between grain-fed and grass-fed beef, Korea is, according to Australia, imposing a condition that within the quota individual limits apply to grass- and grain-fed beef, respectively. Under Article II, any other "terms, conditions or qualifications" with respect to the quota must be set forth in Korea's Schedule. Given that Korea made no such qualification, the administration of the LPMO quota is less favourable than that provided for in its Schedule. Further, by imposing a quality differential between the two, the tendering system undermines the concession for beef provided in Korea's Schedule.

289. Panels have interpreted Article II as not only requiring no less favourable treatment in the Schedule, but also no less favourable treatment for *each* exporting country. The 1981 panel report on *EEC - Beef* examined the EEC's tariff quota for high quality grain-fed beef. A footnote to the concession provided that "entry under this subheading is subject to conditions to be determined by the

competent authorities". Its administration was through certificates of authenticity. The sole issuing authority for such certificates was the US Department of Agriculture. The panel found:

> "The words, 'terms, conditions or qualifications' in paragraph 1(b) of Article II could not be interpreted to mean that countries could explicitly or by the manner in which a concession was administered actually limit a given concession to the products of a particular country. The Panel further found that the fact that in Annex II there was only one certifying agency for the meat in question and that this agency only certified meat of United States origin *in effect prevented access of high quality meat from other countries.*" [Emphasis added.]
>
> "Consequently, the Panel concluded that the manner in which the EEC concession on high quality beef was implemented *accorded less favourable treatment to Canada than that provided for in the relevant EEC Schedule,* thus being inconsistent with the provisions of paragraph 1 of Article II of the General Agreement." [Emphasis added.][152]

290. Australia rejected the evidence provided by Korea which shows an increase in grass-fed imports by LPMO in 1999 (see paragraph 323). Australia considered that those figures are incorrect. Australia can show, based on information provided by the LPMO in the last three years, that total purchases of grass-fed beef by the LPMO in 1999 have fallen to approximately 15,000 tonnes, down from 44,000 tonnes in 1997 because information for 1999 was based on customs-cleared, not purchase data and because for all years Korea attributed purchases to the LPMO which had actually been made by both the LPMO and super-groups. This is a drop of nearly 60 per cent. As a consequence of LPMO discrimination against grass-fed beef, Australia has seen its share of LPMO tenders fall from 47.7 per cent in 1998 to 20.4 per cent in 1999, a fall of more than half. On the other hand, in the SBS sector of the market, where a range of cuts and grades of grass-fed beef are purchased, Australia's market share has risen.

291. Korea has not rebutted Australia's claim that the distinction imposed by Korea between grass-fed and grain-fed beef provides less favourable treatment than that contained in its Schedule, contrary to Article II. Australia assumes that Korea therefore accepts those claims. Moreover, Korea has not rebutted Australia' claim in paragraph 287. Origin neutrality is not at issue since Australia is not claiming a violation of Article I. Furthermore, the grass-fed / grain-fed distinction is not a measure of customer demand but a distortion imposed by the Korean government contrary to its Schedule commitments.

292. **Korea** submitted that the LPMO operates its tendering procedures on the basis of commercial considerations. The LPMO consistently purchases its full quota amount, according to an open bidding procedure and according to origin-

---

152 *EEC - Beef*, at page 99, paras. 4.5-4.6.

neutral criteria. The LPMO purchases on the basis of consumer demands and preferences and Korea applies no regulatory measure which discriminates against grass-fed beef. Korea is under no obligation to affect its purchases of beef according to sub-groupings of various beef types. Therefore, for the purposes of the present dispute, the distinction between grass-fed and grain-fed beef is artificial and the question of discriminatory or less favorable treatment with respect to grass-fed beef does not arise.

2. *Application of a Mark-Up on SBS Imports*

293. **Australia** submitted that Korea applies a mark-up on beef imported under the SBS system which is not included in its Schedule of Concessions or applied to domestic beef, and hence no "qualification or reservation" which would permit Korea to impose the mark-up. The mark-up constitutes "other duties or charges of any kind imposed on or in connection with the importation" of beef. That Korea has no Schedule coverage for the imposition of the mark-up on imported beef is indicated by the fact that a mark-up on other products is shown in the Korean Schedule. The imposition of the mark-up on beef imported through the SBS system, therefore, constitutes less favourable treatment than that provided in the Korean Schedule and is inconsistent with Article II:1(a) and (b). Korea cannot claim a justification for the mark-up on the basis of a Record of Understanding with Australia that expired in 1995, or a Record of Understanding with the United States to which Australia is not a signatory, nor on the basis of a schedule which contains neither reference to the mark-up, or indeed to any of the Record's of Understanding. Australia also noted that Korea appears to have introduced a mark-up on purchases of the LPMO quota in 2000, which the Korean government is proposing to auction. The mark-up is an unspecified amount and is payable to the Livestock Development Fund.

294. The **United States** submitted that Korea collects a mark-up on beef imported both through the SBS system and by the LPMO. In the opinion of the United States, these mark-ups are in each instance inconsistent with Korea's obligations under Article II:1. One of the fundamental objectives of the GATT 1994 is "the substantial reduction of tariffs."[153] To ensure that tariff concessions, once made, have the full force and effect intended, Article II directs that the duty rates set forth in bindings are maximum limits that may not be exceeded. Specifically, Article II:1(a) requires that "[e]ach contracting party shall accord to the commerce of other contracting parties treatment no less favorable than that provided in ... the appropriate Schedule." Moreover, Article II:1(b) provides that products subject to a schedule of concessions are "exempt from ordinary customs duties in excess of those set forth and provided for therein." Similarly, Article II:1(b) directs in pertinent part that "Such products shall also be exempt from all other

[153] Preamble to the GATT 1994, para. 3. Panels should address issues in light of the underlying purposes of the GATT 1994. See *US – Sugar Head Note*, para. 5.2-5.3.

duties or charges of any kind imposed on or in connection with importation in excess of those imposed at the time of this Agreement". The United States also referred to the Appellate Body's interpretation of the requirements of the first sentence of Article II:1(b) in its report in *Argentine - Textiles* as pertinent to the construction of the second sentence.

295. Article 31 of the *Vienna Convention,* the United States continued, provides that treaty terms are to be given their ordinary meaning in their context and in light of the object and purpose of the treaty. The mark-up is certainly a "charge" within the meaning of Article II:1(b), particularly as Article II:1(b) expressly includes "charges of any kind". Korea's mark-up is a liability to pay money to Korea's Livestock Development Fund. Furthermore, the mark-up is a charge imposed at the time of importation. Indeed, entries of imported beef may not leave Korean Customs until the mark-up is paid.[154] Korea's Schedule makes no provision for the imposition of any duty or charge on imports of beef other than the bound rate of duty, which is currently 42 per cent and will decline to 40 per cent on 1 January 2004. The mark-ups levied since 1993 have been applied in addition to the bound rates in Korea's Schedule.[155] As Korea did not identify any other charges or other duties in its Schedule as applicable to imported beef, there is no justification for the mark-up. By collecting a mark-up on all imported beef in addition to the ordinary duty provided for in its Schedule, Korea violates Article II:1 by imposing "other duties or charges" that exceed its bound tariff rate.

296. A tariff binding in a Member's Schedule provides an upper limit on the amount of duty that may be imposed. The application of customs duties or other charges in excess of those provided for in a Member's Schedule, inconsistent with the second sentence of Article II:1(b), constitutes "less favorable" treatment under the provisions of Article II:1(a). As the Appellate Body has concluded, "[a] basic object and purpose of the GATT 1994, as reflected in Article II, is to preserve the value of tariff concessions negotiated by a Member with its trading partners, and bound in that Member's Schedule. Once a tariff concession is agreed and bound in a Member's Schedule, a reduction in its value by the imposition of duties in excess of the bound tariff rate would upset the balance of concessions among Members.[156] This conclusion is no less valid with respect to "other charges" and the commitment set forth in the second sentence of Article II:1(b).

297. In this connection it is also relevant that the WTO Understanding on the Interpretation of Article II:1(b) of the General Agreement on Tariffs and Trade 1994 provides that:

---

154 Operational Guidelines for Imported Beef Under the SBS System, 26 December 1997, Article 9; Guidelines for Handling Imported Beef, 1 October 1999, Article 25 .

155 Korea had bound the rate for beef at 20 per cent in the Tokyo Round of Negotiations.

156 Appellate Body Report, *Argentina – Measures Affecting Imports of Footwear, Textiles, Apparel and Other Items* ("*Argentina – Textiles and Apparel*"), WT/DS56/AB/R and Corr. 1, adopted 22 April, 1998, DSR 1998:III, 1003, para. 47.

> the nature and level of any "other duties or charges" levied on bound tariff items, as referred to in that provision, shall be recorded in the Schedules of concessions annexed to GATT 1994 against the tariff item to which they apply.

298. Since Korea did not reflect the mark-up charged on imported beef in its Schedule as either an other duty or charge, its imposition is contrary to Article II:1(b).

299. **Korea** replied that 'Schedule LX-Republic of Korea NOTE to PART I: MOST FAVOURED NATION TARIFF Section I: Agricultural Products' contains an item 6 which provides: 'According to the results of the 1989 consultation with GATT/BOP Committee and the Uruguay Round multilateral trade negotiation, the remaining restrictions on the items marked as '*Note 6(a)', '*Note 6(b)', '*Note 6(c)', '*Note 6(d)', or '*Note 6(e)' in column 5 of Section I-A of Part I of this schedule shall be eliminated or brought into conformity with GATT provisions from the dates specified as follows: *Note 6(a): 1995; *Note 6(b): 1 Jan. 1996; *Note 6(c): 1 Jul 1996; *Note 6(d): 1 Jul. 1997; *Note 6(e): 1 Jan. 2001.'

300. Korea explained that the products at issue in the current dispute (02.01 and 02.02) are marked with the Note 6(e), thus meaning that the "remaining restrictions" shall be eliminated or be brought into conformity with GATT provisions from 1 January 2001. Item 6 of the Note, Korea continued, does not enumerate which "remaining restrictions" are meant. However, the plain meaning of the words suggests that the "remaining restrictions" at issue are not necessarily in conformity with the provisions of the GATT. Otherwise there would be no need to provide that they should be eliminated or be brought into conformity with GATT provisions by 1 January 2001.

301. It is not disputed by the Complainants, Korea continued, that at the time of conclusion of the Uruguay Round, a mark-up on imported beef of 95 per cent was applied in 1994. Hence, this mark-up was at that time a *'remaining restriction'*. Korea, therefore, submitted that this mark-up would only need to be eliminated or be brought of into conformity with GATT provisions by 1 January 2001 for the products at issue in the current dispute. Consequently, Korea submitted, its Schedule LX clearly allowed it to maintain "remaining restrictions" on beef until 1 January 2001. Maintaining the mark-up (which was phased out on 1 January 2000) cannot be considered a violation of its obligations under Article II. In addition, "Note 6(e)" is clearly indicated in Korea's Schedule with regard to tariff item numbers 0201 and 0202 subject to this dispute.

302. This, Korea submitted, thus clarifies that, among others, the "mark-up" is one of the "remaining" restrictions referred to in Note 6 of Korea's Schedule which existed at the time of conclusion of the Uruguay Round. This Annex also clarifies that the United States was very well aware of the existence of this mark-up and its intended phase-out schedule at the time of negotiation of the Uruguay Round. At the same time, it should be noted that nothing in this Annex suggests that it intends to exhaustively list all remaining restrictions in existence at the time of conclusion of the Uruguay Round. Korea considered that it has strictly

observed the phase-out schedule of the mark-up as agreed in the December 1993 Record of Understanding with the United States, according to which Korea have until 1 January 2001 to eliminate or bring into conformity with GATT the remaining restrictions. Accordingly, Korea is not in violation of its obligations under Article II:1. Furthermore, Korea submitted, the claims brought by the United States and Australia with regard to this issue are contrary to Article 26 of the *Vienna Convention* (see paragraph 108).

303. For the sake of argument, Korea continued, to demonstrate that the mark-up was one of the "remaining restrictions" existing at the time of the conclusion of the Uruguay Round, should the Panel consider that this issue is not clear and further interpretation is necessary, Korea referred to *Japan -Alcoholic Beverages (AB)*, in which case the Appellate Body held that there can be no doubt that Article 32 of the Vienna Convention has attained the status of customary rules of interpretation of public international law[157] and can be applied according to Article 3.2 of the DSU. Article 32 of the Vienna Convention stipulates that recourse may be had to supplementary means of interpretation, including the preparatory work of a treaty and the circumstances of its conclusion, in order to confirm the meaning resulting from the application of Article 31, or to determine the meaning when the interpretation according to Article 31 (a) leaves the meaning ambiguous or obscure; or (b) leads to a result which is manifestly absurd or unreasonable.

304. Korea submitted that the preparatory works of the treaty and the circumstances of its conclusion with regard to Note 6 of Part I of Schedule LX can be found in two Records of Understanding between the United States and Korea[158] The December 1993 Record of Understanding contains an Annex entitled "Beef" which states that: "The current July 15, 1993 Record of Understanding (L/7270) shall continue to apply except as modified to incorporate the provisions of the new understanding." The United States seems to acknowledge the amendment of the 15 July 1993 Record of Understanding by the Annex in the December 1993 Record of Understanding containing the new timetable. The United States further seems to acknowledge that: " This timetable was ultimately made a part of Korea's WTO Schedule of Concessions". The United States therefore seems to accept the existence of a certain linkage between the Annex attached to the December 1993 Record of Understanding and Korea's WTO Schedule of Concessions.

305. The schedule for the phase-out of the mark-up on beef in the Annex to the December 1993 Record of Understanding is as follows:

1993 – 100; 1994 – 95; 1995 – 70; 1996 – 60;
1997 – 40; 1998 – 20; 1999 – 10; 2000 – 0.

---

157 Appellate Body Report, *Japan - Alcoholic Beverages*, *supra*, footnote 98, at 104.

158 Record of Understanding between the Government of the Republic of Korea and the Government of the United States of America on market access for beef initialed on 26 June 1993; and Record of Understanding between Korea and the United States on agricultural market access in the Uruguay Round initialed on 13 December 1993.

306. Korea has submitted a document provided by the official of the United States Department of Agriculture on 24 February 1994 which leaves no doubt that there was a clear agreement on the application of a mark-up on beef by Korea in the Uruguay Round[159]. The application of a mark-up was, therefore, consistent with Korea's obligations under Article II:1 and not contrary to Article III:2. Furthermore, Korea implemented its December 1993 Record of Understanding obligations in good faith and has since 1 January 2000 eliminated the mark-up in accordance with the schedule agreed in the December 1993 Record of Understanding.

307. The **United States** retorted that the parties to the Records of Understanding expressly preserved all of their WTO rights, which includes the right conferred by Article II to be free from additional charges not provided for in the importing country's schedule. Korea never provided for the mark-up in its Schedule; nor did Korea refer to the Records of Understanding therein. Second, the bilateral agreement is not one of the Agreements annexed to the Marrakesh Protocol to the General Agreement on Tariffs and Trade 1994, is not otherwise annexed to the WTO Agreement, and is not a "covered agreement" listed in Appendix 1 of the Dispute Settlement Understanding. Thus, it does not create rights or obligations under the WTO; nor is it enforceable either by the United States or Korea in proceedings under the DSU.

308. In response to Korea's arguments in paragraph 306, the United States submitted that the "talking points" annexed to Korea's 13 December 1999 oral statement underscore that the mark-up on beef was viewed as a *quid pro quo* granted to Korea in the 1993 Record of Understanding in exchange for market opening undertakings, including a minimum access commitment. The mark-up was scheduled to end as specified in the Record of Understanding on 31 December 1999, unlike the "remaining restrictions" referenced in Korea's Schedule which must be terminated by 1 January 2001. Consistent with the US position, the penultimate "talking point" questions whether mark-ups are consistent with Korea's bilateral and multilateral obligations and suggests that Korea review this subject before submitting its country Schedule.

G. Claims under Article III:2 of GATT

309. **Australia** contended that alternatively to being inconsistent with Article II (see paragraph 293 above), the mark-up constitutes an internal tax or other internal charge on SBS imported beef. Given that domestic beef is not subject to a similar charge, the mark-up infringes Article III:2. Australia referred to the report of the Appellate Body in *Japan - Alcoholic Beverages (AB)* as providing guidance on the interpretation of Article III:2, first sentence. The words of the first sentence require an examination of the conformity of an internal tax measure with

---

[159] "Talking Points", annexed to Korea's oral statement at first Panel meeting in December 1999.

Article III by determining, first, whether the taxed imported and domestic products are "like" and, second, whether the taxes applied to the imported product are "in excess of " those applied to the like domestic products. If the answer is "yes" to both questions, then the measure is inconsistent with Article III:2, first sentence. In accordance with Article 3.8 of the DSU, such a violation is *prima facie* presumed to nullify or impair benefits under Article XXIII.[160] Australia submitted that it has already been established that domestic and imported beef are like products (see paragraphs 168-170).

310. Australia claimed that the mark-up imposed on SBS imports constitutes an internal charge for the purposes of Article III:2. The question of the applicability of Article III to mark-ups was considered by the panel in *Canada - Marketing Agencies.* The panel was of the view that Article III:2 applied to mark-ups levied by Canadian Provincial Liquor Boards because they constituted internal governmental charges borne by products.[161] Australia observed that no mark-up or any equivalent charge is applied to domestic beef. This fact was confirmed by Korea in its consultations with Australia on 28 May 1999.

311. **Korea** reiterated that since in accordance with its Schedule of Concessions agreed to by the United States and Australia, Korea benefits from a transition phase until 1 January 2001 to eliminate or bring into conformity all remaining restrictions with regard to beef, which includes the mark-up, there can be no violation of Article III:2 as argued by Australia. If the DSB were to rule that the mark-up violates Article III:2 and it would need to be eliminated or brought into conformity with GATT provisions before 1 January 2001, the DSB would impose upon Korea an additional obligation beyond its obligations under Article II:1, reducing its rights to a transition phase as provided for in its Schedule of Concessions. Such a DSB ruling would violate Article 3.2 of the DSU which provides in relevant part that: "Recommendations and rulings of the DSB cannot add to or diminish the rights and obligations provided in the covered agreements" (see also paragraphs 299-302).

H. Claims under Article XVII of GATT

1. LPMO Tendering Opportunities

(For arguments under this section, see paragraphs122-125. (Cf. also 287-289.)

2. Measures with Respect to the Allocation of Imported Beef in the Wholesale Market

312. **Australia** submitted that the tender process operated by LPMO, as well as the discharge procedures operated by LPMO and NLCF, are contrary to Article

[160] Appellate Body Report, *Japan - Alcoholic Beverages, supra,* footnote 98, at 112.

[161] Para. 5.24.

XVII. A claim of infringement under Article XVII:1(a) and (b) requires proving two elements: (1) the body or organization falls within the definition of a state trading enterprise; (2) it acts in a manner inconsistent with the general principles of non-discriminatory treatment. Article XVII:1(c) requires evidence that an enterprise has been prevented from acting in accordance with the principles of non-discrimination, including behaving in accordance with commercial considerations.

313. Australia submitted further that manipulation of the kind described in paragraphs 205-206 above is also contrary to the obligation contained in Article XVII:1(a) which requires LPMO and NLCF to conduct their business in a non-discriminatory fashion, on the basis of normal commercial considerations. The fact that these measures are required by law to be carried out by LPMO and NLCF also results in a breach of Korea's obligations under Article XVII:1(c). Australia argued that LPMO has favoured some supplier countries over others, and domestic producers over producers of imported products on the basis of beef production methods and an arbitrary quality distinction between grain-fed and grass-fed beef. It has done so as part of its beef stabilization policies. Such policies are inconsistent with the application of commercial considerations required by Article XVII:1(a).

314. Article XVII:1(a) applies to a "State enterprise", or "any enterprise" that has been granted "formally or in effect, exclusive or special privileges". The Interpretative note to paragraph 1 extends this to "Marketing Boards" which are engaged in purchasing or selling. The 1960 final report of the panel on *Notification of State Trading Enterprises,* (paragraph 8 of L/1146, dated 24 May 1960) considered that Article XVII and the Interpretative Notes provided sufficient guidance on which enterprises were covered. Australia pointed out that both the LPMO and the NLCF are notified as state trading enterprises. The LPMO is notified as a state trading enterprise in relation to beef. Its purpose is stated as to stabilize domestic livestock markets. Its exclusive rights or privileges are stated to be: "authorization to purchase foreign beef used to stabilize domestic beef market, and conduct the tasks of approval and post-import management of the beef quota purchase allocated to private companies under the SBS system".[162] The NLCF has been granted exclusive or special privileges to control the discharge of beef on behalf of the LPMO, including establishment and implementation of regional and purchaser-based sales plans, discretion to decide daily discharging volumes, and to adjust auction volumes in consideration of price movements of domestic beef/cattle.[163]

315. Furthermore, Australia continued, Article XVII:1(a) requires a state trading enterprise to act in a manner consistent with the "general principles of non-discriminatory treatment". What constitutes "non-discriminatory treatment" is not

---

[162] G/STR/N/4/KOR, Working Party on State Enterprises, 10 December 1998, page 6.

[163] *Regulations Concerning Imported Beef,* Articles 4, 6(1), 6(2), 9(2).

defined. Article 3.2 of the DSU stipulates that provisions of the covered agreements be interpreted in accordance with the customary rules of interpretation of public international law. The Appellate Body in the *US – Gasoline (AB)* case took this to mean that the WTO Agreements, including Article XVII , are to be interpreted in accordance with Articles 31 and 32 of the Vienna Convention.[164]

316. Australia submitted that the purpose and object of the GATT is increasing freedom in trade through the removal of barriers to trade as expressed in the preamble. The "elimination of discriminatory treatment in international commerce" refers to the GATT's fundamental principle of non-discrimination.[165] Hence, Article XVII must be read according to this object and purpose. Under Article XVII, each Member undertakes that its state trading enterprises shall, with respect to its purchases or sales involving either imports or exports, act in a non-discriminatory manner and make such purchases or sales solely in accordance with commercial considerations. Article XVII recognises that state trading enterprises have the potential for distorting international trade through explicit or implicit subsidy policies or artificial pricing strategies. Australia referred to the panel in the *Japan - Film* case which acknowledged "a risk that WTO obligations could be evaded through a Member's delegation of quasi-governmental authority to private bodies."[166]

317. This also goes towards the security and predictability of concessions under the WTO system. In this context, Australia also referred to *EC - Computer Equipment (AB)* which agreed with the panel that the security and predictability of "the reciprocal and mutually advantageous arrangements directed to the substantial reduction of tariffs and other barriers to trade" is an object and purpose of the WTO Agreement, generally, as well as of the GATT 1994.[167] The value of concessions would be undermined if countries could avoid the national treatment requirement of Article III through the activities of state trading enterprises,.

318. Finally, the interpretative note provides: "Throughout Articles XI, XII, XIII, XIV and XVIII, the terms "import restrictions" or "export restrictions" include restrictions made effective through state-trading operations." This indicates, in the opinion of Australia, that the prescriptions applying to state trading enterprises are *not* limited to the MFN treatment in Article I. As concerns the "general principles of non-discriminatory treatment" in Article XVII:1(a), Australia submitted that the term must be read in the context of paragraph 1 of the Understanding on the Interpretation of Article XVII. This provides a working definition of state trading enterprises as:

---

[164] Page 17.

[165] In *The Regulation of International Trade*, Rutledge, 1995, page 26, Trebilcock and Howse states this principle as embracing both MFN and national treatment.

[166] Panel Report, *Japan – Film, supra*, footnote 99, para. 10.328.

[167] Appellate Body Report, *European Communities – Customs Classification of Certain Computer Equipment* ("*EC – Computer Equipment*"), WT/DS62/AB/R, WT/DS67/AB/R, WT/DS68/AB/R, adopted 22 June 1998, DSR 1998:V, 1851, para. 82.

"Governmental and non-governmental enterprises, including marketing boards, which have been granted exclusive or special rights or privileges, including statutory or constitutional powers, in the exercise of which *they influence through their purchases or sales the level or direction of imports or exports*."

319. This working definition captures the object and purpose of the provisions on state trading enterprises, i.e. regulate their activities where they influence the *level or direction of imports or exports*. Discriminating between different exporting countries is only one way in which the level or direction of imports is influenced. Composition and levels of imports can also be influenced by discrimination between imported and domestic goods. Excluding national treatment would void Article XVII of much of its scope as revealed in the working definition. The term must also be read in the context of Article XVII:1(b). This refers *inter alia* to affording the enterprises of other Members adequate opportunity, in accordance with customary business practice, to compete for participation in such purchases or sales. Such opportunity would be rendered illusory where state trading enterprises discriminate against imported goods in a way which restricts imports eg. by imposing restrictions on cuts and types of beef permitted to enter the market. Moreover, "having due regard to the other provisions of this Agreement" implies that Article III is relevant to an Article XVII:1(a) examination.

320. Paragraph (b), Australia continued, provides that the provisions of (a) "shall be understood to require" *inter alia* commercial considerations. Paragraph (b) therefore *defines* the application of (a). The wording "shall be understood to require" supports this. An entity infringes the general principles of non-discriminatory treatment where it fails to act on commercial considerations, or afford importers adequate opportunity to compete. Infringement of MFN occurs, in the opinion of Australia, when the LPMO favours the imports of one member over those of another on the basis of an arbitrary distinction applied between the types of beef produced by different members. The statement "having due regard to the other provisions of this Agreement" suggests that the requirements are not limited to those specified in paragraph (b). State trading enterprises must also comply with the other provisions of GATT, for example Article III. Likewise, infringement of non-discrimination can be implied when requirements are imposed on imported product that are not imposed on domestic product and are applied for reasons inconsistent with commercial considerations. Article XVII does not provide a definition of "commercial considerations but essentially, Australia contended, "commercial" connotes buying and selling for financial gain or profit.

321. Referring to Article XVII, Australia considered further that by creating a distinction between grass-fed and grain-fed beef and by excluding grass-fed beef from the three tenders in 1999, the LPMO has limited the supply of imported grass-fed beef at a time when sales of grass-fed beef were growing significantly. The basis of the distinction is the policy of using imported beef to assist in the stabilization of the prices of domestic cattle and beef. Both the LPMO and the NLCF have acted to withhold release of beef imported by the LPMO onto the

wholesale market, either by supplying under demand or by setting minimum prices for imports. This has the effect of artificially restricting the supply of imported beef. Article 1 of the *Regulations Concerning Sales of Imported Beef* refer to the stabilization of the prices of cattle and beef in Korea. By engaging in beef price stabilization, neither the NLCF nor the LPMO are operating on the basis of commercial considerations.

322. In conclusion and referring to Article XVII:1(c) , Australia submitted that the actions by the LPMO/NLCF are governed by laws imposed by the Government of Korea, as part of its polices to protect domestic beef. The discharge procedures adopted by LPMO and NLCF are in accordance with the requirements imposed by the *Regulation Concerning Sales of Imported Beef,* pursuant to the Minister of Agriculture and Forestry's powers under Article 25 of the *Livestock Act.* The regulations impose upon both the LPMO and the NLCF the obligation of acting to stabilize the prices of domestic beef. In doing so, both organizations are therefore required by the Government of Korea to take measures which are discriminatory towards imported beef and are inconsistent with commercial considerations.

323. Referring in particular to paragraph 321 above, **Korea** replied that the distinction between grass-fed and grain-fed beef does not by itself constitute discriminatory treatment or an infringement of MFN principles. Korea explained that all tenders are open to all supplying countries and perfectly origin neutral. Australian exporters are free to participate both in tenders for grass-fed and grain-fed beef and Australia has not adduced any evidence that Australian products have been discriminated against based on their origin. If Australia's producers are operating on a commercial basis, they can be expected to adjust to the customers' demand, rather than expecting the customer to change its demand based on their supply. Second, Korea continued, Australia's allegation that in excluding grass-fed beef from the three tenders in 1999, LPMO has constricted the supply of imported grass-fed beef at a time when sales of such beef were growing significantly, appears unfounded. Korea referred to the following purchase figures (customs cleared) by the LPMO

Year	Australia		Canada		New Zealand		United States		Total	
	MT	%	MT	%	MT	%	MT	%	MT	%
1997	50,567	33.3	5,097	3.3	13,093	8.6	83,232	54.8	151,989	100
1998	21,209	30	3,391	5	2,185	3	43,160	62	69,945	100
1999*	33,152	44	2,827	3,7	3,770	5	35,535	47,2	75,284	100

*first 6 months

324. Korea reiterated that it was clear from the above data that total purchases from Australia in the first 6 months of 1999 represented a 44 per cent share of all purchases which is much higher than their previous shares of 33.3 per cent in 1997 and of 30 per cent in 1998. Therefore, these data do not suggest any *de facto* discrimination of Australian products. (Cf paragraph 123.)

325. Furthermore, Korea considered that Australia's allegation that by engaging in beef price stabilization, LPMO is not operating on the basis of commercial considerations and that price stabilization and stability for consumers/producers is an extraneous consideration that goes beyond engaging in buying and selling for financial gain is not substantiated by any *prima facie* evidence demonstrating the alleged inherent conflict between price stabilization and commercial considerations in the LPMO operations. Korea is of the opinion that the two policies are not inherently contradictory. Indeed, it makes perfect commercial sense to sell more products when there is a shortage and market prices are high, while selling less products at a moment when there is oversupply and prices are low. This is obviously a marketing strategy to maximize profits which at the same time can have the effect of stabilizing prices (see also paragraph 207).

326. **Australia** submitted that Article XVII incorporates an obligation for state trading enterprises to abide by the national treatment principle. In creating a distinction between grass-fed and grain-fed beef for imported product, but not for domestic product, this principle has been breached by the LPMO in its tendering processes. The quality differential applied between the two for the purposes of stabilising domestic beef prices is also contrary to commercial principles.

327. Korea has not addressed the Article XVII claims made by Australia in respect of these measures (minimum prices, withholding beef from market by NLCF) except to claim that LPMO's policies of stabilising domestic beef prices is not inherently in conflict with commercial consideration. Australia rejected this argument. When imported beef is priced, not on the basis of profitability, but with the aim of protecting domestic beef prices, which may or may not be a profitable exercise, the requirements of Article XVII have been breached. Australia also rejected Korea's claim that the pricing of imported product in reference to the price of domestic product is evidence of normal commercial behaviour. It is not normal commercial behaviour to artificially raise the price of imported product to improve the sale potential of competing domestic product. The reverse is true. Australia referred the Panel to the findings of the panel on *Canada - Marketing Agencies.* (See also arguments in paragraph 292.)

I. Claims under the Agreement on Licensing Procedures

328. Korea's import licensing regime for imported beef is based on the issuance of import recommendations by the LPMO, and is, in the view of the **United States**, totally discretionary and, therefore, constitutes a non-automatic licensing procedure for purposes of the *Licensing Agreement.* Approval is not granted in all cases; no import recommendation is accorded by right. Indeed, Article 24 of the *Final Livestock Act* provides that the criteria for import recommendations, i.e. import licences, shall be established by the MAF. The Act specifies no criteria for issuing licences. Moreover, the licensing procedures are administered in such

a manner as to have restrictive effects on the imports in question. Only the LPMO and the super-groups are eligible to apply for import recommendations.[168] No actual user or reseller of imported beef, unless a super-group, is permitted to import beef directly or to obtain an import approval.

329. These restrictions are in addition to the resale and use limitations that apply to customers and end-users of the respective super-groups. The United States submitted further that the LPMO, as administrator of the licence approval and SBS system, has delayed quota allocations, postponed the invitation of tenders, and discouraged licence approval requests which have resulted in additional impediments to the entry and sale of imported beef. Each of these licensing procedures is inconsistent with the requirements contained in the *Licensing Agreement.*[169] Specifically, Article 3.2 provides that "Non-automatic licensing shall not have trade-restrictive or –distortive effects on imports additional to those caused by the imposition of the restrictions."

330. Article 3.1 defines non-automatic import licensing procedures as import licensing not falling within the definition contained in Article 2.1. Article 2.1 in turn defines "automatic import licensing" as "import licensing where approval of the application is granted in all cases, and which is in accordance with the requirements of paragraph 2(a)." In the case of Korea, no party can automatically import beef. Moreover, only the LPMO and the super-groups can import beef through discretionary licensing. From the foregoing, the United States argued, it follows that Korea's regime is a non-automatic licensing system and that, therefore, it is subject to the obligations contained in Article 3 of the *Licensing Agreement.* The obligation encompassed in Article 3.2 reflects the *Licensing Agreement's* objectives that the flow of international trade not be "impeded by the inappropriate use of import licensing procedures" and that "licensing procedures should be no more administratively burdensome than absolutely necessary to administer the relevant measure."[170]

331. The United States considered that Korea's discretionary licensing approval regime has trade restrictive effects additional to those created by the approval regime itself, by *inter alia* imposing severe limitations on the scope of importers' business activities, i.e. confining an individual super-groups' import authority to importation on behalf of a designated set of customers, as well as restrictions on the use and resale of imported beef by the importers' customers.[171] The effect of these restrictions can be seen in the substantial decline in the volume of beef imported during 1998. Korea's imports of beef fell from 166,092 to 92,026 metric

---

168 Guidelines for Handling Imported Beef, Articles 2.3, 11, 26 December 1999.

169 The Appellate Body found in *EC - Bananas III, supra*, footnote 97, paras.193-194 that import licensing procedures for the administration of tariff quotas are subject to the *Licensing Agreement* and to the obligations thereby established.

170 Preamble, *Licensing Agreement*, paras. 8 and 9.

171 Operational Guidelines for Imported Beef under the SBS System, Article 12; Guidelines for Handling Imported Beef, 1 October 1999, Article 27.

tonnes (product weight basis) between 1997 and 1998. Thus, just 49 per cent of the available quota was imported in 1998, whereas such imports had comprised fully 99 per cent in 1997. Imports of beef declined *vis-à-vis* Korean beef both in terms of relative quantities shipped and market share as a result of the LPMO's administrative procedures. Thus, whereas production of Korean beef increased by 12 per cent from 236,527 to 264,074 metric tonnes (boneless weight basis) between 1997 and 1998, imports of beef declined by 45 per cent from 166,092 to 92,026 metric tonnes (product weight basis). As a percentage of Korean consumption, imported beef also decreased from 46 to 27 per cent over the same period, while Korean producers increased their market share from 54 to 73 per cent of domestic consumption.

332. The United States submitted that the low volume of beef imported by the LPMO during the first five months of 1999, less than 10 per cent of its quota,[172] suggests that the LPMO was again refraining from inviting tenders for beef. In addition, the LPMO withheld over 32,000 metric tonnes, or approximately 22 per cent, of the SBS quota, refusing to allocate it until well into the second calendar quarter of 1999. This action meant that no import licences could be sought for that quota amount, a situation compounded by what the United States understood was active interference in the import approval process. Trade sources reported that the LPMO requested and obtained a reduction of 30 per cent in the import recommendation requests that were made by the super-groups in January 1999. These trade disruptive licensing procedures, viewed cumulatively, had precisely the trade restrictive effect that Article 3.2 of the *Licensing Agreement* is intended to forestall. The LPMO's licensing procedures during 1998 and 1999, thus, constitute a violation of Article 3.2 of the *Agreement.*

333. While the financial crisis that affected much of Asia, including Korea, during 1998 contributed to this decline, the United States was of the view that a substantial portion of this decrease can be attributed to the LPMO operating procedures during 1998 and the first half of 1999, and the restrictions on access to import licences under Korea's regime for importation of beef. Because the LPMO in 1998 still directly controlled 40 per cent of the import quota for beef, its failure to initiate tenders for imported beef until approximately mid-year altogether precluded any possibility that its portion of the quota would be filled that year. Because of the LPMO's role as both importer and administrator of Korea's licensing system, its failure to initiate tenders for imports of beef is, in the opinion of the United States, the equivalent of a refusal to issue import licences, as no import approval for beef within the LPMO's quota share can occur without an invitation for tenders for beef imports. .In addition, by refusing to reallocate quota share among the super-groups, or to qualify any other entities as super-groups

[172] No other qualified importer, other than the producer-dominated NLCF, entered a comparatively small percentage of its quota share. Many of the super-groups had entered a third or more of their allocation by May 1999.

eligible to import beef, the LPMO also reduced the ability of the private sector to utilize its quota share.

334. Replying to the United States arguments in paragraphs 328-333 above, **Korea** submitted that it does not operate a 'discretionary licensing system' contrary to the *Licensing Agreement*. The cases cited by the United States in support of its allegations are, according to Korea, not relevant in the present situation since in all of the cases cited, without exception, there was no legally valid quota or quantitative restriction in place in the importing Member country. The Korean licensing procedures have not had "trade-distortive effects on imports additional to those caused by the imposition of the restriction." Korea reiterated that it applies and administers a quota on beef products, the legality of which is not in dispute. To this end, Korea maintains an import licensing regime which is designed to enable full allocation of the quota and which is in full compliance with Article 3, including Article 3.2. Article 3 recognizes the necessity of non-automatic import licensing procedures as a means of administering restrictions such as quotas and, subject to compliance with the provisions of Article 3 (as well as those of Article 1), recognizes the legality of such procedures. Korea submitted that both the legal and factual arguments advanced by the United States are fundamentally flawed and seriously mischaracterize the import system maintained by Korea. The first mistake in the United States' reasoning is that it appears to equate the mere existence of a non-automatic licensing regime with a violation of Article XI:1. This implication is erroneous. Article 3 expressly recognizes the legality of discretionary licensing systems, subject to compliance with the applicable provisions of that Agreement.

335. Article 3.2, Korea continued, foresees and sanctions the use of non-automatic licensing procedures in the context of administering an otherwise WTO-consistent restriction. As regards Article XI:1 of GATT, the question of whether Korea's licensing system with respect to enforcing the beef quota may be termed discretionary is entirely irrelevant, to the extent that the Complainants cannot establish that the licensing system operates as a separate restriction on the importation of beef products additional to the legal quota, and acts to intensify the quota effect. In the opinion of Korea, neither of the Complainants has furnished any evidence that this is the case. In particular, contrary to the assertion by the United States that import approval by the LPMO is *"not granted in all cases,"*(see paragraph 328) the LPMO has never refused to issue an import recommendation.

336. Moreover, the assertion by the United States that "[t]he licensing procedures are indeed administered in such a manner as to have restrictive effects on the imports in question" (see paragraph 328) is inaccurate. The so-called restriction of eligibility to apply for import recommendations to the LPMO and supergroups is designed to ensure an efficient and transparent allocation of the available quota and in no way constitutes a restriction within the meaning of Article XI:1 of GATT additional to the restriction imposed in the form of the legal quantitative restriction. The LPMO has consistently purchased its entire allocated quota amount, including during the height of the financial crisis in 1998. With

respect to imports of allocated quota share through the SBS system, these imports are effected on the basis of market factors and the import demands of the members of the various super-groups. The import licensing system applied by Korea does not, therefore, in any way constitute a restriction on importation in addition to the legal quantitative restriction applied by Korea.

337. Furthermore, Korea considered that the United States has not established any causal link between Korean licensing procedures and US loss of market share. The restrictions cited by the United States relate to measures which implement the quota. However, the alleged restrictions do not fall within the scope of the *Licensing Agreement*. Korea referred to the *EC - Poultry* case, in which it was clearly established that the complaining party must demonstrate not only trade distortive effects beyond those caused by the imposition of the restriction within the meaning of Article 3.2, but also a clear causal relationship between import licensing procedures maintained by a Member and any injury suffered by the complaining Member. The panel in the *EC - Poultry* case held that the complaining party had failed to establish that its fall in market share could be attributed to trade-distortive import licensing procedures maintained by the respondent.[173]

338. Similarly, the United States seeks to demonstrate the alleged trade distortive effects by reference to the fall in overall import share during 1998 (see paragraph 331). Korea reiterated that this argument substantially underplays the crucial significance of the market conditions prevailing at that time in the context of the Asian crisis. Indeed, the decisive nature of this factor in leading to an overall decreased import share can conclusively be demonstrated by the fact that, while Korea has operated the same or similar licensing procedures for several years, a system which is recognized in the US/Korea Record of Understanding, the quota has, with few exceptions, been fully utilized. In the view of Korea, and referring to the *EC - Poultry* case, the United States has not established a causal link between import licensing procedures maintained by Korea and a fall in beef imports in 1998.

339. Furthermore, Korea submitted, the US allegations does not establish that the Korean licensing regime has had "trade-restrictive or distortive effects on imports additional to those caused by the imposition of the restriction" within the meaning of Article 3.2 of the Agreement. In the view of Korea, the United States fails to recognize the distinction between import licensing *rules* on the one hand, and import licensing *procedures* on the other hand. While the latter is subject to the disciplines of the *Licensing Agreement*, the former has consistently been held not to fall within the scope of the *Licensing Agreement*. Korea referred to *EC - Bananas III(AB)*, in which case the Appellate Body stated that the *Licensing Agreement* was concerned with the application and administration of import li-

173 Panel Report, *European Communities – Measures Affecting the Importation of Certain Poultry Products* ("*EC – Poultry*"), WT/DS69/R, adopted 23 July 1998, DSR 1998:V, 2089, para. 249.

censing procedures, and required that this application and administration be "neutral [...] fair and equitable."[174] The Appellate Body went on to state that:

> "As a matter of fact, none of the provisions of the Licensing Agreement concerns import licensing rules, per se. As is made clear by the title of the Licensing Agreement, it concerns import licensing procedures. The preamble of the Licensing Agreement indicates clearly that this agreement relates to import licensing procedures and their administration, not to import licensing rules. Article 1.1 of the Licensing Agreement defines its scope as the administrative procedures used for the operation of import licensing regimes".[175]

340. Applying this principle to Article 1.3, the Appellate Body considered the question of whether the imposition of different licensing systems on like products when imported from different Members was prohibited under the Agreement. The Appellate Body (overruling the panel) determined that such a system was related to import licensing rules and not to procedures. It was, therefore, concluded that such a system was not precluded by the *Licensing Agreement*. This principle was also applied in the *EC - Poultry* case where, the panel examined claims by Brazil that the EC allocated import licences on the basis of, among others, export performance. The panel, quoting from the *EC - Bananas III (AB)* Appellate Body report and applying the distinction between import rules and import procedures in the context of Article 1.3, stated that:

> "By its very terms, Article 1.3 of the Licensing Agreement clearly applies to the application and administration of import licensing procedures, and requires that this application and administration be 'neutral ... fair and equitable'. Article 1.3 of the Licensing Agreement does not require the import licensing rules, as such, to be neutral, fair and equitable. Furthermore, the context of Article 1.3 – including the preamble, Article 1.1 and, in particular, Article 1.2 of the Licensing Agreement – supports the conclusion that Article 1.3 does not apply to import licensing rules."[176]

With respect to the requirement under consideration in that case, the panel concluded that:

> In our view, the issue of licence entitlement based on export performance is clearly that of rules, not that of application or administration of import licensing procedures. Thus, Article 1.3 is not applicable to this specific issue."[177]

341. The general provisions of Article 1 of the *Licensing Agreement*, Korea continued, shed light on the type of procedures and administrative issues with which the Agreement is concerned. These include the requirement to notify in-

---

174 Appellate Body Report, *EC – Bananas III, supra*, footnote 97, para.197.

175 *Ibid.*

176 Op.cit. para. 197.

177 Appellate Body Report, *EC – Bananas III, supra*, footnote 97, para. 254.

formation concerning procedures for the submission of applications, eligibility, the administrative bodies to be approached and the list of products subject to the licensing requirement in order that traders and governments can become familiar with them (Article 1.4(a)); the requirement that application forms or renewal forms should be as simple as possible (Article 1.5); requirements on the minimum time for submitting applications (Article 1.6); the requirement that applications shall not be refused in cases where minor documentation errors have occurred (Article 1.7), etc.

342. In light of the cases cited above (paragraphs 339-340), Korea submitted that the only issue before the Panel in this case is whether Korea's licensing regime for the quota complied with the administrative procedures set out in the *Licensing Agreement*. In this regard, the United States has not identified any procedures or administrative elements of Korea's licensing regime that are in any way contrary to Article 3.2. Moreover, the United States has not established that any of the alleged measures or practices complained of constitute import licensing procedures within the meaning of the Agreement, as opposed to, at most, import licensing rules. Specifically, the system under which licence entitlement occurs in the context of SBS super-groups and the LPMO clearly relates to import licensing rules and not procedures. This element is, therefore, not subject to challenge under the *Licensing Agreement*. Similarly, the United States has not established how its allegations that constraints are placed on the class of entities which can conduct business with each super-group relate to import licensing procedures covered under the Agreement, or how such alleged procedures are inconsistent with Article 3.2.

343. In addition, the United States provides an inaccurate characterization of the conduct and role of the LPMO. With regard to the allegation that the LPMO has delayed quota allocations and postponed invitations of tenders (paragraph 333 above), Korea noted that the LPMO has consistently procured the share of the quota attributable to the LPMO, even in the difficult circumstances surrounding the Asian crisis and despite the very considerable foreign exchange losses incurred by the LPMO. While, at the height of this crisis, some unavoidable delays occurred due to collapsing demand and the inability to contain the build-up of beef stocks, this cannot be attributed to import licensing procedures maintained by Korea.

344. The allegation by the United States that the LPMO discouraged licence approval requests (paragraph 331 above), Korea continued, misrepresents the actual facts. In the Records of-Understanding concluded with the United States, Korea has undertaken to progressively expand the role of the SBS system by further increasing the number of super-groups under the system. This was done at the specific request of the United States. It was in furtherance of this objective that the LPMO requested that the super-groups make appropriate adjustments to their import demands, so as to be able to expand the number of participating super-groups. Far from constituting an import licensing procedure having additional trade-restrictive or distortive effects on imports, these actions were undertaken with the specific objective of further liberalizing trade with respect to im-

ported beef. For these reasons, the arguments that Korea violated the *Licensing Agreement* must be rejected.

345. The **United States** retorted that Korea has not substantiated its contention that Korea's licensing authority's delays in tendering for imports and allocation of quota share do not constitute procedures under the *Licensing Agreement*. The LPMO's decision not to tender for imported beef for the six month period from November 1997 through April 1998 constitutes, in the opinion of the United States, a procedure as that term is commonly construed.[178] On the same basis, the withholding of quota allocation for four months at the beginning of 1999 is also a licensing procedure for purposes of the *Licensing Agreement*. Korea's assertion that there is no causal link between these LPMO procedures and the resulting distortion to trade (see paragraph 337 above) is likewise erroneous. The withholding of quota allocations for new super-groups when several of the super-groups already possessing quota share were on track to fully utilize their distributed shares meant that the new super-groups were denied an opportunity to participate in the market during a period when commercial activity was recovering. The delay in allocation meant that for the period of the delay Korea, in essence, was maintaining the quota at the level set for earlier years despite its Schedule commitment to enlarge the quota on an annual basis. This, according to the United States, resulted in trade restrictions beyond those associated with the quota.

346. The delay in tendering, the United States continued, kept imports of beef out of the Korean market until tenders resumed in May 1998. It explains in part why the LPMO filled a far smaller percentage of its quota share than some of the super-groups operating under the SBS system. Three of the super-groups, KMIA, LCTM, and KMPA, filled virtually 100 per cent of their quota in 1998. In comparison, the LPMO's late tenders meant that, while the LPMO ultimately tendered for 100 per cent of its allotted quota during 1998, over 30 per cent of the beef for which tenders were invited did not enter Korea until sometime in 1999. The United States submitted that the LPMO's tendering procedures deteriorated further in 1999. Thus, while it's quota share in 1999 is 61,800 MT, LPMO did not tender for 30,000 MT of that total until late in November 1999, ensuring that most of those imports would not enter Korea until sometime in 2000. The LPMO's delayed tendering cannot be attributed to lack of market demand for beef imports since several of the super-groups will fill their 1999 quotas.

347. Korea's suggestion that the situation of beef imports in the Korean market is similar to the circumstances prevailing in the *EC - Poultry* case (see paragraph 340), is also unfounded in the opinion of the United States. Whereas imported beef entering Korea declined both in absolute terms and as a percentage of total Korean beef consumption between 1997 and 1998, in the *EC - Poultry* case Brazil's exports to the EC had remained stable as a percentage of the TRQ and had

178 Cf. The New Shorter Oxford English Dictionary (1993 ed.).

increased overall. Perhaps more importantly, the EC poultry TRQ was being fully filled. In contrast, imports of beef were held to just 45 per cent of the Korean quota in 1998. Thus, there is no basis for a determination here that trade in imported beef is not distorted within the meaning of Article 3.2 by Korea's procedures in administering its beef quota.

348. **Korea** responded that in the *EC - Poultry* case, Brazil made several claims with regard to import licensing procedures maintained by the EC, including the failure to notify relevant procedures to the Licensing Committee, frequent changes in licensing rules which allegedly made it difficult for traders and governments to become familiar with such procedures, overall lack of transparency and the issuance of licences in economic quantities. Brazil argued that its market share had dropped in recent years and alleged that this was due to the trade-distortive effects of the EC's import licensing procedures, including those mentioned above.

349. The panel concluded that Brazil had failed to establish that its fall in market share could be attributed to any trade-distortive import licensing procedures maintained by the EC. The Panel noted that:

> "*[T]he licenses issued to imports from Brazil are fully utilized, which strongly suggests that any trade-distortive effects of the operation of the licensing rules have been overcome by exporters. [...] Therefore, we fail to understand the relevance of the decline in the percentage share in total trade to a violation of the Licensing Agreement.*"[179]

The panel's findings in the *EC - Poultry* case on this point were upheld by the Appellate Body.

350. With reference to the United States arguments in paragraph 346, Korea submitted that these substantially downplay the crucial significance of the market conditions prevailing at that time. Korea stressed again that, while it has operated the same or similar licensing procedures for several years, the quota has, with few exceptions, been fully utilized. The fall in the import share in 1998 is clearly attributable to the severe economic crisis affecting Korea during this period. In the opinion of Korea, the United States has not established that any of the alleged measures or practices complained of constitute import licensing procedures within the meaning of the Agreement, as opposed to import licensing rules. Korea reiterated that the system governing licence eligibility in the context of SBS super-groups and the LPMO clearly relates to import licensing rules and not procedures. As such, they are not subject to challenge under the *Licensing Agreement*. For these reasons, the arguments that Korea violated the *Licensing Agreement* must be rejected.

[179] Panel Report, *EC - Poultry*, *supra*, 173, para. 249.

J. Claims under the Agreement on Agriculture[180]

1. Article 4.2 of the Agreement on Agriculture

351. **Australia** noted that Article 4.2 of the *Agreement on Agriculture*[181] has not been the subject of a detailed examination by a WTO panel or the Appellate Body. However, in *India - Quantitative Restrictions*, the panel found that a range of Indian measures were quantitative restrictions which violated Article XI:1 and Article 4.2 of the *Agreement on Agriculture.*[182] The Appellate Body in *EC - Bananas III(AB)* also made some comments on the relationship between Article 4.2 and the provisions of other multilateral trade agreements in Annex 1A to the WTO Agreement.[183] The panel found that the *Agreement on Agriculture* does not permit measures which are contrary to the obligations imposed by GATT 1994, except where specifically provided. The relationship between the provisions of the GATT 1994 and of the *Agreement on Agriculture* is set out in Article 21.1 of the *Agreement on Agriculture.*[184]

352. Article 4.2 expressly prohibits the maintenance, reversion or resort to measures of the kind required to be converted to ordinary customs duties. Footnote 1 of Article 4.2 provides an indicative list of the kinds of measures required to be converted into ordinary customs duties. These include quantitative import restrictions, variable import levies, minimum import prices, discretionary import licensing, non-tariff measures maintained through state-trading enterprises, voluntary export restraints, and similar border measures other than ordinary customs duties.

353. The provisions of the GATT 1994 apply to market access commitments concerning agricultural products, except to the extent that the *Agreement on Agriculture* contains specific provisions dealing with the same matter. Therefore, Australia argued, if a measure is a quantitative restriction for the purposes of Article XI:1, then it is also a quantitative restriction in violation of Article 4.2. The approach of the panel in *India - Quantitative Restrictions* reflects this view. As argued below (paragraph 354), the discharge system for beef imported by the LPMO is a quantitative import restriction and is therefore in violation of Article 4.2 of the *Agreement on Agriculture.*

---

180 Note: when not otherwise stated, article numbers in this section refer to those of the Agreement on Agriculture.

181 "Members shall not maintain, resort to, or revert to any measures of the kind which have been required to be converted into ordinary customs duties, except as otherwise provided for in Article 5 and Annex 4".

182 Panel Report, *India – Quantitative Restrictionson Imports of Agricultural, Textile and Industrial Products* ("*India – Quantitative Restrictions*"), WT/DS90/R, adopted 22 September 1999, as upheld by the Appellate Body Report, DSR 1999:V, 1799, para. 5.241.

183 Appellate Body Report, *EC – Bananas III, supra*, footnote 97, paras. 154-157.

184 "The provisions of GATT 1994 and of other Multilateral Trade Agreements in Annex 1A to the WTO Agreement shall apply subject to the provisions of this Agreement".

354. Footnote 1 of Article 4.2 also lists non-tariff measures maintained through state trading enterprises as measures of the kind prohibited under Article 4.2. In the view of Australia, the discharge system for beef imported by the LPMO is also a non-tariff measure maintained through state trading enterprises. Furthermore, the maintenance of minimum wholesale prices for LPMO imports and withholding of stocks from sale are non-tariff measures maintained by the LPMO and the NLCF which artificially constrict the supply of imported beef into the market and, as a consequence, restricts imports through delays in holding tenders and deferred shipping dates. Australia added that the measures referred to in paragraph 128 above are also contrary to Article 4.2 of the *Agreement on Agriculture* since they constitute both quantitative restrictions and non-tariff measures maintained by state trading enterprises and are, therefore, measures of the kind expressly prohibited by Footnote 1 of Article 4.2.

355. The **Complainants** noted that during the negotiation of the WTO *Agreement on Agriculture*, the participants in the Uruguay Round agreed to eliminate their non-tariff barriers to trade in agricultural products and to replace them with tariffs, which would be subject to reduction over time. The Complainants submitted further that Korea has kept in place a number of non-tariff measures that by virtue of the footnote to Article 4.2 should have been eliminated. These measures include Korea's discretionary import approval system, its maintenance of other import restrictions including, but not limited to, the LPMO's establishment of minimum bid prices for imported beef and MAF's prohibitions on the sale and distribution of imported beef outside of the rigid channels of the SBS system. The **United States** was of the view that Korea's continued maintenance of such measures is inconsistent with Korea's obligations under Article 4.2 of the *Agreement on Agriculture.*

356. **Korea** replied that the Complainants' arguments with respect to Article 4.2 of the *Agreement on Agriculture* contain the same mistakes presented in their arguments under Article XI:1 of GATT 1994. For the reasons outlined above (see paragraphs 146-156 and 150-153) no *prima facie* case of violation has been established since no causality was demonstrated between the alleged additional restrictions and the restrictions ensuing from the legal quota itself. Korea submitted that Article 4.2 should be read in conjunction with Article 4.1 which recognizes explicitly that in the Schedules there may be "other market access commitments as specified therein". Korea reiterated that its Schedule LX contains a note 6(e) for beef which provides that Korea benefits from a transition period and is required to eliminate or bring into conformity all remaining restrictions on beef only by 1 January, 2001.

2. *Article 6 of the Agreement on Agriculture*

(i) De minimis

357. **Australia** submitted that in 1997, Korea provided domestic support to its beef industry which exceeded the *de minimis* levels and which therefore were

required to be included in its calculations of its Current Total Aggregate Measure of Support (AMS). This resulted in Korea's Current Total AMS for 1997 being in excess of its reduction commitments for that year, contrary to Articles 3, 6 and 7 of the *Agreement on Agriculture*.

358. The **United States** argued that Korea's determination that the support it provided to its domestic cattle industry in 1997 and 1998 was *de minimis* is not consistent with the provisions of Article 6.4.(a)(i) of the *Agreement on Agriculture*. Korea's failure to include that support in its Current Total AMS for 1997 and 1998 violated the requirements of Article 7.2.(a) of the *Agreement on Agriculture*. Finally, adding the amount of support Korea provided to the cattle industry into its Current Total AMS for 1997 and 1998, Korea has exceeded its domestic support commitments under the *Agreement on Agriculture*.

(ii) 1997

359. Australia noted that Article 6.4 of the Agreement of Agriculture provides that "A member shall not be required to include in the calculation of its Current Total AMS ... product specific domestic support which would otherwise be required to be included in a Member's calculation of its Current AMS where such support does not exceed 5 per cent of that Member's total value of production of a basic agricultural product during the relevant year" and that for developing country members the *de minimis* percentage under this paragraph shall be 10 per cent.

360. **Australia** submitted that in each year that Korea has made domestic support notifications to the WTO, it has claimed that product-specific support for beef was *de minimis,*[185] i.e. not exceeding 10 per cent of the total value of beef production for that year, even though the notified level of support for beef has increased substantially from 1.12 billion won in 1995 to 195.27 billion won in 1997 and 183.06 billion won in 1998. For this reason, domestic support for beef

---

185 Article 6.3 provides: "A Member shall be in compliance with its domestic support reduction commitments in any year in which its domestic support in favour of agricultural producers expressed in terms of Current Total AMS does not exceed the corresponding annual or final bound commitment level specified in Part IV of the Member's Schedule."
Article 6.4 provides:

(a) "A Member shall not be required to include in the calculation of its Current total AMS and shall not be required to reduce:

(i) product-specific domestic support which would otherwise be required to be included in a Member's calculations of its current AMS where such support does not exceed 5 per cent of that Member's total value of production of a basic agricultural product during the relevant year; and

(ii) non-product specific domestic support which would otherwise be required to be included in a Member's calculation of its current AMS where such support does not exceed 5 per cent of the value of that Member's total agricultural production.

(b) For developing country Members, the *de minimis* percentage under this para. shall be 10 per cent."

has not been included in calculations of the Current Total AMS. However, calculations based on figures published by the OECD and the MAF show that for 1997, Korea's domestic support for beef was above the *de minimis* level and should have been calculated as part of Korea's Total AMS.

361. Australia noted that Article 1 of the *Agreement on Agriculture* defines "Aggregate Measurement of Support" and " AMS" as the annual level of support, expressed in monetary terms, provided for an agricultural product in favour of producers of the basic agricultural product or non-product-specific support provided in favour of agricultural producers in general, other than support provided under programmes that qualify as exempt from reduction under Annex 2 to this Agreement, which is:

(i) "with respect to support provided during the base period, specified in the relevant tables of supporting material incorporated by reference in Part IV of a Member's Schedule, and

(ii) with respect to support provided during any year of the implementation period and thereafter, calculated in accordance with the provisions of Annex 3 of this Agreement and taking into account the constituent data and methodology used in the tables of supporting material incorporated by reference in Part IV of the Member's Schedule".

362. With respect to (i) above, Korea has specified no product-specific support for beef in its tables of supporting materials contained in G/AG/AGST/KOR. In relation to (ii) above, product specific support in favour of producers of beef provided in 1997 must be calculated in accordance with the provisions of Annex 3 which presents the methodology for calculating the AMS. The AMS is required to be calculated on a product-specific basis for each basic agricultural product receiving market price support, non-exempt direct payments or any other subsidy not exempted from the reduction commitment. Market price support, such as that provided by Korea to its domestic beef industry, Australia submitted, is to be calculated using the gap between a fixed external reference price and the applied administered price multiplied by the quantity of production eligible to receive the applied administrative price.[186] (Cf. paragraph. 420.)

(iii) Eligible Production

363. **Australia** submitted that in its Notification to the Committee on Agriculture for 1997, Korea indicates that eligible production for price support measures for beef was 35,127 tonnes. However, on the basis of Korea's own conversion rates, Australia submitted that eligible production was in fact 56,615 tonnes of beef based on the eligibility for support of 170,000 cattle in 1997.

---

[186] Annex 3.8, *Agreement on Agriculture*.

364. Australia considered that Annex 3.8 of the *Agreement on Agriculture* is unambiguous in its reference to "eligible production" being the basis upon which to calculate levels of domestic support. The definition of "eligible" is "fit, suitable or qualified".[187] The calculation of the level of market price support on actual purchases is clearly inconsistent with this requirement and results in a lower level of support for beef than if all production "eligible" for the payment were included. Thus, the eligible production figure used by Korea in its notification should show the number of cattle (or tonnage of beef) that was qualified and could possibly have been purchased under its support programme for 1997. It is not sufficient to show only what was *actually* purchased in that period. On this basis Australia continued, market price support for beef in 1997 was 281.9 billion won, rather than the 194.2 billion won notified by Korea. Adding the 1.09 billion won in other budgetary outlays for beef notified by Korea in G/AG/N/KOR/18, this pushes Korea's total AMS for beef in 1997 to 282.9 billion won rather than the 195.27 billion won notified.

365. **Australia** and the **United States** noted that in 1997, the domestic support programme for beef began on 26 January when the Korean government started to purchase cattle to prevent the falling of cattle prices. The programme continued throughout 1997 (340 days) with 500 head of 500 kg. Hanwoo steers (cattle) at 2,400 thousand won per head, per day, eligible to be purchased by NLCF and KCSC. Under the most conservative approach, therefore, eligible production should be no less than the quantities announced by MAF as eligible for daily procurement, which in this case would be 170,000 head of Hanwoo steers (500 head per day x 340 days). This quantity, [170,000 head of 500 kg. steers,] would yield 52.615 thousand tonnes of beef, carcass basis, and not the 35,127 tonnes announced by Korea in its notification to the Committee on Agriculture for 1997.[188] Therefore, Korea's 1997 market price support should have been calculated as follows:

AAP (1,000 *won*/tonnne)	FERP (1,000 *won*/tonnne)	EP (1,000 tonnes)	Market Price Support (billion *won*)	Quality Incentive Programme (billion *won*)	TOTAL Support for Beef (billion *won*)
7,754	1,823	52.615	312.082	1.09	313.173

366. **Australia** submitted that it cannot agree with Korea's claim that the words "quantity of production eligible to receive the applied administered price" in Annex 3:8 can be interpreted to mean actual procurement. Presumably, if the drafters of the Agreement had intended actual procurement rather than eligible production, they would have chosen those words instead, since the words eligible

187 *Collins Concise Dictionary*, William Collins and Son, page 403.

188 (170,000 x 500 kg. = 85 million kg. beef live basis, multiplied by 61.9 per cent = 52,615,000 kg. or 52.615 thousand tonnes beef.)

and actual have clearly different meanings. Australia noted Korea's statement in paragraph 384 that its market price support also extended to dairy and hybrid cattle. Australia, therefore, assumed that production eligible for support is even higher than that shown by Australia. Nor does Australia accept Korea's claim that its determination of eligible production is consistent with the methodology applied in its tables of supporting materials incorporated by reference in Part IV of its Schedule. The fact remains, that domestic support programmes for beef do not appear in Korea 's supporting materials. This being the case, the methodology provided in Annex 3 of the *Agreement on Agriculture* must apply.

367. Furthermore, the **Complainants** concurred with the analysis provided by New Zealand on the concept of eligible production in paragraph 479.

368. In the opinion of Australia, Korea has not substantively rebutted the definition of "eligible production" claimed by Australia. Eligible production is not actual production as claimed by Korea. Korea has failed to provide any alternative definition of the term "eligible production". The fact that Korea has always used actual production figures to calculating the base AMS is irrelevant given the specific requirements of the *Agreement on Agriculture*. Australia noted that Korea did not provide product specific support for beef in the base period and consequently it can not be claimed that the way that beef is calculated is consistent with the approach to base period calculations. Australia supported the views expressed by New Zealand that, in the absence of a calculation for product specific support for beef in the base period, there is no "constituent data and methodology" for beef contained in Korea's Schedule. Hence, Annex 3 of the *Agreement on Agriculture* needs to be the starting point for determining the appropriate calculation method of the support level for beef.

369. The **United States** submitted that Korea also has disregarded the prescriptions contained in Annex 3 of the Agreement regarding the manner of calculation of current total AMS for beef. Despite the mandatory direction in paragraph 8 of Annex 3 that the calculation of domestic support be based on total eligible production, Korea instead computed domestic support for beef based on actual procurement. Korea's approach, thus, also contravenes Annex 3. Korea offers no reasons to justify its substantial departure from the methodology set forth in Annex 3 of the Agreement.

370. Eligible production means, the United States continued, either total production or, in those situations where a specific quantity is identified as subject to support, the entire amount so designated, regardless of the quantity actually purchased. This computational method is necessary because market price support is meant to measure the effect of government policy on agricultural producers, rather than the cost of the measure to government. This method of calculating a subsidy's effect, moreover, is consistent with the Appellate Body's finding under the Subsidies Agreement in the *Aircraft* dispute where the Appellate Body concluded that the existence of a subsidy benefit is determined based on the benefit to the recipient, not the cost to the government.

371. Referring to the arguments in paragraph 363, 368 and 369, **Korea** noted that the distinction between *"eligible"* and *"actual"* production is somewhat imaginary in the case of Korea's measures. The production which is *"eligible"* is the production for which there is *"actually"* money available to receive the applied administered price. Production which cannot *"actually"* receive the administered price is, in Korea's view, also not *"eligible"* to receive the administered price. In simple terms, [for example,] if Korea has a budgetary outlay which allows it to actually purchase 1,000 heads of live cattle, it seems logical to conclude that 1,000 heads of live cattle were actually eligible. It would be absurd to hold that Korea should have reported all heads of live cattle in Korea in this calculation as the eligible production on the basis of the fact that any cow in Korea could have been among those 1,000 heads of live cattle which could be actually purchased and, therefore, was theoretically *"eligible"*. This would contravene the language in paragraph 8 of Annex 3 that it should be the *"quantity of production eligible to receive the applied administered price"*, because not all live cattle in Korea could actually receive the administered price. The quantity of production which actually received the applied administered price was obviously also the quantity of production which was actually *"eligible"*. The term *"applied administered price"* also indicates that it refers to money actually spent and prices actually applied. This is further confirmed by the material produced by the GATT Secretariat during the Uruguay Round, quoted in the submission by New Zealand as: "For an open-ended intervention or buy-in scheme, this [eligible production] may be total production. If the scope of the measure is limited to a particular quantity, it is this limited quantity that should be used."[189] Due to its limited budget, Korea continued, Korea does not apply an open-ended intervention or buy-in scheme, but the scope of the measure is limited to particular quantities in accordance with the limited budget available. Accordingly, it is appropriate to refer to the limited quantity which is actually eligible to receive the applied administered price.

372. **Australia** submitted that the calculation of whether an amount of product specific domestic support is *de minimis* is done by calculating the ratio of support to the total value of production of that commodity. While the total value of production for beef in 1997 is not shown by Korea in its notifications, a 1997 figure is available from the OECD, which calculates the total value of domestic beef production for that year at 1,886 billion won.[190] The OECD calculation is based on the carcass weight equivalents for domestic beef production and farm gate prices, using MAF and NLCF information.

373. Australia further submitted that the data used by Australia was sourced from the OECD. The OECD data is publicly available and is a transparent calculation of the value of production. It should also be noted that the OECD calcula-

---

189 See para. 479.

190 OECD *Review of Agricultural Policies in Korea*, 1999, pages 146, 148.

tion is based on data provided by Korea to the OECD. Korea indicates that the total value of production is "calculated based on actual sales prices of the live cattle sold by the producers at 80 livestock markets in producing areas" (see paragraph 387). However, Korea has not provided either the methodology or any raw data to show how it reached this alternative figure. Korea further indicates that the "government official statistical data is calculated through a precise statistical technique" (see paragraph 388). Australia believes there is a clear burden of proof on Korea to demonstrate why the data used by Australia and the United States is not the appropriate method to calculate the total value of production.

374. Referring to Korea's claims that there is no requirement to include the total value of production in the Committee on Agriculture notifications (G/AG/2)(see paragraph 387), Australia contended that the notification requirements under the Committee on Agriculture do not stem from the binding obligations under the *Agreement on Agriculture*. Rather, these notification requirements were agreed to assist the Committee to undertake the review of implementation of commitments set out in Article 18 of the *Agreement on Agriculture*. Whether the notification requirements require total value of production data to be included is not relevant. Article 6.4 of the *Agreement on Agriculture* provides for Members to be able to exclude from the AMS calculation support which is below *de minimis* levels. In the case of Korea, a developing country, the *de minimis* level is set at ten per cent of the total value of production of a basic agricultural product for product specific support. The right of Members to claim that support is *de minimis* is not disputed, this is clearly the intention of Article 6.4. If, however, a Member claims that the support level is *de minimis*, there is a clear obligation that the Member is required to provide the necessary data to substantiate the claim. Without this information other Members have no way of assessing the validity of claim.

375. The total value of beef production used in Korea's notification to the OECD for the calculation of the producer subsidy equivalent (PSE) for beef is, in the opinion of the **United States**, a more accurate measure for determining *de minimis* status. The value of production used by the OECD is carcass weight equivalent at the farm gate level. The OECD method is a well-established and universally accepted method for calculation of total production value. According to the OECD data, Korea's 1997 value of beef and veal production was 1.886 billion *won*. Using the formula in Article 6.4.(a)(i) of the *Agreement on Agriculture*, dividing 1.886 billion won value of 1997 beef production into the 313.173 billion won of support for beef results in a quotient of 16.61 per cent (cf. paragraph 372). Accordingly, had Korea implemented the provisions of Article 6.4.(a)(i) of the *Agreement on Agriculture*, it would have determined that the support it provided to the cattle industry in 1997 was not *de minimis*.[191] Under

[191] On a live animal basis, the calculation used to determine whether the support was *de minimis* would be as follows:

Article 7.2.(a) of the *Agreement on Agriculture*, that support should have been included in Korea's Current Total AMS calculations for that year, which would have resulted in Korea failing to meet its reduction commitment for 1997.

376. The **United States** considered that Korea had not included the total value of beef production in its 1997 notifications. The value of 2.105 billion won was eventually provided at the request of the United States and other countries. However, this was the value for 1996 production.[192] It appears likely that it is based on the average wholesale carcass price for beef. Since Korea's price support programme actually supports the price of live cattle, the appropriate total value of production should be the farm gate price for cattle. Use of carcass price at wholesale markets would overstate the value by incorporating costs of slaughter, as well as any other value added.

377. Using its alternative figure for eligible production and the OECD figure for the total value of production, **Australia** submitted that domestic support for beef in 1997 was 15.47 per cent of the total value of production. For this reason, domestic support for beef should have been included in Korea's calculations of its AMS for that year. Australia noted that even using Korea's own figures for eligible production and the OECD figure for the total value of production, domestic support for beef was 10.35 per cent of the value of total production and should likewise have been included in Korea's Current Total AMS calculation for 1997.

378. As concerns the total value of production, Australia contended that it used the OECD figure because the methodology is clear and is based on data provided by the Korean government itself. Australia also used the OECD calculation in the absence of a reference to the total value of production in Korea's domestic support notification to the WTO for 1997. Australia acknowledges that Korea has now supplied a figure which it considers represents the total value of production. However, Korea has not provided either the methodology or any raw data to show how it reached this alternative figure.

379. Australia contended that Korea's 1997 market price support should have been calculated as follows:

2.4 million *won*/head (AAP) - 543,456 *won*/head (FERP) x 170,000 head (EP) = 315.6 billion won (Market Price Support for Live Cattle) + 1.90 billion won Quality Incentive Program = 316.7 billion won total support for cattle. 316.7 billion won divided into 1.886 billion won (value of production) = 16.79 per cent

Under Article 6.4(a)(i) of the *Agreement*, any quotient of 10 per cent or higher would not be *de minimis*.

192 See 25 January 1999, Summary report, Meeting of 17 November 1998.

1997 Calculation of Market Price Support for Beef							
	A	B	C	D	E	F	G
	AAP (1) (000 on/MT)	FERP (2) (000 won/MT)	EP (3) (000 MT)	*MPS (A-B)*C billion won*	*Other Support (4) billion won*	*Value of Production (5) billion won*	*Support as a % of production*
Beef	*7351.1*	*1,823.0*	*52,615 s*	*290.9*	*1.09*	*1,886.5*	*15.47*
Notified by Korea	*7,351.1*	*1,823.0*	*35,127*	*194.18*	*1.09*	*1,886.5*	*10.35*

1. Source: G/AG/N/KOR/18, supporting table DS:5.
2. MT = metric tonne.
3. Programme operated from 26 January to 31 December, 1997 with authority to purchase 500 head per day. (340 days x 500 head per day = 170,000 head). Converted to beef tonnage using carcass conversion rate of 61.9 per cent.
4. Source: G/AG/N/KOR/18, supporting table DS:7.
5. OECD Review of Agricultural Policies in Korea1999; Annex 7, pages 146-148.

(iv) Applied Administered Price and Fixed External Reference Price

380. **Australia** contended that it's calculations did not factor in anomalies relating to Korea's calculations of the applied administered price or the fixed external reference price raised by the United States and New Zealand. This is because the correction of these anomalies did not in Australia's opinion materially affect the outcome - that Korea has exceeded *de minimis* levels of support for beef. However, Australia considered that these are important issues for determination by the Panel in its deliberations on the methodology that Korea is required to use to calculate its domestic support for beef. Australia considered that the *Agreement on Agriculture*, in particular Annex 3 of that Agreement, provides the methodology which must be followed by Korea. The result of Korea's failure to calculate domestic support for beef correctly resulted in its subsequent failure to include this support in its calculation of its total AMS for 1997. When beef is included, Australia has shown that Korea exceeded its total permitted support levels for 1997 by 191.2 billion Won.

381. The **United States** submitted that when the beef AMS for 1997 (based on beef, not live cattle) is included in Korea's Current Total AMS for that year, Korea exceeds the level of domestic support contained in its Schedule (those identified in both data series in Column 2 of its Schedule). As explained in paragraph 420, the United States continued, Korea posited two distinct AMS amounts for 1997: 2,028.65 billion won and 1,650.03 billion *won.*[193] Korea's Current Total

[193] Schedule LX, Part IV, Section I at I-1 and Korea's notification, Table DS:1 at 1 (G/AG/N/KOR/18) 16 September 1998.

AMS for 1997 was 1,936.95 billion *won*.[194] Adding the 1997 beef AMS (313.17 billion *won*), which Korea omitted as *de minimis* to Korea's Current Total AMS for 1997, increases the latter to 2,250.12 billion *won*, significantly more than either of the AMS figures set forth in Korea's Schedule for 1997. Accordingly, Korea exceeded the level of domestic support provided for in its reduction commitments for 1997 and, thus, violated Articles 3.2. and 6.3 of the *Agreement on Agriculture*.

382. Korea did not use the 1986 to 1988 base years to calculate the FERP as required by Annex 3.11 of the *Agreement on Agriculture*, the United States continued. Further, Korea did not use the 1986 to 1988 base period for calculating the AAP. The United States submitted further that Korea's calculations are incorrect for several reasons including the use of values for beef production rather than cattle production and an erroneous amount for eligible production. With regard to 1997, in calculating the AAP of 7,351.10 thousand *won* per tonne of beef (presumably carcass basis), Korea uses an average price per kilogram based on actual purchases. Korea's programme called for the purchase of live cattle at a price of 2,400 thousand *won* per head for a 500 kg. steer. However, Annex 3, paragraph 7, of the *Agreement on Agriculture* specifies that "The AMS shall be calculated as close as practicable to the point of first sale of the basic agricultural product concerned." Even if we were to accept Korea's conversion of the live cattle procurement to a beef basis, the calculation is still flawed, the United States continued. According to MAF data, the conversion of live weight to carcass basis for steers is 61.9 per cent.[195] Therefore, the AAP for 1997 should have been 7,754.4 thousand *won* per tonne.

383. The United States submitted that Korea's 1997 market price support should have been calculated as follows:

AAP (1,000 won/tonne)	FERP (1,000 won/tonne)	EP (1,000 tonnes)	Market Price Support (billion won)	Quality Incentive Programme (billion won)	TOTAL Support for Beef (billion won)
7,754	1,823	52.615	312.082	1.09	313.173

384. Concerning the Complainants arguments in paragraph 360 *et sequitur* that Korea's domestic support for beef in 1997 was not *de minimis,* **Korea** submitted that it's calculation of the AMS for the domestic cattle purchase programme for 1997 was correct. Korea explained that it's cattle purchase programme was based on actual purchases at the standard price of 2,400 thousand won per head for a 500 kg. steer. The said programme was implemented not only for the Hanwoo but also for dairy cattle and hybrid cattle of Cheju Island and an amount different

194 Korea's notification, Table DS:1 at 3 (G/AG/N/KOR/18).

195 Conversion rate per "Major Statistics for Agriculture and Forestry", Republic of Korea Ministry of Agriculture and Forestry, 1999, page 328. (2,400 thousand *won*/500 kg. steer = 4,800 thousand won per tonne live basis; divided by 61.9 per cent = 7,754.4 thousand won per tonne carcass basis.)

from that for Hanwoo beef was applied as well. To calculate the market price support, the AAP and the FERP are computed on the basis of carcass weight even though live cattle is purchased. Korea's live cattle purchase programme in 1997 was implemented as follows:

(i) Domestic cattle (live cattle):

88,891 head multiplied by average weight 564.1 kg. multiplied by 61.91 per cent (the conversion of live weight to carcass basis for Hanwoo steers) = 31,043,528 kg.

(ii) Dairy cattle (carcass):

9,150 head multiplied by average weight 385.5 kg. = 3,527,838 kg.

(iii) Hybrid cattle of Cheju Island (live cattle):

1,500 head multiplied by average weight 639.4 kg. multiplied by 57.9 per cent (the conversion of live weight to carcass) = 555,359 kg.

(i) plus (ii) plus (iii) equals 35,127 tonnes.

Korea accordingly purchased Hanwoo steers at a price of 4,800 thousand won per head, dairy cattle at market prices and Cheju Island hybrid cattle at a price of 3,800 thousand won per head. The total amount required for the purchase programme was 258,221,547 thousand won.

385. Hence, the AAP is calculated as follows:

258,221,547 thousand won divided by 35,127 tonnes equals 7,351.1 thousand won/ton.

The external reference price of beef is 1,823 thousand won/ton and, therefore, the market price support is calculated as follows:

(7,351.1 thousand won/ton-1,823 thousand won/ton) X 35,127 tonnes = 194.18 billion won.

If the 1.09 billion won for the Quality Improvement Programme is included, the AMS for cattle is 195.27 billion won.

386. As pointed out by the Complainants, Korea has been using actual purchase quantities, or the actual eligible quantities, as eligible production for calculation of the market price support amount. Korea noted that it also computed its Base AMS and annual reduction level, by using actual purchase quantities in preparing Part IV of the Uruguay Round Schedule LX. This Schedule has been reviewed by the Member countries. Referring to Article 1(a)(ii) of the *Agreement on Agriculture* which specifies that the AMS shall be calculated in consideration of the "*constituent data and methodology used in the tables of supporting material incorporated by reference in Part IV of the Member's Schedule*", Korea was of the view that it has adequately implemented its reduction commitment since a method identical with that of the Schedule LX has been used.

387. With regard to the support amount, Korea continued, the WTO notification form did not provide for the inclusion of the total value of production Furthermore, Korea pointed out that the total value of production is not calculated on the basis of the wholesale carcass price for beef, as the Complainants argued (see

paragraph 376), but on the basis of the actual sales price of live cattle sold by the producers at 80 livestock markets in producing areas.

388. Referring to the OECD figures presented by the Complainants (paragraphs 372 and 375), according to which the 1997 value of Korean beef and veal production was 1,886 billion won, Korea replied that the OECD values are provisionally estimated values. In calculating the OECD values, the production quantity was based on the weighted average of the carcasses of locally produced beef. The production price was the amount adjusted to convert the average price of beef traded in three wholesale markets in Seoul to the price at the farm gate. Accordingly, estimated values computed on the basis of such assumptions are not as accurate as the government's official statistical data calculated through a precise statistical technique. Korea submitted that its 1997 value of cattle was 2,107 billion won. Hence, the AMS for cattle in 1997 did not exceed 10 per cent of the total value of cattle production and Korea's 1997 Current Total AMS did not exceed its reduction commitment level specified in Schedule LX.

389. Another argument, **Korea** contended, set forth in particular by New Zealand[196], is that Korea should have based the fixed external reference price for beef on 1986 to 1988 c.i.f. unit values. Korea has based the fixed external reference price on the average c.i.f. unit values for beef imported in the period 1989-1991, because Korea has used the 1989 to 1991 base period in its Schedule (with the exception of rice for which 1993 has been used as the base period). Again, in accordance with its obligations under Article 1 (a)(ii) of the *Agreement on Agriculture*, Korea has taken into account the methodology and data used in its Schedule to calculate its support in 1997 and 1998 on a comparable and consistent basis. Further, Korea pointed out that since beef imports were prohibited for most of the period 1986-1988 in Korea, no foreign beef was imported during that period. Accordingly, it is impossible for Korea to calculate the fixed external reference price on reliable and representative data on c.i.f. unit values for the period 1986-1988. Finally, because the applied administered price under Korea's cattle purchase programme is calculated by converting live cattle to carcass, the administered price and fixed external reference price are at the same stage of processing and it is not necessary to convert the fixed external reference price to live cattle as argued by New Zealand.[197]

(v) 1998

390. Furthermore, Korea's Total AMS commitment for 1998, the United States submitted, appears to be 1,951.70 billion *won.*[198] Korea notified the Current To-

---

196 See paras. 472-476.

197 See para. 476. (It is also not clear to Korea why necessarily Korean slaughtering costs, rather than slaughtering costs in the country of origin of the beef for which c.i.f. unit values are determined should be used in this exercise by New Zealand).

198 1998 notification at Table DS:1, column 1.

tal AMS for 1998 as 1,562.77 billion *won.*[199] Adding the correct amount of 919.2 billion won of beef support for 1998, because, in the opinion of the United States, it is not *de minimis*, results in a Current Total AMS of 2,481.97 billion *won*. In addition, Korea incorrectly calculated its rice AMS for 1998, understating the rice AMS by approximately 280 billion won meaning that its Current Total AMS for 1998 should be 2,761.97 billion *won.* As in 1997, Korea's correct Current Total AMS for 1998 exceeds both of the AMS reduction levels reflected in Schedule LX, Part IV. Thus, for 1998, Korea violated the domestic support reduction commitments contained in Articles 3.2 and 6.3 of the *Agreement on Agriculture*, as well.

391. As concerns the year 1998, the United States argued that the price and animal eligibility criteria for Korea's cattle procurement programme appear to have changed as follows:

- July 8: The procurement price is lowered to 1,900 thousand won per 500 kg. steer, and size parameters changed to include medium size (300-399 kg.) steers.
- July 16: Procurement price is reduced to 1,800 thousand won per 500 kg. steer.
- July 19: Eligibility is limited to "small-medium" (200-399 kg.) Hanwoo steers.
- July 27: Eligibility is increased to 600 head per day of which 250 would be "half-grown" animals (200-350 kg.), and 350 would be small-medium steers.

Under these parameters, 125,000 head of various size Hanwoo steers were eligible for Korea's domestic support programme in 1998. Market circumstances and Korea's modifications to the programme suggest that actual procurement may have been near the maximum eligible.

392. Moreover, the United States noted that Korea does not include in its notification of Current AMS for 1998 several other beef support programmes that were implemented in that year.[200] These programmes include a Calf Production Stabilization Programme implemented in certain parts of the country in June of 1998, and expanded to the entire country in August of 1998; the purchase of breeding cows on Cheju Island, and support provided through the delay of loan repayments for up to three years.[201] Up to 5,000 head of breeding cows were to

---

199 *Ibid* at column 3.

200 These other programmes consisted of the following: Quality Improvement Subsidy (as notified): 1.4 billion *won;* Purchases of Cheju Island breeding cows: 7.5 billion *won*; Calf production stabilization programme: 8.6 billion *won*; loan extensions: 570.0 billion *won*; Supplementary Livestock Management Fund: 150.0 billion *won.* These additional programmes involved support equal to a total of 737.5 billion *won.*

201 See, "Calf Production Stabilization System to be in place on a trial basis", 30 June 1998, in "Agriculture, Livestock and Fishery News", and "Government to compensate the Difference if the

be purchased on Cheju Island for 3,000 won per kilogramme, 570 billion won was spent for loan extensions, and 150 billion won was spent for a supplemental livestock management fund.[202] In addition, the United States continued, according to the 1998 "Korea Livestock Yearbook" published by the Agriculture, Fisheries and Livestock News, 8.6 billion won was budgeted for the calf production stabilization programme. Though these may be incorrectly included in the "non-product specific support" supporting table of Korea's 1998 notification, the extent of these programmes based on this information appears to be in excess of what was reported.[203] The United States considered, therefore, that the 183.06 billion won that Korea notified to the WTO as domestic beef support in 1998 understates the actual value of support provided. An additional 737.5 billion won should have been reported, bringing total beef support to at least 919.2 billion won to account for the programmes listed above.

393. Furthermore, the United States continued, Korea did not include the total value of beef production for 1998 in its domestic support notification. Upon questioning by WTO Members, Korea provided a value of production that Korea claimed to represent the 1997 value of production. However, as with the previous year, the United States was of the opinion that this value is not for the correct time period, nor is it calculated correctly. No OECD data for purposes of calculating Korea's PSE for beef is as yet available for 1998. The only known published value of Korean beef production for 1998 was provided in a seminar sponsored by the Korean Meat Industry Association's Meat Journal on 2 April 1999. According to materials provided at the seminar, the value of Korean beef production in 1998 was 1.8106 billion *won.*[204] Using the formula in Article 6.4 (a)(i) of the *Agreement on Agriculture*, dividing the 919.2 billion won of support for beef by the 1.8106 billion won value of 1998 beef[205] production results in a quotient of 50.77 per cent or 51.92 per cent on a live cattle basis. Therefore, (on the basis of the data provided at the Meat Journal seminar), it appears that Korea's support to the beef industry was not *de minimis* in 1998, either. Hence, Korea failed to meet its reduction commitment for domestic support for 1998. The level of support provided is thus inconsistent with Korea's obligations under the *Agreement on Agriculture*.

Price of Calves Falls below 700,000 Korean *won*," Chosun Ilbo (12 August 1998), and MAF June 1998 Press Release. June 1998 Press Release, News Articles dated 2 February 1998, 30 June 1998, and 2 August 1998.

202 The loan deferment and supplemental livestock management fund probably also applied to livestock other than cattle, so the cattle numbers may be overstated. Until the Korean government is responsive to request for specific information, the amounts dedicated to cattle only remains unknown.

203 See 1998 notification at Supporting Table DS:9.

204 The Meat Journal is published by Choon-Shil Hwang and was registered as a magazine on 3 December 1991. The Journal's address is: Meat Journal Building, fourth floor, 221-31, Soongnap-dong, Songpah-ku, Seoul. Home page: HTTP:/www.meat.co.kr.

205 This calculation uses the same value of beef production for both 1997 and 1998.

394. Korea's cattle purchase programme was implemented again in 1998 for Hanwoo, dairy cattle and hybrid cattle of Cheju Island. However, there were several changes in the cattle purchase programme, as mentioned by the United States above (paragraph 391) Until completion of the cattle purchase programme on 31 August, 1998, Korea's cattle purchase programme in 1998 was implemented as follows:

*Total purchase quantity:*112,774 head or 35,899,193 kg.

(1)	Hanwoo (live cattle):	98,941 head or 31,444,756 kg.
	- Large steer:	70,565 head multiplied by 589.29 kg./head multiplied by 61.9 per cent (carcass rate) = 25,740,031 kg.
	- Medium steer:	19,925 head multiplied by 362.97 kg./head multiplied by 58.6 per cent (carcass rate) = 4,238,056 kg.
	- Medium cow:	8,451 head multiplied by 296.16 kg./head multiplied by 58.6 per cent (carcass rate) = 1,466,669 kg.
(2)	Hanwoo (carcass):	9,601 head multiplied by 335.97 kg./head = 3,225,648 kg.
(3)	Dairy steer (carcass):	668 head multiplied by 308.84 kg./head = 202,965 kg.
(4)	Hybrid cow:	3,564 head multiplied by 481.32 kg./head multiplied by 59.8 per cent (carcass rate) = 025,824 kg.

Total purchase amount: 247,098,680 thousand won.

Accordingly, Korea submitted, the AAP is 6,883.2 thousand won/ton. Therefore, the market price support is calculated as follows: (6,883.2 thousand won/ton minus 1,823 thousand won/ton) multiplied by 35,899 tonnes = 181.66 billion won.

395. Replying to the United States argument concerning the Calf Production Stabilization Programme in 1998 (paragraph 392), Korea explained that 3 billion won was budgeted for that programme in 1998 but the actual payments under the programme to individual farmers started only in January 1999. Therefore, in Korea's view, this programme should not be included in the notification of 1998. As concerns the United States argument in respect of the Cheju Island breeding cow procurement programme (paragraph 392), Korea asserted that such a programme was never implemented in Korea. The United States possibly mistook the purchase of the hybrid cattle of Cheju Island in the above mentioned purchase programme as the breeding cow purchase programme. Korea has included the purchase of the hybrid cattle of Cheju Island in its AMS for cattle.

396. As concerns the delay in loan repayments mentioned in paragraph 392, Korea stated that this was only planned. The actual amount of loan extensions for the purpose of relieving economic hardships facing livestock farmers totaled 435.6 billion won out of the originally planned 570 billion won. The amount was 68 billion won under the Livestock Development Fund, 41.2 billion won under the special account fund for rural development and 326.4 billion won under livestock management funds. Since they were all loans, Korea included these in its AMS notification for 1998. The calculation of the AMS for the loans is (market interest rate on loan minus average interest rate on loan) multiplied by loan amount multiplied by average loan period, and the result is 19.3 billion won. Of the total loan extension amount, 14.5 billion won under the livestock management fund was included as a non-product specific support in the notification.[206] The remaining 4.8 billion won under the livestock development fund and special account fund for rural development was included as a Green Box support in the same notification.[207] Of the total amount of 150 billion won which was originally planned to be spent by the Livestock Management Fund, 146 billion won was spent. Moreover, this amount was for loan interest subsidy for livestock farming and this corresponded virtually to loan extensions. Therefore, the AMS for the loan is 6.5 billion won[208], and is included as a non-product specific support in the same notification.[209] Finally, including the 1.4 billion won of the Quality Incentive Programme in 1998, the AMS for cattle was 183.06 billion won. Korea's 1998 total value of cattle production is 1,836 billion won. Accordingly, Korea's 1998 AMS for cattle represents 9.97 per cent which is *de minimis*.

397. The 183,06 billion won that Korea notified to the WTO, Korea continued, was the exact amount and the argument of the United States that an additional 737.5 billion won should have been reported is erroneous. Further, referring to the arguments in paragraph 393, Korea explained that the reason for Korea to provide 1997 data is because Korea's official statistics for total value of cattle production require some time to be computed and the calculation method is based on accurate data calculated on the basis of actual sales price of live cattle realized at the cattle source markets throughout the country. The data presented at the seminar mentioned by the United States is nothing but an estimated value for reference announced by an individual.

398. In conclusion, Korea's 1998 AMS for cattle is 183.06 billion won which represents 9.97 per cent of 1,836.1 billion won being the total value of cattle production for 1998 and such value is *de minimis*. Accordingly, Korea's 1998 Cur-

---

206 Loan interest subsidy for livestock farming in Supporting Table DS:9, G/AG/N/KOR/24.

207 Infrastructural services and structural adjustment assistance provided through investment aid in supporting table DS:1.

208 Market interest rate on loan-average concessional interest rate on loan) x loan amount x average loan period.

209 Loan interest subsidy for Livestock Farming in Supporting Table DS:9.

rent Total AMS of 1,562.77 billion won does not exceed 1,951.7 billion won being the commitment level as provided in Schedule LX.

399. Regarding the issue of total value of production as a basis for compliance with the *de minimis* percentage, Korea recalled the United States assertion that it derived the total value from information contained in the OECD data. However, as Korea explained in paragraph 388, the data provided by Korea on its total value of production come from the official statistics which Korea's statistical authority has produced on the basis of farm gate prices identified with respect to 80 livestock markets in producing areas across the country. In contrast, Korea wishes to highlight that the OECD data are only estimates that had been produced based on the prices prevailing in a limited number of wholesale markets in Seoul.

(vi) Annex 3 of the Agreement on Agriculture

400. The **United States** submitted that Korea attempts to justify its violation of its reduction commitments by arguing that its inclusion of an erroneous approach in its Schedule removes it from challenge is untenable in light of paragraph 3 of the Marrakesh Protocol which provides:

> The implementation of the concessions and commitments contained in the schedules annexed to this Protocol shall, upon request, be subject to multilateral examination by the Members. This would be *without prejudice to the rights and obligations of Members under Agreements in Annex 1A of the WTO Agreement.* (emphasis added)

The *Agreement on Agriculture* is one of the listed Agreements. Korea's inclusion of an erroneous methodology in its Schedule and supporting material cannot nullify the rights of other Members under the Agreement or diminish Korea's obligations under the Agreement.

401. Furthermore, the United States was of the opinion that Korea exceeded the commitment level for 1997, regardless of which base computation is used. Based on the data supplied by Korea, it appears that the eligible production for 1998 may be higher than reflected in the calculations the United States has provided (see paragraphs 390-393). The United States at that time had believed that actual and eligible production for that year may have been the same. Now it appears that dairy steer and hybrid cows may have also been eligible for the support, which would increase the current total AMS for beef. Also, Korea has incorrectly computed the fixed external reference price by relying on a price that is not specified at an equivalent stage of processing as that used for establishing the applied administered price. The resulting apples to oranges comparison distorts the result. The United States referred the Panel to the discussion of this issue made by New Zealand.[210]

---

[210] See paras. 468-476.

402. **Korea**, referring to the United States' arguments in 358, submitted that those does not really contradict Korea's position. Indeed, it is precisely the *Agreement on Agriculture* itself which clearly provides in Article 6.3 and Article 3.2 that compliance should be judged by reference to the commitment levels specified in Part IV of a Member's Schedule, rather than the general calculation methods set forth in Annex 3 of the *Agreement on Agriculture*. As concerns the arguments in paragraph 425, Korea submitted further that it is the United States rather than Korea which negates the provisions of the *Agreement on Agriculture*. Article 1(a) of the *Agreement on Agriculture* explicitly defines, first, that for the base period it is the support "*specified in the relevant tables of supporting material incorporated by reference in Part IV of a Member's Schedule*" which is decisive. It is not disputed that the base periods used by Korea are clearly identified in the supporting Table 6 of Part IV of Korea's Schedule.

403. Second, Korea continued, with regard to the *"support provided during any year"*, Article 1(a)(ii) clearly contradicts the arguments by the Complainants that these should be based exclusively on the Annex 3 methodology, but specifies that in addition to the provisions of Annex 3, one should also take into account *"the constituent data and methodology used in the tables of supporting material incorporated by reference in Part IV of the Member's Schedule."* If the *Agreement on Agriculture* intended to provide that only the methodology set forth in Annex 3 could be considered and used, it would be inappropriate and superfluous to define in Article 1(a)(ii) the need to take into account in addition the data and methodology used in the supporting tables. Nor would Annex 4 to the *Agreement on Agriculture* exist which provides for alternative calculation methods "*where market price support as defined in Annex 3 exists but for which calculation of this component of the AMS is not practicable.*" Korea submitted that the *Agreement on Agriculture* also explicitly recognizes the possibility of *"differential and more favourable treatment"* for developing country Members as embodied in their Schedule of Concessions, as well as the fact that there is scope for *"flexibility"* to implement reduction commitments over a period of up to ten years.

404. Furthermore, the methodologies in Annex 3 are not the only methodologies to take into account under the *Agreement on Agriculture* because Article 1(a)(ii) mandates the need to take into account *in addition* the *data and methodology* used in the supporting tables in a Member's Schedule. As a matter of data and methodology, Korea also used actual quantities of production in the supporting tables in its Schedule. Therefore, in accordance with its obligations under Article 1(a)(ii) of the *Agreement on Agriculture* with respect to calculation of support provided during any year of the implementation period of its AMS reduction commitments, Korea takes into account the data and methodology in its supporting tables by also using actual production figures. Needless to say, to fairly gauge compliance of Korea with its commitments, one should compare like with like and the reduction of total AMS based on actual quantities in Korea's Sched-

ule should be judged with annual AMS calculations based on the same use of actual quantities. The arguments by the Complainants that higher eligible quantities - potentially total beef production in Korea[211]- should be used as eligible quantities and then be compared with data based on actual quantities used in the Schedule of Korea, must be rejected because it would result in an illogical and manifestly unfair comparison (see also arguments in paragraph 389).

405. In conclusion, Korea submitted that the calculations for the annual support of beef in 1997 and 1998 have been made taking into account *the data and methodology* used in its Schedule of Concessions in accordance with Article 1(a)(ii) of the *Agreement on Agriculture*. As already shown in detail elsewhere, the support amounts for beef in 1997 and 1998 were *de minimis* and therefore were not required to be included in the total AMS calculation in accordance with Article 6 (4)(b) of the *Agreement on Agriculture*. The alternative estimated calculations presented by New Zealand fail to take into account the data and methodologies used in Korea's Schedule of Concessions, in violation of Article 1(a)(ii) of the *Agreement on Agriculture*. The comparison provided by New Zealand of the annual AMS in 1997 and 1998 with the reduction commitments in Korea's Schedule[212] is manifestly inaccurate and unfair, because the 1997 and 1998 annual data have been calculated using completely different data and methodologies from those used to determine the Base AMS amount from which Korea's reduction commitments have been derived.

406. **Australia** submitted that Korea's claim that the reference to "constituent data and methodology" in Article 1 of the *Agreement on Agriculture* provides the justification for an alternative methodology to that in Annex 3 was inconsistent with the rules of interpretation of public international law. According to Australia, Article 1 of the *Agreement on Agriculture* is clear and unambiguous that support in any given year shall be calculated in accordance with Annex 3, taking into account the constituent data and methodology. The reference to constituent data and methodology does not remove the obligation to calculate support in accordance with Annex 3.

407. Australia submitted that the terms of Article 1 make sense if one understands that the calculations of AMS are product specific. In this respect, "constituent data and methodology" has an important role to play in ensuring that the calculation of support on any given commodity is calculated in subsequent years consistently with support calculated in the base period. For products where no support was included in the base period calculation, there is no constituent data or methodology in the tables of supporting material to a Member's Schedule. Annex 3 calculations are therefore mandatory.

408. The United States submitted that the language from the definition of AMS in Article 1 of the *Agreement on Agriculture* refutes Korea's contention that it is

---

211 See para. 481.

212 See para. 483-485.

bound only by the AMS computation reflected in its Schedule and the methodology contained in the supporting material referenced in the Schedule. Korea's construction of the *Agreement on Agriculture's* AMS provisions would render substantial portions of the text of the *Agreement on Agriculture* meaningless. As a consequence, Korea's interpretative approach is contrary to customary rules of treaty interpretation and must be rejected.

409. Consideration of the specific language used in Article 1(a)(ii) requires, in the opinion of the United States, the rejection of Korea's interpretation. The provision explicitly directs that the AMS calculation be made in the manner prescribed in Annex 3; no conditions or exceptions are provided for. The only additional guidance set forth is that the calculation also take into account the data and methodology contained in the supporting tables. This guidance cannot be construed to nullify the express requirement that the AMS calculation be performed in accordance with the provisions of Annex 3. Similarly, Korea's reliance on Article 1(a)(1) is, in the view of the United States, misplaced. Again, Korea suggests that the language there set forth referencing the tables of supporting material incorporated by reference in a Member's Schedule should be construed in isolation from the remainder of the *Agreement on Agriculture*. However, the customary rules of interpretation of public international law as reflected in the *Vienna Convention* require that treaty terms be given their ordinary meaning in their context and in light of the object and purpose of the treaty. The other provisions of the *Agreement on Agriculture* pertinent to the AMS computation are part of the context of paragraph (a) of Article 1.

410. Since the term "base period" is not defined in Article 1(a)(i), and its ordinary meaning does not assist in determining the specific period that is intended to be captured, it is necessary to expand the inquiry to consider other provisions in the *Agreement on Agriculture* that provide the context for the term. The most pertinent provision in this regard is paragraph 5 of Annex 3 which directs that the "AMS calculated as below for the base period shall constitute the base level for the implementation of the reduction commitment on domestic support". Paragraph 5 is important as it provides guidance not only as to how the AMS base level will be computed, but also indicates what the relevant base period is. Thus, it is clear why Korea argues so strenuously for the Panel to disregard Annex 3.

411. Paragraphs 9 and 11 of the Annex specify, respectively, the United States continued, that the base period to be used for the computation of the fixed external reference price and the fixed reference price consists of the years 1986 to 1988. As the United States explained in response to a Panel question, it would be inappropriate to use a different base period for establishing the other elements of the calculation of market price support. Moreover, the historical background to this provision, as contained in the *Modalities*, supports the US proposition that the base period for fixing the applied administered price and eligible production must also be the years 1986-1988.

412. Korea's argument that it was free to select the base period that would provide the highest level of domestic support throughout the implementation period,

thus, flies in the face of the pertinent provisions of the *Agreement on Agriculture*, interpreted in their context, and in light of the object of the treaty. Indeed, if the domestic support reduction commitments, a core aspect of the *Agreement on Agriculture,* are not to be undermined, a common base period must be used by the Members. Clearly, a construction of the obligation that permitted Members to elect a base period that represents the highest level of domestic support would defeat, in part, the purpose of those very reduction commitments.

413. The third party submission of New Zealand provides, in the view of the **Complainants**, a well reasoned explanation of issues associated with the calculation methodology and the consistency of this methodology with Annex 3 of the *Agreement on Agriculture.* The Complainants agreed with the New Zealand views and believed these views are a useful adjunct to the points raised by Australia and the United States. The New Zealand submission also provides some alternative calculations which provide a useful guide to the Panel as to the AMS level if an alternative calculation were used.

(vii) Total AMS-Current Total AMS

414. **Australia** considered that Korea cannot exclude support for beef either on the basis that it is justified under Annex 2 or that support levels are 10 per cent or less of the total value of production as permitted under Article 6. For this reason, and consistent with Article 7.2(a) of the *Agreement on Agriculture*, the domestic support for beef provided by Korea in 1997 must be included in its calculation of its Current Total AMS for that year. Australia noted that Korea's Total AMS Commitment for 1997 was 2,028.65 billion won. Its notified Current Total AMS for that year was 1,936.95 billion won. Korea's Current Total AMS figures for 1997 include support for barley, maize, rapeseed, rice and silk-worm. For the reasons stated in paragraph 372, the support for beef must also be included. Australia submitted that the calculation of Korea's Current Total AMS for 1997 therefore should be as follows:

Commodity	Current Total AMS (billion Won)
Ric	1884.34
Barley	46.02
Maize	5.67
Rapeseed	0.91
Silk-worm	0.01
Beef	282.9
Total	2219.85

415. The **United States** noted that Korea's most recent notifications with respect to its Current Total AMS were G/AG/N/KOR/18 (16 September 1998) for 1997 and G/AG/N/KOR/24 (25 August 1999) for 1998 in which it classified, incorrectly in the opinion of the United States, the support provided to its cattle industry as *de minimis, i.e.* it did not exceed 10 per cent of the total value of cat-

tle or beef production. However, the United States argued, an accurate accounting, which would include the amount of support provided to the cattle industry, shows that in 1997 and 1998, Korea failed to meet its commitments for reducing domestic subsidies. In its 1997 and 1998 notifications[213], Korea apparently used a formula based on the one in Annex 3.8. to the *Agreement on Agriculture* to calculate market price support.[214] Hence, the 1997 and 1998 AMS for beef was reportedly 195.27 billion won and 183.06 billion *won*, respectively.[215]

416. The **Complainants** submitted that it is not for Korea to determine its reduction commitments under the *Agreement on Agriculture* by unilaterally determining a different calculation to that required explicitly by the *Agreement on Agriculture*. Korea adopted a different methodology to that adopted by other WTO Members in calculating an alternative commitment level for domestic support, reflected in the column in parenthesis in Part IV, Section I of the Korean Schedule. Korea cannot rely on this error to justify the consistency with the *Agreement on Agriculture* of its later calculations and its failure to meet its commitments. The Complainants submitted further that the approach adopted by Korea results in a lower level of AMS commitment, and in effect the AMS level for the years concerned is higher than for the base period used by Korea. The base used by Korea is 1989-1991, not the 1986-1988 period provided for in the Uruguay Round, reflected in the use of 1986-1988 in Annex 3, paragraph 11 of *the Agreement on Agriculture*.

417. **Korea** submitted that it is not correct that Korea's Schedule LX does not identify which of the two sets of figures constitutes Korea's binding obligation. Korea's Schedule LX clearly contains a Note 1 stating that: "Refer to Note 1 of Supporting Table 6 about the numbers in parentheses." It seems clear that the purpose of the supporting tables is to contain supporting material relating *to commitments* on agricultural products contained in Schedule LX-Korea (as explicitly stated below). Supporting Table 6 again contains a Note 1 which states:

> "*The AMS for rice has been calculated based on 1993 market price support instead of 1989-1991 average. The Final Bound Commitment level in 2004, however, is the level reduced by 13.3% from the 1989-1991 average Base Total AMS.*"

---

213 See Korea's 1997 and 1998 Notifications at Table DS:4 where beef is identified as *de minimis*.

214 Applied Administered Price (AAP) minus Fixed External Reference Price (FERP) multiplied by Quantity of Production Eligible for Support (EP) equals Total Market Price Support for Beef.

215

	AAP(1)	FERP(1)	EP(2)	Market Price Support (3)	Quality Incentive Program (3)	TOTAL Support for Beef(3)
1997	7,351.1	1,823	35.127	194.18	1.09	195.27
1998	6,883.2	1,823	35.90	181.66	1.4	183.06

(1) 1000 won/tonne; (2) 1000 tonnes; (3) billion won.

418. In the supporting table, the calculation method of the AMS reduction commitments, by use of the 1993 market price support for rice, is explicitly explained and it is noted that the end-result of the Final Bound Commitment level in 2004 results in the same level reduced by 13.3 per cent from the 1989-1991 average Base Total AMS. The reference to this calculation method would be wholly meaningless if it was not clearly intended to base Korea's commitments on that basis.

419. Furthermore, Korea contended that the said calculation methods and annual commitment levels of AMS had been reviewed and agreed upon by the Member countries in March 1994. Article 6.3 very clearly refers to the commitment level specified in Part IV of a Member's schedule as a basis for judging compliance, rather than the general calculation methods set forth in Annex 3 as the United States argued. Article 3.2 of the *Agreement on Agriculture* confirms this point. The US argument on this point must therefore be rejected.

420. The **United States** submitted that Article 6.3 of the *Agreement on Agriculture* specifies when a Member shall be considered in compliance with its domestic support obligations. The commitment levels in Member's Schedules were established in accordance with a Base Total AMS which, except for support that is exempt, is the total amount of support (Total AMS) provided by a WTO Member to its domestic agricultural producers from 1986 through 1988.[216] (For definition of "AMS" see paragraph 361).[217] Annex 3 of the *Agreement on Agriculture* provides the methodology for calculating the AMS, which is required to be computed on a product-specific basis for each basic agricultural product receiving market price support, non-exempt direct payments or any other subsidy not exempted from the reduction commitment. Once the AMS was established, Members included in their Schedules corresponding domestic support ceilings for each year of the implementation period, calculated on the applicable reduction formula for each Member. Developing countries agreed to reduce their domestic support in annual steps by 13 per cent.

421. Moreover, the United States noted that Korea provides, in Part IV of its Schedule, two separate numbers with respect to the total current AMS for each year of the implementation period (1995-2004). These figures are set forth in two separate columns, the second of which is set off by parentheses. An examination of the respective columns of expenditure amounts reveals, in the opinion of the United States, that the first column approached conformity with the formulae

---

216 See Annex 3 to the *Agreement on Agriculture*.

217 Support which is exempt from the base AMS includes support which (i) satisfies the requirements of Annex 2 to the Agreement ("Green Box") because it has no or minimal trade-distorting effects or because it limits domestic production ("Blue Box") or (ii) is exempt from reduction by an *Agreement on Agriculture* provision. See Articles 1 (h) and 7.2.(a), *Agreement on Agriculture*.

contained in Annex 3 to the *Agreement on Agriculture,*[218] whereas the expenditure ceilings in the second column did not. In the second column, Korea has inflated the amount of the annual Current Total AMS by basing the largest component of Korea's total AMS, that for rice, on a 1993 base year when domestic support for rice peaked.[219] Korea's methodology resulted in a Current Total AMS in 1995 that is 28 per cent higher than it would be using the procedure provided for in the *Agreement on Agriculture*. This distortion is then carried throughout the implementation period in each succeeding year. Korea attempts to justify this approach, the United States continued, by suggesting that the final current total AMS in the last year of the implementation period, 2004, is the same as if calculated consistently with the *Agreement on Agriculture* (see paragraph 426).[220] Korea's alternative reduction commitment, which is not in accordance with the requirements of Annex 3 of the *Agreement on Agriculture,* must be rejected as inconsistent with Korea's obligations.

422. The untenable nature of Korea's AMS commitment, the United States argued, is underlined by a comparison of Korea's Base Total AMS and the Current Total AMS reported by Korea in its Schedule as an alternative approach. Korea's Base Total AMS[221] is 1,718.6 billion *won*. This is less than the expenditure level that Korea includes in the amounts in parentheses in column 2 of Korea's Schedule for 1997 (2,028.65 billion *won*) and for 1998 (1,951.70 billion *won*). Based on its notifications to the Committee on Agriculture for 1997 and 1998, Korea appears to consider the AMS levels included in the parentheses as its commitments.[222]

423. Korea has provided two inconsistent sets of support amounts for Current Total AMS in its Schedule.[223] Nowhere in its Schedule does Korea identify which of the sets constitutes Korea's binding obligation. Through its 1997 and 1998 notifications, Korea appears to be following the less onerous "commitments" contained in the second column. If this is indeed the case, Korea would be ignoring the commitments in the first column of its Schedule which more closely coincide with the methodology for establishing the Base Total AMS as reflected in the *Agreement on Agriculture.* The United States submitted that the parenthetical data in column 2 in Korea's Schedule represents an admission by Korea

---

218 Even the figures in Korea that most closely approximate the Annex 3 methodology suffer from such defects as reliance on a time period other than the 1986-1988 period specified in para. 9 of the Annex.

219 See Note 1 of Supporting Table 6 and statistics provided there.

220 Note 1 to Supporting Table 6 states: The AMS for rice has been calculated based on 1993 market price support instead of the 1989-1991 average. The Final Bound Commitment level in 2004, however, is the level reduced by 13.3 per cent from the 1989-1991 average Base Total AMS.

221 (column 1, Schedule LX, Part IV, Section I).

222 See, 1997 and 1998 Notifications at Table DS:1, column 1.

223 See, column 2, "Annual and Final bound commitments level: 1995-2004", Schedule LX, Part IV, Section I (Korea Schedule) at I-1.

that it is reducing its support based on criteria not found in the *Agreement on Agriculture.*

424. It is a well-founded principle, the United States continued, that Korea is free to incorporate into its Schedule "acts yielding rights", "additional commitments", and qualifications to those additional commitments. However, Korea cannot use its Schedule to "diminish ... obligations ... [or] reduce ... commitments under other provisions of that Agreement."[224] Korea cannot avoid its domestic support reduction in this unilateral manner. To accept Korea's position that it should be able to fulfill its reduction commitments by complying with a reduction schedule based on a Base Total AMS that represents a composite of those approaches most favorable to Korea, but none of which is consistent with Annex 3 of the *Agreement on Agriculture*, would be to permit Korea to evade the disciplines of the *Agreement on Agriculture* relating to domestic support levels.

425. The United States argued that by claiming that it possesses the freedom to choose whatever base period best suits its interests, Korea effectively negates the provisions of the *Agreement on Agriculture* relating to the manner in which the reduction commitments were to be developed, as well as the reduction commitment itself. Korea's approach to the construction of its domestic support commitments leads to the absurd result that for the first seven years of the implementation period (from 1995 through 2001) the annual AMS levels claimed by Korea to be permitted under its Schedule are higher than the base AMS computed using an approximation of the calculation methodology set forth in the *Agreement on Agriculture*. Korea's construction of its Schedule also makes the first set of reduction commitments contained in its Schedule, and which are generally computed in accordance with the requirements of the *Agreement on Agriculture* provisions, completely meaningless, contrary to principles of treaty interpretation.

426. Korea also offers no explanation, the United States continued, for why it based the calculation of the fixed external reference price for beef on a period other than 1986-1988 as paragraph 9 of Annex 3 requires, or failed to compute the fixed external reference price based on the farm-gate price, which would be at an equivalent stage of processing to the cattle prices used by Korea for its applied administered price. Again, by electing a fixed external reference price that is inconsistent with the methodology provided for in the *Agreement on Agriculture*, Korea distorted the calculation of domestic support. The fixed external price used by Korea is higher than would have resulted using the correct methodology. The effect of Korea's departure from the prescribed methodology is a narrowing of the difference between its applied administered price and the fixed external reference price and, consequently, an understatement of the amount of domestic support.

427. Referring to the United States' allegations in paragraph 421, **Korea** submitted that it's Schedule LX contains a Note 1 stating that: "Refer to Note 1 of

[224] *US - Sugar Head Note* at 342.

Supporting Table 6 about the numbers in parentheses." Korea submitted that the purpose of the supporting tables is to contain supporting material relating to *commitments* on agricultural products contained in Schedule LX-Korea. The note in Supporting Table 6 states: "The AMS for rice has been calculated based on 1993 market price support instead of 1989-1991 average. The Final Bound Commitment level in 2004, however, is the level reduced by 13.3 per cent from the 1989-1991 average Base Total AMS." Therefore, it is evident that the numbers in parentheses constitute Korea's commitment levels on Total AMS reflecting the exceptional calculation method for rice which is based upon the 1993 market price support. In the supporting table, the calculation method of the AMS reduction commitments, by use of the 1993 market price support for rice, is explained and it is noted that the end-result of the final bound commitment level in 2004 results in the same level reduced by 13.3 per cent from the 1989-1991 average Base Total AMS. The reference to this calculation method would be totally meaningless if it was not clearly intended as a basis for Korea's commitments.

428. Korea, referring to the *US - Gasoline* case[225], noted that the said calculation methods and annual commitment levels of AMS had already been reviewed and agreed upon by the Member countries in March 1994. Moreover, Korea noted that Article 6.3 of the *Agreement on Agriculture*[226] refers to the commitment level specified in Part IV of a Member's schedule as a basis for judging compliance, rather than the general calculation methods set forth in Annex 3, as the United States argues. Korea considered that Article 3.2 of the *Agreement on Agriculture* confirms this point.[227]

V. SUMMARY OF THE ARGUMENTS PRESENTED BY THIRD PARTIES

A. *Arguments Submitted by Canada*

429. Canada submitted that certain measures undertaken by Korea with respect to the importation of fresh, chilled and frozen beef are inconsistent with Korea's obligations under Articles II, III and XI of GATT 1994 and Article 4 of the *Agreement on Agriculture*. Amongst these measures are restrictions on the retail sale of beef, the imposition of a mandatory mark-up on imports of beef and certain aspects of Korea's system of distribution of imported beef. In the view of

225 Appellate Body Report, *United States – Gasoline* , *supra*, footnote 117, at 21; see also Appellate Body Report, *Japan - Alcoholic Beverages, supra,* footnote 98, at 105.

226 "A Member shall be in compliance with its domestic support reduction commitments in any year in which its domestic support in favour of agricultural producers expressed in terms of Current Total AMS does not exceed the corresponding annual or final bound commitment *level specified in Part IV of the Member's Schedule*". (Emphasis added.)

227 "Subject to the provisions of Article 6, a Member shall not provide support in favour of domestic producers in excess of the commitment levels specified in *Section I of Part IV of its Schedule*." (Emphasis added.)

Canada, it is apparent that the common purpose and effect of all of these measures is to provide support and protection to the Korea's domestic beef industry.

1. Article III of GATT

430. Canada claimed that the restriction of retail sales of imported beef to a limited number of separate retail outlets compared to the significantly greater number of retail outlets available to domestic beef is a violation of the national treatment principle, as embodied in Article III:4 of GATT 1994. Previous GATT and WTO panels have interpreted this provision as "establishing the obligation to accord to imported products competitive opportunities no less favourable than those accorded domestic products."[228] In this regard, Article III:4 requires that imported products "shall be accorded treatment no less favourable than that accorded to like products of national origin in respect of all laws, regulations and requirements affecting their internal sale, offering for sale, purchase, transportation, distribution or use." Article III:4 applies where the following elements are satisfied: (1) there must be a law, regulation or requirement; (2) it must affect the internal sale, purchase, transportation, distribution or use of the product; (3) the imported product and the domestic products must be like products. If these elements are satisfied, the measure must accord the imported product treatment no less favourable than the like domestic product in order to comply with Article III:4.

431. First, the Korean measures restricting sales of imported beef to specialized outlets are without question "laws, regulations or restrictions". Second, these measures clearly "affect the internal sale, purchase, transportation, distribution or use" of imported beef. Third, it is equally clear that imported beef and domestic Korean beef are like products. It is also evident that the measures in question accord imported beef treatment that is less favourable than that accorded to the like domestic beef product. By restricting the retail outlets available to imported beef relative to domestic beef, the effect is to deny the imported product "competitive opportunities" that are "no less favourable" than those available to domestic beef. In effect, by restricting the number of retail outlets at which imported beef can be sold, the access to the Korean market available to imported beef is impaired relative to the competing domestic product. This is inconsistent with the obligation to provide "equal conditions of competition" once imported goods have cleared customs.

432. Canada claimed further that, in addition to Korea's limitation on the retail sale of imported beef to specialized retail outlets, a number of other measures and practices also appear to violate the national treatment principles of Article III:4 of GATT 1994:

---

228 *US - Section 337,* at para. 5.11.

(a) all beef imported by the LPMO, not sold directly by the LPMO to processors, must be sold through wholesale markets. Wholesale purchasers may then sell to specialized stores for retail purposes. Neither of these restrictions apply to sales of domestic beef;

(b) while regulations contemplate the possibility of sales of LPMO imported beef on a credit basis, this is discretionary, a discretion that has not been exercised. The availability of sales on a credit basis provides greater commercial opportunities in the marketplace. Sales of domestic beef are not similarly restricted to a cash basis;

(c) in order to import beef under the Simultaneous Buy/Sell (SBS) system, end-users must belong to one of a number of designated super-groups. In addition to the resulting imposition of a middleman, such super-group membership also results in increased expenses through membership fees and other additional costs; and

(d) in addition to country of origin requirements that apply to all beef, domestic and imported, Korea has imposed new additional labelling requirements that apply only to imported beef. Boxes of imported beef must also display labels that indicate commodity name, contract number and the super-group importer's name. This requires re-labelling in Korea, resulting in additional costs to imported beef.

433. Canada argued that each of these measures meets the requirements of Article III:4 of GATT 1994 as set out above with respect to retail sales. In each case, obligations are imposed on imported products that are not applicable to the like domestic products. Hence, each measure constitutes a violation of Korea's obligations under GATT 1994.

2. *Article II of GATT*

434. Canada submitted that Korea's imposition of a mark-up on imports of beef under the SBS system is inconsistent with Korea's obligations under Article II:1 of GATT 1994. In the alternative, it is a violation of Article III:2 of GATT 1994.

435. Korea collects a mandatory mark-up on all beef imported under the SBS system. This mark-up is collected by Korean Customs and the product is not released from customs control until the mark-up is paid. On its face, the collection of this mark-up constitutes the imposition of a charge on beef imports. Article II.1 of GATT 1994 states that on importation, products shall be subject only to those "ordinary customs duties" and "other duties or charges of any kind imposed on or in connection with the importation" specifically provided for in a Member's Schedule. The mark-up imposed by Korean authorities would appear to fall clearly within the plain meaning of the word "charge": i.e. "a pecuniary burden;

cost; a liability to pay money laid on a person or estate."[229] Its payment appears to operate as a condition of import. There is no reference to this mark-up as a "charge" in Korea 's Schedule.

436. As a result, the imposition of the mark-up upon importation is inconsistent with Korea's obligation under Article II.1(a) to provide "treatment no less favourable" to goods on importation than provided for in Korea's Schedule and in particular to be free of "all other duties or charges of any kind imposed on or in connection with importation", pursuant to Article II.1(b).

437. In the alternative, the mark-up constitutes an "internal tax or other internal charge" as contemplated by Article III:2. If it is an internal tax or charge, then its application only to imported beef and not to the like domestic product would constitute a violation of the national treatment principle and would be inconsistent with Korea's obligations under Article III:2 of GATT 1994.

3. Article XI of GATT and Article 4.2 of the Agreement on Agriculture

438. Canada submitted further that the following aspects of the Korean imported beef distribution system, individually or taken together, restrict and distort access to the Korean market contrary to Article XI of GATT 1994:

(a) arbitrary limitation of access to imported beef to "super-group" members;

(b) LPMO discourages potential applicants from seeking access to imported beef;

(c) resale of imported beef by end-users is not permitted;

(d) significant delays in invitations to foreign suppliers for LPMO allocation;

(e) inadequate reallocation of unused quota access; and

(f) restrictions on retail sale outlets of imported beef.

439. In Canada's view, to the extent that any of the measures or practices noted above constitute quantitative restrictions pursuant to Article XI:1 of GATT 1994, it follows that they must also be quantitative restrictions maintained in violation of Article 4.2 of the *Agreement on Agriculture*.

440. Canada was concerned that the principles underlying Article XI:1, as they relate to discretionary import licensing, not be misunderstood in their application to the facts of this case. The submissions of the United States and Australia may be read as suggesting that the mere use of a discretionary import licensing system in allocating access to imports within a quota or a tariff quota, by itself, constitutes a "restriction ... on ... importation" contrary to Article XI. Canada believes

[229] The New Shorter Oxford English Dictionary.

that the essential thrust of the submissions of the Complainants is that use of particular measures *in the operation* of a discretionary licensing system can constitute "restrictions" in the context of Article XI:1, where those measures result in a limitation on imports that would not otherwise exist.

441. Canada submitted that in support of their submissions on these points, both Complainants rely on the recent panel report in *India –Industrial Products*. The panel in the India case considered the application of Article XI:1 to India's practices in its operation of its discretionary import licensing system.[230] The panel found that the import licensing system maintained by India operated "as a restriction on imports within the meaning of Article XI:1".[231] In Canada's view, the factual background of this finding is very significant. Under the Indian licensing system, a range of products had been added to a "Negative List of Imports" and such products could only be imported with a licence. These licences were issued on a discretionary basis. There was no other quantitative restriction or tariff quota associated with the licensing system. In the absence of the discretionary licensing system, there would be no restriction on imports.

442. In these circumstances, the discretionary licensing system was found to be, by itself, a restriction on imports because the imposition of a discretionary licensing system, where licences are issued to some applicants but not to others, will necessarily provide some check on the potential flow of imports where there are no other impediments such as a quota or tariff quota. The result will be a smaller quantum of imports than would otherwise have occurred. (An automatic licensing system would not provide such a check.) On the other hand, where a quota or a tariff quota is in place, the use of discretionary licensing to allocate access within the limits imposed by the quota or tariff quota need not result in any further lessening in the flow of trade already constricted by the imposition of the quota or tariff quota. Indeed, in certain circumstances, discretionary licensing may be the most effective means of enforcing other GATT requirements applicable to the administration of otherwise lawful import restrictions (e.g., Article XIII:2).

443. Where a discretionary licensing system is implemented in conjunction with other restrictions, such as a quota or tariff quota, the manner in which the discretionary licensing system is operated may create additional restrictions to trade independent of those imposed by the quota or tariff quota. Since this issue was not considered in the India case, that case does not provide authority for the proposition that a discretionary licensing system, used in conjunction with a quantitative restriction or a tariff quota, necessarily provides some additional level of restriction over and above the inherent restriction on access created through the imposition of a quantitative restriction or a tariff quota. Indeed, the panel's decision clearly indicates that its conclusion that the Indian discretionary

---

230 Panel Report, *India – Quantitative Restrictions*, *supra*, footnote 65, paras. 5.122-142.

231 *Ibid.*, para. 5.131.

licensing system in question amounted to a "restriction" was reached "in the light of" the factual circumstances of that particular case.[232]

444. As suggested above, Canada would also note that the use of discretionary licensing in the allocation of a quota or tariff quota for example, if properly conducted, may be less distorting to trade patterns that the use of another type of licensing system such as "first-come, first-served". A discretionary system should attempt to allocate access to a quota or a tariff quota based on replicating as closely as possible the pattern of trade that would exist in the absence of such a restriction. This reflects the principles found in Article XIII of GATT 1994 with respect to allocation of quantitative restrictions or tariff quotas between exporting countries. In both cases, the purpose is to limit the disruption to trade inherently created by the imposition of the quantitative restriction or the tariff quota.

445. More relevant to the circumstances of this case, the panel in the India case did go on to find that by restricting issuance of licences to a limited class of ultimate end users ("Actual Users"), and excluding all other potential importers such as wholesalers, traders and other "intermediaries", India had created a restriction as contemplated in Article XI.[233] It is this finding that is the principle authority cited by the Complainants in their submissions as support for their arguments that actions by the Korean government in the operation of the Korean discretionary licensing system constitute "restrictions" pursuant to Article XI. Canada argued that the application of this principle in the case of the Korean measures in question is appropriate.

B. Arguments Submitted by New Zealand

446. New Zealand was concerned that, despite the progress made to date, Korea continues to rely on GATT-inconsistent trade restrictions to protect its domestic producers from the increased market access for imported beef provided for in Korea's Schedule. Korea has recently consolidated a number of these trade restrictions in new legislation. New Zealand considers that these measures are inconsistent with Korea's obligations under the WTO, including Articles II, III and XVII of GATT 1994. New Zealand's objective in joining in this dispute is to ensure that all illegal non-tariff measures are removed, so that by the year 2001 when the last quantitative restrictions are phased out, Korea's beef market will be fully and effectively liberalized, thereby ensuring that New Zealand's access to the Korean beef market is fair and equitable.

447. New Zealand was especially concerned over the following measures:

(a) retail restrictions on imported beef imposed by Korea;

(b) use of the LPMO tendering and grading system by Korea to discriminate against imported grass-fed beef; and

---

232 *Ibid.*, paras. 5.130-131.

233 *Ibid.*, paras. 5.141-143.

(c) maintenance by the LPMO of minimum auction prices for imported beef that are contingent on the price of domestic product.

1. Article III of GATT

448. New Zealand considered that the restrictions imposed by Korea on imported beef at the retail level constitute a violation of Article III:4 of GATT 1994. Korea has in place a number of measures which restrict the retail opportunities for imported beef. These include a requirement that imported beef may only be sold in specialised imported beef stores or in large-scale department stores or supermarkets with separate sales areas for imported beef.[234] Imported beef is effectively denied access to the existing retail infrastructure for beef. In order to sell imported beef, a meat retailer must seek permission for, and establish a separate retail facility. In 1998, there were only 5498 retail outlets for imported beef compared with over 45,000 retail outlets for domestically produced beef.

449. These measures fall within the scope of Article III:4, being "laws, regulations and requirements affecting [the] internal sale, offering for sale, purchase, transportation, distribution or use" of imported beef. The measures are mandatory, with penalties for violations in many cases.[235] There can be no doubt that imported beef and domestically-produced beef are "like" products for the purposes of Article III:4.[236] Nor does Korea dispute that imported and domestic beef are "like" products.

450. Korea's retail restrictions treat imported beef less favourably than domestic beef. The phrase "treatment no less favourable" in Article III:4 encapsulates the core intent of this provision of GATT: "to provide equal conditions of competition", or in other words to provide "effective equality of opportunities" between domestic goods and imported goods once they are cleared through customs.[237] Korea's retail restrictions do not offer equal conditions of competition or effective equality of opportunities for imported beef. Retail sale of imported beef in Korea is effectively confined to a relatively small number of retail outlets - around one tenth of the number of the existing domestic beef retail outlets. Korea has an extensive existing retail infrastructure for beef. The retail restrictions limit access to that infrastructure to domestic beef only. The only way that imported

---

[234] See Articles 15 and 9.5 of the *Management Guideline for Imported Beef.* Prior to 1 October 1999, these measures were contained in Articles 5C and 3A of the *Guidelines Concerning Registration and Operation of Specialized Imported Beef Stores.*

[235] See the table entitled "Criteria for Punishment for Violation" at page 15 of the *Management Guideline for Imported Beef* .

[236] Appellate Body Report, *Japan - Alcoholic Beverages, supra,* footnote 98, at 112, summarises the approach to any examination of the question of "like" products under Article III.

[237] See *Italian Agricultural Machinery,* paras. 11-13; *US - Section 337,* paras. 5.11-5.13; Panel Report, *US - Gasoline, supra,* footnote 97, para. 6.10; Appellate Body Report, *Japan - Alcoholic Beverages, supra,* footnote 98, at 109

beef can enter the retail market is if shop-keepers are prepared to establish separate new retail facilities. Only the very largest existing retailers can sell imported beef under the same roof as domestic product, and even then they may do so only if physically separate display units for imported product are set up. The costs associated with the requirement of establishing separate retail facilities for imported beef clearly limit the competitive opportunities *vis-à-vis* domestic product.

451. Restricting access for imports to fewer points of sale than domestic products was considered in *Canada - Marketing Agencies*. In that case, the panel concluded that exclusion of imported beer from points of sale where domestic beer could be sold represented a denial of competitive opportunities for imported beer. While in that case the panel did not consider it necessary to make a finding under Article III:4 on this point, the panel nevertheless "saw great force in the argument that the restrictions on access to points of sale were covered by Article III:4".[238]

452. Korea's retail restrictions cannot be defended on the basis that they are merely the result of there being a legitimate quantitative restriction in place at the border. The quantitative restrictions in Korea's Schedule allow Korea to limit the quantity of imported beef entering its territory. This cannot be interpreted as an entitlement to then restrict the way in which those imports can be sold in the domestic market. Once imported beef is imported under the quota, there must be no less favourable treatment than that accorded like domestic product.

453. Likewise, Korea's arguments that when the quota is filled, there can be no breach of Article III are also invalid. Just because the import quota is filled does not mean that imported beef enjoys equally competitive opportunities in the domestic market. Even when imports are at a competitive disadvantage as a result of trade restrictions, they may still sell. But it is the competitive disadvantage itself that is relevant to the consideration of Article III:4. In accordance with Article III:4, imported beef must be allowed to realise its full competitive potential in the domestic market.[239]

454. In addition to the measures at the retail level, Korea also maintains other measures throughout the distribution chain which treat imported beef less favourably than domestic product, and which are therefore in breach of Article III:4. These include:

(a) restriction of beef sold through the LPMO system primarily to wholesale markets;[240]

---

[238] *Canada - Marketing Agencies*, paras. 5.5-5.6.

[239] In this regard, the panel in *US - Section 337* (para. 5.13) found that treatment no less favourable requires an assessment of the potential impact rather than the actual consequences for competitive opportunities.

[240] See Article 5 of the Management Guideline for Imported Beef (previously Article 3 of the Regulations Concerning Sales of Imported Beef).

(b) controls on the marketing of beef imported through the SBS system, including limitations on the range of consumers eligible to make purchases through the system;[241] and

(c) reporting, record-keeping, and labelling requirements that are imposed in respect of imported beef.[242]

455. None of these restrictions apply to domestic beef. New Zealand considered that such measures limit the competitive opportunities for imported beef to the domestic market. These measures deny exporters of beef to Korea the opportunity to choose their preferred method of marketing, and impose additional compliance costs on imports relative to like domestic product. To this end, the measures subject imported beef to treatment that is less favourable than that given to like domestic product. It follows that these measures also are inconsistent with Article III:4 of GATT 1994. Furthermore, like the retail restrictions, New Zealand also contended that these measures cannot be justified under Article XX(d) of GATT 1994.

456. New Zealand submitted further that under Article 11.1 of the *Management Guideline for Imported Beef* (and formerly under Article 9.1 of the Regulations Concerning Sales of Imported Beef), the LPMO is required to determine a minimum price for imported beef sold at auction. In practice, the minimum price is set with reference to the price of the competing domestic product, and is used by the LPMO as a means of influencing domestic market prices. Rather than being able to compete freely on the basis of its duty paid price at the border, imported beef prices are manipulated by the LPMO using its minimum price-setting powers.

457. Domestic beef is not subject to minimum price controls. Within the constraints of the highly managed Korean domestic market, the price of domestic beef is able to respond to changes in supply levels, consumer demand, prices of other competing protein sources, and so on. Conversely, the price of imported beef sold through LPMO auctions is maintained at a controlled minimum, and

---

241 Article 26.4 of the *Management Guideline for Imported Beef* (formerly Articles 2 and 11 of the *Operational Guidelines for Imported Beef under the SBS System*) restricts access to imported beef under the SBS system to a limited range of defined "end users". "End users" are members of the SBS super-groups specified in Article 20 (formerly Article 4 of the *Operational Guidelines*) . It is, therefore, not possible for purchasers or groups of purchasers who are not "end users" to purchase imported beef through the SBS system. Purchasers of domestic beef do not have to be "end users", nor do they have to be members of super-groups. Article 21 of the *Management Guideline* (Article 11 of the *Operational Guidelines*) also provides that "end users" may only use imported beef for the purposes specified in that provision. The same restrictions do not apply to domestic beef.

242 At the wholesale level, Article 17 of the *Management Guideline for Imported Beef* (and formerly Article 19 of the *Regulations Concerning Sales of Imported Beef*) require wholesale markets, dealers and sales agents to keep records for two years. In the SBS system, monthly reporting and two year record keeping requirements are required by Articles 27.3, 27.4 and 28.1 of the *Management Guideline* (and formerly by Articles 12.3, 13 and 16.1 of the *Operational Guidelines for Imported Beef under the SBS System*). The supervisory powers of Korean MAF and the LPMO have also been used to apply mandatory and restrictive labelling requirements on imported beef.

cannot decrease in response to changes in other market conditions unless the LPMO decides to re-fix a new (lower) minimum price.[243] The minimum price auction system means that imported beef cannot enter the Korean market on the basis of normal commercial considerations. The large build-up of stocks of imported beef in LPMO freezers is indicative of the fact that minimum price controls do inhibit the ability of imported beef to respond to market signals.

458. The minimum price requirement is a law affecting the internal sale or offering for sale of imported beef which accords treatment less favourable to that which is accorded like domestic product, in contravention of Article III:4 of GATT. The inability of imported beef sold through the LPMO to respond to changing market conditions as a result of the operation of the minimum price law means that imported beef does not enjoy "equal conditions of competition"[244] *vis-à-vis* domestic beef. LPMO-imported beef is subjected to a competitive constraint which does not apply to domestic beef.

2. *Article XX of GATT*

459. New Zealand considered further that Korea's retail restrictions cannot be justified as "necessary to secure compliance with laws or regulations [...] relating to [...] the prevention of deceptive practices" in accordance with Article XX(d) of GATT 1994. The burden of proof is on Korea to show that its retail restrictions fall within the scope of Article XX(d).[245] New Zealand contends that Korea has failed to discharge this burden.

460. Notwithstanding that Korea has failed to discharge this burden of proof, New Zealand further contended that it is not possible for Korea to do so. The retail restrictions are not measures that fall within the scope of subparagraph (d) of Article XX. The panel in *EEC - Parts and Components* found that Article XX(d) covers only measures related to the *enforcement* of obligations under laws or regulations consistent with the General Agreement.[246] The regulations relating to separate retail distribution channels do not serve to enforce any Korean laws relating to fair trading or deceptive practices. Even if the retail restrictions are "to secure compliance" with Korea's fair trading laws, they are not "*necessary*" for this purpose. There are a range of alternative measures that would be less trade restrictive than the maintenance of separate retail channels. Measures such as the maintenance of effective audit trails regarding country of origin, more comprehensive monitoring of the activities of beef retailers, and stricter penalty provi-

[243] The price data presented by Australia demonstrates that minimum prices set by the LPMO often remain fixed for long periods of time, despite large movements in demand for beef and price levels of domestic beef.

[244] See *Italian Agricultural Machinery,* paras. 11-13.

[245] The panel in *US - Section 337* (para. 5.27) found that "...it is up to the contracting party seeking to justify measures under Article XX(d) to demonstrate that those measures are 'necessary' within the meaning of that provision."

[246] L/6657, adopted on 16 May 1990, 37S/132, 195-197, paras. 5.14-5.18.

sions in Korea's fair trading laws would all be effective measures that would be considerably less trade restrictive than the retail restrictions.

461. Should Korea's retail restrictions be found to fall within the scope of subparagraph (d) of Article XX, contrary to New Zealand's assertion, then New Zealand contends that in any case, the measures do not comply with the chapeau of Article XX. The retail restrictions are applied in a manner which constitutes a means of arbitrary or unjustifiable discrimination between countries where the same conditions prevail, or a disguised restriction on international trade.[247] Korea seeks to rely on Article XX in order to "frustrate or defeat" its legal obligations under the substantive rules of the GATT.[248] Such reliance is therefore unjustified.

3. *Article II of GATT*

462. Through its import tendering system, the LPMO maintains an artificial distinction between grain-fed and grass-fed beef. In calling for tenders under the import quota set out in Korea's Schedule of Concessions, the LPMO specifies either grain-fed or grass-fed beef. It has called recently for tenders of grain-fed beef only. This practice effectively divides the import quota into two subcategories, and discriminates against New Zealand, an exporter of grass-fed beef,[249] *vis-à-vis* other exporters who produce primarily grain-fed beef. There is no justification for the maintenance of such a distinction.

463. New Zealand contended that the division of Korea's import quota for beef into two sub-categories, and the resulting discrimination against exporters of grass-fed beef in filling the quota represents "treatment less favourable" than that provided for in Korea's Schedule of Concessions, and thus contravenes Article II:1(a) of GATT 1994. Korea's Schedule contains no "other terms or conditions" that allow it to distinguish between grain-fed and grass-fed beef. The maintenance of this distinction has led Korea to administer its concession for beef in a way which grants the benefit of that concession to the products of one group of countries (grain-fed beef exporters), at the expense of others (grass-fed beef exporters, including New Zealand). This has had the effect of preventing access of high quality grass-fed beef from New Zealand to the Korean market under the quota. This restriction also inhibits New Zealand's ability to develop the market for its grass-fed beef in Korea.

---

247 Appellate Body Report in *US – Shrimp, supra*, footnote 38, paras. 146 *et seq* refer in respect of any examination of the chapeau of Article XX.

248 See Appellate Body Report, *United States – Gasoline, supra*, footnote 117, at 22.

249 New Zealand is an exporter of predominantly grass-fed beef. Only 2 per cent of New Zealand beef exports are grain-fed, and this product is supplied exclusively to niche markets in Japan.

4. *Article XVII of GATT*

464. New Zealand also contended that the LPMO, a state trading enterprise notified to the WTO as such by Korea, has not acted in a manner consistent with the general principles of non-discriminatory treatment prescribed in GATT 1994. Korea has accordingly contravened Article XVII:1(a) of that Agreement.

465. By distinguishing between grass-fed and grain-fed beef in the tendering for imported beef under the quota, the LPMO has made purchases that are not solely in accordance with commercial considerations. The LPMO has favoured some supplier countries over others on the basis of a distinction between beef production methods which is not related to commercial considerations. Such practices are accordingly discriminatory treatment which is not based on commercial considerations, and is a contravention of Article XVII:1(a).

5. *Agreement on Agriculture - Domestic Support*

466. New Zealand submitted that the Korean Government significantly increased the amount of domestic support it provided to its beef producers in 1997 and 1998. While Korea notified increased levels of support for beef to the WTO Committee on Agriculture, the notifications did not account for all the support provided and the calculations were not in conformity with the methodology set out in the Agreement on Agriculture. As a result, Korea incorrectly excluded beef from the calculation of its Current Total Aggregate Measurements of Support (AMS) in 1997 and 1998. Had it included beef support in the Current Total AMS, Korea would have exceeded the annual reduction commitment set out in its Schedule for 1997.

467. New Zealand was especially concerned over the incorrect calculation of *market price support* for beef by Korea through the use of incorrect *eligible production* levels. In the same market price support calculation, New Zealand was also concerned over the use of a *fixed external reference price* which differs in terms of its stage of processing from that of the *applied administered price*.

(i) The Fixed External Reference Price for Beef

468. According to paragraph 8 of Annex 3 of the Agreement on Agriculture, the calculation of market price support involves the subtraction of a fixed external reference price from an applied administered price with the result multiplied by eligible production (minus associated fees or levies). Korea's applied administered price for beef was, as set out in the Korean MAF press statement of 27 January 1997, 2,400 thousand won per 500 kg. Hanwoo steer for the remainder of the 1997 calendar year.

469. It appears, as stated by Korea, that "the said programme was implemented not only for the Hanwoo but also for [dairy] cattle and hybrid cattle of Cheju

Island and an amount different from that for Hanwoo beef was applied as well ...". As a result, Korea has apparently used a weighted average applied administered price encompassing the different categories.[250] In doing so, Korea has also converted the base unit for the calculations from a *per head* basis to a *per kilogram carcass weight basis*. While there is a change in measurement unit, it does not affect the stage of processing of the applied administered price. That stage of processing represents live animals for the bulk of the programme.[251] This is consistent with paragraph 7 of Annex 3 of the *Agreement on Agriculture* which specifies that the "AMS shall be calculated as close as practicable to the point of first sale of the basic agricultural product concerned". However, the fixed external reference price Korea has used is not specified at an equivalent stage of processing.

470. Article 1(a)(ii) of the *Agreement on Agriculture* is applicable when a Current AMS is being calculated, i.e. an AMS for any year during the implementation of the *Agreement on Agriculture* and thereafter. It provides that the AMS means "with respect to support provided during any year of the implementation period and thereafter, [support] calculated in accordance with the provisions of Annex 3 of this Agreement and taking into account the constituent data and methodology used in the tables of supporting material incorporated by reference in Part IV of the Member's Schedule".

471. However, in the case of Korean beef, as there was no applied administered price used to support beef in the Uruguay Round base period, no market price support calculation was undertaken and consequently no fixed external reference price for beef is included in G/AGST/KOR which is then to be taken account of. Annex 3 of the *Agreement on Agriculture* must, therefore, be used to determine how the fixed external reference price is derived. Paragraph 9 of Annex 3 provides: "The fixed external reference price shall be based on the years 1986 to 1988 and shall generally be the average f.o.b. unit value for the basic agricultural product concerned in a net exporting country and the average c.i.f. unit value for the basic agricultural product concerned in a net importing country in the base period. The fixed reference price may be adjusted for quality differences as necessary."

472. Korea is a net beef importing Member thus the c.i.f. unit value represents the correct starting point. New Zealand submits that the reference to "the average c.i.f. unit value *for the basic agricultural product concerned* ..." (emphasis added) requires that the applied administered price and the fixed external reference price must both be for the "basic agricultural product". This is reinforced by Annex 3 paragraph 7, which provides that the AMS "shall be calculated as close

250 While a weighted average is a logical approach for aggregating a number of different beef categories, New Zealand contends that the weighting should have been calculated on the basis of eligible production rather than actual purchases for the reasons discussed below.

251 Purchases designated "carcass" accounted for only 10 per cent of total purchases in 1997 and 1998 according Korea.

as practicable to the point of first sale of the basic agricultural product concerned". Since the AMS is calculated by reference to the applied administered price and the fixed external reference price, both of these calculations must be at the same stage of processing. In other words, the fixed external reference price must be at (or converted to) the same stage in the processing chain as the applied administered price for the basic agricultural product concerned – in this case live animals. As live cattle destined for consumption as meat (as opposed to breeding) are not widely traded, New Zealand contends that the correct approach in this instance would have been for Korea to convert its fixed external reference price to the point of first sale – the level of its applied administered price. Korea failed to do so and has thus over-estimated the fixed external reference price for beef.

473. The principle of comparing like with like is also made clear in the context of Annex 3 by the WTO Secretariat's technical note for acceding countries which states with reference to the calculation of market price support: "This price [an external reference price, e.g. an estimate of the world price such as the c.i.f. price or f.o.b. price] should be adjusted to a similar stage of processing as the administered price".[252] In the sense that there is no "constituent data and methodology"[253] provided by Korea on beef in its AGST tables, the Secretariat's advice on Annex 3 for acceding countries is particularly relevant in this case.

474. In its calculations, Korea is effectively comparing live animals in carcass weight equivalents (the administered price), with meat (the external reference price). In terms of the Harmonised System, this is comparing products in 0102 (live bovine animals) with 0201-0202 (meat of bovine animals, fresh, chilled or frozen).

475. In order to have a rational calculation of the effect of Korea's beef price support, the fixed external reference price must be converted to the same stage in the processing chain[254] as the applied administered price. C.i.f. unit values are generally considered to correspond most closely to domestically produced products at the wholesale level and much of the difference between wholesale and the point of first sale (farm gate) prices represents processing costs. In the case of beef, this indicates that slaughtering costs should be deducted from the c.i.f. unit value in order to reflect the same stage of processing as Korea's applied administered price which is measured in carcass weight equivalents of live animals.

476. New Zealand has calculated the external reference price at the appropriate stage of processing based on Korean slaughtering costs from information from

[252] Accession to the World Trade Organization: Information to be Provided on Domestic Support and Export Subsidies in Agriculture: Technical Note by the Secretariat, WT/ACC/4, para. 15.

[253] As provided in Article 1(a)(ii) of the *Agreement on Agriculture*.

[254] The different stages of processing of some agricultural products represent only a minor change in some cases, but for many livestock products such as beef, the products are very different - live animals versus a slaughtered, processed and often further prepared product.

the Korean MAF.[255] The fixed external reference price thus calculated is 1,514 won per kilogram carcass weight.

(ii) The Eligible Production of Beef

477. New Zealand submitted further that Korea has also used an incorrect figure for the quantity of *eligible production* in its calculation of market price support. Market price support can exist through a variety of means, but in all cases it results in transfers from consumers to producers which provide support to those producers. Often state purchases will be used in order to maintain the government-set prices of products, effectively ensuring the transfers from consumers to producers. But the *actual* quantity of purchases is not relevant in the calculation of market price support. The language of Annex 3 makes it clear that it is the quantity of production which is *eligible* to receive the applied administered price which is relevant.

478. In situations where governments only enter the market as "buyers of last resort", i.e. in order to take "excess" product off the market to ensure farmers receive the price set by governments, government purchases may be minimal or even zero. But agricultural producers are "eligible" to receive the government-set

[255] As the price support measure (applied administered price) was specified at the point of first sale on the basis of carcass weight equivalents of live animals, the fixed external reference price should have been converted to the same basis. This can be achieved by deducting those costs necessary to transform beef from the live animal to a carcass, i.e. the slaughtering costs.

Table 1 - Fixed external reference price for beef at point of first sale

Item	Description	Years	Value (won/kg)
(a)	c.i.f. unit values	1989	1,784
		1990	1,828
		1991	1,858
		Average	1,823
(b)	Slaughtering costs	1989	287
		1990	305
		1991	337
		Average	310
(c)	c.i.f. at point of first sale equivalent	1989	1,497
		1990	1,523
		1991	1,521
		Average	1,514

Source:
(a) Answers by Korea in the Committee on Agriculture, G/AG/R/13, page 37.
(b) Korea MAF as reported by OECD in "Electronic Data Product on Producer and Consumer Subsidy Equivalent (PSE/CSE)", Statistics on Diskette, (revised annually), Table 2.7, referred to in OECD, Agricultural Policies in OECD Countries: Monitoring and Evaluation.
(c) The figures in (c) are those in (a) less those in (b), in other words c.i.f. unit values less slaughtering costs. (Slaughtering costs appear to have been estimated as representing a consistent 4.6 per cent of the Korean wholesale price for beef in each year).

price for *all* of their production because, in order to secure supplies, consumers must be prepared to match or better the government-set price.

479. The ordinary meaning of "eligible" is also at odds with Korea's use of actual purchases of beef. The meaning of eligible is "fit, suitable or qualified". It is not related to the more restricted amount implied by *actual* purchases. This is also confirmed by material produced by the GATT Secretariat during the Uruguay Round in order to assist in the preparation of Uruguay Round participants' initial lists of specific binding commitments.[256] These initial lists eventually became the basis for Korea's (and others') domestic support reduction commitments. In that note, the Secretariat clarified that: "For an open-ended intervention or buy-in scheme, this [eligible production] may be total production. If the scope of the measure is limited to a particular quantity, it is this limited quantity that should be used".[257] There is no reference in the explanatory note to the *actual* quantity bought-in – in fact, unless a measure was limited to a particular quantity, it is clear the presumption was that eligible production would equal total production. The note did not "interpret" the text, but gave "further clarification where possible."[258]

480. In the case of Korea's beef support, the measure was apparently limited to a particular quantity. In 1997, for example, that quantity was 500 head per day of Hanwoo cattle above 500 kg. within the 27 January to 31 December 1997 period (340 days). A total of 170,000 head of Hanwoo cattle were thus eligible in the 1997 calendar year as used by Korea for its domestic support commitments. In carcass weight terms, this amounts to 52,615 tonnes for Hanwoo cattle alone.[259] But, as stated by Korea "the said programme was implemented not only for the Hanwoo but also for [dairy] cattle and hybrid cattle of Cheju Island ... as well ."

481. The fact that Korea notified a total figure of 35,127 tonnes in 1997 is clear evidence that eligible production, and thus market price support, has been underestimated. Indeed, given that the purchase programme covered such a wide category of beef cattle, there would be justification in assuming that, in fact, eligible production should equal total beef production. Consumers had to compete with the government-set price to buy stock – this is what resulted in a transfer from consumers to producers rather than the actual purchases made by the government

---

256 "Explanatory notes on the formats for the establishment of lists of specific binding commitments under the agriculture reform programme", Informal technical note by the [GATT] Secretariat, 27 January, 1992. While the note was prepared in relation to the "Draft Final Act Embodying the Results of the Uruguay Round" (MTN.TNC/W/FA), the language concerning the calculation of market price support is identical in that document and the Agreement on Agriculture.

257 *Ibid*, page 21.

258 *Ibid*, para. 2. It went on to say "It does not constitute a basis for evaluating or assessing specific binding commitments by any participants".

259 170,000 head at 500 kg.(0.5 tonne) per head multiplied by the conversion coefficient of 61.9 per cent, i.e. ((170,000*0.5)*.619) = 52,625 tonnes carcass weight equivalent. The conversion coefficient is the one used by Korea.

– and this affected all production. Total beef production in 1997 was around 237,000 tonnes.[260]

482. For 1998, the situation was more complex. There were several changes in the cattle purchase programme. Nevertheless, New Zealand has attempted to estimate the 1998 eligible production level for Hanwoo beef (only) on the basis of information provided in Korean press releases.[261] The resultant figure is 35,328

260 [Korean] MAF, Statistical Yearbook of Agriculture and Forestry (1998) and MAI (1998) as reported in the MAF web site http://152.99.166.2/english/maf_03_12.html.

261 Korea generally specified its price support programme in terms of a maximum number of Hanwoo animals which would be eligible for purchase each day - sometimes in particular weight ranges. By calculating the number of days each of the variations applied to, it is possible to estimate the total number of Hanwoo animals eligible for purchase and the carcass weight equivalent of those animals. The following tables present this information. The quantities of dairy and hybrid cattle of Cheju Island are not included below because detailed information is not available.

Table 2 - Eligible production for Hanwoo Beef in 1997

Period	Duration (days)	Head per day	Eligible Production (Total Head)	Carcass weight equivalent (tonnes)
25.1.97-31.12.97	340	500	170,000	56,615

Table 3 - Eligible production for Hanwoo Beef in 1998

Period	Duration (days)	Head per day/ (weight kg.)	Eligible Production (Total Head)	Carcass weight equivalent (tonnes)
1.1.98-15.6.98	167	500 (500 kg.)	83,500	25,843
16.6.98-7.7.98	21	340 (500 kg.)	7,140	2,210
	21	160 (399 kg.)	3,360	786
8.7.98-15.7.98	7	340 (500 kg.)	2,380	737
	7	160 (399 kg.)	1,120	262
16.7.98-18.7.98	4	340 (500 kg.)	1,360	421
	4	160 (399 kg)	640	150
19.7.98-26.7.98	7	160 (399 kg)	1,120	262
27.7.98-31.12.98	35	350 (399 kg)	12,250	2,864
	35	250 (350 kg)	8,750	1,795
Total	241		121,620	35,328

Source:

Information provided in various Korea MAF press statements. Carcass weight equivalents reflect the weight of the animal category (top end of the range where a range was given) multiplied by eligible production and the relevant carcass/live-weight ratios. The ratios were 61.9 per cent in 1997 and, in 1998, 61.9 per cent for 500 kg. steers and 58.6 per cent for other (medium) steers.

tonnes for Hanwoo beef alone. New Zealand's calculation comes out marginally lower than the total beef figure of 35,899 tonnes given by Korea for 1998. This simply reflects an under-estimation resulting from a lack of data on the eligible number of dairy steers and hybrid cows.

(iii) The AMS Calculation for Beef

483. On the basis of the adjusted fixed external reference price determined by New Zealand and New Zealand's improved calculation of eligible production levels (but for Hanwoo beef alone), the following table recalculates Korea's beef AMS for 1997 and 1998. The product-specific AMS are then compared to the values of production supplied by Korea for 1997 and 1998:

Table 4 - Calculation of the product-specific AMS for Hanwoo beef and *de minimis* calculation

Year	AAP	FERP	EP	MPS	OS	Total AMS	VP	*Percentage*
	won/kg.		tonnes	billion won				%
1997	7,351.1	1,514	52,615	307.1	1.09	308.2	2,107	14.6
1998	6,883.2	1,514	35,328	189.7	1.40	191.1	1,836	10.4

Key:
AAP - Applied administered price – Source: Notifications of Korea
FERP - Fixed external reference price - from Table 1
EP - Eligible production - from Tables 3 and 3
MPS - Market price support – Source: ((AAP-FERP)*EP)
OS - Other support – Source: Notifications of Korea
VP - Value of production – supplied by Korea

484. By simply adding the *actual* purchases of dairy cattle and hybrid cattle of Cheju Island[262] to the eligible Hanwoo production as set out in the previous table, the proportion of the total value of beef production accounted for by the beef product-specific AMS increases to 15.8 per cent and 11.7 per cent in 1997 and 1998 respectively. Of course, including the *eligible* production of dairy cattle and hybrid cattle of Cheju Island would result in even higher figures. Given the nature of the scheme, eligible production could even be argued to be total beef production.[263] Despite the under-estimation resulting from data deficiencies concerning dairy steers and hybrid cows, therefore, Korea's product-specific beef AMS significantly surpassed the 10 per cent *de minimis* level in both years. Thus the

[262] Non-Hanwoo purchases amounted to 4,083 tonnes in 1997 and 4,454 tonnes in 1998.

[263] According to [Korean] MAF, Statistical Yearbook of Agriculture and Forestry (1998) and MAI (1998) as reported in the MAF website http://152.99.166.2/english/maf_03_12.html, total Korean beef production (Hanwoo plus other) was 237,000 tonnes in 1997. The use of total production as eligible production yields a Total beef AMS of around 1,300 billion won in that year.

product-specific AMS for beef should have been included in the calculation of Korea's Current Total AMS in both years. With no other changes to Korea's notified Current Total AMS, the correct Totals should therefore be as follows:[264]

Table 5 - Adjusted Current Total AMS for Korea 1997 and 1998

Year	Current Total AMS as notified by Korea (billion won)	Product Specific AMS for Beef (billion won)	Correct Current Total AMS (billion won)
1997	1,936.95	308.2	2,245.2
1998	1,562.77	191.1	1,753.9

485. In 1997, the correct Current Total AMS for Korea as calculated by New Zealand exceeds the annual commitment level as notified by Korea of 2,028.65 billion won contrary to Article 3.2 of the Agreement on Agriculture. In 1998, the correct Current Total AMS (but including only Hanwoo beef instead of total eligible beef) falls below the notified commitment level of 1,951.70 billion won. New Zealand does not have information at its disposal to assess whether, if *all* eligible beef production was included, the Current Total AMS would have been surpassed. Nevertheless, Korea still failed in 1998 to include beef in its Current Total AMS contrary to Article 7.2(a) of the *Agreement on Agriculture*.[265]

6. *Conclusion*

486. For the reasons cited above, New Zealand requested the Panel to find that:

(a) the restrictions imposed by Korea on the sale and distribution of imported beef constitute a violation of Article III:4 of GATT 1994;

(b) the tendering process adopted by the LPMO for the import of beef results in treatment less favourable than that provided for in Korea's Schedule of Concessions, in breach of Article II:1(a) of GATT 1994, and constitutes conduct by the LPMO that is in breach of the non-discriminatory treatment requirement in Article XVII:1(a) of GATT 1994; and

(c) the maintenance by the LPMO of minimum auction prices accords to imported beef treatment less favourable than that accorded to domestic beef, in contravention of Article III:4 of GATT 1994.

---

264 As noted above, this still under-estimates the product-specific AMS for beef because of the under-estimation of eligible production.

265 Article 7.2(a) provides: "Any domestic support measure in favour of agricultural producers, including any modification to such measure, and any measure that is subsequently introduced that cannot be shown to satisfy the criteria in Annex 2 to this Agreement or to be exempt from reduction by reason of any other provision of this Agreement shall be included in the Member's calculation of its Current Total AMS".

487. Concerning domestic support, New Zealand submitted that, through incorrectly applying Annex 3 of the *Agreement on Agriculture* in calculating product-specific support for beef producers, Korea has erroneously excluded support to beef producers from the calculation of its Current Total AMS in 1997 and 1998 in violation of Article 7 of the *Agreement on Agriculture*. Had Korea correctly included support for beef producers in its Current Total AMS in 1997, the commitment level specified in Section I of Part IV of its Schedule would have been exceeded, thus Korea was also in violation of Article 3.2 of the *Agreement on Agriculture* in that year. New Zealand requested that the Panel recommend to the DSB that Korea bring these measures into conformity with the provisions of GATT 1994 and the *Agreement on Agriculture*.

VI. INTERIM REVIEW[266]

488. On 24 May 2000, the United States and Korea requested the Panel to review sections of the Interim Panel Report which had been issued to the parties on 10 May 2000. None of the parties requested an additional meeting with the Panel. Invoking WTO panel practice, the parties reserved the right to respond to other parties' comments on the Interim Panel Report. On 24 May the Panel invited the three parties, should they so wish, to respond to each others' comments by 12 noon on Tuesday, 30 May 2000. On 30 May the three parties sent responses to each others' comments.

489. It is mainly Korea that has submitted review comments on various aspects of the interim report including those relating to the legal tests under Article III:4 of GATT, the consequence of Korea's legal beef import quota on the Article III:4 claims, the Panel's refusal to consider that the dual retail system is a measure necessary to secure compliance with Korea's *Unfair Competition Act*, the Panel assessment of the LPMO's practices between the end of October 1998 and the end of May 1999, the Panel's considerations of the Complaining parties claims pursuant to Articles 3,4,6 and 7 of the Agreement on Agriculture and the Panel's use of the provisions of Annex 3 as well as the Panel's consideration that its first duty, in light of the Complaining parties claim that Korea exceeded its scheduled commitments with respect to domestic support, was to identify such commitments in Korea's Schedule. The United States requested the Panel mainly to review some of its legal analysis under Article XX(d).

490. In addition, Korea pointed the Panel to factual errors in the data used by the Panel and initially provided by the United States. Since all parties agree on these mistakes and since the correction of these errors does not affect the reasoning developed in the panel report, the Panel has decided to revise such data ac-

[266] Pursuant to Article 15.3 of the DSU, the findings of the panel report shall include a discussion of the arguments made at the interim review stage. Consequently the following section entitled Interim Review is part of the Findings of this Panel report.

cordingly. Parties have also pointed to some linguistic and typographical mistakes which the Panel has taken into account when revising its findings.

491. On a few occasions, Korea claimed that in its findings, the Panel did not fully reflect Korea's arguments or refused to take them into account. The Panel would like to insist that it has always taken into account all Korea's arguments but the Panel has summarized only those arguments which it considered particularly relevant to its legal analysis. The Panel recalls that Korea was given ample opportunity to comment on the descriptive part of this Panel report. To ensure full transparency and due process, the Panel agrees to revise the descriptive part of its report with a view to reassuring Korea that all its arguments are fully reflected in the Panel report.

492. The Panel would like to add the following comments on the parties' review requests and responses: Korea argues that the Panel is inconsistent in its findings that there is no "trade effect" test required to prove a violation of Article III:4 of GATT. The Panel would like to reiterate that the GATT/WTO jurisprudence has clearly established that when establishing a violation of Article III:4, the Complaining parties do not need to demonstrate any actual or future specific trade effects caused by the measure challenged. This does not limit the obligation for the Panel to discuss whether the said measure is treating imported products less favourably than domestic products. This is why the Panel's discussion is focussed rather on the main features of the dual retail system and the "architecture"[267] of the measure challenged rather than the factual or economic context of the Korean market, including the effect of its beef import quota, its financial crisis or the health scares.

493. Korea submits that the Panel did not properly reflect its arguments with regard to the fact that it had filled its import quota. The Panel has revised its findings to use the very wording of Korea. The Panel would like to reiterate three points. First, the Panel considers that Korea was under ***no obligation*** to import any amount of beef but rather, pursuant to its annual import quota, Korea had a right to limit importation to the level of its scheduled quota. Second, the Panel considers that in 1997 and 1998 imports of beef into Korea were below its quota limits. Third, the existence of such scheduled beef import quota does not affect the legal assessment of the WTO compatibility of Korea's dual retail system for beef. It is always for the Complaining parties to bear the burden of proof that Korea's dual retail system, in segregating imported and domestic beef, is violating the WTO national treatment obligation. There was no need to further address the actual trade effects of such dual retail system or whether the low level of imported beef was rather the consequence of the import quota or the financial crisis or the health scares. There was no need to examine whether there was a correla-

[267] See for instance in the context of an Article III:2 analysis, *Japan – Alcoholic Beverages*, *supra*, footnote 98, at 120: "Although it is true that the aim of a measure may not be easily ascertained, nevertheless its protective application can most often be discerned from the design, the *architecture*, and the revealing structure of a measure" (emphasis added).

tion between the level of imported beef and the dual retail system since the level of imports and the actual commercial impact of the dual retail system need not be demonstrated in an Article III:4 analysis. As such, the dual retail system is inconsistent with Article III:4 of GATT and the existence of Korea's import quota does not alter the normal GATT evidentiary rules or those relating to the burden of proof. Finally, the Panel did not conclude that the number of imported beef stores was in any manner "the reliable indicator of the effect of the dual retail system on imported beef" as the Panel was, and still is, of the view that it was under no obligation to assess the trade effects of the dual retail system.

494. Korea claims that it never agreed that its dual retail system "affects" trade since Korea is of the view that its dual retail system is not discriminatory. Korea is misquoting the Panel findings and confusing two concepts, i.e. (1) whether the measure at issue is an internal regulation – a regulation or a requirement affecting the internal sale, offering for sale, purchase or distribution of imported and/or domestic products – and (2) whether such internal regulation is discriminatory against imported products. Clearly, the dual retail system for beef affects the sale, offering for sale and distribution of beef in the Korean market. In addition, and in a separate analysis, the Panel reached the conclusion that such dual retail system was indeed discriminatory by treating imported beef less favourably than domestic beef.

495. Korea submits that it does not understand the Panel's discussion on national treatment in paragraphs 611 to 614 of the Interim Panel report. The Panel would like to reiterate that the object of the national treatment obligation is to ensure that imported products are not treated less favourably than domestic products. In this sense, Article III:4 is not concerned with the treatment (or mistreatment) that WTO Members may impose on their domestic products but rather whether, through the application of an internal mandatory regulation, imported products are treated less favourably than domestic products. In this context the Panel is of the view that segregation of imported products in the Korean domestic market is inherently less favourable to imported products which are excluded from the normal domestic distribution system, limiting thereby consumers choices as further developed in the Panel's findings. This conclusion is independent from the effect of the Korea's beef import quota which also reduces the availability of imported beef. Again, the Panel reiterates that when assessing the compatibility of the dual retail system with the national treatment obligation of Article III:4 of GATT, the Panel is under no obligation to assess the actual trade effects of the quota on the availability of imported beef or the trade effects of the dual retail system. In such a determination, the Panel is not required to examine any specific data and is authorized to discuss the potential consequences of such a system on the imported products relying on hypothetical situations[268], always

[268] See for instance what was done by the panel in *Canada – Certain Measures Concerning Periodicals* ("*Canada – Periodicals*"), WT/DS31/R and Corr. 1, adopted 30 July 1997, DSR 1997:I, 481, paras. 522-524 and Appellate Body Report, *Canada – Certain Measures Concerning Periodi-*

with a view to better understand the functioning of the Korean dual retail system and the less favourable treatment to imported products caused by the segregation of imported products into the Korean domestic market. Finally, basic economic principles suggest that the segregation of imported products into the Korean market is certainly one of the factors that facilitate the maintenance of the price differential between imported and domestic beef. In any case, with a view to ensuring clarity, the Panel has slightly revised the wording of its findings accordingly.

496. Korea submits that, in its discussion on the applicability of Article XX(d), the Panel did not reflect fully Korea's arguments relating to the "primitive" state of Korea's beef retail stores which would make it difficult for Korea to effectively prosecute the perpetrators of fraud. The United States argues that the dual retail system and the Korean *Unfair Competition Act* had been found only to share similar objectives and that the Panel should have concluded that the Korean dual retail system was not adopted to secure compliance with the *Unfair Competition Act*, pursuant to Article XX(d) of GATT. The Panel is of the view that although not necessary, and disproportionate, the Korean dual retail system does more than simply share the same objectives as the *Unfair Competition Act*, to the extent that it reduces the opportunities and thus the temptations for butchers to misrepresent foreign beef for domestic beef. In this sense, the dual retail system ensures compliance with the prohibition against misrepresentation as to the origin of beef pursuant to the *Unfair Competition Act*. With a view to ensuring clarity, the Panel has slightly revised the wording of its findings accordingly.

497. With reference to the Panel's discussion that no dual retail system is in place in other sectors of the Korean economy, Korea has pointed to factual errors as to the level of imported beef in 1990 and the proportion between dairy cow meat and imported beef during the same period. The United States admits the errors. Under the circumstances (in light of the agreement of all parties) the wording the findings has been slightly revised accordingly.

498. Korea also submits that the Panel does not understand the background material it provided or misrepresents the fact when the Panel states that the December 1989 report for the National Assembly can be used to substantiate that there are alternatives available to Korea to combat fraud. Korea adds that this 1989 report was submitted in the process of a one-time, special investigation of fraudulent practices. Korea submits that its main argument relates to the cost of continuous policing. The Complaining parties agree with the findings and note Korea's admission that it has the capacity to investigate fraud. First, the Panel would like to insist that it had clearly understood that the December 1989 report was the result of a special investigation. Korea had thus demonstrated that it has

---

cals ("*Canada – Periodicals*"), WT/DS31/AB/R, adopted 30 July 1997, DSR 1997:I, 449, at 466. See also the Panel Report on *Indonesia – Certain Measures Affecting the Automobile Industry* ("*Indonesia – Autos*"), WT/DS54/R and Corr. 1,2,3,4, WT/DS55/R and Corr. 1,2,3,4, WT/DS59/R and Corr. 1,2,3,4, WT/DS64/R and Corr. 1,2,3,4, adopted 23 July 1998, DSR 1998:VI, 2201, para.14.113.

the capacity to investigate. As to the related costs, the Panel has addressed this matter separately and concluded that compliance with the WTO Agreement may sometimes require demanding and even costly adjustments, as the WTO Agreement is a bargain. As stated by the Appellate Body in its report on *Japan – Alcoholic Beverages*:

> "The *WTO Agreement* is a treaty -- the international equivalent of a contract. It is self-evident that in an exercise of their sovereignty, and in pursuit of their own respective national interests, the Members of the WTO have made a ***bargain***. In exchange for the benefits they expect to derive as Members of the WTO, they have agreed to exercise their sovereignty according to the commitments they have made in the *WTO Agreement*."[269] (Emphasis added.)

The Panel has deleted what was paragraph 654 of the Interim Panel report.

499. With reference to the Panel's discussion on the LPMO's tender practice to make a distinction between grass-fed and grain-fed imported beef, Korea submits that the Panel seems to imply that the fact that the LPMO failed to purchase grass-fed beef on one or two occasions would constitute an import restriction. The Panel would like to reiterate that WTO Members are not obliged to import any amount of foreign products, but they are prohibited, as a general principle, from interfering with any import-export flows and from imposing any discriminatory distinctions between like imports. To the extent that Korea imposes import conditions, not otherwise contained in its Schedule, such import conditions do necessarily constitute import restrictions for grass-fed beef contrary to Articles XI and II of GATT. The LPMO, a state-trading enterprise, was under no obligation to import grass-fed beef, but it is prohibited from making any discrimination against grass-fed beef. To the extent that such grass-fed/grain-fed distinction was never negotiated as a condition to its Schedule, Korea, through its state-trading enterprise, is prohibited from introducing such discrimination. WTO Members cannot avoid their tariff and other scheduled obligations through the use of a state-trading enterprise.

500. With reference to the fact that the LPMO did not call for tenders and did not discharge its beef imports between the end of October 1998 and the end of May 1999, Korea submits that the Panel should have taken into account the fact that if it would not have been commercially reasonable for Korea to discharge its stocks at a time when replacement purchases would have needed to be made at very high prices, owing to the currency devaluation. The Panel would like to insist that during that same period the level of beef stocks was very high and not commercially reasonable. There was therefore no need for Korea to "replace" all such stocks. Moreover, in not inviting tenders, the LPMO had no way of knowing whether imported beef was available at prices that would permit the LPMO to import without incurring any financial losses. In not inviting tenders the LPMO

---

[269] See the Appellate Body Report in *Japan – Alcoholic Beverages, supra*, footnote 98, at 108.

effectively closed the Korean market to imported beef to the extent of LPMO's allocated quota share. Korea also claims that the Panel ignored the fact that there were health scares during the same period. The Panel would like to add that Korea did not offer any evidence, other than newspapers clippings, that the cited health scares had any impact on import levels during the relevant period or that they affected the prices of imports or the prices Korean consumers were willing to pay for imported beef.[270] With a view to ensure clarity the Panel has slightly revised the wording of its findings accordingly.

501. Concerning the claims relating to Korea's domestic support to its beef industry, Korea submits that the Panel misrepresented Korea's argument that it was suffering prejudice from the fact that the Complaining parties had not listed Annex 3 in their request for establishment of a panel, although they referred to Annex 3 in their submissions and arguments. The Panel would like to add that although Korea did submit generally that it could not adequately prepare its defense, the precise point made by the Panel is that Korea never claimed nor argued that it had ever been uncertain about the nature of the Complaining parties' claims regarding Korea's domestic support obligations. In fact, Korea in its first submission submitted detailed explanations on how it had calculated its aggregate measurement of support for beef. In addition the Panel recalls that in the recent report on *US - FISC* the Appellate Body insisted that "good faith"[271] was a necessary component of any challenge of a panel's terms of reference. This implies that a party's claim that it has misunderstood a request for consultation or a request for a panel should be raised as soon as possible. In the present dispute, Korea alluded to this point only in its rebuttals and made a formal request one day before the second meeting of the Panel with the parties. With a view to ensuring clarity, the Panel has slightly revised its findings accordingly.

502. Moreover, the Panel would like to reiterate that it considers that a claim that the level of aggregate measurement of support was greater than that provided for in Korea's Schedule necessitates a calculation of the current support using the methodology prescribed in the *Agreement on Agriculture*. Annex 3 contains one of those methodologies which is applicable in the present dispute for the reasons set out in Section I hereafter.

503. Korea submits that the Panel should not have decided which of the two columns of figures set out in its Schedule constituted Korea's committed levels of domestic support. Korea even claims that none of the Complaining parties have

---

270 The Panel cannot see any link with an alleged health scare of September 1997 or June 1999 and the period of the end of October 1998 and the end of May 1999.

271 See the Appellate Body Report, *United States – Tax treatment for "Foreign Sales Corporations"* ("*US – FSC*"), WT/DS108/AB/R, adopted 20 March 2000, DSR 2000:III, 1619, para.166: "The same principle of good faith [Article 3.10] requires that responding Members seasonably and promptly bring claimed procedural deficiencies to the attention of the complaining Member, and to the DSB or the Panel, so that corrections, if needed, can be made to resolve disputes. The procedural rules of WTO dispute settlement are designed to promote, not the development of litigation techniques, but simply the fair, prompt and effective resolution of trade disputes."

argued the relevance of the unbracketted numbers. The Panel would like to insist that the United States, throughout its submissions, has always referred to the unbracketted column, as containing the proper list of commitment levels. But more importantly, the Panel considers that it was obliged to determine first which were Korea's scheduled commitments in order to comply with its mandate to determine whether Korea exceeded such commitments. The Complaining parties have claimed that Korea violated Article 3 of the *Agreement on Agriculture* which states that a Member shall not provide domestic support in excess of the commitment levels contained in its Schedule. Therefore, the first obligation of this Panel was to identify which were the commitment levels contained in Korea's Schedule. Since Korea's Schedule contained two columns, only one of them was to be identified as the right one. Korea's reference to footnote 1 of its Schedule only explains the different base year used for each column Korea's statement to the *Committee on Agriculture* mentioned in footnote 410 of the Interim Panel Report (footnote 428 of this Panel report) does not help Korea: statements to the *Committee on Agriculture* do not "legalize" measures otherwise incompatible with the WTO. Moreover, the document entitled "Notification Requirements and Formats" provides clearly that the "Information submitted under these formats is without prejudice to the consistency of the arrangements notified with the relevant provisions of the WTO".[272]

504. On this matter, the Panel would like to insist that it is not expanding its terms of reference; it is only complying with its mandate. Korea submits that the Panel is inconsistent when it decided not to examine the Base Total AMS itself or the related data and methods of calculation used by Korea. The Panel indeed refused to re-open the calculation of Korea's scheduled commitments. The Panel has not examined how Korea arrived at those two sets of numbers. However, the Panel was under the obligation to identify which was Korea's set of commitment levels in order to determine whether Korea has exceeded them. The Panel decided that the unbracketted set of numbers was the only set of commitment levels that bore any relation to the initial Base Total AMS.

505. Korea also submits that it should be allowed to follow the commitment levels contained in its bracketted column because the commitment level for year 2004 is the same for both sets of numbers. The Panel would like to reiterate that where the drafters of the *Agreement on Agriculture* intended to allow for flexibility in the amount of an annual reduction commitment, they made specific provision for it, such as in Article 9.2(b) relating to export subsidy commitments. No similar provision exists in respect of domestic support.

506. Finally, the Panel would also like to stress that, of course, it is not questioning Korea's good faith attempt to comply with its notification commitments.

---

[272] See Document G/AG/2 adopted by the Committee on Agriculture on 8 June 1995.

VII. FINDINGS

A. *General Considerations*[273]

1. *Brief Description of the Beef Import Regime in Korea*

507. Korea's import regime for beef has a long history. In 1989 Australia, the United States and New Zealand requested that a GATT Panel be established to examine Korea's import regime for beef, claiming that the Korean restrictions could no longer be justified for reasons relating to the protection of Korea's balance-of-payments and were otherwise GATT inconsistent. Prior to this panel request, there had been no commercial imports of beef into Korea between 1985 and 1988.

508. The 1989 panel findings[274] called on Korea to bring into consistency with the GATT 1947 a number of specific measures taken in 1984 and 1985, and to enter into consultations with Australia, New Zealand and the United States with a view to establishing a timetable for the elimination of the remaining import restrictions on beef.

509. Consultations between Korea, Australia, New Zealand and the United States resulted in the conclusion of separate and parallel bilateral "Records of Understanding" (ROUs) in 1990 and 1993 intended to implement the findings of the 1989 panel and the consultations undertaken by Korea in the GATT Committee on Balance-of-Payments Restrictions (hereafter called the "Committee on Balance-of-Payments") in 1989.

510. The 1990 ROUs established a system of annual quotas for the period 1990 to 1992 and a "Simultaneous Buy/Sell" (SBS) mechanism intended to distribute a proportion of the annual quotas to entities other than the LPMO, the public body established by Korea in 1988 to administer the importation of beef. Additional ROUs, which entered into force in July 1993, continued the system of annual quotas to the end of 1995 and significantly expanded the scope of, and participation in, the SBS system. Korea and the United States entered into another ROU in December 1993. Following the ROUs, import authority within the quota was divided between the LPMO and the SBS system, with the amounts allocated to LPMO decreasing annually. The SBS system was meant to furnish foreign beef suppliers with the opportunity to sell directly to end users and customers through super-groups representing different sectors of Korea's industry.

---

273 The Panel has taken into account and considered all arguments submitted by the parties. However, throughout these findings, only the parties' arguments particularly relevant to the Panel's legal analysis have been summarized. A more exhaustive description of the parties arguments is contained in the previous sections of this Panel report.

274 The 1989 panel reports on *Korea – Beef*, complaint by Australia and complaint by the United States are hereinafter referred to as the "1989 Panel reports". There was also a similar panel report involving New Zealand.

2. *Brief Description of the Claims*

511. The United States and Australia submit claims with reference to seven main measures,[275] including some more specific measures. In general terms, the Complaining parties have claims against: (i) the dual retail system for beef; (ii) the alleged restrictions and less favourable treatment imposed by the LPMO on the importation and distribution of foreign beef; (iii) the alleged restrictions and less favourable treatment imposed by the functioning of the SBS system; (iv) the LPMO's minimum auction prices and other discharge and tendering practices as well as the LPMO's alleged refusal to import. In addition, Australia claims that (v) the grass-fed/grain-fed distinction imposed by the LPMO in its importation of beef is incompatible with various provisions of the WTO Agreement. The United States also has a general claim that, (vi) Korea's import licensing system constitutes a restriction which is inconsistent with WTO provisions. Finally, the Complaining parties have also submitted claims, (vii) regarding Korea's domestic support to its bovine industry.

512. Korea challenges the general and more specific claims. In addition to its various specific defences, Korea submits, as a general defence, that pursuant to its Schedule of Concessions, many, if not all, of the 17 measures[276] challenged by the Complaining parties, constitute "remaining restrictions" which benefit from a "transition period" and are required to be eliminated only by 1 January 2001.

3. *Methodology Followed by the Panel*

513. In view of the nature of the general defence submitted by Korea, which requires this Panel to interpret the WTO obligations of Korea in the light of the term "the remaining restrictions" contained in Korea's Schedule, taking into account the historical context surrounding the inclusion of this term, the Panel shall proceed in the following way. The Panel will start by analysing the meaning and scope of the terms of Korea's Schedule which provides that "the remaining restrictions shall be eliminated or brought into conformity with GATT from 1 January 2001". This will allow the Panel to identify which of the disputed measures, if any, can be considered as "covered" by these words and hence benefit from a "transition period".

514. Measures that do not benefit from such a transition period will then be examined by the Panel for a determination on their consistency with various provisions of the WTO according to the following sequence. The first set of measures that the Panel examines are those relating to the dual retail system for beef. All parties have emphasised the importance of such measures. Moreover, the effect of the dual retail system will be further amplified once the beef import

---

[275] See for instance, paras. 49 and 51 of this Panel report.

[276] Except the measures covered by the claims relating to the domestic support provided to Korea's beef industry.

quota is phased out. The Panel thereafter examines claims relating to specific aspects of the SBS system and the LPMO rules. The WTO compatibility of certain import and distribution practices by the LPMO/NFCL, in 1997 and 1998 - namely the refusal to discharge imported beef into the Korean market and the refusal to call for tenders – and the grain-fed and grass-fed distinction practiced by the LPMO when it calls for tenders, is then determined. Finally, claims relating to the alleged excessive domestic support provided to the Korean beef industry are assessed.

515. The Panel notes that this single panel was mandated by the DSB to examine both the requests of the United States and Australia[277]. On occasion, the Complaining parties have differed in their description of the Korean measures they challenge and they have sometimes submitted different claims on the same measures. In view of the provisions of Article 9.2 of the DSU, the Panel has ensured that the "rights which the parties to the dispute would have enjoyed had separate panels examined the complaints are in no way impaired".

B. Korea's Defence that "the remaining restrictions" Should Benefit from a Transition Period as Established in its Schedule LX

516. The Panel first examines the status and the scope of the term, "the remaining restrictions".

1. Legal Status of Note 6(e) to Korea's Schedule LX

(a) Arguments of the Parties

517. In support of its claim that its Schedule of Concessions provides for a transition period until 1 January 2001 to eliminate or bring into conformity with the WTO all "the remaining restrictions" on beef imports, Korea relies on Note 6(e) in its Schedule which reads:

> "*According to the results of the 1989 consultation with GATT/BOP Committee and the Uruguay Round multilateral trade negotiation, the remaining restrictions* on the items marked as "* Note 6(a)", "* Note 6(b)", "* Note 6(c)", "* Note 6(d)", or "* *Note 6(e)"* in column 5 of Section I-A of Part I of this schedule shall be eliminated or be brought into conformity with GATT provisions from the dates specified as follows: * Note 6(a): 1995; * Note 6(b): Jan. 1, 1996; * Note 6(c): Jul. 1, 1996; * Note 6(d): Jul. 1, 1997; and * Note 6(e): *Jan. 1, 2001.*" (emphasis added)

277 See para. 3 of this Panel report.

518. According to Korea, Note 6(e), which specifically covers beef products - the subject of this dispute - defines the extent of its WTO commitments on the liberalization of its market for imports of the beef products in question. In support of this contention, Korea refers to Article II:1 of the GATT which provides that WTO Members shall accord to the commerce of other Members treatment no less favourable than that provided for in the appropriate part of the appropriate Schedule annexed to this Agreement.

519. Korea argues that the reference to "the remaining restrictions" in Note 6(e) can only possibly be interpreted as meaning that "all limitations placed on actions which continue to exist at the time of conclusion of the treaty (the Uruguay Round) and which are not in conformity with GATT should be eliminated or brought into conformity with GATT by January 1, 2001." Korea submits that almost all of the measures challenged by the Complaining parties were already in existence at the time of the Uruguay Round, implying that the measures in dispute are "remaining restrictions" within the ambit of Note 6(e).[278]

520. The Complaining parties submit that Members' schedules annexed to the Marrakesh Protocol to the General Agreement on Tariffs and Trade 1994 are integral parts of the GATT 1994.[279] However, both Complaining parties reject Korea's claim that its commitments under Note 6(e) of its Schedule provide a transition period until 1 January 2001 for the measures at issue in this dispute to be brought into conformity with GATT/WTO.[280]

521. In Australia's view, the significance of the Note is limited, not only to GATT-inconsistent measures, but also to restrictions which are quantitative in nature, which were in existence at the time of the 1989 report of the GATT Committee on Balance-of-Payments[281] and the 1989 GATT panel reports[282], and which are specified in Korea's Schedule. Australia contends that the Uruguay Round negotiations only lengthened the transition period for these measures, but did not permit the maintenance of new, post-1989, GATT-inconsistent, measures.[283] Australia also argues that the Panel should first determine whether the measures at issue in the present dispute are *prima facie* inconsistent with the WTO Agreement and then examine Korea's claim based on this so-called transition period.[284]

522. The United States argues that the term "remaining restrictions" interpreted in accordance with Article 31 of the *Vienna Convention on the Law of Treaties* ("Vienna Convention") leaves enough ambiguity to justify recourse to supple-

---

[278] Paras. 54 and 105 of this Panel report.

[279] Para. 60 of this Panel report.

[280] Paras. 63 and 66, for instance, of this Panel report.

[281] BOP/R/183.1, 27 October 1989.

[282] Panel reports *Korea – Beef*, complaint by Australia; and complaint by the United States. (A similar panel exists with New Zealand. All three of which were adopted on 7 November 1989.)

[283] Para. 77 of this Panel report.

[284] Australia, Rebut. paras. 1.4-1.5.

mentary means of interpretation in accordance with Article 32 of the Vienna Convention. In this regard, the United States submits that in order to establish the true meaning of "remaining restrictions", the 1987 report of the GATT Committee on Balance-of-Payments, the 1989 GATT panel report, the 1989 report of the GATT Committee on Balance-of-Payments with respect to Korea's balance-of-payment measures, and the 1990 and 1993 Records of Understanding (ROUs) between the United States and Australia on the one hand and Korea on the other hand should all be examined as documents forming the historical background to the use of the words "remaining restrictions" in the Note to the Schedule. For the United States, the term "remaining restrictions" covers only restrictions that existed at the time of the balance-of-payment consultations and that have continued until the end of the Uruguay Round.[285] For the United States, Korea's assertion of a transition period is in effect a unilateral reduction in its obligations under the WTO. According to the United States, Korea may not exempt itself from specific GATT obligations and to do so through reliance on a Note to its Schedule of Concessions would be inconsistent with the *US - Sugar Head Note*[286] and *EC - Bananas III*[287] cases in 1993.

(b) Relevant Jurisprudence on the WTO Schedules

523. The legal status of a Member's Schedule of Concessions was addressed by the Appellate Body in *EC – Computer Equipment*, where it was held that:

> "...A Schedule is ... an integral part of the GATT 1994 ... Therefore, the concessions provided for in that Schedule are part of the terms of the treaty. As such, the only rules which may be applied in interpreting the meaning of a concession are the general rules of treaty interpretation set out in the *Vienna Convention*."[288]

524. In the *Canada – Dairy* dispute, which was concerned with the interpretation of a schedule in the area of agriculture (where schedules are of particular relevance), the Appellate Body confirmed that the provisions of schedules are terms of the treaty and should be interpreted together with the other relevant WTO treaty provisions. The Appellate Body also recognized that "although Canada's commitment on fluid milk was made unilaterally, both Canada and the United States understood that this commitment represented a continuation by Canada of current access opportunities ...".[289]

525. More recently, the Appellate Body in *Korea – Safeguards* insisted on the fact that the WTO is "one treaty" and therefore all provisions (including Sched-

---

285 Paras. 69 -70 of this Panel report.

286 Panel report on *US – Sugar Headnote*, paras. 5.2-5.3.

287 Appellate Body report on *EC – Bananas III, supra*, footnote 97, paras. 154-158.

288 Appellate Body report on *Canada – Dairy, supra*, footnote 40, para. 131.

289 Ibid., para. 139.

ules) ought to be interpreted harmoniously, in an effective manner, in order to ensure that no clause or provision is reduced to "inutility".[290]

(c) The Panel's Assessment

526. The Panel considers that Note 6(e), as it relates to the beef products in question, is a specific elaboration of Korea's Schedule of concessions for the liberalization of its market for agricultural products. Therefore, Note 6(e) of Korea's Schedule must be read together with the other WTO obligations. The Panel cannot ignore Note 6(e) and cannot reduce its "utility". The Panel therefore does not agree with Australia's interpretation that the term "remaining restrictions" refers only to the quotas already listed in Korea's Schedule. To interpret "remaining restrictions" to cover the restrictions already agreed upon and reflected in Korea's Schedule would reduce Note 6(e) to inutility.

527. The Panel does not agree with Australia's contention that the Panel should first determine whether the measures at issue are *prima facie* inconsistent with the WTO Agreement and then examine Korea's claim based on the transition period. As noted above, Note 6(e) must be read together with the other WTO obligations which the Complaining parties claim have been violated. The Panel needs to proceed to a determination of the obligations of Korea under "the WTO Agreement as a whole" with regard to each measure. Korea's Schedule does not constitute an exception to other GATT provisions, but rather qualifies Korea's obligations under the WTO Agreement. The Panel considers, therefore, that it is more appropriate to determine first the scope of the term "remaining restrictions". It would be a waste of its judicial function to assess the WTO compatibility of measures which will be phased out or otherwise brought into conformity with the WTO by 2001.

528. In this regard, the Panel notes that, in response to its questions, Korea stated that the coverage of remaining restrictions under Note 6(e) is "limited to all GATT-inconsistent measures that existed at the conclusion of the Uruguay Round". In the same answer, Korea also stated that if there are any remaining restrictions which have not yet been eliminated or brought into conformity with GATT, Korea still has one full year of time remaining to do so.[291] Read together, these responses imply a recognition by Korea that all the measures characterized as "remaining restrictions" under Note 6(e) are GATT-inconsistent and are to be eliminated or brought into conformity with the WTO Agreement by 1 January 2001.

529. The Panel shall therefore first analyse the meaning and the scope of the terms of Korea's Note 6(e), and then identify which of the measures challenged in

---

290 Appellate Body Report on *Korea – Definitive Safeguard Measures on Imports of Certain Dairy Products* ("*Korea – Dairy*"), WT/DS98/AB/R, adopted 12 January 2000, DSR 2000:I, 3, para. 81.
291 Para. 59 of this Panel report.

the present dispute are "covered" by the provisions of Note 6(e) and, therefore, benefit from a transition period until 1 January 2001, by which date they shall be eliminated or otherwise brought into conformity with the WTO Agreement.

2. *Scope and Interpretation of the Term "the remaining restrictions"*

530. At the outset, the Panel would like to emphasize that this dispute deals with issues arising out of a case from the past, in other words, the consequences of a dispute over alleged balance-of-payment problems that took place before the entry into force of the GATT 1994 Understanding on Balance-of-Payments Provisions (hereafter called the "GATT 1994 Understanding on Balance-of-Payments"). As mentioned by the Panel in *India – Quantitative Restrictions*[292], prior to the WTO and the GATT 1994 Understanding on the Balance-of-Payments, the GATT Committee on Balance-of-Payments would often grant to a contracting party disinvoking Articles XII or XVIII:B of GATT, long periods for the phasing out of balance-of-payments restrictions, during which period the legal status of these remaining import restrictions was not altogether clear.[293] Paragraph 13 of the GATT 1994 Understanding on Balance-of-Payments now clearly provides that:

> "In those cases in which a time-schedule has been presented for the removal of restrictive measures taken for balance-of-payments purposes, the General Council may recommend that, in adhering to such a time-schedule, a Member shall be deemed to be in compliance with its GATT 1994 obligations."

531. In the present dispute, as will be further explained below, the 1989 report of the GATT Committee on Balance-of-Payments concluded that Korea, after disinvoking Article XVIII:B of GATT[294], had until 1 July 1997 to remove its remaining restrictions. The report recommended that Korea, Australia, New Zealand and the United States consult with a view to developing an *orderly programme of liberalization* which would phase out the *remaining restrictions*. The 1989 Panel report also recommended that "Korea hold consultations with the United States, Australia and New Zealand to work out a timetable for the removal of import restrictions on beef justified since 1967 by Korea for balance-of-payments reasons ..."[295] This led to the negotiation of various Records of Understandings (ROUs). Before the expiry of the transition period envisaged in the

---

[292] Panel Report on *India – Quantitative Restrictions*, *supra*, footnote 65, paras. 5.28 to 5.53.

[293] See for instance para. 13 of the Balance of Payments Report (BOP/R/183/Add.1): "The Committee understood that, on the basis of the implementation of these undertakings by Korea, other contracting parties will exercise due restraint in the application of their rights under the General Agreement in relation to products included in the programmes of liberalization".

[294] See para. 7 of the 1989 BOP report: "Members of the Committee welcomed Korea's commitment to disinvoke Article XVIII:B."

[295] Panel report on *Korea – Beef* (Australia) at para. 109, and *Korea – Beef* (US) para. 131.

ROUs, the WTO Agreement was concluded in which Korea's "remaining restrictions" are again referred to in Note 6(e) to Korea's Schedule which provides that the remaining restrictions shall be eliminated by 2001. This is the context to which the Panel needs to refer in order to determine the scope of the term "the remaining restrictions".

532. The Panel must determine the meaning of the term "the remaining restrictions" in accordance with Article 3.1 of the DSU - which provides that: "Members affirm their adherence to the principles for the management of disputes heretofore applied under Articles XXII and XXIII of GATT 1947, and the rules and procedures as further elaborated and modified herein" - and with Article XVI:1 of the Agreement Establishing the WTO, which provides that: "...the WTO shall be guided by the decisions, procedures and customary practices followed by CONTRACTING PARTIES to GATT 1947 and the bodies established in the framework of GATT 1947." In addition, the Panel should be guided by Article 3.2 of the DSU, by applying customary rules of interpretation of public international law, including the provisions of Articles 31 of the *Vienna Convention* referring to the ordinary meaning of the terms, and those of Article 32 of the same convention referring to the preparatory work and the circumstances surrounding the conclusion of the Note 6(e) to Korea's Schedule.

533. Referring to the wording of Note 6(e) quoted above, the Panel notes that a "restriction" means "a thing which restricts someone or something, a limitation on action, a limiting condition or regulation".[296] Korea's Schedule refers to "restrictions on the items marked..." in plural, so it clearly contemplates having application to more than one "limiting condition or regulation". This must be read together with the use of the term "the" in "the remaining restrictions on the items marked". Note 6(e) does not refer to "any" restrictions existing at the end of the Uruguay Round but only to "*the*" remaining restrictions. The use of the term "the" implies identified and specified restrictions. Korea admits that the remaining restrictions are not an unspecified range of measures.[297] The term "remaining restrictions" can, therefore, only be interpreted to mean "restrictions" other than the import quota that is set forth in the Schedule. To equate the term "the remaining restrictions" with the import quota identified in the Schedule would leave the Note meaningless. If the Note referred to "these" or "those" remaining restrictions, such terms could have been interpreted to mean the restrictions mentioned in the Schedule, but the deliberate choice of the term "the" implies restrictions other than those already listed in Korea's Schedule.

534. The "restrictions" envisaged under the Schedule must be "remaining restrictions".[298] What amounts to a remaining restriction must therefore be deter-

---

[296] *The New Shorter Oxford English Dictionary.*

[297] See para. 65 of this Panel report.

[298] *The New Shorter Oxford English Dictionary* defines "remain" as meaning "to be left behind or over after others or other parts have gone or been removed, used, or dealt with; be in the same place or condition during further time; continue to stay or exist".

mined with reference to a specific point in time. There are two points in time referred to by Note 6(e): the results of the balance-of-payments consultations; and the results of the Uruguay Round. The Panel notes that all parties to the present dispute have identified these two events as the relevant temporal periods for determining what amounts to a "remaining restriction" and must be determined with reference to a specific point in time.

535. Note 6(e) refers to "the results of the 1989 consultation with BOP Committee and the Uruguay Round of multilateral trade negotiations" as the basis for eliminating or bringing the "remaining restrictions" into conformity with the GATT. The Schedule thus creates a relationship between the elimination of the "restrictions" and the "results" of two events - the 1989 consultation in the GATT/BOP Committee and the Uruguay Round negotiations. "According to" relates to both parts of the sentence, i.e. the BOP consultations **AND** the Uruguay Round (i.e. the use of a conjunction between the BOP consultations and the Uruguay Round). If the remaining restrictions had no link with the BOP consultations the words "according to" and "and" would be meaningless. Therefore a remaining restriction must at least bear a relation to the results of the BOP consultations and still be in place when the Schedule was finalized as the result of the Uruguay Round.

536. A "result"[299] is "the effect, consequence, issue, or outcome of some action, process, or design". The "results" envisaged in the Note may, therefore, be characterized as the "effects, consequences or outcomes" of the 1989 consultations and the Uruguay Round. It follows that "remaining restrictions" should be interpreted as meaning "restrictions" envisaged or at least bearing a relation to the "results" of the 1989 consultations and the "results" of the Uruguay Round, and therefore still in place in March 1994 when the Uruguay Round schedules were filed with the Secretariat.

537. The interpretation of Note 6(e) in accordance with Article 3.1 of the DSU and Article 31 of the *Vienna Convention* does not allow the Panel to come to a definitive finding on the list of "the remaining restrictions", identified by Korea as benefiting from a "grace period" until 1 January 2001.

538. Article 32 of the Vienna Convention allows the Panel to have recourse to "supplementary means of interpretation" when the interpretation according to Article 31 leaves the meaning of a treaty provision ambiguous or obscure.[300] In the present case, it is evident that in order to come to a more precise definition of the term "remaining restrictions", it will be necessary to determine what is meant by the "results" or "effects, consequences or outcomes" of the 1989 balance-of-

[299] According to *the New Shorter Oxford English Dictionary*.

[300] See Appellate Body Report on *Canada – Dairy, supra*, footnote 40, para. 138: "In our view, the language in the notation in Canada's Schedule is not clear on its face. ... For this reason, it is appropriate, indeed necessary, in this case, to turn to 'supplementary means of interpretation' pursuant to Article 32 of the Vienna Convention".

payments consultations and the Uruguay Round. To the extent necessary to make an objective assessment of the matter before the Panel[301], it needs to ascertain the meaning of the term used in the various legal instruments mentioned above where the term "the remaining restrictions" appeared before and until the conclusion of the Uruguay Round.

539. In *EC - Banana III*, the Appellate Body upheld the panel's statement that it "had no alternative but to examine the provisions" of a non-WTO agreement "in so far as it is necessary" to interpret the WTO rules (the Lomé waiver referred to the Lomé Convention).[302] The Panel shall therefore proceed along the same line as in *EC - Bananas III*. In this respect, the Panel emphasizes that its role is limited to interpreting the term "the remaining restrictions" as used in Korea's Schedule, to find the objective meaning of the terms of Note 6(e), the inclusion of which was agreed to by Members by the end of the Uruguay Round. The Panel recalls that in *EC – Poultry*, the Appellate Body concluded that the bilateral agreement between the European Communities and Brazil could be examined when interpreting the provisions of the EC Schedule.[303] In *EC – Computer Equipment*, reference was made to the *practice of one state* to interpret the provision of a Member's schedule.[304] In *US – Shrimp*, reference was made to treaties not even ratified by the parties in dispute in order to interpret provisions of Article XX.[305] In addition to the 1989 Panel reports and the GATT Committee on Balance-of-Payments reports, the various bilateral agreements between Korea and the disputing parties, the ROUs, will thus be examined, not with a view to "enforcing" the content of these bilateral agreements, but strictly for the purpose of interpreting an ambiguous WTO provision, i.e. Note 6(e) to Korea's Schedule.

---

[301] Article 11 of the DSU.

[302] Appellate Body Report on *EC – Bananas III, supra*, footnote 97, para.167: " ... since the GATT CONTRACTING PARTIES incorporated a reference to the Lomé Convention into the Lomé waiver, the meaning of the Lomé Convention became a GATT/WTO issue, at least to that extent. Thus, *we have no alternative but to examine the provisions of the Lomé Convention ourselves in so far as it is necessary to interpret the Lomé waiver*." (Emphasis added.)

[303] Appellate Body Report on *EC – Poultry, supra*, footnote 61, para. 83: " ... Therefore, in our view, the Oilseeds Agreement may serve as a *supplementary means* of interpretation of Schedule LXXX pursuant to Article 32 of the *Vienna Convention*, as it is part of the historical background of the concessions of the European Communities for frozen poultry meat."

[304] In Appellate Body Report on *EC - Computer Equipment, supra*, footnote 167, it was stated: "93 ... The purpose of treaty interpretation is to establish the *common* intention of the parties to the treaty. To establish this intention, the prior practice of only *one* of the parties may be relevant, but it is clearly of more limited value than the practice of all parties". (Emphasis added.)

[305] In *United States - Shrimp, supra*, footnote 38, the Appellate Body used a variety of non-WTO international rules to interpret WTO provisions. As noted above in Part I, the Appellate Body examined the use of the term "natural resources" in a number of international conventions (paras. 127-134). It referred to other international conventions when assessing the meaning of sustainable development referred to in the Preamble of the WTO Agreement (para. 154). It referred to international (and regional) treaties when assessing whether the US measure had been applied in unjustifiable discrimination, in particular with reference to the way consultations had been conducted and ought to be conducted under other international conventions (paras. 166-177).

(a) Negotiating History and Circumstances that Led to the Inclusion of the Words "According to the results of the 1989 consultation with BOP Committee and the Uruguay Round multilateral trade negotiation, the remaining restrictions" in Note 6(e) of Korea's Schedule.

540. The Panel now proceeds to a detailed examination of the legal documents referred to above.

(i) The 1989 GATT Committee on Balance-of-Payments Restrictions Consultations

541. The 1989 BOP Committee undertook consultations with Korea to review import restrictions imposed by Korea for the purpose of protecting its balance-of-payments position.[306] These consultations followed an earlier set of consultations undertaken in 1987 between the BOP Committee and Korea on the same issue, which found that improvements in Korea's balance-of-payments position were such that "import restrictions could no longer be justified under Article XVIII:B" of the GATT. In reaching this conclusion, the 1987 Committee expected that Korea would "establish a timetable for phasing out balance-of-payments restrictions, and ... consider alternative GATT justifications for any *remaining measures*, ..." (emphasis added).[307]

542. During the 1989 consultations, Korea communicated its intention to disinvoke restrictions imposed through Article XVIII:B by January 1990. In a statement to the BOP Committee on Balance-of-Payments, Korea proposed this course of action on the proviso that the CONTRACTING PARTIES:

> "(i) agree to a grace period of ten years from the date of disinvocation;
>
> (ii) allow Korea to phase out during the grace period the existing balance-of-payments restrictions in a progressive manner, but having due regard to the interests of other contracting parties; and
>
> (iii) reach an understanding not to take any unilateral or multilateral legal actions against Korea's *remaining restrictions* during the given grace period." (statement by Korea 23 October 1989, Annex I to BOP/R/183/Add.1) [308]

543. During the consultations, it had been noted by Members of the Committee that:

306 BOP/R/183/Add.1, 27 October 1989.

307 BOP/R/171, 10 December 1987.

308 BOP/R/183/Add.1, para. 10.

> "Korea was encouraged ... to develop, in consultation with other Contracting Parties, an *orderly program of liberalisation* which would phase out *remaining restrictions* in a reasonably short period of time." (Emphasis added.)[309]

This observation was maintained in the Committee's conclusion that:

> "... appropriate *flexibility* was necessary for Korea to phase out, or bring into conformity with other GATT provisions, its *remaining restrictions* ... largely in the agricultural sector." (Emphasis added.)[310]

544. The conclusions of the Committee required Korea to:

> "... eliminate its *remaining restrictions* or otherwise bring them into conformity with GATT provisions by 1 July 1997 ... in a generally even manner, on a most-favoured-nation basis, over two three-year programmes beginning on the expiry of the current liberalization programme." (Emphasis added.)[311]

545. Thus, it is evident that the results of the 1989 consultations were that Korea should, "in consultation with other Contracting Parties," develop a programme that would phase out the import restrictions remaining after Korea's disinvocation of Article XVIII:B over a ten year period starting from the date of the actual disinvocation. The consultations identified no list of such measures and provided no general description. In this regard, the findings of the Committee are clear that Korea should "consult" with contracting parties on the substance of the programmes proposed to phase out the "remaining restrictions".

(ii) The 1989 Panel Reports

546. It is important to note that the ROUs entered into by the above parties were also the result of recommendations made by two 1989 GATT panels which specifically examined Korea's alleged balance-of-payments restrictions as they related to beef products in the respective complaints by Australia and the United States.[312] In both panels, parties challenged the existence of an import quota on beef and the role of the LPMO, established in 1988, in setting imported beef prices (mark-up) and in its distribution activities.

547. The panel held that there were essentially two sets of restrictions on beef imports maintained by Korea:

> "(a) measures amounting to a virtual suspension of imports introduced in November 1984 and May 1985 and subsequently

[309] Ibid. para. 7.

[310] Ibid. para. 11.

[311] Ibid. para. 12.

[312] A similar and parallel panel was also established following the complaint of New Zealand.

> amended in August 1988. These measures were neither notified to, nor reviewed by, the GATT Committee on Balance-of-Payments;
>
> (b) restrictions on beef existing since Korea's accession to the General Agreement in 1967, which were notified to, and reviewed by the Balance-of-Payments Committee."[313]

548. After finding that Korea should eliminate or otherwise bring into conformity with the GATT import measures on beef "introduced in 1984/85 and amended in 1988", the panel recommended that Korea hold consultations with Australia and the United States and other interested contracting parties in order to:

> "work out a timetable for the removal of import restrictions on beef justified since 1967 by Korea for balance-of-payments reasons and report the result of such consultations within a period of three months following the adoption of the Panel report to the Council".[314]

549. It is thus evident that those panel reports form part of the background to the results of the 1989 Committee on Balance-of-Payments consultations. Not only were the panel reports issued prior to the 1989 consultations, but also, the need for GATT Committee on Balance-of-Payments consultations was referred to in each of the panel reports. Indeed, both the panel reports and the results of the Committee consultation were adopted by the Council on the same day, 7 November 1989.

550. Korea's consultations with some of the contracting parties (representing for that purpose the CONTRACTING PARTIES) led it to adopt a number of individual Records of Understanding (ROUs) with Australia and the United States between 1990 and 1993.[315] As will be shown, these ROUs formed the basis of Korea's Schedule of Concessions at the end of the Uruguay Round. The Panel's examination of the ROUs for the purpose of determining the meaning of the term "remaining restrictions" is therefore not only consistent with the "results" of the 1989 consultations, but also with the specific wording of Note 6(e), which calls for an examination of the "results" of both the 1989 consultations and the Uruguay Round.

551. It follows that the next step in the Panel's investigation into the meaning of "remaining restrictions" must necessarily involve examination of the consultations and understandings reached by Korea with the CONTRACTING PARTIES. The Panel recalls that it does so only to the extent necessary to interpret the terms of Note 6(e) to Korea's Schedule.

313 Panel report on *Korea – Beef* (Australia), para. 91.

314 Panel reports on *Korea – Beef* (Australia), para. 109, and *Korea – Beef* (US), para. 131.

315 Korea also concluded an ROU with New Zealand.

(iii) The Records of Understanding

The 1990 Records of Understanding Between Korea and Australia; and Korea and the United States

552. The first of the Records of Understanding between Korea and Australia and Korea and the United States[316] was entered into in 1990. Both the 1990 ROUs were circulated to all GATT contracting parties. The terms of the respective ROUs were almost identical and will, therefore, be examined together. Consistent with the results of the 1989 BOP Committee consultations, the 1990 ROUs manifest an intention on the part of Korea to:

> " ... eliminate its *remaining import restrictions* or otherwise bring them into conformity with GATT provisions as included in the conclusion of the report of the GATT/BOP Committee...."

553. To this end, the ROUs provide, generally, for the creation of a "joint study" team to:

> " (1) examine the structural weakness of the Korean livestock industry and to review the effects of the industry structure on the appropriate timing of market liberalisation; and
>
> (2) review the functions of the LPMO and make recommendations for improvements in marketing and pricing practices in the future." (Paragraph I.D.)

554. The ROUs call for the implementation of a "simultaneous buy/sell" (SBS) system, composed of super-groups that would control a gradually increased share of the imports of beef into Korea (now 70 per cent of Korea's import quota). The purpose of this mechanism was to increase access to Korea's beef market. The SBS is to replace gradually the activities of the LPMO. In the 1990 ROUs, it is envisaged that the details of the SBS mechanism is left to be determined through further consultations between the parties (paragraph II.C). Provision is also made for "industry-to-industry dialogue" on issues associated with the beef trade (paragraph III).[317]

555. As such, the 1990 ROUs did set up a framework for Korea to eliminate its remaining import restrictions in accordance with the results of the GATT/BOP Committee consultations. In doing so, it is clear that the ROUs result from the 1989 consultations and identify the general nature of "the remaining restrictions" referred to in Note 6(e) of Korea's Schedule.

---

316 See attached to the present Panel report, as Annex 1 (the ROU between Korea and Australia).

317 In addition, the ROUs stipulate that Parties are to reserve their rights under the GATT (para. V).

The July 1993 Records of Understanding Between Korea and Australia; and Korea and the United States

556. Korea's second set of Records of Understanding (ROUs) with Australia and the United States was entered into in July 1993. These ROUs were also circulated to all contracting parties. As with the 1990 ROUs, the terms of the respective 1993 ROUs were almost identical and will therefore be examined together. The main objective of the July 1993 ROUs, as of the 1990 ROUs, was to eliminate all remaining import restrictions[318] in accordance with the results of the 1989 GATT/BOP Committee consultations and the 1989 GATT panel reports.[319]

557. In the July 1993 ROUs, the link between the 1989 panel's conclusion, the inconsistencies of certain Korean measures and the transition period through the ROUs, is emphasised. The July 1993 ROUs add considerably more detail on the operation of the SBS system, created in the 1990 ROUs.[320]

The December 1993 Record of Understanding Between Korea and the United States

558. A further ROU was entered into between Korea and the United States in December 1993. The title of this ROU, in referring to "agricultural market access in the Uruguay Round", suggests that it was reflective of Korea's agriculture negotiations under the Uruguay Round. Indeed, the December 1993 ROU sets out specific understandings on the importation of a number of agricultural products. In relation to beef, the ROU presents a schedule of quota volume for beef imports increasing until the year 2000. The ROU further sets out the amounts of duty and mark-up to be imposed on the beef quota in each year and established a corresponding percentage share of the annual quota for the SBS system.

559. The December 1993 ROU also expressly provided that:

> "all balance-of-payments restrictions on beef shall expire no later than December 31 2000. In the year 2001, there shall be no quota, no mark-up, no LPMO involvement, and complete private sector autonomy regarding product quantity, price, quality, and supplier. There shall be no government restrictions on product utilisation".

---

[318] See para. I:C of the July 1993 ROUs: "This Understanding is the second Understanding between the ROKG and USG concerning market access for beef. This Understanding reflects the desire of the parties to implement the GATT dispute settlement panel recommendations and Balance-of-Payments Committee determinations." The same commitment is reiterated in para. 3 - front page – and in para. VI.A.

[319] In addition, the July 1993 ROUs stipulate that parties are to reserve their rights under the GATT (para. VI.B).

[320] For instance, para. IV:C.7(c) of the July 1993 ROU is a recognition of the continuity between the panel's conclusion and the object of the ROUs when it provides that "*in further implementation of the findings of the GATT dispute settlement panel on beef*, during 1993 the [SBS] mark-up on beef shall not exceed 100 per cent ..." (emphasis added).

560. Like the 1990 ROUs, the July 1993 ROUs, in establishing specific rules for the importation of beef into Korea with a view to implementing the results of the BOP Committee consultations, identified the "remaining restrictions" referred to in Note 6(e) to Korea's Schedule. The Panel notes that nowhere in the July or December 1993 ROUs is there a reference to the effect that the contents of the 1993 ROUs should replace the 1990 ROUs. The July 1993 ROUs are an elaboration of parts of the 1990 ROUs. Indeed, the December 1993 ROU expressly provides that:

> "the current July 15, 1993 record of understanding (L/7270) shall continue to apply except as modified to incorporate the provisions of the new understanding".

561. The December 1993 ROU between the United States and Korea was not circulated to GATT contracting parties. However, the link between this ROU and the Uruguay Round seems to have been admitted by the United States. For the United States, the effect of the December 1993 ROU was to extend the duration of the quotas until 2001, and that this was ultimately made part of Korea's WTO Schedule of Concessions.[321] The fact that the content of the ROUs was reflected in Korea's Uruguay Round concessions is also admitted by Korea.[322] Australia also recognizes the link between the Schedule and the closing of the Uruguay Round, but does not agree to the meaning given by Korea to Note 6(e).

562. The Panel considers that the December 1993 ROU, even if concluded only between Korea and the United States, is relevant to assist the interpretation of the ambiguous terms of Note 6(e). The Panel recalls that in *EC – Computer Equipment*, the practice of one single WTO Member was stated to be relevant when interpreting the provisions of the Schedule of the European Communities.[323] In particular, the Panel notes that the reference to a phasing out period until 1 January 2001 appears for the first time in the December 1993 ROU. It seems reasonable to try to understand the relationship between a first transition period to phase-out "remaining restrictions" until 1997 (provided to Korea by the Committee on Balance-of-Payments) and the reference in Korea's WTO Schedule to the "remaining restrictions" to be phased-out by 2001. The Panel underlines again that here it is not enforcing the bilateral agreement between the United States and Korea but simply reading and interpreting it in order to interpret a provision in a Member's Schedule.

---

[321] Para. 99 of this Panel report.

[322] Para. 87 of this Panel report.

[323] Appellate Body Report on *EC – Computer Equipment*, *supra*, footnote 167, para. 93.

(b) Material to be Consulted in Order to Interpret Note 6(e) of Korea's Schedule

563. The Panel recalls that in its efforts to interpret the ambiguous terms of Note 6(e) of Korea's Schedule, the circumstances of the conclusion of Korea's Schedules lead it to examine: the 1989 panel reports on beef; the 1989 report of the Committee on Balance-of-Payments; and the various ROUs negotiated by some GATT contracting parties upon recommendations of the GATT CONTRACTING PARTIES in the wake of the reports just mentioned.

564. The Panel is thus called upon to determine the extent to which the measures at issue can be found to exist in the 1989 panel reports on beef, in the 1989 report of the GATT Committee on Balance-of-Payments or in the ROUs which were governing the beef trade relations between Korea, the United States, Australia and New Zealand. To the extent they are mentioned in these documents and were still in place at the time of the conclusion of the Uruguay Round, the measures must be part of "the remaining restrictions" within the meaning of Note 6(e). As a consequence, such measures benefit from a "transition period" until 1 January 2001 and until then, they cannot be successfully challenged. At the same time, as the Panel has determined above, the same measures found to be part of "the remaining restrictions" would also be considered inconsistent with the WTO Agreement – save for the transition period - and will, therefore, have to be phased-out by 1 January 2001. Conversely, measures falling outside the scope of restrictions envisaged or identified in the ROUs or in the 1989 panel reports and Committee on Balance-of-Payments reports could not have been intended to be included in the reference to "the remaining restrictions" in Note 6(e) to Korea's Schedule.

(c) Determination of the Measures which Qualify as "remaining restrictions"

565. Before proceeding to the determination as to whether the specific measures at issue in the present dispute are "remaining restrictions" within the meaning of Note 6(e), it is worth recalling them in detail.

(i) Measures Challenged

566. The measures challenged by the Complaining parties are the following:

Restrictions on the retail sale of imported beef

- the requirement that imported beef be sold in specialized beef stores;
- separate sales areas for the sale of imported beef in department stores; and
- obligation to display an imported beef store sign.

Restrictions on purchases and sales in the wholesale market (for the LPMO's imports)

- mandatory acquisition of imported beef through established distribution channels (middlemen);
- supply from imported beef wholesale markets is restricted to specialized imported beef stores only;
- imported beef to be supplied only on a cash payments basis; and
- wholesale markets required to retain records of the supplies of imported beef for at least two years.

Limitations on participation in the SBS import system

- end-users (customers) not members of super-groups excluded from the system;
- range of end-users is restricted;
- end-users can only import beef through the super-group to which they belong and can belong to only one super-group;
- quotas and sub-quotas allocated to super-groups according to annual plans rather than demand; and
- labelling, reporting and record-keeping requirements not imposed on domestic beef.

Restrictions on discharge of LPMO's imports

- the LPMO's monthly and daily discharge practices;
- minimum wholesale price at auctions of imported beef.

Restrictions resulting from LPMO tendering practices

- refusal or delays in calling for tenders
- the LPMO's tendering practice restricting the type of beef that may fill a tender to grain-fed beef to the exclusion of grass-fed beef.

Price mark-up applied to imports through the SBS system that is additional to the tariff

Discretionary licensing system

567. The Panel now proceeds to examine whether the above measures were envisaged or can be said to originate in the ROUs negotiated between the parties, and thus constitute "remaining restrictions" within the meaning of Note 6(e).

(ii) Disputed Measures that were in Place in 1989 or Originate in the ROUs and which therefore Constitute "remaining restrictions" within the Meaning of Note 6(e)

Restrictions on purchases and sales in the wholesale market (for the LPMO's imports)

- mandatory acquisition of imported beef through established distribution channels (middlemen);

568. The Panel recalls that state-trading enterprises as such are consistent with the WTO Agreement but their operations may be restrictive within the meaning of the WTO Agreement. To the extent that a Korean regulation (or guidelines) requires the LPMO to sell its imports or some of them through the wholesale market (and therefore prohibits it from selling to any consumers contrary to what would otherwise be permitted for like domestic products), such a requirement is restrictive. However, it appears from the 1989 panel reports that the LPMO has always sold beef predominantly through the wholesale market.[324] The Panel concludes, therefore, that this measure falls within the meaning of the term "the remaining restrictions" mentioned in Note 6(e).[325]

Limitations on participation in the SBS import system

569. In giving effect to the results of the 1989 BOP consultations, the ROUs setting up the SBS system were intended to assist Korea in establishing an "orderly program of liberalisation" with "appropriate flexibility" to allow Korea to phase out its "remaining restrictions" by the year 2001. By its very nature, an "orderly program of liberalisation" may contain some temporary restrictions.

570. To this extent, the Panel considers that restrictions inherent to the SBS system[326] put in place at the time of the ROUs were intended to be covered by the term "the remaining restrictions" and, therefore, were to be tolerated until 2001. However, this intention must be viewed in the light of the more general requirements of the July 1993 ROUs in Paragraph IV.C.6(a) that:

---

[324] See for instance paras. 23-24 and 39 of the panel report on *Korea – Beef* (US): "Korea recalled that virtually all imported beef was resold through wholesale market auctions."

[325] The Panel also recalls that, in the ROUs parties have agreed that as of 2001, the LPMO would no longer be involved in the beef market and that with the disappearance of the beef import quota, the LPMO practices will have to be brought into conformity with the WTO Agreement.

[326] The Panel considers it a governmental measure. It was set up by the Korean government in the ROUs, it creates a system of incentives and disincentives if one is interested in importing beef and it is monitored by the MAF and the LPMO. The Panel notes that the LPMO not only possesses the exclusive right to import a substantial portion of the imported beef quota, but also exercises considerable control over the use of the remaining portion of the quota through its authority to allocate quota shares to the SBS super-groups and to approve their import requests. See the panel report on *Japan – Semi-Conductors*, para. 108.

"except as otherwise specified in this understanding, there shall be no restrictions placed by the ROKG or any super-group on beef (regardless of country of origin, product type, or specification, whether grass-fed or grain-fed or whether fresh, chilled or frozen) imported under the SBS system, including processing requirements, labelling, pricing, marking or packaging requirements or other barriers to legitimate importation, distribution and sale that create *unnecessary obstacles to trade or otherwise undermine the objectives* of the understanding."[327]

- Super-group membership requirement

571. Some limitation on membership was envisaged in the 1990 ROUs in that it was stipulated that "the mechanism will be used initially by tourist hotels, tourist restaurants, the NLCF and the Korean Cold Storage company ... Both governments will consult concerning future expansion of the SBS system". (Paragraph II.C) More specifically, both the July 1993 ROUs prescribe rules for adding "new super-groups" implying that there is indeed a membership requirement (paragraphs IV.A.1 and IV.A.2). The Panel concludes that this measure falls within the meaning of the term "the remaining restrictions" mentioned in Note 6(e); it thus benefits from a transition period until 1 January 2001, by which date it shall be phased out or otherwise brought into conformity with the WTO.

- Restrictions on range of end-users

572. The Panel considers that some restrictions on the range of end-users are inherent to the SBS system. This is confirmed in the definition of an end-user provided in both the July 1993 ROUs as "any individual private enterprise, firm, business, or grouping thereof, and/or their buying agents that has the *right* to import beef through any supergroup except NLCF and KCSC." (paragraph II, emphasis added). Therefore, the restrictions limiting the range of end-users who can import directly from Australia and the United States existed at the time of the ROUs and can be viewed as some of the "remaining restrictions" for the purpose of Note 6(e); these thus benefit from a transition period until 1 January 2001, by which date they shall be phased out or otherwise brought into conformity with the WTO.

- Prohibition on cross-trading between end-users, and between end-users and super-groups

573. The July 1993 ROUs envisage cross-trading between certain end-users and two specific super-groups. For instance, KOSCA members not eligible to import through the KOSCA super-group "shall have the right to participate in the SBS system as customers under the NLCF *and* KCSC." (paragraph IV.B.2(d), emphasis added). The ROUs also establish that "... beginning in January 1995,

[327] In this light, the Panel considers that restrictions not inherent to the SBS system or creating otherwise "unnecessary obstacles to trade" could not have been intended to be part of "the remaining restrictions".

any butcher shops that are or become registered dealers of imported beef shall have the right to participate in the SBS system as customers under NLCF *and* KCSC." (Paragraph IV.B.2(e) emphasis added). Further references exist to all KOSCA members being allowed to participate in the SBS system as customers under NLCF *and* KCSC (ParagraphIV.C.1 (a)).

574. The specific inclusion of provisions permitting cross-trading between certain end-users and super-groups, together with the membership requirement, implies the existence of a prohibition of cross-trading with other super-groups. If the parties had intended to permit cross-trading between end-users and any other super-groups they would not have limited the super-groups allowed to do so to NLCF and KCSC. To this extent, the Panel finds that the prohibition on cross-trading between end-users, other than those within the KOSCA group, and super-groups other than NLCF and KCSC, is inherent to the SBS system established in the ROUs and therefore is a "remaining restriction". Hence, the Panel finds that it constitutes a "remaining restriction" within the meaning of Note 6(e) to Korea's Schedule and benefits from a transition period until 1 January 2001, by which date it shall be phased out or otherwise brought into conformity with the WTO.

575. The ROUs also envisaged that there would not be any cross-trading between super-groups as their allocation of shares was pre-determined annually and issued on a quarterly basis. In addition, it was provided in paragraph IV.C.6(b) of the July 1993 ROU that "any SBS sub-share that is not fully utilised by a super-group by the end of the third calendar year quarter shall be reallocated to all other super-groups on a *pro rata* basis ... Such reallocation shall be made no later than October 15". The very existence of the need to provide for the re-allocation of non-utilized quota shares is evidence that cross-trading was otherwise understood to have been prohibited. Thus, the Panel finds that the prohibition on cross-trading between super-groups is inherent to the SBS system as then envisaged. Therefore, the Panel finds that it constitutes a "remaining restriction" within the meaning of Note 6(e) to Korea's Schedule and benefits from a transition period until 1 January 2001, by which date it shall be phased out or otherwise brought into conformity with the WTO.

576. The ROUs do not, however, make any reference to the existence of any restriction on trading between end-users.

- quotas and sub-quotas allocated to super-groups according to annual plans rather than demand

577. The allocation and re-allocation of quotas to super-groups was expressly envisaged in the 1993 ROUs which specifically provide for the allocation of "shares and sub-shares" to super-groups existing at the time of the ROUs (e.g. paragraph IV). This, coupled with the possibility of the entry of new super-groups into the SBS system, implies that allocation and re-allocation of quotas must be inherent to the system. The needs of new super-groups could not be satisfied without re-allocation of quotas.

578. The existence of a mechanism of allocation of quota amounts is not only inherent to the SBS system but it is also consistent with the general objective of

the whole system to assist Korea to establish an "orderly program of liberalisation" with "appropriate flexibility" to allow Korea to phase out its "remaining restrictions" by the year 2001. The Panel, therefore, finds that this measure is a "remaining restriction" for the purpose of Note 6(e) and benefits from a transition period until 1 January 2001, by which date it shall be phased out or otherwise brought into conformity with the WTO.

- recording requirements

579. Paragraph IV.C.14 of the July 1993 ROUs provide for record keeping measures to be introduced along with the SBS system:

> "approved super-groups shall administer record keeping of purchases to ensure compliance with the annual and quarterly SBS shares."

580. The Panel finds that the record keeping requirements of the type actually imposed by Korea, being practically the same as those explicitly referred to in the ROUs, were accepted by the parties as being inherent to the SBS system and thereby fall within the meaning of "the remaining restrictions" of Note 6(e); they thus benefits from a transition period until 1 January 2001, by which date it shall be phased out or otherwise brought into conformity with the WTO.

Restrictions on discharge of imports through the wholesale system

- minimum wholesale price[328] (auction/target price)

581. This form of pricing practice has been in place for many years. The 1989 panel first noted that a minimum bid price at wholesale auction, or derived price for direct sale, was set by the LPMO with reference to the wholesale price for domestic beef.

582. The 1990 ROUs (paragraph D.(2)) provide that the joint study team, established by agreement, should:

> "review the functions of the LPMO and make recommendations for improvements in marketing and pricing practices in the future."

This passage reveals a concern with the LPMO's role in the "marketing and pricing practices" of beef imports. The LPMO's restrictive pricing practices, such as the so-called minimum wholesale price, appears to be amongst the types of practices, which falls within this concern.

583. Paragraph IV:C.7(c) also reveals the concern of the parties over Korea's import pricing practices: "in further *implementation of the findings of the GATT dispute settlement panel on beef*, during 1993 the mark-up on beef shall not exceed 100 per cent" (emphasis added).

584. The LPMO's pricing practices, including its minimum wholesale price, are therefore to be considered as one of "the remaining restrictions" within the mean-

[328] Also called "target price" or "minimum auction price" by the parties.

ing of Note 6(e), needing to be addressed during Korea's transition period under the ROUs. To this extent, the LPMO's minimum wholesale price constitutes a "remaining restriction" which benefits from a transition period until 1 January 2001, by which date it shall be eliminated or otherwise brought into conformity with the WTO Agreement.

Price mark-up applied to imports through the SBS system that is additional to the tariff

585. Both sets of 1993 ROUs contain the following reference to the determination of prices through the SBS system:

> "The ROKG shall take no action to increase the price of beef entering under the SBS system above the price of similar beef imported under general tender." (Paragraph IV.A.3.)

586. In addition, paragraph IV.C.7 of the 1993 ROUs specifically address the existence of an SBS mark-up in the following terms:

> " (a) A single, uniform percentage mark-up shall be applied to all types of beef purchased under the SBS system and shall be equal to the difference between the duty-paid price, c.i.f. Korea, and the price for all boneless cuts of imported grain-fed high quality beef, based on the purchases of the LPMO sold in the general tender system."
>
> ...
>
> " (c) ... in further *implementation of the findings of the GATT dispute settlement panel on beef*, during 1993 the mark-up on beef shall not exceed 100 per cent of the weighted average percentage mark-up applied to imported bone-less grain-fed high quality beef during calendar year 1992, as derived from data in Attachment I."[329]

587. This passage, in particular, indicates that the existence of an SBS-like mark-up was indeed contemplated at the time of the ROUs. Korea has also submitted "talking points"[330] from an official of the US Department of Agriculture on 24 February 1994, which shows that the United States had accepted the imposition of the mark-up as an integral part of the 1993 ROU on beef and the Uruguay Round market access. The Panel finds, therefore, that the SBS mark-up is a "remaining restriction" within the meaning of Note 6(e) and benefits from a transition period until I January 2001, by which date it shall be eliminated or otherwise brought into conformity with the GATT/WTO.

---

329 It happens that in 1992, as can be seen from Attachment 1, the LPMO mark-up expressed as a percentage of duty paid export price was almost 100 per cent of the import price.

330 Para. 306 of this Panel report.

Discretionary Licensing System

588. In addition to the measures listed by the Complaining parties, the United States claimed that Korea's import licensing regime for imported beef, based on the issuance of import recommendations by the LPMO, is totally discretionary and, therefore, constitutes a non-automatic licensing procedure for the purposes of the *Agreement on Import Licensing Procedures* ("*Licensing Agreement*"). The United States submitted that the licensing procedures are administered in such a manner as to have restrictive effects on the imports in question.

589. To the extent that imports are restricted through the application of a WTO compatible import quota, a licensing system is necessary. Indeed, the very nature of the SBS system set up under the ROUs regulates the manner in which foreign beef enters Korea's market. Therefore, the existence of a licensing system *per se*, as distinct from its operation, must be one of the "remaining restrictions" envisaged in Note 6(e). In addition, since the beef import quota of the LPMO and the super-groups benefit from a transition period until 1 January 2001, the provisions of its licensing system inherent to the administration of the same beef quota must benefit from the same transition period.[331]

590. The Panel is, therefore, of the view that it is appropriate to examine each of the specific measures identified by the United States and reach a conclusion on each of them rather than examine Korea's import licensing system generally. In the context of these specific determinations, the Panel will necessarily examine the US arguments and suggested evidence that Korea's *administration* of its licensing system was more trade-restrictive than necessary and contrary to the *Licensing Agreement*.

(iii) Disputed Measures not associated with the administration of the beef quota as of 1989 and not envisaged in the ROUs

591. In entering into the ROUs, it is evident that the parties intended to keep open the possibility of challenging any measures which were not inherent to those permitted in the ROUs. To this extent, it is the view of the Panel that the term "the remaining restrictions" could not have been intended to allow reliance on restrictions under the ROUs, if such restrictions were not inherent to those permitted thereunder.

592. In support of the above, the Panel notes that, although providing for the existence of certain restrictions, the July 1993 ROUs also set up a mechanism for consultations between the parties should there be any disputes or problems of

331 However, other aspects of Korea's import licensing system, such as those features not inherent to any remaining restriction – thus not benefiting from the transition period - can be successfully challenged and considered WTO incompatible.

implementation.[332] This envisages precisely the kind of situation described in the previous paragraph, namely, the existence of restrictions not inherent to those prescribed.

593. The Panel, therefore, considers that the following measures or practices were not covered by the wording of any of the ROUs and do not appear to be necessary or inherent to measures (restrictions) otherwise explicitly envisaged in those agreements for the purpose of phasing out the import quota.

Restrictions on the retail sale of imported beef

- the requirement that imported beef be sold in specialized beef stores;
- separate sales areas for the sale of imported beef in department stores; and
- obligation to display an imported beef store sign.

594. With reference to its dual retail system for beef, Korea claims that it is not discriminatory. In the alternative, Korea claims that it benefits from the protection of Article XX. Finally, Korea also claims that it is one of "the remaining restrictions", (thus admitting its restrictive nature) because it existed at the time of the conclusion of the ROUs and this fact is, according to Korea, recognized in the ROUs. Korea draws this conclusion from Section IV B2(e) of the July 1993 ROU which provides that: "Also beginning January 1, 1995, any butcher shops that are or become registered dealers of imported beef shall have the right to participate in the SBS system ... Such individual butcher shops shall have the right to negotiate and place collective orders through NLCF and KCSC."

595. The Panel fails to see why the fact that butchers who sell foreign beef must be registered implies that such butchers cannot also sell domestic beef or why this reference would imply that domestic supermarkets must have different cabinets or areas for foreign beef.

596. Moreover and more importantly, it is difficult to see how a dual retail system that did not exist at the time of the 1989 panel reports or the 1989 balance-of-payments consultations and which was not negotiated in the context of the ROUs could have any relation with the phasing-out of balance-of-payments restrictions, the issue at the centre of the consultations and the ROUs.

597. The Panel is, therefore, of the view that the above measures do not fall within the meaning of "remaining restrictions".

Restrictions on purchases and sales in the wholesale market (for the LPMO's imports

332 Para. VI of the July 1993 ROU between Korea and the United States and para. VII of the July 1993 ROU between Korea and Australia.

- supply from imported beef wholesale market is restricted to specialised beef stores only;
- imported beef to be supplied on a cash payment basis; and
- wholesale markets required to retain records of the supplies of imported beef for at least two years.

598. Although the LPMO has existed for many years, there is no indication anywhere that the above three measures are inherent to any state-trading activities or to the LPMO's marketing or pricing activities as discussed in the 1989 panel report, the balance-of-payments consultations and in the 1990 and the July 1993 ROUs. The Panel finds, therefore, that the three measures do not fall within the meaning of "remaining restrictions".

Limitations on participation in the SBS import system

- Prohibition on cross-trading between end-users

599. As mentioned above, the July 1993 ROUs envisage some restriction on cross-trading between super-groups and between super-groups and end-users. The ROUs do not, however, make any reference to the existence of any restriction on trading between end-users. In addition, such a restriction would be more trade restrictive than necessary to achieve the objectives of the ROUs. The Panel, therefore, finds that the prohibition on cross-trading between end-users is not a restriction envisaged by the parties to fall within the meaning of "the remaining restrictions".

- Labelling requirements

600. Paragraph IV.C.6 of the July 1993 ROUs, prescribes that:

> "except as otherwise specified in this understanding, there shall be no ... labelling, pricing, marking, or packaging requirements or other barriers to legitimate importation, distribution and sale that create unnecessary obstacles to trade or otherwise undermine the objectives of the understanding."

There is no provision for special labelling requirements in the ROU. The Panel, therefore, finds that any additional or specific labelling requirements, if any, imposed on beef imported through the SBS system are not "remaining restrictions".

Restrictions on discharge of imports

- the LPMO's monthly and daily discharge practices

601. Some aspects of the LPMO's role in the marketing of beef imports were envisaged as a "remaining restriction". However, according to the United States and Australia, behaviour which effectively led to restrictive practices additional to and independent of the otherwise legal import quota on beef, could not have been intended by the parties to be "remaining restrictions" referred to in Note 6(e). The type of marketing practices envisaged within "remaining restrictions"

could not have been those which effectively added to the normal restrictions of the beef import quota.

602. To the extent that the United States and Australia claim that the Korean authorities have imposed time constraints and administered the auctioning system in an abusive and non-commercial manner, such restrictions could not have been considered by the parties to the ROU as acceptable temporary restrictions inherent to any state-trading activity of the LPMO. Such behaviour would be rather additional to and independent from what was envisaged under the ROUs.

603. The Panel is, therefore, of the view that such practice could not have been considered to be a "remaining restriction" within the meaning of Note 6(e).

Restrictions resulting from LPMO tendering practices

- refusal or delays in calling for tenders

604. The United States claims that by refusing to call for tenders from the end of October 1997 to the end of May 1998, (and keeping stocks of imported beef too high), Korea imposed import restrictions, contrary to Article XI of GATT. This type of measure is neither dictated by the existence of an import quota, nor contemplated by the ROUs.

605. The Panel shall discuss this measure together with Australia's claims that the LPMO's discharge of imports through the wholesale system, in particular LPMO's alleged refusal to release imports into the Korean market together with its stocking of imported beef, violated Article XI and its Ad Note.

- grain-fed/grass-fed distinction

606. Although not expressly mentioned in terms of the LPMO tendering activities, the problem does surface in Attachment 3 to Australia's 1990 ROU in relation to the operation of the SBS system, and again more specifically in Part V of Australia's 1993 ROU. The Attachment to the 1990 ROU provides that:

> "All imports of beef under the simultaneous buy/sell system will receive equal, non-discriminatory treatment without regard to country of origin and without regard to whether it is grass-fed or grain-fed; fresh, chilled or frozen; bone-in or bone-out."

607. Paragraph IV.C.6(a) of the 1993 ROU provides:

> "Except as otherwise specified in this Understanding, there shall be no restrictions placed by the ROKG or any super-group on beef (regardless of country of origin, product type, or specification, whether grassfed or grain-fed ...)."

608. The existence of the above references to grass-fed beef reveals that Australia was concerned with discrimination between grass-fed and grain-fed beef in the wholesale market through the operation of the SBS system. It is clear that no such restrictions could be tolerated by Australia. Thus, the alleged discrimination between grass-fed and grain-fed beef which, according to Australia, characterized

the LPMO's tendering requirements for imports on several occasions, is not one of the envisaged "remaining restrictions".

(iv) Summary of the Panel's Conclusions with Respect to the Measures in Dispute and Note 6(e) of Korea's Schedule

609. The Panel has found the following measures to be part of "the remaining restrictions" within the meaning of Note 6(e):

Limitations on participation in the SBS import system

- super-group membership requirement;
- restriction on range of end-users;
- prohibition on cross-trading between end-users and super-groups;
- quotas and sub-quotas allocated to super-groups according to annual plans rather than demand; and
- record booking requirements.

Restrictions on purchases and sales into the wholesale market (for the LPMO's imports)

- mandatory acquisition of imported beef through established distribution channels (middlemen)

Restrictions on LPMO's discharge of imports

- minimum wholesale price

Price mark-up applied to imports through the SBS system that is additional to the tariff

Per se Existence of a Discretionary Licensing System relating to remaining restrictions (as distinct from its operation)

610. The consequence of this finding is that all of the above measures, being covered by the term "the remaining restrictions", benefit from the transition period until 1 January 2001 as prescribed under Note 6(e). At the same time, this finding also implies that all of the above measures are GATT inconsistent and will need to be eliminated or otherwise brought into conformity with the WTO Agreement by 1 January 2001.

611. The Panel also reaches the conclusion that the following measures are not "remaining restrictions" within the meaning of Note 6(e):

Restrictions on the retail sale of imported beef

- the requirement that imported beef be sold in specialized beef stores;

- separate sales areas for the sale of imported beef in department stores; and
- obligation to display imported beef store sign.

Restrictions on purchases and sales in the wholesale market (for the LPMO's imports)

- supply from imported beef wholesale markets is restricted to specialised beef stores only;
- imported beef to be supplied on a cash payments basis; and
- wholesale markets required to retain records of the supplies of imported beef for at least two years.

Limitations on participation in the SBS import system

- prohibition on cross-trading between end-users;
- discriminatory labelling requirements.

Restrictions on discharge of imports through the wholesale system

- the LPMO's monthly and daily discharge practices.

Restrictions resulting from the LPMO's tender practices

- refusal or delays in calling for tenders;
- the grain-fed/grass-fed distinction imposed when calling for tenders.

612. The consequence of these findings is that all of the above measures do not benefit from the transition period set out in Note 6(e), and can, therefore, be challenged in the present procedure.

613. In the light of the above findings, the Panel will now proceed to determine the validity of the Complaining parties' claims in relation to the above measures which do not constitute "remaining restrictions" within the meaning of Note 6(e) of Korea's Schedule.

C. *Claims Against the Dual Retail System and Related Measures*

1. *General Claims and Defence of the Parties*

614. Australia and the United States claim that the dual retail system (and related measures[333]) violate Article III:4 of GATT as it results in imported beef being treated less favourably than domestic beef.

---

[333] Throughout these findings, a reference to the dual retail system includes: (1) the requirement that imported beef may not be sold in the same outlet as domestic beef but may only be sold in specialized imported-beef shops (Article 5C of the Guidelines Concerning Registration and Operation of

615. Korea's first defence is that the dual retail system for beef does not impose less favourable treatment on imported beef as domestic and imported beef are both sold in separate shops. Korea adds that there are no limitations on the number of imported-beef shops and that decisions to open imported-beef shops are determined exclusively on the basis of commercial considerations within the context of the WTO compatible beef import quota. Korea contends that, in order to substantiate their claims under Article III of GATT, the Complaining parties must show that the measures in question result in actual prejudice to them in addition to the market access limitations resulting from Korea's beef quota. According to Korea, where a legal import quota is in place two situations are possible. If the quota is fully absorbed, the claim that the WTO Agreement has been violated and as a result the Complaining parties' rights have been prejudiced has to be rejected.[334] If the quota is not fully absorbed the Complaining parties would have to show that the Korean regulation imposing on traders the obligation to sell domestic and imported beef in separate stores is the very reason why the quota has not been absorbed. According to Korea, the Complaining parties must show injury resulting from the dual retail system independent of the protection afforded to domestic production through the negotiation of the import quota for beef.[335] Korea recalls that its considers that it import quota was fully absorbed in 1997 and 1998. Korea's alternative defence is that the dual retail system is necessary for the enforcement of its domestic law prohibiting fraudulent practices. Therefore, should it be found *prima facie* to be inconsistent with Article III:4, the dual retail system should benefit from the application of Article XX(d) of GATT and be declared WTO compatible.

2. *Article III:4 of GATT and the Dual Retail System*

616. Article III:4 of the General Agreement requires that imported products:

> "The products of the territory of any contracting party imported into the territory of any other contracting party shall be accorded treatment no less favourable than that accorded to like products of national origin in respect of all laws, regulations and requirements affecting their internal sale, offering for sale, purchase, transportation, distribution or use. The provisions of this paragraph shall not prevent the application of differential internal transportation charges which are based exclusively on the economic operation of the means of transport and not on the nationality of the product."

Specialized Imported Beef Stores); (2) the obligation for department stores and supermarkets authorized to sell imported beef to hold a separate display (Article 3A of the same Guidelines). The obligation for foreign beef shops to bear a sign "Specialized Imported Beef Stores" is a related measure which the Panel addresses separately in Section 3 thereinafter.

[334] Para. 228 of this Panel report.

[335] Para. 229 of this Panel report.

617. Article III:4 is violated if the Complaining parties demonstrate (a) that imported and domestic products are "like"; (b) that the measure at issue is either a law, regulation, or requirement affecting their internal sale, offering for sale, purchase, transportation, distribution, or use; and (c) which provides to imported products a treatment less favourable than that accorded to like domestic products. Korea is essentially offering arguments relating to the third aspect, i.e. that imported beef is not less favourably treated than domestic beef.

(a) Like Product Determination

618. This dispute is about imports into Korea of fresh, chilled and frozen beef which, the Complaining parties argue, are "like" Korean beef. It has not been contested that imported and domestic beef are "like products".[336] Korea argues, in its Article XX defence, that imported and domestic beef are even indistinguishable. There is an important price differential between Korean beef and imported beef. However, according to Korea, such price differential is "mainly due to the relative cost of production, quality differences, consumer preferences and the existence of a legal quota".[337] The Panel notes that almost 45 per cent of the imported beef is sold in restaurants, where no distinction is made between any origin of beef offered.[338] The Panel concludes, therefore, that imported beef and Korean beef are like products within the meaning of Article III:4 of GATT.

(b) Law, Regulation, or Requirement Affecting their Internal Sale, Offering for Sale, Purchase, Transportation, Distribution, or Use

619. The measures at issue are clearly internal regulations, i.e. laws and/or regulations affecting the internal sale, offering for sale, purchase and distribution of imported and domestic products.

---

336 Paras. 168-170 of this Panel report. "It is also well to remember that a *prima facie* case is one which, in the absence of effective refutation by the defending party, requires a panel, as a matter of law, to rule in favour of the Complaining party presenting the *prima facie* case." Appellate Body Report , *EC Measures Concerning Meat and Meat Products (Hormones)* ("*European Communities – Hormones*"), WT/DS26/AB/R, WT/DS48/AB/R adopted 13 February 1998, DSR 1998:I, 135, para. 104.

337 (Korea, comment on response no 1, 28 February 2000). The Panel notes, however that the effect of the import quota should be to increase the price of imported beef. The Panel understands that Korea wanted to refer to the idea that in limiting the volume of imported beef, the competition in the domestic market is thus reduced.

338 Para. 193 and footnote 140 of this Panel report.

(c) Less Favourable Treatment

(i) Arguments of the Parties

620. The Complaining parties argue that, contrary to Article III:4, the purpose of which is to provide equal conditions of competition once goods had been cleared through the customs[339], the Korean dual retail system imposes less favourable treatment for imported beef. By requiring that imported beef be sold in stores that cannot sell Korean beef, Korea denies imported beef the opportunity to be sold in the vast majority of meat stores. Imported beef is sold in approximately 5,000 stores, whereas there are approximately 45,000 stores where Korean beef is sold.[340] The result is that imported beef is excluded from the ordinary retail system where Korean consumers shop for meat. The Complaining parties refer to the adopted panel reports on *Canada - Marketing Agencies (1992),* and on *US - Malt Beverages,* where it was concluded that by excluding imported beer or wine from points of sale where domestic beer or wine could be sold, the imported products were denied certain competitive opportunities enjoyed by domestic products. Australia adds that the separate display requirements in larger outlets also discriminates against imported beef because it has the effect of emphasising any perception of quality differences between domestic and imported products. In Australia's view, the fact that foreign beef is sold either in separate shops or in separate cabinets has a negative effect on the marketability of imported beef. The overall limited availability of imported beef relative to domestic beef exacerbates this problem.

621. Korea argued that its dual retail system for imported and domestic beef does not offer less favourable treatment to imported beef. Korea submits that the United States and Australia have not been able to demonstrate how the system of separation of stores selling beef prejudices their rights under the WTO Agreement independently of the injury resulting from the very existence of the Korean quota on beef. For Korea, in situations where a WTO compatible import quota is in place and has *been fully utilised*, the claim that the WTO Agreement has been violated must be rejected. In situations where the quota has *not been fully utilised*[341], the Complaining parties, according to Korea, have to show that this was the very result of the dual retail system, something which, according to Korea, the Complaining parties have failed to do.

622. Korea adds that to impose identical regulatory requirements on both categories of stores is in full compliance with Article III:4 of GATT. Indeed, the same restrictions apply to domestic beef stores (they cannot sell imported beef except pre-packed, although a few Korean supermarkets have a separate section

---

339 Panel reports on *Italian Agricultural Machinery*, paras. 11-13; *US - Section 337*, paras. 5.11-5.14; *Canada – FIRA*, para. 6.6.

340 According to Korea the number of foreign beef shops were as follows: in 1995: 7,713; in 1996: 7,569; in 1997: 7,026; in 1998: 5,498. See footnote 111 of this Panel report.

341 Which is not the case in this dispute according to Korea.

for foreign beef) as to imported beef stores (they cannot sell domestic beef, except pre-packed): all stores must respect identical regulatory requirements. The fact that there are more stores selling domestic rather than imported beef does not constitute discrimination and does not engage the responsibility of Korea. The limited volume of imported beef circulating in the Korean market (a government choice which is consistent with Korea's WTO obligations) explains why there are fewer stores selling imported beef in the Korean market. Korea argues that imported beef can be sold anywhere in Korea, and is subject to the same regulatory requirements. The decision whether to open a store selling domestic or imported beef is left to private operators. The number of stores selling imported beef has evolved freely over the years since the quota was established.

(ii) The Relevant GATT/WTO Jurisprudence

623. There is no doubt that there is no "effect test" requirement under Article III, the national treatment principle of GATT. GATT panels have consistently concluded that the pertinent criterion under Article III:4 is whether Members "provide equal conditions of competition" once goods are cleared through customs. To cite the *US – Section 337* panel report:

> "Article III:4 would not serve this purpose if the United States interpretation [referring to the US defence advanced in the *Section 337* dispute] were adopted, since a law, regulation or requirement could then only be challenged in GATT after the event as a means of rectifying less favourable treatment of imported products rather than as a means of forestalling it ... [The panel] noted that this approach is in accordance with previous practice of the CONTRACTING PARTIES in applying Article III, which has been to base their decisions on the distinctions made by the laws, regulations or requirements themselves and on their *potential* impact, rather than on the *actual* consequences for specific imported products." (Emphasis added; footnotes omitted.)[342]

624. As the panel on *US – Section 337* emphasised, Article III:4 is concerned with the effective equality of opportunities in the application of laws, regulations and requirements. The same applies to the national treatment provision of Article XVII:3 of GATS, which explicitly provides that formally identical legal provisions, may, in some cases, have the effect of according less favourable treatment to imported products.

625. In *Japan – Alcoholic Beverages* it was reiterated that "the broad and fundamental purpose of Article III is to avoid protectionism in the application of ... regulatory measures".

---

342 Panel report on *US – Section 337*, para. 5.13.

> "Towards this end, Article III obliges Members of the WTO to provide equality of competitive conditions for imported products in relation to domestic products.... Moreover it is irrelevant that the trade effects of the tax differential between imported and domestic products, as reflected in the volumes of imports, are significant or even non-existent; Article III protects expectations not of any particular trade volume but rather of the equal competitive relationship between imported and domestic products."[343]

626. Similarly, in *Canada – Marketing Agencies (1992)*, the panel stated that:

> "The Panel recalled that the CONTRACTING PARTIES had decided in a number of previous cases that the requirement of Article III:4 to accord imported products treatment no less favorable treatment than that accorded to domestic products was a requirement to accord imported products competitive opportunities no less favourable than those accorded to domestic products. The Panel found that, by allowing the access of domestic beer to points of sale not available to imported beer, Canada accorded domestic beer competitive opportunities denied to imported beer".[344]

627. Any regulatory distinction that is based exclusively on criteria relating to the nationality or the origin of the products is incompatible with Article III and this conclusion can be reached even in the absence of any imports (as hypothetical imports can be used to reach this conclusion) confirming that there is no need to demonstrate the actual and specific trade effects of a measure for it to be found in violation of Article III.[345] The object of Article III:4 is, thus, to guarantee ef-

---

[343] Appellate Body Report on *Japan – Alcoholic Beverages*, *supra*, footnote 98, at 109. In *EC – Bananas III*, *supra*, footnote 97, para. 252 the Appellate Body reiterated the conclusion of the GATT panel report *US – Superfund*: "Article III:2, first sentence, cannot be interpreted to protect expectations on export volumes; *it protects expectations on the competitive relationship between imported and domestic products.* A change in the competitive relationship contrary to that provision must consequently be regarded *ipso facto* as a nullification or impairment of benefits accruing under the General Agreement." (Emphasis added.)

[344] Panel report on *Canada – Marketing Agencies (1992)*, para. 5.6.

[345] See for instance the Panel Report on *Indonesia – Automobiles*, *supra*, footnote 268 where it was concluded that: "14.112 ... The distinction between the products, which results in different levels of taxation, is not based on the products *per se*, but rather on such factors as the nationality of the producer or the origin of the parts and components contained in the product. As such, an imported product identical in all respects to a domestic product, except for its origin or the origin of its parts and components or other factors not related to the product itself, would be subject to a different level of taxation." "14.113 ... Under the Indonesian car programmes the distinction between the products for [domestic] tax purposes is based on such factors as the nationality of the producer or the origin of the parts and components contained in the product. Appropriate hypotheticals are therefore easily constructed. An imported motor vehicle alike in all aspects relevant to a likeness determination would be taxed at higher rate simply because of its origin or lack of sufficient local content. Such vehicles certainly can exist (and, as demonstrated above, do in fact exist). In our view, such an origin-based distinction in respect of internal taxes suffices in itself to violate Article III:2, without the need to demonstrate the existence of actually traded like products."

fective market access to imported products and to ensure that the latter are offered the same market opportunities as domestic products.

628. The Panel takes this to mean that like products are to be offered the possibility to compete in the framework of an integrated market.

(iii) The Panel's Assessment

629. Korea's main argument is that its domestic beef is prohibited access to imported-beef shops and, therefore, imported and domestic beef are treated equally. Korea adds that to require the dismantling of its dual retail regime would imply that GATT requires deregulation, which, according to Korea, is not the case.

630. The Panel wants to stress first that Article III:4 of GATT is not concerned with the treatment of domestic products as such but whether imported products are treated less favourably than domestic products. In this regard, the Panel considers that, contrary to what Korea asserts, the measure Korea applies to imported beef since 1990, whereby imported beef cannot be sold at the retail level through the same outlets or in the same areas (in the case of department stores) as domestic beef, constitutes in itself differential treatment and, what is decisive under Article III:4, such differential treatment unavoidably results in the imported products being less favourably treated on the Korean market than the like domestic products.

631. Regulations providing for the segregation of imported products on the domestic market limit the possibility for consumers to compare imported and domestic products and effectively base their consumption choice on the differences in quality, characteristic and prices of products (either domestic or imported). Thereby they reduce opportunities for imported products to compete directly with domestic products.

632. Suppose an exporter wishes to increase its share of a foreign market. It has to convince distributors, and ultimately consumers, that it has a worthwhile product to sell at an attractive price, in the same way as a domestic manufacturer. In the case of a domestic manufacturer, he must persuade the retailer to stock his product, which may mean replacing an existing domestic product, but will usually involve the two products being sold side by side on a trial basis. However, under a dual retail system, the only way the imported product can get on the shelves is if the retailer agrees to substitute it, not only for one but for all existing like domestic products. This is clearly an added burden on the imported product in principle, which will be particularly severe when imports have a small share of the market in the first place. It cannot be accepted that a dual retail system for beef, even if formally identical for both domestic and imported goods, is in principle compatible with Article III:4. Moreover, even assuming there could be a functioning dual retail system for imported goods, such that its restrictive effects may appear to be minimal, this does not condone the inherently discriminatory nature of such a dual retail system.

633. In the present case, the notion of equal competitive opportunity implies, at the very least, that there be a possibility for imported beef to be physically present with like domestic beef at the point of sale to the consumer. By excluding imported beef from the existing retail system for domestic beef (which comprises the vast majority of sales outlets), the dual retail system limits the potential market opportunities for imported beef. This is particularly evident since beef is a product which is consumed on a daily basis, and for which consumers may not be willing to "shop-around" before making their final purchase.

634. The dual retail system limits the competitive opportunities for imported beef in other ways. In the context of a market mostly dominated by the domestic product, the costs associated with the implementation of the dual retail system bear more heavily on imported than on domestic beef. Indeed, one may expect that the latter will continue to be sold from existing retail facilities whereas the former will require the establishment of new retail facilities.[346] Requiring that imported beef be sold in specialized stores, or in separate display cabinets in large stores, encourages the perception that imported beef and domestic beef are different, when they are in fact like products belonging to the same market, as admitted by Korea. The segregation of domestic and imported beef provides the domestic product with a competitive advantage over the imported product based on criteria not related to the products themselves. It also facilitates the maintenance of a price differential to the advantage of domestic beef. Overall, the segregation of domestic and imported beef tends to shelter the high priced domestic products from the competition coming from the lower priced imported products.

635. Article III:4 of GATT is concerned with state measures and not with the autonomous behaviour of economic operators. Private firms, if they so wish, may decide on commercial grounds to distribute either domestic or imported goods alone. However, a government regulation contravenes Article III:4 if, as in the present case, it **forces** distributors to make such a choice.

636. The dual retail system enforced by Korea in the case of beef is particularly unfavourable to the imported products, if one considers that it was established at a time when the import quota was being phased out. Against this background, the dual retail system can be seen as a potential brake on the market access prospects normally open to less expensive imported beef, the effect of which will be fully felt the day the quota is lifted.

637. Actually, the jurisprudence on Article III makes it clear that no consideration needs to be given to the effects of any less favourable treatment or the im-

[346] Korea argues that there are no start-up costs for new outlets since existing domestic-beef shops may be converted into imported-beef shops. However, Korea does not indicate the proportion of imported-beef shops that have resulted from the conversion of former domestic-beef shops. Such converted shops would in any case have lost the right to continue to sell domestic beef to Korean consumers who want to buy such beef.

pact of such discriminatory regulation on trade volume.[347] In order to demonstrate the Article III violation, there is, thus, no need to prove that the dual retail system is having any effect on the Korean market distinct from that of the WTO compatible quota. The existence of a WTO compatible import beef quota is of no relevance to the claims that the Korean dual retail system provides less favourable treatment to imported products. Therefore, the Panel disagrees with Korea that it was for the Complaining parties to show that the dual retail system causes them prejudice additional to (and independent of) that resulting from the WTO compatible beef import quota, as there is no need to demonstrate any such prejudice.

638. As to the relationship between the existence of a WTO compatible quota and the possibility of claims under Article III, it is well established that WTO Members are bound by all WTO provisions simultaneously:

> "... the WTO Agreement is a "Single Undertaking" and therefore all WTO obligations are generally cumulative and Members must comply with *all of them simultaneously* ..."[348] (emphasis added).

That is to say that even if Korea benefits from a WTO compatible import quota on beef, all Korea's measures, such as the distinct dual retail system for beef, must respect all the other relevant provisions of the WTO Agreement, including Article III of GATT.

(d) Conclusion

639. The Panel finds that under the Korean dual retail system imported beef is treated less favourably than domestic beef. Accordingly, the Korean dual retail system for beef is inconsistent with Article III:4 of GATT. Having reached this conclusion, the Panel considers that it is unnecessary to determine whether this same measure also violates Article XI of GATT, as claimed by Australia.

3. *Article III:4 and the Requirement to Display a Special Sign*

(a) The Arguments of the Parties

640. The Complaining parties claim that the requirement for specialized imported-beef shops to display a sign "Specialized Imported Beef Store" constitutes

[347] Although there is no need to prove any trade effect to win a claim of Article III violation, the effects of the Korean dual retail system can be seen when during the financial crisis (1998) the importers of foreign beef were not able to "adjust" as well as the domestic producers because the retail (and the SBS) systems in place limited their flexibility to search for additional and new points of sales. It is reported that in 1997 and in particular 1998 the number of foreign-beef shops went down importantly (in 1995: 7,713; in 1996: 7,569; in 1997: 7,026; in 1998: 5,498. See footnote 111 of this Panel report.

[348] Appellate Body Report on *Korea – Safeguards*, supra, footnote 290, para. 74.

a less favourable treatment for imported beef, imposing a requirement that does not exist for domestic beef. Australia adds that the sign "*Specialized Imported Beef Store*" has the effect of emphasising any negative perceptions about the quality of imported beef; this has detrimental effect on the marketability of imported beef and a dampening effect on prices. Australia recalled that in 1955, it had complained that an Hawaiian regulation requiring firms which sold imported eggs to display a sign stating: "We sell foreign eggs", violated Article III:4. The complaint was withdrawn when a US domestic court decision declared the law unconstitutional and contrary to Article III:4 of GATT.

(b) The Panel's Assessment

641. The Panel is of the view that such a sign display requirement being essentially ancillary to the dual retail system, itself is inconsistent with Article III:4, is necessarily also inconsistent with Article III:4.

642. In addition, the requirement to display the sign "*Specialized Imported Beef Store*" goes beyond the indication of origin on products and therefore is in violation of Article III:4 of GATT. The Panel recalls that the 1956 Working Party report on "Certificates of Origin, Marks of Origin, Consular Formalities" noted that "requirements *going beyond the obligation to indicate origin* would not be consistent with the provisions of Article III, if the same requirements did not apply to domestic producers of like products".[349]

643. The Panel finds, therefore, that the requirement imposed on shops selling imported beef to display a sign " Specialized Imported Beef Store" is *prima facie* in violation of Article III:4 of GATT.

644. The Panel now proceeds to examine Korea's defence based on Article XX(d) of GATT.

4. Korea's Defence Based on Article XX(d) of GATT

(a) Arguments of the Parties

645. Korea claims that its dual retail system for beef, if found in violation of Article III:4, as is the case, should benefit from the protection of Article XX(d) of GATT.[350] Korea submits that it is necessary to have domestic and imported beef sold through separate stores in order to counteract fraudulent practices prohibited by the *Unfair Competition Act*. Because imported beef is cheaper than domestic beef, traders have a strong incentive to sell imported beef as domestic beef since by doing so they can profit from the higher sales price. In 1990, in

[349] The *1956 Working Party report on "Certificates of Origin, Marks of Origin, Consular Formalities"*, BISD 5S/102, para. 13.

[350] Korea also argues that the dual retail system is a remaining restriction, something the Panel does not accept. See paras. 593 to 597 above.

order to stop these deceptive practices, Korea enacted the dual retail system and decided to eliminate the previous simultaneous sales system which had been in place since 1988 when imports of beef first resumed. Korea argues that it seriously considered the choice of instrument in order to reach its regulatory objective to ban fraudulent practices by individual traders with respect to sales of beef. In Korea's view, continuous policing of the shops was not an option in view of the substantial costs to the government.[351] On the other hand, Korea stated that the dual retail system relies on policing only domestic-beef shops whilst ensuring that stores selling imported beef indicate that they do so. In Korea's view, this indication is sufficient to remove the risk that imported beef be sold as domestic beef, as consumers know that in foreign beef shops cheaper imported beef is offered.[352]

646. Korea refers the Panel to its *Unfair Competition Act*, which addresses commercial practices which are considered unfair *vis-à-vis* competitors and consumers (including fraudulent practices). The purpose of the Act, as stated in Article 1, is to "maintain the order of sound transactions by preventing unfair competitive acts."

647. In paragraph 1 of Article 2, the term "unfair competitive act" is defined as follows:

> "(1) Act misleading the public to understand the place of origin of any goods either by falsely marking that place on any commercial document or communication, in said goods or any advertisement thereof or in any manner of misleading the general public, or by selling, distributing, importing or exporting goods bearing such mark;
>
> (2) Act making a mark misleading people to understand as if any goods were produced or processed in an area other than that where said goods are produced, manufactured or processed, on any commercial document or communication, in said goods or any advertisement thereof, or in any manner of misleading the general public, or act selling, distributing, importing or exporting goods bearing such mark;"

Korea submits that the system of separation of sales outlets is necessary to enforce this Act and that Article XX(d) GATT provides an appropriate legal framework to justify the dual retail system.

648. Australia and the United States submit that, contrary to paragraph (d) of Article XX, the dual retail system for beef was not put in place to secure compliance with a WTO compatible regulation on deceptive practices; at best the dual retail system has the same objective as the *Unfair Competition Act*. Australia also

351 See para. 244 of this Panel report.
352 See para. 255 of this Panel report.

submits that Korea's substantial market price support and the dual retail system are actually exacerbating the price differential between domestic and imported beef, and therefore increasing the likelihood of fraud. In Australia's view, fraud will cease only when this artificial price differential disappears. In Australia's view, it is pertinent that record-keeping requirements that are imposed on imported beef stores are not imposed on domestic beef stores. Therefore, Korea cannot ascertain the sources of supply for domestic beef and hence whether fraud takes place in domestic shops.

649. In addition, the Complaining parties argue that the dual retail system is not "necessary" to avoid fraudulent practices. They also suggest WTO consistent alternatives to the dual retail system that would allegedly ensure the prevention of deceptive practices. In support of their allegations, the Complaining parties point to the manner in which Korea dealt with similar situations involving domestic beef (misrepresentation of dairy beef for Hanwoo beef) or other sectors of the Korean economy where frequent fraudulent practices are reported to occur. Finally, the Complaining parties claim that the Korean dual retail system for beef is in any event inconsistent with the provisions of the chapeau of Article XX, in that it imposes a disguised restriction on international trade since its only purpose it to protect Korean beef production.

(b) Article XX(d) of GATT and the GATT/WTO Jurisprudence

650. GATT Article XX (d) provides:

> "Subject to the requirement that such measures are not applied in a manner which would constitute a means of arbitrary or unjustifiable discrimination between countries where the same conditions prevail, or a disguised restriction on international trade, nothing in this Agreement shall be construed to prevent the adoption or enforcement by any contracting party of measures:
>
> ...
>
> (d) necessary to secure compliance with laws or regulations which are not inconsistent with the provisions of this Agreement, including those relating to customs enforcement, the enforcement of monopolies operated under paragraph 4 of Article II and Article XVII, the protection of patents, trade marks and copyrights, and the prevention of deceptive practices;"

651. Korea concedes that it bears the burden of showing that its retail restrictions fall within the scope of Article XX.[353] To satisfy its burden under Article XX, Korea must thus show that the requirement for sale of imported beef in separate stores is "necessary to secure compliance with laws that are themselves con-

[353] Appellate Body Report in *United States – Gasoline*, *supra*, footnote 117, page 22.

sistent with the GATT 1994" and further that the dual retail system is not "applied in a manner which would constitute a means of arbitrary or unjustifiable discrimination between countries where the same conditions prevail or a disguised restriction on international trade".

652. With reference to Article XX(d), the GATT panel report on *US – Section 337* provided that the first issue to be determined is whether a GATT consistent alternative could have been employed:

> "It was clear to the Panel that a contracting party cannot justify a measure inconsistent with another GATT provision as "necessary" in terms of Article XX(d) if *an alternative measure which it could reasonably be expected to employ and which is not inconsistent with other GATT provisions is available to it*".[354] (Emphasis added)

653. In *US – Gasoline*, the Appellate Body also considered the existence of WTO consistent alternative courses of action, concluding that the US measure did not benefit from the application of Article XX[355]:

> "*There was more than one alternative course of action available* to the United States in promulgating regulations implementing the CAA. These included the imposition of statutory baselines without differentiation as between domestic and imported gasoline. This approach, if properly implemented, could have avoided any discrimination at all."[356] (emphasis added)

(c) The Panel's Assessment

654. In order to benefit from the protection of Article XX(d), Korea must demonstrate that the dual retail system (including related measures), although inconsistent with Article III:4:

(i) is in place in order to "secure compliance" with a domestic GATT consistent law or regulation which, here, means to enforce the Korean law against deceptive practices; and if this is the case,

(ii) is "necessary" to prevent deceptive practices from occurring in the Korean beef market (and more particularly the passing of foreign beef as domestic beef); and if this is the case,

(iii) is not applied in a manner which would constitute a means of arbitrary or unjustifiable discrimination between countries where the same conditions prevail, or a disguised restriction on international trade.

---

354 See Panel report in *US - Section 337*, para. 5.26.

355 In that case however, the Appellate Body, proceeded to the examination of alternatives under the provision of the chapeau of Article XX.

356 Appellate Body Report on *United States – Gasoline*, *supra*, footnote 117, page 25.

(i) "... secure compliance with GATT consistent regulation"

655. The Panel must first identify and characterize the alleged GATT consistent regulation. In this case, the regulation referred to by Korea, is the Korean *Unfair Competition Act*, which among other things, aims at the prevention of deceptive practices. At face value, this is a GATT consistent regulation. Secondly, the Panel must identify the practices that Korea considers deceptive and aims to prevent. In the present case, the alleged deceptive practices are the misrepresentation of the origin of beef, i.e. selling imported beef as domestic beef, a practice which is commercially profitable because of the price differential. The Panel acknowledges that, whatever is the cause of such fraudulent practices, selling imported beef as domestic beef constitutes misrepresentation as to the origin of the beef, contrary to Article 2 of the *Unfair Competition Act*.[357] The Panel recognizes that there can be good reasons – apart from any protectionist motives – why a WTO Member might want information to be provided as to the origin of products, and particularly meat products, at the retail level.

656. As the Panel understands it, the application of the Korean *Unfair Competition Act* is initiated either by private parties or by public authorities and takes the form of policing, investigations, desist orders, fines, etc. The normal application of the *Unfair Competition Act* would not have given rise to an issue under Article III:4 and thus would not have required any justification under Article XX(d), provided that the same degree of enforcement applies in the case of domestic and imported products. The Korean measure under discussion does not pertain to the normal enforcement of the *Unfair Competition Act*. The establishment of a dual retail system is not among the tools, the use of which the *Unfair Competition Act* envisages or mandates for the purpose of deterring acts of misrepresentation or other types of fraudulent practices.[358]

657. Korea submits that in the case of foreign beef, it had to discard the normal application of the *Unfair Competition Act* since this proved to be too difficult and too costly in late 1989 and early 1990 in view of the number of fraud cases which occurred at that time in the context of the single retail system and where foreign beef was misrepresented as domestic beef. The cases of misrepresentation were themselves induced by the large difference between the respective prices of domestic and foreign beef.[359] Thus, according to Korea, the arrival of less expen-

---

[357] The Panel recalls that Article 1 of the *Unfair Competition Act* prohibits any "act misleading the public to understand the place of origin of any goods either by falsely marking that place on any commercial document or communication, in said goods or any advertisement thereof or in any manner of misleading the general public, or by selling, distributing, importing or exporting goods bearing such mark."

[358] The Panel notes that in the Guidelines Concerning Registration and Operation of Specialized Imported Beef Stores, no reference is made to the need to combat fraud, as the basic rationale for the implementation of such dual retail system.

[359] Korea reports that the price of Korean-bred cattle was 12,000-15,000 won per kilogram while imported beef was sold at 4,800 won per kilogram.

sive foreign beef on the Korean market, after imports resumed in 1989, created an exceptional situation due to the frequency of deceptive practices. In order to prevent such practices from occurring, Korea decided to segregate foreign beef at the retail level. In other words, the dual retail system is presented by Korea as being an exceptional remedy and a substitute to the normal manner of preventing practices forbidden by the *Unfair Competition Act.*[360] The Panel considers that the dual retail system is indeed an exceptional remedy for the purpose of preventing acts of misrepresentation. In addition to being discriminatory, it is a measure of a permanent and fixed character, which, once taken and until removed, cannot easily be adjusted to changing circumstances.[361] This is in contrast with the flexibility afforded by the *Unfair Competition Act.*[362]

658. However, despite these troublesome aspects, the Panel accepts that the dual retail system was put in place, at least in part, in order to secure compliance with the Korean legislation against deceptive practices to the extent that it serves to prevent acts inconsistent with the *Unfair Competition Act.* First, the system was established at the time when, as stated by Korea and not refuted by the Complaining parties, acts of misrepresentation were widespread in the beef sector. Second, it must be conceded that the dual retail system does appear to reduce the opportunities and thus the temptations for butchers to misrepresent foreign beef for domestic beef, when compared with the situation where all domestic and imported beef could officially be supplied to the same shop. The Panel notes that its interpretation of the words "measure ... to secure compliance with laws and regulations" is not inconsistent with the approach taken by the panel on *EEC – Parts and Components* and later followed by the panel on *Canada – Periodicals.*[363] If

---

360 The Panel notes that it is not a complete substitute to the enforcement of the *Unfair Competition Act* to the extent that, as recognized by Korea, the dual retail system does not eliminate the need to prevent through traditional means the large number of domestic-beef shops from trying to sell foreign beef as domestic beef. Also, the need to police large department stores remains high due to, in this case, the physical proximity of imported and domestic beef.

361 For instance the price differential has been diminishing since 1990, and to the same extent the incentive to engage in fraudulent practices. However, the dual retail system has not been altered.

362 While Korea could claim that it made efforts to be somehow flexible in allowing imported packaged beef to be sold in beef domestic shops, the Panel notes that Korean consumers are not asking for packaged beef, as evidenced by the very low level of consumption (and imports of such prepackaged beef).

363 In the *EEC- Part and Components*, the EEC had argued that Article XX(d) could cover a measure (in that case, the imposition of anticircumvention duties) which prevented actions that were consistent with laws and regulations (in that case, the EEC's antidumping regulation) but undermined their objectives. That panel took the view that it was not enough for the measure to share the same objective as the "laws and regulations". That panel considered that the measures covered by Article XX(d) "must prevent actions inconsistent with the obligations set out in laws or regulations" (para. 5.15). That panel referred to "The examples of the laws and regulations indicated in Article XX(d), namely 'those relating to customs *enforcement*, the *enforcement* of monopolies ..., the *protection* of patents ... and the *prevention* of deceptive practices" (emphasis added) ... [which] suggest that Article XX(d) covers only measures designed to prevent actions that would be illegal under the laws or regulations." (para. 5.16). Panel Report, *Canada – Periodicals, supra,* footnote 268 concerned an import ban, which did no more than share the same objective, i.e. the channelling of ad-

one admits that the dual retail system was established in part to secure compliance with the Korean statute against deceptive practices, the crucial question is whether the measure is "necessary" to prevent misrepresentation of imported beef for domestic beef. Here again the burden of proof is on Korea.

(ii) "necessary to prevent misrepresentation as to the origin of beef"

659. To demonstrate that the dual retail system is "necessary", Korea has to convince the Panel that, contrary to what was alleged by Australia and the United States, no alternative measure consistent with the WTO Agreement is reasonably available at present in order to deal with misrepresentation in the retail beef market as to the origin of beef. The Panel considers that Korea has not discharged this burden for two inter-related reasons. First, Korea has not found it "necessary" to establish "dual retail systems" in order to prevent similar cases of misrepresentation of origin from occurring in other sectors of its domestic economy. Second, Korea has not shown to the satisfaction of the Panel that measures, other than a dual retail system, compatible with the WTO Agreement, are not sufficient to deal with cases of misrepresentation of origin involving imported beef. The Panel will detail each of these two reasons, noting that the first turns on facts – what does Korea do to prevent misrepresentation in cases other than the one at hand? The second rests both on factual findings, some of those facts being the same as are relevant to the first question, as well as on projections, based on those facts, regarding what Korea reasonably could do to prevent misrepresentation involving imported beef at the retail level?

Absence of dual retail systems in other sectors of the Korean economy

660. Deceptive practices similar to those which affected, in 1989 and 1990, the sale of foreign beef at the retail level are reported to occur or may occur in other sectors of the Korean economy. However, in those instances, Korea did, or does, not require that the products involved be sold through separate channels as a means to secure compliance with the Korean law on deceptive practices.

661. For instance, Korea has treated differently situations involving similar risks of fraud such as between domestic Hanwoo and domestic dairy cattle beef (dairy steer beef and dairy cow beef). However, there is no dual retail system for

---

vertising revenue towards Canadian periodicals, as a tax provision granting tax deduction for expenses, (paras. 5.8 to 5.10).

The interpretation given by the present Panel to the words "measure to secure compliance ..." would be inconsistent with the *EEC - Parts and Components* only if one were to interpret the approach taken by the panel in that case as requiring that measures coming within the scope of Article XX(d) be technically part of the "laws and regulations" themselves. The reading of the *EEC – Parts and Components* does not warrant such an interpretation and if it would, which is not the case, the present Panel would disagree with so narrow an interpretation of Article XX(d).

domestic dairy cattle beef. Korea's justification is that the amount of such dairy beef is negligible. In 1990, the year the dual retail system was established, beef from domestic dairy cattle represented somewhat less than half the amount of imported beef and about 25 per cent of total beef consumption in Korea.[364] In 1998, beef from dairy cattle amounted to approximately half of the amount of imported beef and 12 per cent of total beef consumption.[365] Therefore, the Panel considers that the amount of beef coming from dairy cattle is not negligible. Korea also submitted that in late 1998 it discovered a DNA test that apparently distinguishes between the two types of domestic beef. The Panel is not convinced that such a scientific test, if being able to distinguish between domestic Hanwoo beef and dairy beef, would not also be able to distinguish between foreign and Korean beef. Furthermore the discovery of a DNA test in 1998 can not explain the absence of a dual retail system for domestic beef during the period before that date.

662. The Panel notes also that there is no dual retail system for other agricultural products. Korea suggests that it is necessary to resort to the drastic measure of segregating retail sales in the case of beef, but not in the instance of other products, because of beef 's particular importance as a component of the average Korean's diet and the substantial commercial activity in beef. However, Korea did not explain to the satisfaction of the Panel why other sources of protein, such as pork and seafood, which also have been identified as subject to fraudulent misrepresentation of the country of origin, were not made subject to a dual retail system.

663. Moreover, although some 45 per cent of imported beef is sold in restaurants, there is no requirement that domestic and foreign beef be offered in separate restaurants. Restaurants selling imported beef do not need to indicate whether they serve domestic or imported beef, or at least not until 2000. Two types of situations may arise.[366] In the first, some Korean restaurants may serve imported beef as Hanwoo beef, thus suggesting that Korea may not consider the

---

[364] The Panel was not able to make comparisons at the retail level. According to Korea, beef imported in 1990 amounted to 84,000 MT (See para. 258 of this Panel report) in excess of the 58,000 MT quota for that year while according to MAF statistics, Korean beef production amounted to 95,000 MT of which about 42 per cent came from dairy cattle. In 1991, imports of beef amounted to 124,000 MT and domestic beef amounted to 98,000 MT, of which 42 per cent came from dairy cattle. At the Interim review stage Korea and the United States submitted new data indicating that the amount of imported beef in 1991 would have been 127,000 MT. Even if one were to rely on this new data, this would not make the amount of dairy cattle beef less negligible.

[365] In 1998, total consumption in Korea amounted to 345,000MT of which 91,000 MT was imported, and about 254,000MT came from domestic production. According to statistics by the NLCF, dairy cattle represented, in 1998, 18.25 per cent of total Korean slaughter (head). According to Korea, dairy cow beef alone represented 28,000 MT (Annex 11), i.e. 8.1 per cent of total beef consumption, 11 per cent of domestic production and corresponded to 30 per cent of the amount of imported beef. See Annexes 8, 9, 10 and 11 of this Panel report.

[366] The Panel notes that the Livestock Times reported that the deceptive beef marketing practice was widespread in restaurants (where price differential was 58 per cent).

prevention of such acts of misrepresentation to require the establishment of a dual restaurant system. In the second, some restaurants, while not necessarily claiming that their beef is Hanwoo beef, may in fact sell beef without any reference to its origin, thus suggesting that Korea, unlike in the cases of butcher shops, is at least, not preoccupied with the profits restaurants may make from such practices and with precise information to be provided to consumers.

664. The Panel considers that the previous examples taken from outside as well as within the beef sector indicate that misrepresentation of origin can indeed be dealt with on the basis of basic methods, consistent with the WTO Agreement, and thus less trade restrictive and less market intrusive, such as the normal policing under the Korean *Unfair Competition Act*.[367] These examples could leave the impression that only when imported beef is sold at the retail level does misrepresentation of origin become a matter of such concern to Korea. This directly questions the "necessity" of the dual retail system.

Existence of WTO consistent alternative measures to prevent deceptive practices in the beef retail market

665. The Panel considers that in the presence of an alternative measure consistent with WTO rules, it is for Korea to demonstrate that such an alternative measure is not reasonably available or is unreasonably burdensome, financially or technically, taking into account a variety of factors including the domestic costs of such alternative measure, to ensure that consumers are not misled as to the origin of the beef.

666. The Complaining parties have suggested that there exist alternatives measures consistent with the WTO Agreement, including labelling, record-keeping, prosecution and fines that would be effective in detecting and preventing deceptive practices as to the origin of beef.

667. With reference to the suggestion that the Korean government could increase investigations, prosecutions and the use of fines, Korea submits that imposing higher fines does not help to resolve the issue since traders will continue to have an incentive to cheat. Korea also asserts that more traditional means of addressing fraud, such as through investigations and prosecutions, are not practical because imported beef is allegedly nearly impossible to distinguish from domestic beef. Korea's contention is unconvincing for a number of reasons.

668. With reference to Korea's allegation that investigations are impossible[368], the Panel recalls that in the discussions of the December 1989 report (by the National Assembly's Subcommittee on Audits of Agricultural and Livestock Marketing), Korea was able to be very precise in terms of the exact amount of im-

---

[367] The Panel also notes that Korea has not submitted any evidence of similar dual retail systems for the purpose of preventing acts of misrepresentation as to the origin of goods in other WTO Members.
[368] Para. 244 of this Panel report.

ported beef sold in deceptive ways. According to Korea, "a Marketing Association confirmed that 28 per cent of imported beef transacted at general butcher shops have been faked and sold as Hanwoo". It seems that Korea had then, before the entry into force of the dual retail system, an investigation system that allowed it to identify imported beef and to distinguish it from Korean beef. The Report of the Proceedings of the National Assembly's Committee on Agriculture, Forestry and Fisheries (7 March 1990), after investigations, reported fraudulent beef sales in 604 instances. At the time, Korea's investigation system and capacities appear to have been sufficient to detect fraudulent practices even in the beef sector[369], without any need to having recourse to a dual retail system. Contrary to Korea's allegations, therefore, it would seem that Korea had the ability to distinguish imported beef from locally produced beef or at least to detect fraud when the one was passed off for the other. It is unlikely that such capacity would have disappeared in the course of a few years.

669. The effectiveness of fines will depend, on the one hand, on the level of such fines and the probability of being caught and, on the other, on the level of profit margin resulting from such fraud.[370] The Panel considers that the threat of prosecution, which for small butchers would imply an attack on their reputation, would be an effective deterrent.

670. The Complaining parties submit that the auditing of purchase and sale records could supplement Korea's WTO-consistent efforts to identify instances of fraudulent misrepresentation of product origin. The Complaining parties suggest that enforcement of record-keeping requirements, applied universally to sales of beef, would be a WTO-consistent way of combating any fraud, as Korean regulations relating to imported beef already require substantial record-keeping by the various levels of trade.

671. Korea's response is that audit trails are not yet a feasible option for Korea's under-developed system of distribution. With respect to record-keeping, Korea's response is that few merchants in practice maintain comprehensive and accurate book records.

672. The Panel agrees that some forms of audit trailing are a rather sophisticated system of fraud detection. But there are several alternative means available to Korea to ensure the prevention of deceptive practices. For instance, a generally applied record-keeping requirement backed with sanctions would constitute a WTO consistent alternative to the WTO inconsistent dual retail system. If foreign

[369] Some kind of similar system must now be in place with respect to large department stores which can be officially supplied with both domestic and imported beef, even though they are supposed to sell them in separate areas.

[370] If fines were commensurate to incentives to engage in fraudulent practices on the Korean market, whether domestic or foreign goods are involved, this would appear consistent with Article III:4 of GATT.

beef shops can keep book-records[371], it is difficult to see why the same could not be requested from domestic shops. Indeed, all beef traders at all levels of trade could be required to keep records so that investigations would easily detect the origin of the beef sold and/or purchased and be able to compare the prices of beef products and the profit made.

673. Korea also argues generally that, in the absence of a dual retail system, the prevention of acts of misrepresentation at the retail level would require the continuous policing of beef stores, something which, according to Korea, would be too costly. However, Korea has not supplied any data as to the costs which, for example, the normal enforcement of the *Unfair Competition Act* would entail. Moreover, as mentioned above, reliance on traditional means does not seem too costly an alternative in those instances where acts of misrepresentation do or may occur on the Korean market. After all, with the WTO Agreement the Members have made a bargain[372] and compliance with the WTO Agreement may sometimes require (costly) adjustments to domestic policies and laws.[373]

674. On the basis of the previous discussion, the Panel considers that Korea has not demonstrated to the satisfaction of the Panel that alternative measures consistent with the WTO Agreement were not reasonably available in order to detect deceptive practices in the beef retail sector.

Non-fulfilment of the "necessity" requirement

675. For the reasons detailed above, the Panel finds that the dual retail system is a disproportionate measure not necessary to secure compliance with the Korean law against deceptive practices. Therefore, it is not justified by Article XX(d) of GATT. Consequently, there is no need for the Panel to examine the relevance of the chapeau of Article XX of GATT.

(iii) Conclusion on Korea's Article XX Defence

676. The Panel has thus not been convinced by Korea's defence that its dual retail system should benefit from the application of Article XX(d) of GATT.

---

[371] A practice which when imposed only on foreign beef shops would be contrary to Article III:4 of GATT.

[372] As stated by the Appellate Body in its report on *Japan – Alcoholic Beverages II*, *supra*, footnote 98, at 108:"The *WTO Agreement* is a treaty -- the international equivalent of a contract. It is self-evident that in an exercise of their sovereignty, and in pursuit of their own respective national interests, the Members of the WTO have made a ***bargain***. In exchange for the benefits they expect to derive as Members of the WTO, they have agreed to exercise their sovereignty according to the commitments they have made in the *WTO Agreement*."

[373] See Article XVI:4 of the Agreement Establishing the WTO.

5. *Conclusion on the WTO Compatibility of the Dual Retail System for Beef*

677. The Panel finds, therefore, that Korea's dual retail system for beef is inconsistent with the provisions of Article III:4 of GATT by treating imported beef less favourably than domestic beef, a discrimination that cannot be justified pursuant to Article XX(d) of GATT. It should therefore be removed or otherwise brought into conformity with the WTO Agreement. It is, however, for Korea to decide which measure(s) consistent with WTO it wants to choose, whether measures already in use in Korea, or measures suggested above, or other measures, to replace the dual retail system.

D. *Claims Against the (LPMO) Distribution System at the Wholesale Level*

1. *General Arguments of the Parties*

678. Australia raises the following specific claims against various requirements pertaining to sales of beef imported by the LPMO: (a) the limitation of sales of imported beef to the wholesale market, unless beef is processed and packaged; (b) the restrictions on supply of beef from the wholesale market to specialized imported-beef stores only; (c) sales on a cash payment basis; and (d) record-keeping requirements, which according to Australia, are imposed only on beef imported by the LPMO and thus accord less favourable treatment to imported beef. The United States does not raise any specific claims on this matter although it has claimed that the dual retail system, generally, is in violation of Article III:4.

679. Korea's counter-arguments with reference to each specific claim above is that: (a) it is impossible to establish comparability between domestic and imported beef since there is a WTO compatible quota; (b) the dual retail system, including the obligation for department stores to have a separate section selling foreign beef, is compatible with the WTO; (c) Korea admitted that the LPMO's sales of imported beef through the wholesale market shall in principle be on a cash basis,[374] however, Korea argues that this requirement is also applied to the NLCF sales of domestic beef to domestic beef stores; (d) Korea did not submit any counter-argument to this claim. Korea concluded that these measures, therefore, do not violate Article III:4. Should the Panel reach a different conclusion, Korea claims that it benefits from the protection of Article XX(d) of GATT.

2. *The Panel's Assessment*

680. The Panel recalls that in paragraph 584, it concluded that the LPMO's sale of imported beef through the Korean wholesale market is a "remaining restriction" which benefits from a transition period until 1 January 2001, by which date

[374] See para. 214 of this Panel report.

it shall be eliminated or otherwise brought into conformity with the WTO Agreement. This measure will therefore not be further discussed.

681. The Panel also recalls its discussion on Article III:4 of GATT in paragraphs 627 to 638 where it concludes that the object of Article III:4 is to guarantee effective market access to imported products and to ensure that the latter are offered the same market opportunities as domestic products.

682. It is not disputed that imported and Korean beef are like products. Nor is it disputed that the above-mentioned measures are regulations or requirements affecting the sale, offering for sale or distribution of imported beef. Article III:4 of GATT is thus applicable to the present situation. The Panel will now proceed to examine Australia's claim that less favourable treatment is imposed on imported beef by the LPMO distribution rules.

(a) Restrictions on Supply of Beef from the Wholesale Market to Specialized Imported-Beef Stores – the Dual Retail System

683. Australia claims that the requirement that beef imported through the LPMO be sold only in specialized foreign beef shops is in violation of Article III:4.

684. The Panel has already reached the conclusion that the Korean dual retail system, whereby imported beef (except pre-packed or processed) can only be sold in "foreign beef shops", is contrary to Article III:4 and cannot benefit from the protection of Article XX.

685. The Panel finds, therefore, that the restrictions imposed on the supply of beef from the wholesale market to specialized imported-beef stores, i.e. an application of the dual retail system, impose on beef imported through the LPMO treatment less favourable than that accorded to domestic beef which is not subject to any such restriction, and thus are contrary to Article III:4 of GATT. For the reasons provided in paragraphs 654 to 676 above, the Panel reaches the same conclusion with regard to the non-application of Article XX(d) to the present measures.

(b) Sales of Imported Beef through the Wholesale Market can Allegedly only be on a Cash Basis

686. Australia claims that the requirement, contained in Article 11 of the Regulation Concerning Sales of Imported Beef, that imported beef be supplied on a cash basis only is in violation of Article III:4.

687. Korea's defence that this requirement is also applied to the NLCF sales of domestic beef to domestic beef stores does not appear to have been contradicted

by Australia. Korea submits that both imported and domestic beef stores sell their products mostly on a cash basis except where a credit relationship is formed between the traders or when the trader has secured a mortgage bond.[375] It is not clear whether a "credit relationship" can legitimately take place in favour of specialized imported-beef shops.

688. The Panel recalls that Australia bears the burden of proving its claim that beef imported by the LPMO is subject to less favourable treatment (such as the requirement that payment take place only on a cash basis) than domestic beef. Considering the evidence before it, the Panel is of the view that Australia has failed to do so and therefore cannot accept this claim.

(c) Record-Keeping Requirements

689. Australia claims that the obligation imposed on those who purchase foreign beef imported by the LPMO to record all purchases and sales and retain such records for at least two years creates compliance costs on distributors of imported beef in terms of time and expense. These costs have an inevitable impact on the price of imported product. For Australia, the absence of similar requirements on domestic beef, impose less favourable treatment on foreign beef imported through the LPMO, contrary to Article III:4 of GATT.

690. Korea submits that under the revised Guidelines, the specialized shops are no longer required to keep records of sales. The Panel is aware that its terms of reference oblige it to examine the factual and legal situation on 26 May and on 26 July 1999, and that such revised Guidelines were adopted after the Panel was established.

691. The Panel recalls Korea's concern with respect to fraudulent practices, that imported beef could be sold as domestic beef. To the extent that such record-keeping requirements were imposed equally on the LPMO, to those who purchase from the LPMO and to distributors of both imported and domestic beef, such record-keeping requirements could be seen as a reasonable and feasible alternative to ensure the prevention of fraudulent practices in Korea.

692. The Panel's appreciation of the evidence relevant to the time when it was given its mandate is that those in Korea who purchased foreign beef imported by the LPMO were subject to more stringent record-keeping requirements than those who purchased domestic beef. There is no doubt that such additional requirements are in violation of Article III:4.

---

[375] Ibid.

E. Claims against the SBS System

1. General Description of the Claims of the Parties

693. The Complaining parties argue that the very existence of the SBS system, the restrictions on who can import, the SBS membership requirement, the prohibition on cross-trading between super-groups, the prohibition on cross-trading between end-users and super-groups and the prohibition on cross-trading between end-users are restrictive and inconsistent with Articles III:4, and XI and its Ad Note.

694. Australia adds that Korea's overall "supervision of imports", i.e. the labelling, reporting and record-keeping requirements, is in violation of Article III:4, as similar requirements do not exist for domestic beef.

695. Korea offers specific defences addressed below.

2. The Panel's Assessment in the Light of Note 6(e)

696. The Panel recalls its conclusion in paragraphs 569 to 580 that the SBS system, including its exclusive membership mechanism, the prohibition on cross-trading between super-groups, and between super-groups and end-users as well as some more onerous record book keeping requirements were "inherent" features of the SBS system[376] as set up by the parties in the ROUs and, thus, constituted some of the remaining restrictions which benefit from a transition period until 1 January 2001, by which date they shall be eliminated or otherwise brought into conformity with the WTO.

697. However, prohibition to cross-trade between end-users cannot be seen as "inherent" to the SBS system as set up in the ROUs, as there is no reference to the existence of any restriction on trading between end-users. The same is to be said of any additional (or abusive) labelling requirement imposed only on imported products as there is no reference to specific labelling requirements in the ROUs. Some of the features of the SBS system relate to the distribution of imported beef. However, the origin of beef should be of no legal relevance to its distribution within Korea. In the Panel's view, such additional labelling requirements are not inherent to the SBS system. The prohibition on cross-trading between end-users and additional labelling requirements of the SBS system are not "remaining restrictions". The Panel proceeds to the examination of these specific measures.

[376] See in particular paras. 579-580 of this Panel report.

3. *Examination of Two Specific Measures of the SBS System*

(a) Prohibition on Cross-Trading between End-Users

(i) Arguments of the Parties

698. The Complaining parties claim that the prohibition on cross-trading between end-users impose a treatment less favourable on imported beef than on domestic beef.

699. Korea's response is that the Revised Management Guideline for Imported Beef prohibit only the resale of imported beef by specialised stores to their counterparts selling domestic beef, but cross-trading between specialized stores is now allowed.

(ii) The Panel's Assessment

700. First, the Panel recalls that, based on its terms of reference, it must examine the situation on and before 26 May and 26 July 1998.

701. Article 11 of the Guidelines prohibits, as previously, the use of imported beef for any purpose other than a use permitted under the Guidelines for the particular end-user or customer. [377] It specifies the permitted uses of beef for the end-users of each of the super-groups and provides that no use or sale other than that provided for in Article 11 shall be authorized.[378] Sanctions for failure to comply with the specified use and sale limitations are severe.

702. The Panel recalls its discussion (see paragraphs 629 to 640 of this Panel Report and the panel report on *US – Section 337*, paragraph 5.13) on Article III:4 of GATT where it concludes that the purpose of Article III:4 is to oblige all domestic laws and regulations to provide equality of competitive conditions to imported products in relation to domestic products.[379]

703. The SBS Operational Guidelines and the December 1997 Guidelines are laws, regulations and requirements affecting the internal sale, offering for sale, purchase, distribution or use of domestic or imported beef. It is not disputed that imported and Korean beef are like products.

704. The Panel recalls that similar restrictions on the internal distribution of domestic beef do not exist. The Panel finds, therefore, that foreign beef imported

---

377 The prohibited activities, formerly identified in Articles 6 and 11 of the December 1997 Guidelines, and previously in the SBS Operational Guidelines, are now contained in Article 26 of the October 1999 Guidelines. Although Korea recently reissued both the Regulations Concerning Imported Beef Stores and the Operational Guidelines for Imported Beef Under the SBS System, and consolidated those directives into a single document, the substance of the requirements is left unchanged.

378 The restrictions on the specific use of imported beef by each end-user and customer are now set forth in Article 21 of the new Guidelines.

379 The panel report on *US - Section 337*, para. 5.13.

through the SBS system is accorded less competitive opportunities to reach potential consumers in the Korean market than those accorded to domestic beef, for which there is no prohibition on cross-trading between end-users.

705. Thus, the prohibition against cross-trading between end-users imposed on foreign beef imported through the SBS system is contrary to Article III:4 of GATT. Having reached this conclusion the Panel does not consider it necessary to examine the Complaining parties' claims that the same measure also violates Article XI and its Ad Note.

(b) Additional Labelling Requirements

(i) Arguments of the Parties

706. Australia argues that the Korean labelling requirements imposed on beef imported through the SBS system are in violation of Article III:4, as similar requirements do not exist for domestic beef. Australia further claims that this requirement imposes an unnecessary, impractical and expensive measure imposed only on the imported product, thereby artificially reducing the competitive ability of the imported product. For Australia, the current labelling of Australian products clearly identifies the origin and product. In Australia's view, many elements of what is required by Korea to be included on the label are of no relevance, impracticable and more restrictive than necessary. For instance, for the end consumer, the contract number and super-group importer adds no information of any relevance as these matters are concerned with the importation of foreign beef. This requirement (to indicate the number of the contract and the super-group) is impractical because the contract number and super-group may be unknown at the time the product is packed by the producer. The measure, therefore, requires relabelling either prior to shipment or in Korea. For Australia, whether re-labelled in Korea or Australia, there will be additional costs for the re-labelling, which will serve to make the imported product less competitive.

707. Korea submits that all imported livestock products including beef are required to be marked with, among other things, the name of the product, importer, the address of the importer, production date, and shelf life. For Korea, these requirements are necessary to facilitate the importation of these products and are used for customs clearance purposes as well as distribution. Korea adds that the domestic beef traders must also mark the name of the products, producer, shelf life, and the production date. For Korea, these requirements aim to protect public health and to establish sound distribution processes.

(ii) The Panel's Assessment

708. The Panel notes that no such additional labelling requirement is inherent to the SBS system. Some of the features of the SBS system relate to the distribution of imported beef. However, under basic WTO national treatment principle, the origin of beef cannot be a factor affecting the distribution of beef within Ko-

rea. The Panel notes also that Korea has not raised any specific defence based on the application of Article XX(b) for the protection of public health.

709. Under Article III:4 of GATT, imported products must not be subject to more stringent requirements affecting their distribution within the Korean market than domestic products. The Panel has already referred to the 1956 Working Party report on "Certificates of Origin, Marks of Origin, Consular Formalities" where it was concluded that the "requirements *going beyond the obligation to indicate origin* would not be consistent with the provisions of Article III:4, if they are not also imposed on domestic products".[380]

710. The Panel, therefore, finds that any additional labelling requirements imposed on foreign beef imported through the SBS system that are not also imposed on domestic beef, such as the requirements that the end consumer, the contract number and super-group importer be marked on the imported beef, are contrary to Article III:4 of GATT.

F. Claims against the LPMO's Minimum Wholesale Price, the Refusal or Delays in Calling for Tenders and the Discharge Practices in 1997-1998

1. General Arguments of the Parties

711. The United States claims that various "operating procedures" of the LPMO, including its alleged establishment of a minimum wholesale price or minimum auction price, the alleged refusal or delays in calling for tenders and the alleged delays selling into the Korean market such imported beef as well as the withholding of quota shares to SBS super-groups, amount to restrictions additional to that of the WTO compatible beef import quota.

712. Australia's focus of concern is the manner in which the LPMO satisfies its mandate of price stabilization. In this regard, Australia submits that the LPMO's alleged practice of imposing a minimum wholesale price or minimum auction price, the establishment and execution of monthly discharge plans, and its control over daily imported beef discharge at the wholesale market are inconsistent with the WTO Agreement.

713. Both Complaining parties point to the fact that Korea's import quota (both the LPMO and SBS shares) were not filled which for them constitutes *prima facie* evidence that Korea's practices in its administration of the beef quota constituted an import restriction.

714. For the Complaining parties, the fact that such practices were those of a state-trading enterprise cannot be used to justify their inconsistency with Article XI of GATT, in view of the Ad Note to Article XI which provides that the re-

380 The 1956 Working Party report on *"Certificates of Origin, Marks of Origin, Consular Formalities"*, para. 13.

quirements of Article XI also apply to measures taken by a state-trading enterprise. Both Complaining parties claim that the same measures, as they restrict imports of agricultural products, are also inconsistent with the provision of Article 4.2 of *the Agreement on Agriculture* and its footnote, which more specifically prohibits restrictions on imports of agricultural products maintained through a state-trading enterprise. Australia claims that the same measures violate Articles XVII and III:4 of GATT, while the United States argues that the same practices also violate Article 3 of the *Licensing Agreement* since the administration of the import licensing procedures are more "administratively burdensome than absolutely necessary to administer the relevant measure". The United States did not further develop its claim that such LPMO's practices violate Article XVII of GATT.

715. Korea's defence to these claims is that, since it has a WTO compatible beef import quota in place, the only way for Australia and the United States to establish a violation is for them to prove that the quota was not fully utilized and that the failure to fill the quota is caused by, or the result of, a separately identifiable prohibition or restriction. Korea argues that even if such a quota is not fully utilized, for the Complaining parties to successfully claim a violation of Article XI, they must establish a clear causal relationship between separately identifiable restrictions and the non-fulfilment of the quota (since the non-fulfilment can be due to a multitude of market factors).

716. In summary, Korea submits that in order to establish a violation of Article XI:1 in this case, the United States and Australia must establish: (1) the existence of a separately identifiable prohibition or restriction (beyond the quota and its implementation) on the importation of product, other than duties, taxes or charges; (2) that such prohibition has been "made effective." In the present case, this would involve establishing that (i) the quota has not been fulfilled, (ii) the restriction has actually had the intended effect of restricting imports to a level below the quota level and that (iii) a clear causal link establishing that the non-fulfilment of the quota is specifically due to the measure at issue and is not attributable to other factors.

717. Korea argues that it fully used its beef import quota so the Australian and US claims should be rejected. Furthermore, Korea argues that the United States and Australia do not properly attempt to explain how any of the alleged restrictions constitute restrictions in addition to the restrictions imposed for the purposes of implementing the legally valid quota. Thus, in Korea's view, the fact that the Complaining parties did not submit any evidence or arguments on the causal relationship between any alleged restrictions and the reduced import levels is fatal to the Complaining parties since the Korean financial crisis provides the commercial and economic reasons for the inability of Korea to fill its import quota.

2. *Minimum Wholesale Price*

(a) Arguments of the Parties

718. The Complaining parties claim that, with a view to stabilizing prices, the LPMO auctions beef which it imports while a minimum wholesale price (or minimum auction price or target price) is fixed with reference to the domestic price. The Panel considers that the basis on which such a minimum wholesale price is established is not clear. In its first submission, Korea argues that the minimum wholesale price for imported beef is fixed by reference to the price of domestic beef.[381] In its second submission Korea argues that the minimum wholesale price is set to "avoid the sale of imported beef below a certain price level".[382] In response to a question by the Panel, Korea responded that "target prices are set based mainly on the import price (duty paid CIF + selling cost) of beef ... thereby aimed at avoiding losses".[383]

(b) Panel's Assessment in Light of Note 6(e)

719. The Panel has already reached the conclusion that some kind of minimum wholesale price or minimum auction price existed (and was indeed condemned by the 1989 Panel) at the time of the 1989 panel reports and must have existed at the time of the conclusion of Korea's Schedule, since the July 1993 ROUs provide for the need to improve LPMO's pricing practices. In the Panel's view, and to the extent that some minimum/target auction price can be viewed as a "remaining restriction", the Panel finds that such a restrictive pricing practice benefits from a transition period until 1 January 2001, by which date it should be phased out or otherwise made WTO compatible. The Panel will not discuss this measure any further.

720. The Panel notes, however, that the Complaining parties have made other and distinct claims against the administration of the beef quota by the LPMO, namely, that the alleged refusal to discharge imported beef into the Korean market resulted in the stocking of imported beef, and that the alleged delays and refusal to call for tenders during certain periods contributed to the non-filling of Korea's import quota. The Panel shall, therefore, address these claims separately, below.

---

381 See para. 207 of this Panel report.

382 See for instance, paras. 130 and 131 of this Panel report.

383 See para. 131 of this Panel report.

3. *The LPMO's Daily and Monthly Discharge Practices; the Withholding of Imported Stocks; and the Refusal or Delays in Calling for Import Tenders*

(a) Arguments of the Parties and Factual Determination Made by the Panel

(i) Were the Beef Import Quotas Filled in 1997 and 1998?

721. In reply to the claims that the LPMO's auctioning and discharge functions are essentially restrictive and led to the non-filling of the import quota for 1997 and 1998, Korea's first defence is that its import quotas have been fully used. In Korea's view, therefore, it cannot be in violation of its WTO obligation and, in particular, its licensing system cannot have any trade-distortive effects as prohibited by Article 1.2 and 3.2 of the *Licensing Agreement*. In support of its arguments, Korea refers the Panel to the conclusions of the panel and the Appellate Body in EC – *Poultry*, where it was said that the full utilisation of import licenses "strongly suggests that any trade-distortive effects of the operation of the licensing rules have been overcome by the exporters."[384]

722. The parties have submitted data with reference to imports of beef by the SBS system and the LPMO. Korea provided the following data:

1997	**LPMO**	**SBS**
Quota amount	83,500 tonnes	83,500 tonnes
Amount Purchased	83,500 tonnes	83,486 tonnes
Amount Customs Cleared	75,266 tonnes	75,666 tonnes
Amount of the quota not cleared	8,234 tonnes	7,509 tonnes

1998	**LPMO**	**SBS**
Quota amount	74,800 tonnes	112,200 tonnes
Amount Purchased	74,800 tonnes	69,933 tonnes
Amount Customs Cleared	26,961 tonnes	94,395 tonnes
Amount of the quota not cleared	47,839 tonnes	17,805 tonnes

723. The Complaining parties submitted more or less similar data except for the non-use of the SBS's share of Korea's import quota in 1998:

[384] Panel Report on *EC – Poultry*, *supra*, footnote 173, para. 249; and Appellate Body Report, *supra*, footnote 61, paras. 119-122.

1997	LPMO	SBS
Quota amount	83,500 tonnes	83,500 tonnes
Amount Purchased	83,500 tonnes	83,175 tonnes
Amount Customs Cleared	75,266 tonnes	76,723 tonnes
Amount of the quota not cleared	8,234 tonnes	6,777 tonnes

1998	LPMO	SBS
Quota amount	74,800 tonnes	112,200 tonnes
Amount Purchased	74,800 tonnes	69,933 tonnes
Amount Customs Cleared	26,961 tonnes	52,128 tonnes
Amount of the quota not cleared	47,839 tonnes	60,072 tonnes

724. In order to assess whether Korea's import quota has been filled, the Panel must determine whether the annual level of imported beef is below the level at which Korea is entitled to limit imports. The date when contracts are signed between commercial actors is of no relevance when assessing whether Korea's annual imports have been restricted. What is relevant is the date of importation of the beef products and the level of those imports. The relevant date is the customs-clearance date, i.e. the date when such beef products are effectively imported into Korea.

725. The Panel notes in particular the different figures submitted by the parties with regard to the amount of customs cleared beef under the SBS in 1998. The Panel notes as well that Korea submits that in 1997 the amount of beef customs cleared under the SBS was 75,666 tonnes and the amount purchased was 83,486 tonnes while in 1998 the amount of beef customs cleared was 94,395 tonnes for 69,933 tonnes purchased. The Panel notes furthermore that, according to these figures, under the SBS system, super-groups were able to customs clear so much more than they purchased in spite of the fact that super-groups, according to Korea, do not carry over stocks.

726. Australia submitted non-refuted evidence that in 1998, 112,200 tonnes was allocated among the SBS super-groups (70 per cent of Korea's quota). Of this amount, only 69,933 tonnes or 62.3 per cent was actually taken up. Among the various super-groups, KMPA, LCTM and KMIA used up 99.8 per cent, 99.3 per cent and 97.0 per cent of their allocations, respectively. However, KTSC, KFMP and KRSC used up only 33.0 per cent, 26.0 per cent and 14.8 per cent of their allocation. This suggests that super-groups with excess demand were prevented from purchasing additional imports whilst other super-groups had unused quotas. Although this appears very restrictive, the Panel has reached the conclusion that such restrictions, i.e. the allocation and re-allocation process of the SBS system, constitute part of "the remaining restrictions" within the meaning of Note 6(e) to Korea's Schedule which, therefore, benefit from a transition period until 1 January 2001, by which date they should be phased out or otherwise brought into

conformity with the WTO Agreement. Therefore, although the SBS system of re-allocation of quotas (in which LPMO and MAF are involved) may explain the non-filling of the SBS 70 per cent share of Korea's beef import quota, such SBS system cannot be successfully challenged at the moment. The Panel will, therefore, limit its discussion to the LPMO practices – delays in selling stocks of imported beef and in calling for tenders – with regard to the LPMO's 30 per cent share of Korea's beef import quota.

727. In respect of the LPMO's share of Korea's beef import quota, the Panel concludes that it was not filled in 1997 and 1998. As such, this is not evidence of any violation of any WTO rules. In this respect, the Panel notes that Korea is not bound by any minimum purchase or minimum import obligation.

(ii) The LPMO's Role in the Non-Filling of the Import Quota

728. Korea admits that the LPMO suspended its tenders for beef of foreign origin between the end of October 1997 and May 1998.[385] In other words, in the Panel's view, while Korea was entitled to limit imports of beef to the level of its import quota (30 per cent of which is exclusively allocated to the LPMO), at the end of October 1997 the LPMO unilaterally decided to further reduce the level of its import quota by part of this 30 per cent.

729. Australia submits evidence of demands for imported beef that remained unsatisfied notwithstanding the fact that there was an important amount of beef in stock. The Complaining parties submit extracts from the Daily Meat News from 1997 to 1999 which show a consistent pattern of supplying a range of imported beef cuts below amounts demanded and below amounts in stock. For example, data from the Daily Meat News on 13 February 1999 shows that although 275 boxes of Excel (EC) brand chuck roll were demanded, only 175 boxes were awarded, despite availability of 500 boxes. Similarly, despite demand for 655 boxes of IBP chuck roll and the availability of 800 boxes, only 555 boxes were sold. Korea responds that these requests were not filled because the price offered would have been below the minimum wholesale price.

730. There is also evidence that, in October 1997, the LPMO had an estimated 28,000 tonnes of imported beef in stock. By the end of 1998, the LPMO had accrued stocks of 67,934 tonnes of imported beef, more than the LPMO's entire quota allocation for 1999. As at July 1999, these stocks had fallen to 61,524 tonnes.[386] The LPMO had, thus, enough beef in stock to respond to the market demand.

---

[385] See para. 138 of this Panel report.

[386] "Cattle Prices and Beef Supply and Demand Trends", issued with MAF Press Release of 22 July 1999. (Attached as Annex 12 of this Panel report.)

731. To the extent that (i) Korea admits that the LPMO did not call for tenders between the end of October 1997 and the end of May 1998; (ii) in 1998 the LPMO had stocks of imported beef amounting to almost one full year of quota which necessarily led to very high stocking costs for the LPMO; (iii) there is evidence that in 1997 and 1998 LPMO/NLCF (hereafter collectively designated as the LPMO) refused to sell imported beef although it had sufficient stock to respond to the demand and that (iv) imported beef is generally cheaper than domestic beef, the Panel considers that the Complaining parties have submitted a *prima facie* case that the LPMO's delays or refusal to call for tenders in 1997 and 1998 and its discharge practices during the same period were, at least in part, responsible for the non-filling of its portion of Korea's beef quota.

(iii) The Issue of the Economic Justifications for Korea to Do So

732. The Panel recalls that in light of the facts mentioned in paragraph 731 above, Korea has the burden of rebutting the *prima facie* case established by the Complaining parties. In this regard Korea submits that in the context of the 1997-1998 financial crisis, it was commercially justified for the LPMO to refuse to discharge (i.e. to sell the beef it had in stock) and to refuse or delay the call for tenders between the end of October 1997 and the end of 1998 because it would have made losses on those sales. Korea adds that the LPMO was already making important losses.[387] The Panel considers that two distinct periods must be examined: first the period between the end of October 1997 and the end of May 1998 and second, the period between June 1998 and the end of December 1998.

From the end of October 1997 to the end of May 1998

733. Korea admits that the LPMO refused to call for tenders between the end of October 1997 and the end of May 1998.[388] It argues that the LPMO's failure to call for tenders for beef imports between November 1997 and May 1998 was the result of stagnant beef sales due to decreased domestic demand for imported beef, resulting in increased imported beef stocks.[389] It noted that, after November 1997, no subsequent purchases were made by the LPMO because it had already purchased the total quota by October 1997. It submits that, after the depreciation of the Korean won towards the end of 1997, import prices in won surged while

[387] The Complaining parties submit that during that period the LPMO was not making real losses. For them, the LPMO's losses (as set forth in Annex 4 to this Panel report) appear to be overstated since they were calculated by comparing the LPMO's selling price to its costs which include, however, selling expenses.
[388] See para. 138 of this Panel report.
[389] See para. 138 of this Panel report.

domestic beef prices fell, leading to a substantial decline in the demand for imported beef.[390]

734. The Complaining parties do not dispute the effect of the financial crisis on the demand for beef in Korea. However, they argue that the main reason for the drop in imported beef consumption was the refusal of the LPMO to supply as part of a deliberate policy to stabilize and support the price of domestic beef.[391] The higher cost of feed had an adverse effect on the profitability of Korean beef farming in 1998, encouraging a sell-off of cattle with a consequent downward pressure on the domestic beef price.[392] They argue that the LPMO's actions in maintaining a minimum wholesale price for imported beef were intended to offset this.

735. Korea's response is that the LPMO would have made losses on the import of beef and that it was justified in maintaining the minimum wholesale price at the level it did in order to prevent losses on sales of imported beef. In support of its allegation, Korea presents price data in Annexes 5 and 6 (KOREA's Exhibits 41 and 45)[393]. These exhibits show average import prices above the LPMO wholesale prices throughout 1998 (especially in the summer, well after the peak of the currency crisis). It argues that purchasers were not prepared to meet the target price level (set by reference to c.i.f. + tariff + selling costs) and thus that it would have made losses if it had sold below this price.

736. The Panel notes some problems with the price data presented in Annex 4. Korea does not indicate how the import prices for the period during which tenders for imports were suspended as shown in its Annex 4, are derived. The Panel also notes that, in calculating the LPMO losses in Annex 4, Korea takes into account the LPMO's selling costs. These selling costs averaged 11.5 per cent in 1998 but were as high as 35 per cent on some cuts in some months. Selling costs appear to vary depending on the type of beef (grain-fed or grass-fed) and the type of cuts; selling costs also change every month. These high selling costs are in striking contrast with the fees charged by the super-groups to their end-users or customers.[394] The Panel is not convinced that the LPMO's selling costs could not have been reduced by selling the beef it had in stock, as some of the very high costs probably were the result of its large stocks of imported beef. The Panel, thus, has difficulty in accepting that these selling costs always represent a legitimate cost item which should be deducted in arriving at the LPMO profit or loss from selling imported beef.

---

390 See para. 138 of this Panel report.

391 See para. 127 of this Panel report.

392 See para. 193 of this Panel report.

393 See Annexe 4 to this Panel report.

394 The Panel is aware that the super-groups are not supposed to keep stocks of beef under the ROUs; the charges and fees that they are allowed to collect are much lower. The United States alleges that SBS super-groups are only allowed by the MAF to charge 2-3 per cent to their end-users/customers. See para. 140 of this Panel report.

737. The Panel notes also that super-groups continued to import beef in 1998 (as the LPMO also did in the second half of 1998): this would not have been the case if, as Korea seems to argue, there was not some demand for beef at prices higher than import prices. While it is true that not all super-groups used their quotas, it is apparent that at the end of 1998, there was an important demand for imported beef, as evidenced by the three reallocations of sub-shares, and the extensive import activities of some super-groups (KMIA, LCTM and KMPA: representing processors, and sales agents to shops and restaurants).

738. Korea also claims that there were health scares during that same period. The Panel considers, however, that Korea did not offer any evidence, other than newspapers clippings, that the cited health scares had any impact on import levels during the relevant period or that they affected the prices of imports or the prices Korean consumers were willing to pay for imported beef.[395]

739. However, in the absence of convincing evidence that these import prices and selling costs are erroneous, the Panel will use the data in Annex 4 to evaluate Korea's claim that the LPMO would have made important losses on imported beef at the end of 1997 and through 1998 on the grounds that demand for imported beef fell and stocks were building up.

740. The sales volume of imported beef at the wholesale level is not independent of the minimum auction price set by the LPMO. In this regard, the Panel notes that, for the specific chuck roll cut, there is evidence that Korea increased the target price considerably between the last quarter of 1997 and January/February 1998 from 3,800 won/kg. to 4,620 won/kg.[396] Korea argues that the target price is set by reference to the c.i.f. import price plus duty plus selling costs in order to avoid selling imported beef at a loss. But, even though it may be the case that a higher import price had to be paid for the beef imported during those months, from the stock-holding perspective the relevant comparison to make is between the price at which the LPMO had bought the beef that was in stock and the price it would be able to get on selling it. As the LPMO did not tender for beef after November 1997, it must be that the beef in stock had been bought before the financial crisis and the devaluation of the won. Therefore, the LPMO would not have made losses as long as it sold beef from its stocks.[397] In the Panel's view, during the period running from the end of October 1997 to the

[395] The Panel cannot see any link between an alleged health scare in September 1997 or June 1999 and the period of the end of November 1998 and the end of May 1999.

[396] The figure of 3,800 won/kg. was the average level of the target price for chuck roll for the last three months of 1997 in Annex 7 to this Panel report in response to the Panel's Question No. 29 on 14 January 2000. In the table in para. 2.28 in Korea's First Submission the target price was given as 4,620 won/kg. in late January 1998 for the same cut of beef.

[397] For example, for chuck roll, the ex-LPMO import price (c.i.f. price + duty + selling costs) in the last quarter of 1997 was 4,311 won/kg. (Annex 7 to this Panel report). The wholesale price in November and December 1997 was very slightly less than this, but was significantly higher in the January through May 1998 period when, according to Korea, stocks were increasing (Annex 8 of this Panel report).

end of May 1998, Korea would not have made all the losses it claims have occurred. The Panel adds that during that same period the level of beef stocks was very high and not commercially reasonable. There was, therefore, no need for Korea to take into account what would have been high "replacement" costs of all such stocks. Therefore, the Panel finds that Korea's delays in discharging its imported beef were not commercially justified.

741. The Panel also finds that the absence of any LPMO tenders for imported beef in the period between the end of October 1997 and May 1998 was not justified by the evidence presented. By not inviting tenders, the LPMO had no way of knowing whether imported beef was available at prices that would permit the LPMO to import without incurring any financial losses. In not inviting tenders the LPMO effectively closed the Korean market to imported beef to the extent of LPMO's quota share.

From June to the end of December 1998

742. With regard to Korea's absence and delays in calling for tenders, the Panel notes that the two most important cuts in volume terms imported in 1998 were chuck roll and grass-fed (bone-in) beef. Korea's figures for 1998 in Annex 4 suggest that it made losses in importing grass-fed (bone-in) beef in each month that year, and on importing chuck roll from April of that year. These losses are calculated as the difference between the actual wholesale price obtained and the ex-LPMO import price (c.i.f. price + duty + selling costs). In this connection, it is relevant to recall that the Complaining parties have argued that the wholesale price obtained by the LPMO was manipulated by the minimum target price system in order to hold it at a higher level than would otherwise have been the case. It therefore follows that, if the LPMO had in fact imported and discharged imported beef in a "normal" manner, the wholesale price of imported beef would have been even lower than the level which prevailed, and the losses incurred would have been even greater.

743. In reaching this conclusion, the Panel has assumed that the auction system for imported beef operates in a transparent way and that all beef which is demanded at the auction price is, in fact, supplied. Australia submits evidence that fewer boxes of beef were awarded than were demanded (on a date in February 1999), despite the general availability of beef on that day. Korea responds[398] that the reason for the release volumes being less than domestic demand is that bid prices for the bulk of imported beef were lower than minimum auction prices. If Korea had released beef at these bid prices, it would have incurred higher losses than those reported in Annex 4. Thus, while the Panel believes that the LPMO import prices, and hence the LPMO losses, may be exaggerated by the level of selling costs included in the import price, the operation of the minimum auction

[398] See para. 138 of this Panel report.

price system acted to offset this and would have reduced the size of reported losses. If it were the case that, even at the price being bid, Korea rationed the award of beef, then the argument in this paragraph would not be valid. However, no evidence was submitted to challenge Korea's explanation on this point.

744. Given the LPMO's ability to influence the level of demand for imported beef through its manipulation of the minimum target price system at auctions[399], it is for Korea to prove that it did not abuse this practice by preventing access to imported beef by domestic consumers who, even after the financial crisis at the end of 1997, might have been prepared to pay the commercial price for that beef. Korea has submitted that the price being bid at the wholesale auction markets for particular cuts of beef was insufficient to cover its import price for most of 1998 and that this justified its delays in tendering and shipping. While the Panel has some reservations about the figures used by Korea to make this point, it accepts that Korea was commercially justified to delay its purchasing of imported beef during 1998.

(iv) Conclusion

745. In sum, with the rather limited evidence before the Panel, it appears to the Panel that Korea did not have an economic reason for not calling for tenders and not discharging imported beef during the period between the end of October 1997 and the end of May 1998. Korea's lack and delays in calling for tenders and its discharge practices of imported beef after May 1998 until December 1998 (the last month for which detailed price data was provided by Korea in Exhibit 45, Annex 4 of this Panel report) may be justified by normal economic considerations.

746. Having reached this factual conclusion, the Panel shall now examine whether the LPMO's refusal to call for tenders between the end of October 1997 and the end of May 1998 and its daily and monthly discharge practices during this period are inconsistent with the WTO Agreement. Before proceeding to its legal discussion, the Panel notes that Korea did not invoke Articles XII or XVIII:B of GATT during the period when it experienced financial difficulties and does not claim, still today, to have had any balance-of-payments difficulties in 1997 and 1998.

(b) The WTO Provisions and Jurisprudence on Restrictions Imposed by State-Trading Enterprises

747. The Panel shall now proceed to examine the law applicable to restrictions imposed by state-trading enterprises. The Complaining parties claim that the LPMO practices violate Article XI and its Ad Note, Articles III and XVII of the

399 A practice which in para. 584, the Panel has already deemed to be a "remaining restriction" having to be phased out or otherwise brought into conformity by 1 January 2001.

GATT 1994 and Article 4.2 of the *Agreement on Agriculture.* Korea's defence is that its import quota was filled in 1997 and 1998 or that in any event all its quota had been purchased in 1997 and 1998 and would receive customs clearance before the end of 2000. In addition, Korea argues that, in any event, the LPMO was justified in its refusal and delays to call for tenders and discharge because it would have incurred losses in doing so. The Panel has already reached the conclusion that Korea has not demonstrated these facts to the satisfaction of the Panel for the period between the end of October 1997 until the end of May 1998. For the rest of 1998, Korea may have been justified to keep some delays in calling for tenders and in discharging its imports as it appears that, if it had not done so, the LPMO would have incurred further losses.

(i) Articles XI, the Ad Note to Articles XI, XII, XIII, XIV and XVIII and Article XVI of GATT

748. Article XI.1 of the GATT provides that:

> "No prohibitions or restrictions other than duties, taxes or charges, whether made effective through quotas, import or export licences or other measures, shall be instituted or maintained by any contracting party on the importation of any product of the territory of any other contracting party … "

The Ad Note to Articles XI, XII, XIII, XIV and XVIII provides that:

> Throughout Articles XI, XII, XIII, XIV and XVIII, the terms "import restrictions" or "export restrictions" include restrictions made effective through state-trading operations.

This is to say that when an import restriction is imposed by a state-trading enterprise, with or without exclusive rights, such restriction would be covered by Article XI[400].

749. In the dispute on *Japan - Agricultural Products* the Panel took note of Japan's contention that quantitative restrictions made effective through import monopolies could not be covered by Article XI:1 and found that:

> "Article XI:1 covers restrictions on the importation of any product, 'whether made effective through quotas, import ... licences or other measures.' The wording of this provision is comprehensive, thus comprising restrictions made effective though an import monopoly. This is confirmed by the note to Articles XI, XII, XIII, XIV and XVIII, according to which the term 'import restrictions' throughout

[400] The Panel notes that the general prohibition against import restrictions contained in Article XI and its Ad Note find a more specific application in Article 4.2 of the *Agreement on Agriculture* together with its footnote with regard to agricultural products. The Panel shall discuss further the relationship between this set of provisions below.

> these Articles covers restrictions *made effective through state trading operations.*" (Emphasis added.)

More specifically, the panel in this case noted that:

> *"The basic purpose of this note is to extend to state-trading the rules of the General Agreement governing private trade and to ensure that the contracting parties cannot escape their obligations with respect to private trade by establishing state-trading operations."*[401] (Emphasis added.)

750. The adopted GATT panel report on *Canada - Marketing Agencies (1988)*, dealt with import and distribution restrictions imposed by a state-trading enterprise which held monopoly rights on both the importation and the distribution. It was found that:

> " 4.24 ... the note to Articles XI, XII, XIII, XIV and XVIII provided that throughout these Articles "the terms 'import restrictions' and 'export restrictions' include restrictions made effective through state-trading operations". *The Panel considered it significant that the note referred to "restrictions made effective through state-trading operations" and not to "import restrictions"*. It considered that this was a recognition of the fact that *in the case of enterprises enjoying a monopoly of both importation and distribution in the domestic market, the distinction normally made in the General Agreement between restrictions affecting the importation of products and restrictions affecting imported products lost much of its significance since both types of restriction could be made effective through decision by the monopoly*. The Panel considered that systematic discriminatory practices of the kind referred to should be considered as restrictions made effective through "other measures" contrary to the provisions of Article XI:1. It also noted that an agreement or arrangement would have to be consistent with the General Agreement."[402] (Emphasis added.)

751. Thus, in the special case where a state-trading enterprise possesses an import monopoly *and* a distribution monopoly, any restriction it imposes on the distribution of imported products will *lead to a restriction on importation* of the particular product over which it has a monopoly. In other words, the effective control over both importation and distribution channels by a state-trading enterprise means that the imposition of any restrictive measure, including internal measures, will have an adverse effect on the importation of the products concerned. The *Ad Note* to Article XI therefore prohibits a state-trading enterprise

---

[401] Panel Report on *Japan – Measures Affecting Agricultural Products* (" *Japan – Agricultural Products II*"), WT/DS76/R, adopted 19 March 1999, DSR 1999:I, 315, para. 5.2.2.2.

[402] Panel report on *(1988) Canada - Marketing Agencies*, para. 4.24.

enjoying monopoly right over both importation and distribution from imposing any internal restriction against such imported products.

752. Article XVII of GATT (and the parallel footnote to Article 4.2 of the *Agreement on Agriculture* further discussed below) is also relevant to state-trading enterprises activities and practices. Article XVII of GATT provides that:

> 1.* (*a*) Each contracting party undertakes that if it establishes or maintains a State enterprise, wherever located, or grants to any enterprise, formally or in effect, *exclusive or special privileges*,* such enterprise shall, in its purchases or sales involving either imports or exports, *act in a manner consistent with the general principles of non-discriminatory treatment prescribed in this Agreement for governmental measures* affecting imports or exports by private traders.
>
> (*b*) The provisions of subparagraph (*a*) of this paragraph shall be understood to require that such enterprises shall, having due regard to the other provisions of this Agreement, make any such purchases or sales solely in accordance with *commercial considerations*,* including price, quality, availability, marketability, transportation and other conditions of purchase or sale, and shall afford the enterprises of the other contracting parties adequate opportunity, in accordance *with customary business practice*, to compete for participation in such purchases or sales.
>
> (*c*) No contracting party shall prevent any enterprise (whether or not an enterprise described in subparagraph (*a*) of this paragraph) under its jurisdiction from acting in accordance with the principles of subparagraphs (*a*) and (*b*) of this paragraph.
>
> 2. ...
>
> 3. The contracting parties recognize that enterprises of the kind described in paragraph 1 (*a*) of this *Article might be operated so as to create serious obstacles to trade*; thus negotiations on a reciprocal and mutually advantageous basis designed to limit or reduce such obstacles are of importance to the expansion of international trade.*

753. Article XVII.1(a) establishes the general obligation on state trading enterprises to undertake their activities in accordance with the GATT principles of non-discrimination. The Panel considers that this general principle of non-discrimination includes at least the provisions of Articles I and III of GATT. This seems to be where the GATT jurisprudence was pointed to when in *Canada - Marketing Agencies (1988)*, the Panel stated:

> "4.26 The Panel then examined the contention of the European Communities that the practices complained of were contrary to Article III. The Panel noted that Canada did not consider Article III to be relevant to this case, arguing that the Interpretative Note to

Articles XI, XII, XIII, XIV and XVIII made it clear that provisions other than Article XVII applied to state-trading enterprises by specific reference only. The Panel considered that it was not necessary to decide in this particular case whether the practices complained of were contrary to Article III:4 because it had already found that they were inconsistent with Article XI. *However, the Panel saw great force in the argument that Article III:4 was also applicable to state-trading enterprises at least when the monopoly of the importation and monopoly of the distribution in the domestic markets were combined*, as was the case of the provincial liquor boards in Canada. This interpretation was confirmed *a contrario* by the wording of Article III:8(a). (Emphasis added.)

754. In the panel report on *Canada - Marketing Agencies (1992)*, the Panel also concluded:

"For these reasons the Panel found that Canada's right under the General Agreement to establish an import and sales monopoly for beer *did not entail the right to discriminate against imported beer inconsistently with Article III:4 through regulations affecting its international transportation*"[403] (emphasis added).

755. The GATT jurisprudence has also made clear that the scope of paragraph (b), which refers to commercial considerations, defines the obligations set out in paragraph (a).

756. In *Canada – FIRA*, the panel concluded:

"5.16 The Panel takes the view that, through its reference to sub-paragraph (a), paragraph l(c) of Article XVII of the General Agreement imposes on contracting parties the obligation to act in their relations with state-trading and other enterprises "in a manner consistent with the general principles of non-discriminatory treatment prescribed in this Agreement for governmental measures affecting imports or exports by private traders". This obligation is defined in subparagraph (b), which declares, *inter alia*, that these principles are understood to require the enterprises to make their purchases and sales solely in accordance with commercial considerations. The fact that *sub-paragraph (b) does not establish a separate general obligation to allow enterprises to act in accordance with commercial considerations, but merely defines the obligations set out in the preceding subparagraph*, is made clear through the introductory words "The provisions of subparagraph (a) of the paragraph shall be understood to require ...". (Emphasis added.)

[403] Panel report on *Canada - Marketing Agencies (1992)*, para. 5.15.

757. In other words the terms "general principle of non-discrimination treatment prescribed in this Agreement" (Art. XVII:1(a)) should be equated with "make any such purchases or sales solely in accordance with commercial considerations" (Art. XVII:1(b)). The list of variables that can be used to assess whether a state-trading action is based on commercial consideration (prices, availability etc...) are to be used to facilitate the assessment whether the state-trading enterprise has acted in respect of the general principles of non-discrimination. A conclusion that the principle of non-discrimination was violated would suffice to prove a violation of Article XVII; similarly, a conclusion that a decision to purchase or buy was not based on "commercial considerations", would also suffice to show a violation of Article XVII.

758. Therefore, when assessing the claim of the WTO compatibility of the LPMO's discharge practices, in particular its practice of refusing or delaying to sell imported beef into the Korean market, the Panel shall also determine whether the LPMO "in ... sales involving either imports or exports, act[ed] in a manner consistent with the general principles of non-discriminatory treatment prescribed in this Agreement for governmental measures" pursuant to Article XVII.

(ii) Article 4.2 of the Agreement on Agriculture

759. The Complaining parties claim that the practices mentioned above are also in violation of Article 4.2 of the *Agreement on Agriculture*, taking into account footnote 1 which extends the prohibition against import restrictions to non-tariff measures maintained through state-trading enterprises.

760. The Panel recalls that Article 4.2 of the *Agreement on Agriculture* provides that:

> "Members shall not maintain, resort to, or revert to any measures of the kind which have been required to be converted into ordinary customs duties ... "

761. Footnote 1 to Article 4.2 clarifies that:

> "These measures include quantitative import restrictions ... discretionary import licensing, *non-tariff measures maintained through state-trading enterprises* ... and similar border measures other than ordinary customs duties, whether or not the measures are maintained under country-specific derogations from the provisions of GATT 1947 ..."

762. Therefore, when dealing with measures relating to agricultural products which should have been converted into tariffs or tariff-quotas, a violation of Article XI of GATT and its *Ad Note* relating to state-trading operations would necessarily constitute a violation of Article 4.2 of the *Agreement on Agriculture* and its footnote which refers to non-tariff measures maintained through state-trading enterprises.

(c) The Panel's Assessment

763. The LPMO is a notified state-trading agency for beef and imports its share of the annual quota through a tendering system.[404] The import, distribution and sale of beef imported by the LPMO was still regulated at the time of the establishment of this Panel by Regulations on Imported Beef and the Imported Beef Dealer Designation and Product Supply the purpose of which was "the establishment of operational guidelines with regard to the storage, sales etc of beef imported in accordance with the government's supply plan implemented in order to stabilize the prices of cattle and beef in Korea".[405] In its notification to the Committee on State-Trading Enterprises, Korea identifies the LPMO as the entity appointed by the MAF to administer the import regime for beef. Moreover, as earlier discussed, MAF has delegated extensive powers to the LPMO to administer Korea's licensing regime for imported beef.

764. From 1988 to 1991, the LPMO was responsible for purchasing 100 per cent of the Korean beef import quota; it was thus a full import monopoly. Its share of the import quota has been reduced over time but the LPMO is still responsible for the import of 30 per cent, over which no other importer has any right. Special rights in relation to the import and discharge of the LPMO beef are shared between two state trading agencies under a "consignment agreement" between the principal, the LPMO and its agent, the NLCF. The NLCF has also been granted exclusive or special privileges under government regulation, to control the daily discharge of beef on behalf of the LPMO. Both organizations have the stated objective of stabilizing the price of domestic beef.[406] The activities of both organizations are also regulated and supervised closely by the MAF.

765. Thus, the LPMO and its agent the NLCF (herein referred to collectively as LPMO) have exclusive rights of import for its 30 per cent share of Korea's beef import quota, to the extent that no other entity can benefit from any of its import rights (as the SBS cannot import more than its 70 per cent share) and therefore exercises full control over that 30 per cent of the Korean beef import market. To the extent that the LPMO has such exclusive import right over the said 30 per cent of Korea's beef quota, and that the LPMO/NLCF also have full control over the discharge into the Korean market for that same 30 per cent of all imported beef into Korea, the Panel considers that, though the LPMO does not control all details of distribution, its powers over the discharge of imported beef into the Korean market give it full control over the quantity distributed in the Korean market of the 30 per cent allocated to it. Therefore, the Panel is of the view that the LPMO has exclusive right of import and distribution over its allocated share of Korea's import quota on beef.

---

404 G/STR/N/4/KOR, 10 December 1998.

405 Regulations Concerning Sales of Imported Beef, Article 1. As of 1 October 1999, they are regulated by the Government through the *Management Guideline for Imported Beef* and Article 3 notes that beef is imported by the LPMO for stabilizing demand and supply in the market.

406 *LPMO*, Foreword, page 1; *Brief Introduction of NLCF*, page 3.

766. Based on the panel findings in the *Canada - Marketing Agencies (1988)* case, the Panel considers that to the extent that LPMO fully controls both the importation and distribution of its 30 per cent share of Korean beef quota, the distinction normally made in the GATT between restrictions affecting the *importation* of products (i.e. border measures) and restrictions affecting *imported* products (i.e. internal measures) loses much of its significance.

767. Therefore, the Panel concludes that the LPMO's lack and delays in calling for tenders and its discharge practices between the end of October 1997 and the end of May 1998, i.e. the LPMO's refusal to discharge into the Korean market imported beef led it to keep important stocks of beef and in turn to reduce imports, were restrictive. As demonstrated above, these LPMO practices are closely connected and have led to import restrictions on foreign beef, contrary to Article XI through the application of its *Ad Note*.

768. Since the Panel has already reached the conclusion that the above measures are inconsistent with Article XI and the Ad Note to Articles XI, XII, XIII, XIV and XVIII relating to state-trading enterprises, the same measures are necessarily inconsistent with Article 4.2 of *the Agreement on Agriculture* and its footnote referring to non-tariff measures maintained through state-trading enterprises.

769. Should the LPMO/NCLF not be viewed as having full control over the distribution of its 30 per cent share of Korea's import quota, the Panel considers that, when it delayed its sales of imported beef into the Korean market while having important stocks, the LPMO was not acting "in a manner consistent with the general principles of non-discriminatory treatment prescribed in this Agreement for governmental measures affecting imports or exports by private traders" (Article XVII:1(a)). The Panel finds therefore that the LPMO's discharge practices after the end of October 1997 and until the end of May 1998, were inconsistent with Article XVII.1(a) of GATT. The LPMO's suspension of calls for any tenders during the same period would still constitute an import restriction, contrary to Article XI through the application of the Ad Note to Articles XI, XII, XIII, XIV and XVIII of GATT.

G. *Claim with Regard to the Grass/Grain Fed Beef Distinction*

1. *Arguments of the Parties*

770. Australia claims that in allocating the LPMO quota between grass-fed and grain-fed beef and in excluding grass-fed beef from three tenders in 1999, on 10 June, 14 July and 10 September[407], the LPMO constricted the supply of imported grass-fed beef at a time when sales of grass-fed beef were growing significantly. Australia claims, therefore, that such restrictive tender practices are inconsistent with Article II, in that it imposes conditions contrary to and additional to the "terms, conditions or qualifications" contained in Korea's Schedule. Australia

[407] See para. 122 of this Panel report.

also claims that such grass-fed/grain fed tendering practices provided less favourable treatment to imported beef than to domestic beef where such a distinction is not made. For Australia, it also constitutes an import restriction on grass-fed beef contrary to Article XI and its Ad Note and contrary to Article XVII of GATT in that it is discriminatory and not based on commercial considerations.

771. Korea responds that the distinction between grass-fed and grain-fed beef does not by itself constitute discriminatory treatment or an infringement of MFN principles. All tenders are open to all supplying countries and perfectly origin neutral. For Korea, Australian exporters are free to participate both in tenders for grass-fed and grain-fed beef and Australia has not adduced any evidence that Australian products have been discriminated against based on their origin. Korea submits that if Australia's producers are operating on a commercial basis, they can be expected to adjust to the customers' demand, rather than expecting the customer to change its demand based on their supply. Korea also argues that import data show that the share of Australian imported beef has grown in 1999, and therefore, no discrimination on the basis of origin has taken place. Australia challenges the Korean data and claims that imports of grass-fed beef by the LPMO in 1999 have fallen by approximately 60 per cent.

2. *Factual Determination by the Panel*

772. The Panel recalls that Korea's Schedule of Concessions includes tariff bindings on all beef imported within the tariff quota of 43.6 per cent reducing to 41.6 per cent by 2000. The Panel notes also that Korea has made no qualification in its Schedule under column 7 "other terms and conditions" and no reference to grain-fed beef or grass-fed beef. The Panel also recalls that on 10 June and 14 July, i.e. before 26 July (date of the establishment of the present Panel for Australia[408]) grass-fed beef was completely excluded from the call for tenders.[409]

773. The evidence shows that as a general matter, grass-fed beef originating in Australia, and grain-fed beef from the United States, are like products. However, in calls for tenders, a distinction is made between these like products and on at least two occasions, i.e. on 10 June and on 14 July, grass-fed beef was excluded from the tenders. In addition, it may be emphasised that imports through the SBS system, a commercially based regime, are not subject to any similar distinction. Such a distinction is not imposed nor ever used in the commercial practices of the Korean domestic market where different types of beef are distinguished according to a grading system using criteria such as marbling, texture, meat colour, fat content and maturing level, pursuant to Article 28 of Korea's Livestock Act. The

[408] See document WT/DS169/6 and the provisions of Article 9.2 of the DSU which provides that one single panel is established: "The single panel shall organize its examination and present its findings to the DSB in such a manner that the rights which the parties to the dispute would have enjoyed had separate panels examined the complaints are in no way impaired".

[409] See para. 122 of this Panel report.

non-refuted evidence also shows that by May and June 1999, the sales of grass-fed beef on the Korean market increased by over three times compared to what had been consumed in 1998.[410]

3. *The WTO Provisions and Jurisprudence*

774. The Panel considers that the LPMO's calls for tenders that impose a distinction between grain- and grass-fed beef constitute *de facto* limits on importation of grass-fed beef, thus amounting to import restrictions. The Panel recalls its discussion on Article XI, the Ad Note to Articles XI, XII, XIII, XIV and XVIII, where it was concluded that the purpose of the Ad Note to Articles XI, XII, XIII, XIV and XVIII is to ensure that WTO Members cannot escape their basic obligations, such as the prohibition against import restrictions, by using a state-trading enterprise.

775. Article II:1 of GATT provides:

> "(a) each contracting party shall accord to the commerce of the other contracting party treatment no less favourable than that provided for in the appropriate Part of the appropriate Schedule annexed to this Agreement.
>
> (b) The products described in Part 1 of the Schedule relating to any contracting party, which are the products of territories of other contracting parties, shall, on their importation into the territory to which the Schedule relates, and subject to the terms, conditions or qualifications set forth in that Schedule, be exempt from ordinary customs duties in excess of those set forth and provided therein."

776. The panel report on *EEC - Beef* found that:

> "The words, 'terms, conditions or qualifications' in paragraph 1(b) of Article II could not be interpreted to mean that countries could (...) by the manner in which a concession was administered actually limit a given concession to the products of a particular country. The Panel further found that the fact that in Annex II there was only one certifying agency for the meat in questions and that this agency only certified meat of United States origin *in effect prevented access of high quality meat from other countries."*
>
> "Consequently, the Panel concluded that the manner in which the EEC concession on high quality beef was implemented *accorded less favourable treatment to Canada than that provided for in the relevant EEC Schedule,* thus being inconsistent with the provisions

---

[410] See para. 122 of this Panel report: 1220 MTs in May/June 1998 compared with 3720 MTs in May/June 1999.

of paragraph 1 of Article II of the General Agreement." (Emphasis added.)[411]

4. *The Panel's Assessment*

777. In the light of the evidence before it, the Panel considers that the LPMO practices to call for tenders on the basis of the distinction between grass-fed and grain-fed beef, constitute an import restriction in violation of Article XI of GATT, through the Ad Note to Articles XI, XII, XIII, XIV and XVIII.

778. The Panel considers that pursuant to Article II, any other "terms, conditions or qualifications" that add to import concessions must be set forth in Korea's Schedule. The Panel recalls that Korea has made no condition concerning grass-fed/grain-fed beef in its Schedule. In administering its import beef quota on the basis of grain-fed and grass-fed beef distinctions, Korea is imposing a condition in the form of individual limits applied to grass and grain-fed beef, within Korea's total import quota. The Panel recalls its conclusion above, that such grass-fed/grain-fed condition constitutes a limit, an import restriction, inconsistent with Article XI of GATT.

779. Given that Korea made no such qualification, and that imports of grass-fed beef by the LPMO are thus restricted, the Panel finds that imports of grass-fed beef are accorded less favourable treatment than that is provided for in Korea's Schedule, contrary to Article II:1(a).

780. Having reached the above conclusions, the Panel does not find it necessary to address Australia's claims that the same measures also violate Articles III:4 and XVII of GATT.

H. *Claim that Korea's Import Licensing System per se Violates Various Provisions of the WTO Agreement*

781. The United States claims that Korea's regulatory regime, and thus its licensing system, by granting exclusive authority to the LPMO and the SBS system to import beef, effectively establishes a non-automatic import licensing system in violation of Article XI:1, Article 4.2 of *the Agreement on Agriculture*, and Article 3.2 of the *Licensing Agreement*. In support of its allegations, the United States refers to the panel and Appellate Body reports on *India – Quantitative Restrictions*.

782. With reference to the US claim that the Korean import licensing system is inconsistent with Article XI of GATT (and Article 4.2 of the *Agreement on Agriculture*), this Panel is of the view, as pointed out by Canada, that the conclusions reached in the *India – Quantitative Restrictions* reports are of no relevance to the present dispute, because the factual context is different. Under the Indian licens-

---

[411] Panel report on *EEC – Beef*, paras. 4.5-4.6.

ing system, a range of products had been added to a "Negative List of Imports" and such products could only be imported with a licence. These licences were issued on a discretionary basis. There was no other quantitative restriction with the licensing system. In other words, in the absence of the discretionary licensing system, there would be no restriction on imports. In these circumstances, the Indian discretionary licensing system was found to be, by itself, a restriction on imports. However, where a quota is in place, the use of a discretionary licensing system need not necessarily result in any additional restriction. Where a discretionary licensing system is implemented in conjunction with other restrictions, such as in the present dispute, the manner in which the discretionary licensing system is operated may create additional restrictions independent of those imposed by the principal restriction. Since this issue was not considered in the *India - Quantitative Restrictions* report, that case does not provide authority for the proposition that a discretionary licensing system, used in conjunction with a quantitative restriction, necessarily provides some additional level of restriction over and above the inherent restriction on access created through the imposition of a quantitative restriction.

783. In addition, the Korean discretionary licensing system has been put in place for the administration of various import measures. The Panel recalls that conclusions on a number of specific measures have been reached in previous sections of this Panel report, including the fact that some of the challenged measures benefit from a transition period until 1 January 2001. The Panel, thus, does not see the need to reach a separate conclusion on Korea's import licensing system, as various aspects of Korea's import licensing system may be amended when Korea adopts new measures in accordance with the conclusions of this Panel report and at the expiry of the transition period, i.e. on 1 January 2001.

784. Finally, the Panel notes that many of the US claims regarding alleged violations of the *Licensing Agreement* are concerned with the substantive provisions of Korea's import (and distribution) regime (by the LPMO or SBS super-groups). It has been said repeatedly that such substantive matters are of no relevance to the *Licensing Agreement* which is concerned with the administrative rules of import licensing systems.[412]

785. For theses reasons, the Panel does not reach any general conclusion on the compatibility of Korea's import licensing system with the WTO Agreement.

I. Claims Against the Alleged Excessive Domestic Support to Korea's Cattle Industry

1. Korea's Request for a Preliminary Ruling on the Panel's Terms of Reference and Lack of Specificity as Concerns

[412] Appellate Body Report on *EC – Bananas III*, *supra*, footnote 97, para. 197.

Claims Relating to Domestic Support of the US and Australian Claims

(a) Arguments of the Parties

786. Korea submits that the terms of reference of this Panel do not allow it to examine all the claims and arguments raised by the Complaining parties[413].

787. Korea argues that since the Complaining parties' request for a panel stated that "Korea has increased the level of its domestic support for its cattle industry to the point that the total domestic support provided by Korea exceeds its Aggregate Measurement of Support (AMS) under the Agreement on Agriculture", the only measures that this Panel can legally examine are the Korean measures of domestic support for its cattle industry. Korea, therefore, argues that the data and calculation methods used to establish its Base Total AMS in Part IV of Korea's Schedule LX, or in broad terms, Korea's Schedule LX by itself, are not mentioned as disputed measures and no violation can be claimed with regard to these additional measures. Korea adds that the US and Australian requests for the establishment of a panel (which form the basis of the terms of reference of this Panel), were insufficiently detailed and specific to encompass the Complaining parties' claims based on Annex 3 of the *Agreement on Agriculture* and on the data and methodology used in Part IV of Korea's Schedule LX. Korea requests the Panel to limit its examination to Articles 3, 6 and 7 of *the Agreement on Agriculture*, i.e. the Articles listed in the Complaining parties' request, and not to allow the Complaining parties to bring claims or arguments which are based mainly on Annex 3 of *the Agreement on Agriculture* because Annex 3 was not identified as a legal basis upon which the Complaining parties wished this dispute to be examined.

788. In support of its request, Korea refers the Panel to the Appellate Body decisions on *EC - Bananas III* and on *Korea – Dairy* where it was concluded that panels must examine the request for their establishment carefully to ensure its compliance with both the letter and the spirit of Article 6.2 of the DSU and that the listing of the Articles claimed to have been violated is a minimum prerequisite if the legal basis of the complaint is to be presented at all.

789. In response, the United States and Australia argue that Korea's request came too late as the Panel's rules of procedure provide that a request for a preliminary ruling should be included in the first written submission, which was not the case in the present dispute, and that Korea did not invoke any just cause in support of its late request. The Complaining parties also argue that the measures at issue, and the specific provisions of the Agreement on Agriculture claimed to have been violated, were included in their requests for establishment of a panel and were developed in their first written submissions. Korea had the opportunity

413 See paras. 30 to 32 of this Panel report.

in its first written submission to raise the issue of adequacy of the panel request, but did not do so.

790. The Complaining parties add that in *Korea – Dairy*, the Appellate Body concentrated on the issue of whether the panel request was specific enough to ensure that Korea's ability to defend itself in the course of the panel proceedings was not prejudiced. The Appellate Body also made it clear that Korea had the burden of proof in claiming prejudice. For the Complaining parties, there is no basis for Korea to contend that it did not understand the claims being made or that it was not accorded an opportunity to respond to these claims, since in its first written submission Korea responded to the Complaining parties' claims regarding Articles 3, 6 and 7, and through Article 6, to Annex 3 and Part IV of its Schedule.

791. Both Complaining parties also insist that a textual analysis of Article 6 makes it clear that, if Article 6 is to have any meaning, it must be considered together with Annex 3 and Part IV of Korea's Schedule. Annex 3 and Part IV of Korea's Schedule are intrinsic to the Panel's interpretation of Korea's obligations under Article 6. The Panel's terms of reference explicitly requires it to examine the consistency of Korea's domestic support measures for beef with its scheduled commitments under Articles 3, 6 and 7, in particular Korea's obligation to include in the calculation of its Current Total AMS product specific support which exceeds the *de minimis* levels, and its obligation not to provide support exceeding its AMS commitments for any given year. For the Complaining parties, it is not possible to make any determination of a Member's compliance with these obligations without reference to the formulations contained in Annex 3, because Annex 3 contains the methodology required to determine the current AMS for specific products as well as the Current Total AMS. Furthermore, it is not possible to decide whether Korea has met its obligations under these Articles without reference to the reduction commitment levels contained in Korea's Schedule.

(b) WTO Provisions and Jurisprudence on Terms of Reference

792. The terms of reference of the present Panel were determined by cross-referring to the Complaining parties' requests for the establishment of a panel.[414] Both Complaining parties' requests for the establishment of a panel contend that:

> "At the same time, Korea has increased the level of domestic support for its cattle industry to the point that [Australia used the term "in amounts which result in"] the total domestic support provided by Korea exceeds its Aggregate Measurement of Support (AMS) under the Agreement on Agriculture.

414 See WT/DS 161-169/5 and WT/DS161-169/6.

[Only the US request contains the following paragraph: Korea's measures appear to be inconsistent with the obligations of Korea under the General Agreement on Tariffs and Trade 1994 (GATT 1994), the Agreement on Agriculture, and the Agreement on Import Licensing Procedures. In particular, the United States considers that Korea's measures are inconsistent with the obligations of Korea under:]

(...)

(2) Articles 3, 4, 6, and 7 of the Agreement on Agriculture, and (...)"

793. Article 6.2 of the DSU provides that

"The request for the establishment of a panel shall be made in writing. It shall indicate whether consultations were held, *identify the specific measures* at issue and provide a *brief summary of the legal basis* of the complaint sufficient to present the problem clearly. (...)" (emphasis added).

794. The Panel notes that the request for the establishment of a panel and, therefore, the terms of reference of a panel, must contain at least two fundamental elements: a description of the specific measure and the identification of the legal basis for the claims, both of which must be sufficient to present the "problem" clearly.

795. The WTO jurisprudence has provided further clarification on these two aspects of a panel's terms of reference, introducing a distinction between the claims and the arguments. In *EC – Bananas III*, the Appellate Body stated:

"141. In our view, there is a significant difference between the *claims* identified in the request for the establishment of a panel, which establish the panel's terms of reference under Article 7 of the DSU, and the *arguments* supporting those claims, which are set out and progressively clarified in the first written submissions, the rebuttal submissions and the first and second panel meetings with the parties.

142 ... It is incumbent upon a panel to examine the request for the establishment of the panel *very carefully to ensure its compliance with both the letter and the spirit of Article 6.2 of the DSU*. It is important that a panel request be *sufficiently precise* for two reasons: first, it often forms the basis for the terms of reference of the panel pursuant to Article 7 of the DSU; and, second, it *informs the defending party and the third parties of the legal basis of the complaint*." [415] (emphasis added.)

[415] In its Report on *European Communities – Hormones*, *supra*, footnote 336, the Appellate Body reiterated its views on the distinction between claims and arguments. See paras. 155-156.

796. In *Korea - Dairy*, the Appellate Body had the opportunity to elaborate its views on this matter:

> "123. Thus, we did not purport in *European Communities – Bananas* to establish the mere listing of the articles of an agreement alleged to have been breached as a standard of precision, observance of which would *always* constitute sufficient compliance with the requirements of Article 6.2, *in each and every case*, without regard to the particular circumstances of such cases. …
>
> 124. Identification of the treaty provisions claimed to have been violated by the respondent *is always necessary* both for purposes of defining the terms of reference of a panel and for informing the respondent and the third parties of the claims made by the complainant; *such identification is a minimum prerequisite if the legal basis of the complaint is to be presented at all.* But it may not always be enough. There may be situations where the simple listing of the articles of the agreement or agreements involved may, *in the light of attendant circumstances*, suffice to meet the standard of *clarity* in the statement of the legal basis of the complaint. However, there may also be situations in which the circumstances are such that the mere listing of treaty articles would not satisfy the standard of Article 6.2. This may be the case, for instance, where *the articles listed establish not one single, distinct obligation, but rather multiple obligations. In such a situation, the listing of articles of an agreement, in and of itself, may fall short of the standard of Article 6.2.* (Emphasis added.)
>
> 127. Along the same lines, we consider that whether the mere *listing of the Articles* claimed to have been violated meets the standard of Article 6.2 must be examined on a case-by-case basis. In resolving that question, we take into account *whether the ability of the respondent to defend itself was prejudiced, given the actual course of the panel proceedings*, by the fact that the panel request simply listed the provisions claimed to have been violated.
>
> 131. … Korea failed to demonstrate to us that the mere listing of the articles asserted to have been violated has prejudiced its ability to defend itself in the course of the Panel proceedings. Korea did assert that it had sustained prejudice, but offered no supporting particulars in its appellant's submission nor at the oral hearing. We, therefore, deny Korea's appeal relating to the consistency of the European Communities' request for the establishment of a panel with Article 6.2 of the DSU." (Emphasis added.)

797. In *US - FISC* the appellate Body insisted that "good faith" was a necessary component of any challenge on Panel's terms of reference which implies that a party's claim that it has misunderstood a request for consultation or a request for a panel should be raised as soon as possible:

"166. Article 3.10 of the DSU commits Members of the WTO, if a dispute arises, to engage in dispute settlement procedures "in good faith in an effort to resolve the dispute". This is another specific manifestation of the principle of good faith which, we have pointed out, is at once a general principle of law and a principle of general international law.[416] *This pervasive principle requires both complaining and responding Members to comply with the requirements of the DSU (and related requirements in other covered agreements) in good fait*h. By good faith compliance, complaining Members accord to the responding Members the full measure of protection and opportunity to defend, contemplated by the letter and spirit of the procedural rules. The same principle of good faith *requires that responding Members seasonably and promptly bring claimed procedural deficiencies to the attention of the complaining Member, and to the DSB or the Panel, so that corrections, if needed, can be made to resolve disputes.* The procedural rules of WTO dispute settlement are designed to promote, not the development of litigation techniques, but simply the fair, prompt and effective resolution of trade disputes."

(c) The Panel's Assessment

798. In the particular circumstances of this case, three principles should govern the determination of the compatibility of a request for the establishment of a panel with Article 6.2 of the DSU. First, the "specific measure" at issue must be clearly identified. Second, the claims must also be clearly identified – in this respect claims should be distinguished from arguments, in which the latter can be developed in written submissions. The obligation to identify the claims implies that at *a minimum* the Articles claimed to have been violated must be listed (but this may not always be sufficient); if an Article contains various distinct obligations, the listing of Articles of an agreement, in and of itself, may fall short of the standard of Article 6. Third, in assessing whether a request for a panel is sufficiently clear and detailed, the Panel ought to take into account whether the ability of the respondent to defend itself was prejudiced, "given the actual course of the panel proceedings".[417]

(i) The Measures at Issue

799. In the present dispute the measure identified by the Complaining parties is Korea's level of domestic support to its cattle industry, resulting in a Current To-

---

[416] [Original] *United States – Shrimp*, *supra*, footnote 38, para. 38. In that report, we addressed the issue of good faith in the context of the chapeau of Article XX of the GATT 1994.

[417] See Appellate Body report in *Korea – Safeguards* (quoted above), *supra*, footnote 290, para. 127.

tal AMS exceeding Koreas' scheduled reduction commitments. Korea's domestic support notifications to the WTO refer to support to its "beef" industry. For the purpose of the present dispute, the Panel shall consider that domestic support in the form of administered support prices is provided in favour of producers of cattle as part of the Korean beef industry.[418] For the Complaining parties, if the actual domestic support for the beef industry had been properly computed, Korea's Current Total AMS would have exceeded its scheduled domestic support reduction commitments in 1997, contrary to Article 3 of the *Agreement on Agriculture*. (The United States has a similar claim for 1998).

800. The United States also claims that the Base Total AMS specified in Section I, Part IV of Korea's Schedule was initially miscalculated and, therefore, continues to invalidate Korea's annual domestic support. The Panel considers that if the United States wanted to challenge the Base Total AMS itself as specified in Part IV of Korea's Schedule LX, and the related data and methods of calculation which are "incorporated by reference" in that Section of Part IV of Korea's Schedule, this should have been adequately identified in the US request for establishment of a panel. However, no such claim is set out in the US request for establishment of a panel. The Panel concludes that the only measure at issue is Korea's current domestic support for its beef industry in the context of Korea's scheduled commitment levels on domestic support under the *Agreement on Agriculture*.

801. This does not mean that the Complaining parties cannot refer, in their arguments, to Part IV of Korea's Schedule LX, since their legal claim is that Korea's Current Total AMS, if properly calculated to include domestic support for beef (according to Article 6 and Annex 3), would have led to a Current Total AMS exceeding Korea's annual commitment levels specified in Part IV of Korea's Schedule (as it stands), contrary to Article 3 of the *Agreement on Agriculture*. In this respect the Panel recalls that Article 3.2 explicitly refers to Part IV of Members' Schedules and that those Schedules explicitly incorporate Members' AGST (constituent data and methodology).

(ii) The Claims under Articles 3, 6 and 7 of the Agreement on Agriculture

802. Regarding Korea's claim that the Complaining parties have limited their challenge to violations of Articles 3, 6 and 7 and, therefore, should not be allowed to raise claims or arguments based on any provisions of Annex 3, the Panel notes that the relevant part of Article 3 of the *Agreement on Agriculture* reads as follows:

---

[418] According to the evidence submitted by Korea, cattle purchases under the Korea's price support programme for beef include Hanwoo steers, dairy cattle and hybrid cattle of Cheju Island. See para. 384 of this Panel report.

"Incorporation of Concessions and Commitments

> ... 2. *Subject to* the provisions of *Article 6*, a *Member shall not provide support in favour of domestic producers in excess of the commitment levels* specified in Section I of Part IV of its Schedule." (Emphasis added.)

803. It is, therefore, clear that Article 3 provides that support in favour of domestic producers (and here explicit reference is made to "*subject to* Article 6") cannot exceed the level of support provided for in a Member's schedule. So, when assessing the WTO compatibility of domestic support, two parameters are indicated: first the provisions of Article 6 which refer to the object of those same "commitments" on domestic support; and second, Section I of Part IV of a Member's schedule. Therefore, the Panel considers that its terms of reference require it to examine Korea's Schedule LX to assess whether its domestic support in 1997 and 1998 exceeded the reduction commitments contained in its Schedule.

804. The relevant provisions of Article 6 read as follows:

"Domestic Support Commitments

> 1. The domestic support reduction commitments of each Member contained in Part IV of its Schedule shall apply to all of its domestic support measures in favour of agricultural producers with the exception of domestic measures which are not subject to reduction in terms of the criteria set out in this Article and in Annex 2 to this Agreement. The commitments are expressed in terms of Total Aggregate Measurement of Support and "Annual and Final Bound Commitment Levels".
>
> 2. (...)
>
> 3. A Member shall be considered to be in compliance with its domestic support reduction commitments in any year in which its domestic support in favour of agricultural producers expressed in terms of Current Total AMS does not exceed the corresponding annual or final bound commitment level specified in Part IV of the Member's Schedule.
>
> 4. (a) A Member shall not be required to include in the calculation of its Current Total AMS and shall not be required to reduce:
>
> (i) product-specific domestic support which would otherwise be required to be included in a Member's calculation of its Current AMS where such support does not exceed 5 per cent of that Member's total value of production of a basic agricultural product during the relevant year; and

(ii) non-product-specific domestic support which would otherwise be required to be included in a Member's calculation of its Current AMS where such support does not exceed 5 per cent of the value of that Member's total agricultural production.

(b) For developing country Members, the *de minimis* percentage under this paragraph shall be 10 per cent."

805. Paragraph 3 of Article 6 elaborates on the prescriptions of Article 3 that domestic support, in any year, in favour of agricultural producers, as expressed in terms of Current Total AMS, cannot exceed the corresponding annual or final bound commitment level specified in Part IV of a Member's schedule. Paragraph 3 adds that "domestic support in favour of agricultural producers" is to be expressed "in terms of Current Total AMS".

806. Article 7.2(a) of the Agreement on Agriculture provides that:

> "*Any domestic support measure in favour of agricultural producers*, including any modification to such measure, and any measure that is subsequently introduced that cannot be shown to satisfy the criteria in Annex 2 to this Agreement or to be exempt from reduction by reason of any other provision of this Agreement *shall be included in the Member's calculation of its Current Total AMS*". (Emphasis added.)

807. Current Total AMS is itself defined in Article 1(h) as representing the sum of (1) AMS for basic agricultural products, (2) all non-product-specific AMS and (3) all equivalent measurements of support for agricultural products, "*calculated in accordance with the provisions of this Agreement, including Article 6*, and with the constituent data and methodology used in the tables of supporting material incorporated by reference in Part IV of the Member's Schedule".[419] This reference to "the provisions of the Agreement" in Article 1(h)(ii) clearly includes the provisions of Annex 3. This is confirmed by the Article 1(a)(ii) definition of the "AMS" as it relates to "support provided during any year of the implementation period and thereafter", or, in other words, as it relates to the "current AMS" which is specifically referred to in the context of the provisions of Article 6.4(a)(i) concerning the product-specific *de minimis*. This definition stipulates that "the current AMS", or "support provided during the implementation period and thereafter" is calculated in accordance with the provisions of Annex 3 and taking into account the constituent data and methodology used in the tables of supporting material incorporated by reference in Part IV of the Member's Schedule.[420] There are no conditions or exceptions placed on these definitions (except if the context may dictate otherwise as provided in the introduction of Article 1). The only guidance additional to that of Annex 3 is that the calculation should

[419] Article 1(h) of the *Agreement on Agriculture*.

[420] Article 1(a)(ii) of the *Agreement on Agriculture*.

also take into account the data and methodology, if any, contained in the supporting tables.

808. It is the Panel's understanding that the general scheme of the domestic support commitments, which are unique to the agriculture sector, is one under which all WTO Members have obligations with respect to non-exempt, generally trade-distorting, domestic support measures. In the case of those Members whose domestic support measures in the 1986-88 base period were fully covered by one or more of the categories of exempt support, and who, therefore, have no Base Total AMS in Part IV of their Schedules, their obligation under Article 7.2(b) of the Agreement is "not to provide support to agriculture producers in excess of the relevant *de minimis* level set out in paragraph 4 of Article 6." Where this was not the case the Members concerned[421] have a "Base Total AMS" in Part IV of their Schedules from which are derived the reduction commitment levels, or "annual commitment levels", for each year of the implementation period and the final bound levels which are applicable thereafter. Although the Base Total AMS reflects the particular complex of non-exempt (mainly product-specific) support in the base period, the annual AMS commitment levels derived therefrom represent a quantum of non-exempt support in monetary terms which may be used, subject to certain constraints as regards "actionability" under Article 13 of the Agreement, to provide support in favour of the producers of any agricultural product. In other words, the annual commitment levels are sector-wide commitments which operate as a ceiling on non-exempt domestic support. The monetary value of these annual ceiling commitments is reduced in nominal terms over the implementation period as specified in the Schedules. In addition, the value of these commitment levels in real terms is further reduced by the fact that the Agreement makes no allowance for inflation, other than in respect of "excessive rates of inflation" in terms of Article 18.4 of the *Agreement on Agriculture*. The overall effect of these commitments is to constrain over time the use of non-exempt, generally product-specific, domestic support and to encourage a shift towards forms of domestic support which are classified, in the case for example of Annex 2 of the *Agreement on Agriculture* ("the Green Box"), as having "no, or at the most minimal, trade-distorting effects or effects on production". This shift away from non-exempt support is facilitated by the fact that there are no monetary ceilings on the exempt categories of support under Article 6, namely: the Green Box under Article 6.1 and Annex 2; the special and differential treatment exemptions under Article 6.2; and direct payments under "production-limiting programmes" (the so-called "Blue Box") in terms of Article 6.5 of the Agreement.

809. In terms of Article 6.3, compliance with the *scheduled* commitment level for any year consists in the Current Total AMS for that year not being in excess

[421] Of the 136 WTO Members 30 have domestic support reduction commitments in Section I of Part IV of their Schedules. This includes 15 developing country Members, all of whom (with the exception of Korea) established their Base Total AMS in relation to a level of support which prevailed in the period 1986-1988.

of that level. If it is, that is a breach of Article 3.2. The Complaining parties must therefore prove that Korea's total domestic support is in excess of the scheduled commitment level.[422]

810. In the first instance, the issue is how the Current Total AMS should have been calculated. One has to rely on what Article 1(a) and (h) stipulate in respect of the calculation of non-exempt current support (as distinct from the base or base total AMS). The Current Total AMS is a composite or aggregate of calculations of non-exempt support in respect of individual basic products and, if any, of non-exempt non-product-specific support under Article 6.4(a)(ii). In other words, the calculation of Current Total AMS is a "bottom-up" process.

811. Article 1(h)(ii) provides for two things: that the "Total AMS" is the "sum" of all the AMS sub-components; and that the Current Total AMS is calculated "in accordance with the provisions of this Agreement, including Article 6, and with the constituent data and methodology used in the tables of supporting material incorporated by reference in Part IV of the Member's Schedule." Article 1(a)(ii), in turn, provides that in any given year the AMS shall be calculated "in accordance with Annex 3, taking into account the constituent data and methodology used in the tables of supporting material incorporated by reference in Part IV of the Member's Schedule". In the calculations of product specific support the "constituent data and methodology" has an important role to play in ensuring that the calculation of support to any given product is calculated in subsequent years consistently with support calculated in the base period. Consequently, where no support was included in the base period calculation for any given product, there is no constituent data or methodology in the tables of supporting material to a Member's Schedule to refer to. In these circumstances, the only means available for calculating such domestic support is that provided in Annex 3.

812. The basic product "beef" was not included in Supporting Table 6 ("Market Price Support") in Korea's base period, i.e. in the product-specific support calculations contained in Korea's Supporting Tables Relating to Commitments on Agricultural Products in Part IV of the Schedule ("AGST/KOR"). Therefore, in the AGST incorporated by reference in Korea's Schedule, there is no "constituent data" or "methodology" for the calculation of support for beef. (The methodology that is used is for other products, with different external reference prices being used for rice (1993) than for other products in Supporting Table 6.) In the absence of AGST "constituent data and methodology" for beef, the relevant calcu-

[422] Article 7 of the *Agreement on Agriculture*: "1. Each Member *shall ensure* that any domestic support measures in favour of agricultural producers which are not subject to reduction commitments because they qualify under the criteria set out in Annex 2 to this Agreement are maintained in conformity therewith. 2.(a) *Any domestic support measure in favour of agricultural producers*, including any modification to such measure, and any measure that is subsequently introduced that cannot be shown to satisfy the criteria in Annex 2 to this Agreement or *to be exempt from reduction* by reason of any other provision of this Agreement *shall be included in the Member's calculation of its Current Total AMS*." (Emphasis added.)

lation has, therefore, to be made "in accordance with the provisions of this Agreement" (Article 1(h)) or "in accordance with Annex 3" (Article 1(a)(ii)). In the circumstances, this means that Annex 3 (which is an integral part of the *Agreement on Agriculture* and which provides specific guidance on AMS calculation) must be applicable for the purposes of calculating current non-exempt support in respect of Korean beef. The same result is arrived at if one approaches the matter via Article 1(a)(ii), which of course specifically refers to Annex 3. In fact, the two approaches are complementary.

813. In addition, all these concepts, e.g. domestic support, AMS, Current Total AMS, and total domestic support and the provisions of Articles 1(a), 1(h), 3.2, 6.4 and 7.2 are organically and inextricably linked. The obligation to respect the annual reduction commitments in Korea's Schedule cannot be read nor understood without an examination of: the level of domestic support provided by Korea; the resulting aggregate measurement of support for the producers of beef; and the consequence of this on the resulting Current Total AMS. Concepts such as "aggregate measurement of support" or "AMS" and "Current Total AMS" have only a meaning within the context of the *Agreement on Agriculture*. There is indeed a definition of such concepts in Article 1 of the *Agreement on Agriculture*. Aggregate measurement of support and Current Total AMS, by their very nature, refer to totals of specific and total domestic support that are arrived at through calculation.

814. The Panel considers that Annex 3 provides for the authoritative method for calculating the components of the Current Total AMS, in the light of the domestic support commitments contained in Article 6. The Panel could not assess whether Korea has met its obligations under Article 6 without examining the calculation prescriptions for AMS contained in Annex 3. There is, therefore, a direct link between Articles 3 and 6 and Annex 3. The titles of Article 3 "Incorporation of Concessions and Commitments", of Article 6 "Domestic Support Commitments" and of Annex 3 "Domestic Support: Calculation of Aggregate Measurement of Support" demonstrate the inherent relationship between these provisions. The first terms of Annex 3 are "subject to the provisions of Article 6". Annex 3 is so intrinsic to the calculation of the AMS that any analysis that ignores those provisions would render substantial portions of the text of the *Agreement on Agriculture* meaningless. As a consequence, Korea's interpretative approach – that unless there is a specific claim under Annex 3, reference cannot be made to the provisions of Annex 3 - is contrary to customary rules of treaty interpretation and must be rejected as it would render Article 6 "inutile."[423]

---

[423] The principle of effective interpretation or "l'effet utile" reflects the general rule of interpretation which requires that a treaty be interpreted to give meaning and effect to all the terms of the treaty. For instance one provision should not be given an interpretation that will result in nullifying the effect of another provision of the same treaty. See for instance the statement of the Appellate Body in *United States – Gasoline*, *supra*, footnote 117, at 15: "An interpreter is not free to adopt a reading that would result in reducing whole clauses or paras. of a treaty to redundancy or inutility".

815. The Panel finds, therefore, that Articles 3, 6 and 7 provide the basis of Korea's obligations relating to domestic support, and it is against the obligations of Articles 3, 6 and 7 that Korea's actions must be judged. In all cases, Annex 3 contains the methodologies to calculate the AMS, by providing a basis for calculating support in respect of products not included in the "Base Total AMS". The Panel finds also that its assessment of the compatibility of Korea's domestic support with Articles 3, 6 and 7 requires that the Panel compares the effective support provided by Korea as determined using the calculation parameters of Annex 3. Only thereafter would the Panel be able to determine whether evidence adduced by the Complaining parties demonstrates that Korea's Current Total AMS exceeds Korea's scheduled commitment levels, contrary to Article 3. The Panel finds, therefore, that Australia and the United States are entitled to rely on Annex 3 to support their arguments that Korea's domestic support for its beef producers was not properly calculated and indeed exceeded the 10 per cent *de minimis*. [424]

(iii) Korea's Prejudice

816. Finally, the Panel notes that, although Korea submits generally that it was not able to prepare adequately its defense because of the lack of specificity of the Complaining parties' requests for the establishment of a panel, Korea has never claimed, and does not now allege, that it has ever been uncertain about, or without adequate notice of, the nature of the Complaining parties' claims regarding Korea's domestic support obligations. In fact, in its first submission, Korea submitted detailed explanations on how it had calculated its aggregate measurement of support for beef.. The Panel recalls that when challenging the terms of reference of a panel, parties must act in "good faith" which implies that their claim should be raised as soon as possible.[425] In the present dispute Korea alluded to this point only in its rebuttals and made a formal request one day before the second meeting of the Panel with the parties. After reviewing Korea's submissions, its answers to the parties' as well as to the Panel's questions during the course of the present proceedings, the Panel remains of the opinion that Korea clearly understood the matter at issue. The Panel considers that Korea was not misled by the requests for establishment of panels because the reference to "Korea has also increased *the level of domestic support* for its cattle industry in amounts which results in[426] the total domestic support provided by Korea exceeding its Aggre-

---

[424] The Panel notes that in *Japan – Alcoholic Beverages, supra*, footnote 106, the panel and the Appellate Body (*Japan – Alcoholic Beverages, supra*, footnote 98) reached conclusions based on the *Ad Note* to Article III:2 even though claims had been raised under Article III only. *Ad Notes* and Annexes are integral parts of the Agreement they relate to.

[425] See the Appellate Body report on *US – FISC, supra*, footnote 271, para. 166.

[426] The US request for establishment of a panel (WT/DS 161/5) used the expression "At the same time, Korea has increased the level of domestic support for its cattle industry to the point that the total domestic support provided by Korea exceeds its Aggregate Measurement of Support (AMS) under the *Agreement on Agriculture*."

gate Measurement of Support (AMS) under the Agreement on Agriculture" could only have referred to domestic support, which under the Agreement on Agriculture, is defined by reference to a Member's domestic support. For the Panel a claim that the level of aggregate measurement of support made available was greater than that provided for in Korea's Schedule necessitates a calculation of AMS using the methodology prescribed in the *Agreement on Agriculture*. In the present case, having omitted any aggregate measurement of support for beef in its constituent data, Korea's current domestic support for beef can only have been calculated on the basis of the methodology contained in Annex 3.

(iv) Conclusion

817. The Panel is, therefore, unable to accept Korea's claim that this Panel is prohibited from examining the Complaining parties' arguments based on the provisions of Articles 3 and 6 and Annex 3 of the *Agreement on Agriculture* to the effect that Korea's Current Total AMS, if properly calculated, exceeded Korea's reduction commitments contained in its Schedule.

2. *Claims that Korea's Domestic Support for Beef Exceeded the 10 Per Cent de minimis and Led to a Total Current AMS for 1997 and 1998 which Exceeded Korea's Scheduled Annual Commitment Levels*

(a) Arguments of the Parties

818. Australia and the United States claim that, as a result of support provided to cattle or beef producers, Korea has exceeded the annual commitment levels specified in Section 1, Part IV of its Schedule in 1997. The same claim is made by the United States in respect of the commitment levels for 1998. The basis of these claims is that, if properly calculated in accordance with the provisions of the *Agreement on Agriculture*, in particular Article 6.4 and Annex 3, support to producers of beef would exceed the *de minimis* level of 10 per cent provided for developing countries and would therefore have to be included in Korea's Current Total AMS for 1997, as required by Article 7.2(a) of the *Agreement on Agriculture*. If so included, the result would be that Korea's Current Total AMS would increase in 1997 from 1,936.95 billion won, as notified, to 2,245.2 billion won, and in 1998, from 1,562.77 billion won, as notified, to 1,753.9 billion, thus breaching the annual commitment levels of 1997 and 1998 which are specified in (the first column of commitment levels in) Section 1 of Part IV of Korea's Schedule. In addition, the United States claims that the Total Base AMS reflected in Korea's Schedule Section I, Part IV was initially miscalculated and, therefore, these initial errors continue to vitiate Korea's annual reduction commitments. In support of its claims of mis-calculation of the Total Base AMS (the initial com-

putation), the United States refers, amongst other elements, to the provisions of the Modalities paper[427] when interpreting provisions of Annex 3.

(b) The Panel's Assessment

819. The Panel has already concluded in paragraphs 799 to 801 that the measure challenged in the Complaining parties' request for a panel is the allegedly excessive domestic support for its beef industry and the resulting excessive Current Total AMS, and not Korea's Schedule itself, nor the methodology followed by Korea with respect to support provided for other products during the base period in the original setting of Section 104 Part IV of its Schedule. The Panel shall, therefore, determine whether, on the basis of Articles 3, 6, 7 and Annex 3, read in conjunction with Articles 1(a)(ii) and 1(h)(ii), Korea provided domestic support to its beef industry in excess of the *de minimis* 10 per cent of its total annual production and whether the resulting Current Total AMS exceeded Korea's scheduled commitment levels.

(i) Korea's Scheduled Commitment Levels of Domestic Support

820. The Panel notes that in Part IV of its Schedule, Korea sets forth the total current AMS for each year of the implementation period (1995-2004). However, unlike any other WTO Member, Korea has provided two separate numbers with respect to the Current Total AMS for each year. These figures are presented in two separate columns, the second of which is set off by parentheses. In the second column, the Total AMS annual commitment levels reflect the use of a 1993 base year for rice when domestic support for rice appears to have peaked; this has inflated the Total AMS annual commitment levels shown in brackets in the second column for the years 1995 through 2003. Nowhere in its Schedule does Korea identify which of the sets of support figures constitutes Korea's binding obligation.[428] Through its 1997 and 1998 notifications, Korea appears to be following the commitments contained in the column where the figures appear in the parentheses:

427 MTN.GNG/MA/W/24, 20 December 1993.

428 However, in a response to a question during a meeting of the Committee on Agriculture as to which of the two sets of figures in Korea's Schedule were dispositive, Korea answered: "The figures in brackets correspond to Korea's real annual commitment level, using the 1993 base period for rice and the 1989-1991 base period for other products, as indicated in the footnote of Korea's Schedule LX. The said calculation and annual commitment level of AMS were already reviewed and agreed upon by the Member countries in March 1994. The other set of figures corresponds to the annual commitment using the base period of 1989-1991 for all products." Summary Report, G/AG/R/9 (17 January 1997) at page 18.

Schedule LX – Republic of Korea

Total Base 1,718.60	1995:	1,695.74	(2,182.55)
	1996:	1,672.90	(2,105.60)
	1997:	1,650.03	(2,028.65)
	1998:	1,627.17	(1,951.70)
	1999:	1,604.32	(1,874.75)
	2000:	1,581.46	(1,797.80)
	2001:	1,558.60	(1,720.85)
	2002:	1,535.74	(1,643.90)
	2003:	1,512.89	(1,566.95)
	2004:	1,490.00	(1,490.00)

821. The Panel first has to determine first which of the two sets of figures listed in Section I of Part IV of Schedule LX constitutes Korea's Total AMS commitment levels for 1997 and 1998 for the purposes of Article 3.2 of the *Agreement on Agriculture*. Given that it would be logically impossible, as well as contrary to the general object and purpose of the provisions of the *Agreement on Agriculture* on domestic support, to have two distinct Total AMS commitment levels for each of these years, the Panel considers that the set of annual figures which are not qualified by brackets must be treated as constituting Korea's commitment levels for the years in question for the purposes of Article 3.2 of the Agreement on Agriculture.

822. In support of this conclusion the Panel notes that, as with Section I of Part IV of other schedules which contains domestic support reduction commitments, the unbracketed figures in Korea's Schedule are derived from, and directly linked to, the "Base Total AMS". In other words, each of the figures in the first column represents a reduction in the annual commitment levels that is calculated by reference to the specified "Base Total AMS" figure of 1,718.60 billion won. On the other hand, the figures in the second column bear no such relationship to the specified "Base Total AMS" of 1,718.60 billion won. In fact, the bracketed figures in the second column for 1997 and 1998 are both higher than the "Base Total AMS" figure. This incongruity in the relationship between the bracketed figures for 1997 and 1998 and the specified "Base Total AMS" figure reinforces the Panel's conclusion that the unbracketed figures alone should be treated as constituting Korea's annual commitment levels.[429] Korea is the only WTO Member whose Part IV domestic support Schedule contains two such sets of annual commitment levels. No provision of the Agreement on Agriculture authorises such a departure from the norm or practice which has been followed by all other developing country members in establishing their domestic support reduction commitments.

---

[429] Where the drafters of the *Agreement on Agriculture* intended to allow for flexibility in the amount of an annual reduction commitment, they made specific provision for it, such as in Article 9.2(b) relating to export subsidy commitments. No similar provision exists in respect of domestic support.

823. The Panel shall now proceed to examine the Complaining parties' claims that Korea's Current Total AMS as calculated violates Articles 3, 6 and 7 of the Agreement on Agriculture, in that the domestic support for Korea's beef industry in 1997 and 1998 was such as to exceed Korea's scheduled reduction commitments.

(ii) Domestic Support for the Beef Industry in 1997 and 1998

824. The Panel noted that Korea's notification of its Current Total AMS for 1997 was 1,936.95 billion won.[430] Korea's bound commitment level for 1997 was 1,650.03 billion won. Korea exceeded the level of domestic support provided under its commitment level for 1997 and, thus, violated Articles 3.2. and 6.3 of the *Agreement on Agriculture*. Even if the WTO compatible commitments were those between parentheses, and therefore, the annual maximum level of support for 1997 was 2,028.65 billion won, the Panel finds that the method employed by Korea to calculate current support in respect of beef is not consistent with the provisions of the *Agreement on Agriculture*.

825. For 1998, Korea's bound commitment level is 1,627.17 billion won while Korea's notified Current Total AMS is 1,562.77 billion won. In the light of its examination, the Panel considers that, properly calculated pursuant to Article 6 and Annex 3, current support for beef would be higher in 1997 and in 1998 than the level notified and defended by Korea. The following errors in Korea's calculations have been identified by the Panel: incorrect calculation of (1) market price support for beef including through the use of a - fixed external reference price for beef relating to the wrong stage of processing; - the use of an incorrect eligible production level; and – the calculation of total production, as well as (2) the omission of other non-exempt support measures from the calculation of the current aggregate measurement of support for the producers of beef.

Market-Price Support

826. The principal form of support for beef producers used by Korea in 1997 and 1998 was "price support for beef,"[431] a form of "market price support". Paragraph 8 of Annex 3 of the Agreement on Agriculture specifies how market price support should be assessed for the purpose of calculating its Current Total AMS. It provides that:

> "market price support shall be calculated using the gap between a fixed external reference price and the applied administered price

[430] Korea's Committee on Agriculture Notification, Table DS:1 at 2 (G/AG/N/KOR/18).

[431] Korea's Committee on Agriculture notifications for 1997 and 1998 refer to "price support" (G/AG/N/KOR/18 and 24 respectively).

multiplied by the quantity of production eligible to receive the applied administered price".

827. It is worth recalling that the quantification of market price support in AMS terms is not based on expenditures by government. Market price support as defined in Annex 3 can exist even where there are no budgetary payments.[432] Market price support gauges the effect of a government policy measure on agricultural producers of a basic product rather than the budgetary cost of that measure borne by government. In general, with market price support programmes, all producers of the products which are subject to the market price support mechanism enjoy the benefit of an assurance that their products can be marketed *at least* at the support price. Therefore, the minimum price support will be available to all marketable production of the type and quality to which the administered price support programme relates, including where actual market prices are above the administered minimum price level. There may, of course, be circumstances where eligible production may be less than total marketable production, as for example where the minimum price support is only available to producers in certain disadvantaged regions. Another possible example would be where there is a legislatively predetermined, non-discretionary, limitation on the quantity of marketable production that a governmental intervention agency could take off the market at the administered price in any year. In the latter case, the particular design and operation of the price support mechanism would have to be taken into account in determining eligible production, since even governmental purchases at a level below the legislatively predetermined quantity limit could, depending on market conditions, suffice to maintain market prices at above the minimum levels for all marketable production. Hence, with these qualifications, eligible production for the purposes of calculating the market price support component of current support should comprise the total marketable production of all producers which is eligible to benefit from the market price support, even though the proportion of production which is actually purchased by a governmental agency may be relatively small or even nil.

828. The market price support is calculated in computing the difference between a fixed external reference price (FERP) and an applied administered price (AAP) with the difference being multiplied by eligible production. Both the FERP and the AAP must be calculated at an equivalent stage of processing or converted accordingly. Since the aggregate measurement of support is calculated by reference to the applied administered price and the fixed external reference price, both of these two variables must be calculated at a comparable stage of production. Paragraph 7 of Annex 3 provides that the AMS shall be calculated as closely as practicable to the point of first sale of the agricultural product. Korea

---

[432] Para. 8 of Annex 3 explicitly notes that "[b]udgetary payments made to maintain this gap [between a fixed external reference price and the applied administered price], such as buying-in or storage costs, shall not be included in the AMS.

admits this.[433] In other words, the fixed external reference price must be at (or converted to) the same stage in the processing chain as the applied administered price for the basic agricultural product(s) concerned.

"Fixed External Reference Price (FERP)"

829. Korea's calculation of its FERP is problematic. In 1997, Korea's applied administered price (AAP) for beef was, as set out in the Korean MAF press statement of 27 January 1997,[434] 2,400 thousand won per 500 kg. Hanwoo steer for the remainder of the 1997 calendar year. Since this programme was offered to different types of beef (with different support prices), Korea used a weighted average applied administered price and converted the base unit for the calculations from a per head basis to a per kilogram carcass weight (bone-in) basis, whereas the FERP is calculated on a (at least partly boneless) "product weight" basis for 1989-1991. The FERP has to be assessed at a practicable, comparable level of trade as close to the first point of sale as possible.[435] The AAP is based on live animals, while the FERP refers to meat on a product weight basis. While both prices purport to be shown on a carcass weight basis, the FERP claimed by Korea includes slaughter costs, whereas the AAP does not. As a result, the FERP used by Korea is overstated. The effect of Korea's error is a narrowing of the difference between its AAP and the FERP, and consequently an understatement of the amount of domestic support.

830. Moreover, the Panel recalls that, by virtue of Articles 1(a)(ii) and 1(h)(ii), Korea is bound by the provisions of Annex 3, since it did not have any "constituent data and methodology" for beef in its Base Total AMS. This means, *inter alia*, that a 1986-88 external reference price has to be used (paragraphs 9 and 11 of Annex 3). Korea's objection that beef was not imported during that period and that it has no relevant import price data is not sustainable, since paragraph 9 of Annex 3 allows the use of proxy prices.[436] Proxy prices were in fact used in Korea's AGST, Supporting Table 6, for rice and two types of barley.[437] The Panel finds, therefore, that in both 1997 and 1998 Korea miscalculated its fixed external reference price contrary to Article 6 and paragraph 9 of Annex 3. Korea, by unilaterally electing to use a fixed external reference price based on data for

[433] See para. 389 of this Panel report.

[434] See para. 384 of this Panel report.

[435] Para. 7 of Annex 3 of the Agreement on Agriculture provides that the AMS "shall be calculated as close as practicable to the point of first sale of the basic agricultural product concerned".

[436] Para. 9: "The fixed external reference price shall be based on the years 1986 to 1988 and shall *generally* be the average f.o.b. unit value for the basic agricultural product concerned in a net exporting country and the average c.i.f. unit value for the basic agricultural product concerned in a net importing country in the base period. The fixed reference price may be adjusted for quality differences as necessary". The reference to "generally" has been interpreted to allow countries to use proxy prices as Korea did for rice and two types of barley.

[437] G/AG/AGST/KOR, page 8.

1989-1991 that is inconsistent with the methodology provided for in the *Agreement on Agriculture*, distorts the calculation of domestic support.

"Eligible/actual production"

831. The Panel finds that Korea has used an incorrect figure for the level of eligible production in its calculation of market price support. Korea argues that it used the actual production to calculate its market support. The language of paragraph 8 of Annex 3 makes it clear that it is the quantity of production which is "eligible" to receive the benefit of the price support provided through the applied administered price which is relevant. The actual quantity of purchases is not relevant in the calculation of market price support. Korea, by indicating its intent to purchase specified quantities, made them eligible to receive the applied administered price, and consequently affected and supported the price of all such products.

832. As mentioned, the fact that not all eligible production was actually purchased by the government is irrelevant. This interpretation of the eligibility of production for price support is confirmed by the language in the last sentence of paragraph 8 of Annex 3 which states that the provision is not concerned with the actual amount of budgetary outlays. It is the market price support provided by the government measure that is the focus of the provision, since as indicated in paragraph 827 above, it is marketable production as a whole which benefits from this type of support.

833. Korea argues that requiring the aggregate measurement of support for beef to be computed based on eligible production would be unfair because actual production was used for computing the base period AMS. The Panel recalls, however, that the Tables of Support Material upon which Korea's Base Total AMS was calculated (AGST/KOR) had no product specific AMS calculation for beef (or cattle) included in its (initial) Total Base AMS. Therefore, Korea is required by the wording of Article 1(a)(ii) of the *Agreement on Agriculture*, in the absence of "constituent data and methodology used in the tables of supporting material", to rely exclusively on the provisions of Annex 3.

834. Korea's underestimation would be even greater if the meaning of "eligible production", which the Panel considers to be appropriate in the light of its interpretation above, were to be applied. For instance, in 1997, based on the evidence submitted, that quantity was 500 head per day of Hanwoo cattle above 500 kg. within the 27 January to 31 December 1997 period (340 days). A total of 170,000 head of Hanwoo cattle were thus eligible in the 1997 calendar year as used by Korea for its domestic support commitments. In carcass weight terms,

this amounts to 52,615 tonnes for Hanwoo cattle alone.[438] However, Korea notified a total figure of 35,127 tonnes in 1997, thereby underestimating the eligible production (let alone any AMS for its beef industry), and thus the market price support, the aggregate measurement of support for producers of beef and the Current Total AMS. There is also evidence that dairy steer and hybrid cows were eligible for support, which would increase the aggregate measurement of support for beef.

"Total value of production"

835. The Panel further notes that there is also evidence that Korea's data for the total value of production was based on the value of 1996 production and not that of 1997.[439] Korea explains that it did not have any available data for 1997. The Panel considers, however, that it would be against the spirit and wording of the Agreement on Agriculture if WTO Members could avoid their obligations to respect annual commitment levels by notifying data from another year.

Product Specific Programmes

836. The Panel also notes that there are other features of Korea's calculation and characterisation of support for beef producers in both 1997 and 1998 which would have warranted closer examination in terms of the explicit provisions of Article 7.2(a) of the *Agreement on Agriculture*. This applies in particular to the programme described as the "Loan interest subsidy for livestock farming" (27.28 and 31.77 billion won in 1997 and 1998 respectively), which on the evidence presented by all parties substantially benefits beef producers (but presumably not only beef producers) and which has been classified by Korea as "non-product specific support" within the non-product-specific *de minimis* level in terms of Article 6.4 (a)(ii). In the Panel's view, given the clear language of Article 1(a), for a measure to be classified as "non-product-specific support" for the purposes of the exemption in Article 6.4(a)(ii), it would have to constitute "support provided in favour of agricultural producers in general", and not to a particular product-specific subset of producers.

(iii) Recalculation of the Aggregate Measurement of Support for Beef in 1997 and 1998 and of the Current Total AMS

837. The Panel considers that Australia and the United States have provided sufficient evidence and arguments in support of their claims that Korea has mis-

---

438 170,000 head @ 500 kg. (0.5 tonne) per head multiplied by the conversion coefficient of 61.9 per cent, i.e. ((170,000*0.5)*.619) = 52,625 tonnes carcass weight equivalent. See para. 480 of this Panel report.

439 See para. 376 of this Panel report.

calculated its annual support to its beef industry in 1997 and 1998. The Complaining parties also submit recalculations of the numerous variables in the product-specific domestic support for beef and Korea's Current Total AMS.[440] The Complaining parties also refer the Panel to the recalculations submitted by New Zealand, as third party, and with which the Complaining parties concur and which they use as an "adjunct" to their own submissions.[441]

838. For reasons of clarity and simplicity of those recalculations, the Panel has decided to rely on the recalculation offered by New Zealand.[442] On the basis of the adjusted fixed external reference price and the recalculation of eligible production levels (but for Hanwoo beef alone), the following table offers revised data on Korea's beef aggregate measurement of support for 1997 and 1998. The beef product-specific aggregate measurement of support is then compared to the values of production supplied by Korea for 1997 and 1998.

Calculation of the product-specific AMS for Hanwoo beef and de minimis calculation[443]

Year	**AAP**	**FERP**	**EP**	**MPS**	**OS**	**Total AMS**	**VP**	***Percentage***
	won/kg.		tonnes	billion won				
1997	7,351.1	1,514	52,615	307.1	1.09	308.2	2,107	**14.6**
1998	6,883.2	1,514	35,328	189.7	1.40	191.1	1,836	**10.4**

839. The Complaining parties suggest that by adding the "actual" purchases of dairy cattle and hybrid cattle of Cheju Island to the eligible Hanwoo production as set out in the table above, the proportion of the total value of beef production accounted for by the beef product-specific domestic support increases to 15.8 per cent and 11.7 per cent in 1997 and 1998 respectively.[444]

---

440 See, for instance, paras. 365, 375, 379, 381, 382, 383 of this Panel report.

441 See para. 413 of this Panel report.

442 The Panel notes that for this recalculation of Korea's FERP, New Zealand even used 1989-1991 data (inflating Korea's legitimate level of domestic support), contrary to the Panel's conclusion that pursuant to Annex 3 a 1986-1988 FERP should have been employed. Para. 9: "The fixed external reference price shall be based on the years 1986 to 1988 and shall *generally* be the average f.o.b. unit value for the basic agricultural product concerned in a net exporting country and the average c.i.f. unit value for the basic agricultural product concerned in a net importing country in the base period. The fixed reference price may be adjusted for quality differences as necessary". Para. 11: "The fixed reference price shall be based on the years 1986 to 1988 and shall *generally* be the actual price used for determining payment rates." (Emphasis added.)

443 AAP - Applied administered price – Source: Notifications of Korea; FERP - Fixed external reference price; EP - Eligible production; MPS - Market price support – Source: ((AAP-FERP)*EP); OS - Other support – Source: Notifications of Korea; VP - Value of production – Source: Para. 483 of this Panel report.

444 Non-Hanwoo purchases amounted to 4,083 tonnes in 1997 and 4,454 tonnes in 1998. See para. 484 to this Panel report.

840. If Korea had included the "eligible" production of dairy cattle and hybrid cattle of Cheju Island in its calculation, its aggregate measurement of support for beef would have certainly resulted in even higher figures, exceeding the 10 per cent *de minimis* referred to in Article 6.4(b) *of the Agreement on Agriculture* by a larger margin.

841. In so miscalculating Korea violated Article 6.4 of the *Agreement on Agriculture*. Thus, since it was above the 10 per cent *de minimis*, the product-specific aggregate measurement of support for beef should have been included in the calculation of Korea's Current Total AMS in both years, as provided for in Article 7.2(a) of the *Agreement on Agriculture*.

842. The Complaining parties also offer their own calculation of Korea's Total Current AMS for 1997 and 1998 (including the recalculation by New Zealand)[445], evidence not refuted by Korea to the satisfaction of the Panel. Such calculations lead to the results set out in the table below:

Adjusted Current Total AMS for Korea 1997 and 1998

Year	Current Total AMS as notified by Korea (billion won)	Product Specific AMS for Beef (billion won)	Correct Current Total AMS (billion won)
1997	1,936.95	308.2	2,245.2
1998	1,562.77	191.1	1,753.9

843. In the light of the evidence and the legal arguments presented, the Panel considers that the Complaining parties have established a *prima facie* case, which has not been rebutted by Korea, that in 1997, the correct Current Total AMS for Korea (2,245.2 billion won) exceeded the annual commitment level, i.e. 1,650.03 billion won (or even the levels referred to in the second column between parenthesis of 2,028.65 billion won) contrary to Article 3.2 of the *Agreement on Agriculture*. In 1998, the correct Current Total AMS - including only Hanwoo beef instead of total eligible beef – also exceeded the annual commit-

Year	AAP	FERP	EP	MPS	OS	Total AMS	VP	*De minimis percentage*
	won/kg		Tonnes	billion won				%
1997	7,351.1	1,514	56,698	331.0	1.09	332.0	2,107	*15.8*
1998	6,883.2	1,514	39,782	213.6	1.40	215.0	1,836	*11.7*

[445] See para. 484 of this Panel report.

ment level, i.e. 1,627.17 billion won, contrary to Article 3.2 of the *Agreement on Agriculture*.

(c) Conclusion

844. The Panel finds, therefore, that Korea's domestic support for beef for 1997 and 1998 was not correctly calculated and exceeded the *de minimis* level, in violation of Article 6 of *the Agreement on Agriculture*. The Panel also finds that, for the same years, Korea's domestic support for beef was not included in Korea's Current Total AMS, in violation of Article 7.2(a). Finally, the Panel finds that Korea's Current Total AMS for 1997 and 1998 exceeded Korea's commitment levels, as specified in Section 1, Part IV of its Schedule, in violation of Article 3.2 of the *Agreement on Agriculture*.

VIII. CONCLUSIONS AND RECOMMENDATIONS

845. In the light of the above findings, the Panel concludes as follows:

(a) The following measures are included in "the remaining restrictions" within the meaning of Note 6(e) of Korea's Schedule and thus benefit from a transitional period until 1 January 2001, by which date they shall be eliminated or otherwise brought into conformity with the WTO Agreement:

(i) The price mark-up applied to imports through the SBS system that is additional to the tariff;

(ii) The limitations on participation in the SBS import system including the super-group membership requirement; the restriction on range of end-users; the prohibition on cross-trading between end-users and super-groups; the quotas and sub-quotas allocated to super-groups according to annual plans rather than demand; and the recording requirements;

(iii) The requirement that the beef imported through the LPMO be distributed only through the wholesale market;

(iv) The LPMO's minimum wholesale price;

(v) The *per se* existence of a discretionary licensing system relating to any of "the remaining restrictions" (as distinct from its operation);

(b) The dual retail system for beef (including the obligation for department stores and supermarkets authorized to sell imported beef to hold a separate display, and the obligation for foreign beef shops to bear a sign "Specialized Imported Beef Stores") is inconsistent with the provisions of Article III:4 in treating imported beef less favourably than domestic beef, a discrimination that cannot be justified pursuant to Article XX(d) of GATT;

(c) The requirement that the supply of beef from the LPMO's wholesale market be limited to specialized imported beef import stores is inconsistent with Article III:4 of GATT and cannot be justified pursuant to Article XX(d) of GATT;

(d) The more stringent record-keeping requirements imposed on those who purchase foreign beef imported by the LPMO than those who purchase domestic beef, is inconsistent with Article III:4 of GATT;

(e) The prohibition against cross-trading between end-users of the SBS system is inconsistent with Article III:4 of GATT;

(f) Any additional labelling requirements imposed on foreign beef imported through the SBS system that is not also imposed on domestic beef, such as the requirement that the end consumer, the contract number and super-group importer be marked on the imported beef, are inconsistent with Article III:4 of GATT;

(g) The LPMO's lack of and delays in calling for tenders and its discharge practices between November 1997 and the end of May 1998, constitute import restrictions on foreign beef, inconsistent with Article XI of GATT through the application of the Ad Note to Articles XI, XII, XIII, XIV and XVIII. The same practices are also inconsistent with Article 4.2 of the *Agreement on Agriculture* and its footnote.

Even if the LPMO had not had monopoly rights over the import and distribution of its 30 per cent share of Korea's beef import, the LPMO's lack of and delays in calling for tenders during the same period constituted an import restriction inconsistent with Article XI through the application of the Ad Note to Articles XI, XII, XIII, XIV and XVIII. The LPMO's discharge practices during the same period were inconsistent with Article XVII.1(a) of GATT.

(h) The LPMO's calls for tenders that are made subject to grass-fed or grain-fed distinctions impose import restrictions inconsistent with Article XI of GATT; they also treat imports of grass-fed beef less favourably than that is provided for in Korea's Schedule, contrary to Article II:1(a) of GATT.

(i) Korea's domestic support for beef for 1997 and 1998 was not correctly calculated and exceeded the *de minimis* level, contrary to Article 6 of the Agreement on Agriculture, and was not included in Korea's Current Total AMS, contrary to Article 7.2(a) of the Agreement on Agriculture.

(j) Korea's total domestic support (Current Total AMS) for 1997 and 1998 exceeded Korea's commitment levels, as specified in Section 1, Part IV of its Schedule, contrary to Article 3.2 of the Agreement on Agriculture.

846. Under Article 3.8 of the DSU, in cases where there is infringement of the obligations assumed under a covered agreement, the action is considered *prima facie* to constitute a case of nullification or impairment of benefits under that agreement. Accordingly, we conclude that, to the extent that the Korea has acted inconsistently with the provisions of covered agreements, as described in the preceding paragraphs, it has nullified or impaired the benefits accruing to the complainants under those agreements.

847. The Panel recommends that the Dispute Settlement Body request Korea to bring its various measures into conformity with its obligations under the covered agreements of the WTO mentioned in paragraph 845 above.

ANNEX 1

1990 RECORDS OF UNDERSTANDING*

RECORD OF UNDERSTANDING BETWEEN THE GOVERNMENT OF THE REPUBLIC OF KOREA AND THE GOVERNMENT OF AUSTRALIA ON BEEF

The Government of the Republic of Korea and the Government of Australia, recognizing the recommendations of the GATT dispute settlement panel report on Korean import restrictions on beef (L/6504) as well as the report of the GATT Balance of Payments Committee (BOP/R/183/Add.1) concerning Korea, have agreed as follows:

I. GENERAL TERMS

A. With regard to beef, the Government of the Republic of Korea (hereinafter referred to as the Korean Government) reaffirms its undertaking to eliminate its remaining import restrictions or otherwise bring them into conformity with GATT provisions as included in the conclusion of the report of the GATT/BOP committee on consultations with the Republic of Korea adopted by the GATT Council on November 7, 1989.

B. Both sides agree that the provisions of this Understanding relating to the import of beef will be implemented on a Most-Favoured-Nation (MFN) basis.

C. Conditions and levels of importation and sale of imported beef provided for in this Record of Understanding and its Attachments will not be impaired or modified by either government without prior consultation.

D. A joint study team will be established in order to:

(1) examine the structural weakness of the Korean livestock industry and review the effects of the industry structure on the appropriate timing of market liberalization;

* The three 1990 ROUs are almost similar.

(2) review the functions of the Livestock Products Marketing Organization (LPMO) and make recommendations for improvements in marketing and pricing practices in the future.

The study will be completed by May 1, 1991. Other details concerning the joint study are set out in Attachment 1.

Representatives of the National Livestock Cooperatives Federation (NLCF) and the LPMO and the Australian Meat and Livestock Industry will respectively select the Korean and Australian members of the study team. Both governments will participate as observers. Third country and industry representatives will be included on the study team. The results of the study team will be taken into consideration by both governments during future consultation.

E. Terms used in this Record of Understanding are defined in Attachment 2.

II. MARKET ACCESS MEASURES

General Consumption

A. The base quota levels of general consumption importation on a customs clearance basis for each of the three years in the period beginning January 1, 1990 and ending December 31, 1992 will be as follows:

1990	1991	1992
58,000 MT	62,000 MT	66,000 MT

B. Bilateral consultations concerning an import régime designed to increase imports following the year 1992 will be initiated no later than July 1, 1992.

Simultaneous Buy/Sell (SBS)

C. A simultaneous buy/sell system will be implemented for seven per cent of the base quota level for the import of beef. This mechanism will be used initially by tourist hotels, tourist restaurants, the NLCF and the Korean Cold Storage Company Ltd. Principles of the operation of this buyer access system are contained in Attachment 3. Details concerning the operation of this system will be determined by both governments no later than October 1, 1990 based upon recommendations from the industry-to-industry dialogue established in section III below. Implementation of the SBS system will be effective no later than October 1, 1990. Both governments will consult concerning the future expansion of the SBS system.

III. INDUSTRY-TO-INDUSTRY DIALOGUE

A. Representatives of the Korean and Australian meat and livestock industries met on 23 April to discuss a range of technical issues. The outcome of these discussions is reflected in Attachment 1.

B. The two industries will meet at the request of either industry to discuss issues associated with the beef trade.

C. The results of industry-to-industry dialogue will be submitted to the Korean and Australian governments for review and consultations, as appropriate.

IV. CONSULTATIONS

Both sides will consult promptly at the request of either party on any matter relating to this Record of Understanding and its Attachments.

V. GATT RIGHTS

Nothing in this Record of Understanding will be interpreted to affect the rights and obligations of either country as contracting parties to the GATT.

VI. STATUS OF ATTACHMENTS

The Attachments to this Understanding form an integral part of it.

Signed on May 31st day of 1990 by the Representatives of the Governments of the Republic of Korea and Australia.

ATTACHMENT 1

INDUSTRY-TO-INDUSTRY DIALOGUE

The following issues were discussed between LPMO, NLCF and the Australian industry (AMLC, AMEFC, CCA).

1. Bid & performance bonds

LPMO could not agree to the elimination of bid & performance bonds because of the difficulties LPMO may face without the bonds. It was agreed that future discussions on the issue would take into account the views of the Australian industry representatives.

2. Bid quantities

The Australian side noted that the minimum bid quantity had been reduced to 18 tonnes for boneless beef and remained at 200 tonnes for bone-in beef.

3. SBS system

The Australian side noted that the SBS system would be implemented no later than October 1, 1990 for 7% of the base quota. Details for the SBS system are not fixed and LPMO invited Australia's participation to assist in the developments of the new system.

The Australian side expressed its desire to meet in the near future to have detailed discussions on the SBS based on the principle of non-discrimination by source and by product type.

4. Technical issues

(a) The LPMO agreed that AMLC technical representatives would be consulted in case problems arose with respect to product quality.

(b) For quality specification, it was agreed that Korea and Australia would jointly develop the specification system. In the first place, the "Ausmeat K1" which codifies the specification of grain-fed beef that LPMO established shall be used. And the "Ausmeat P1" which codifies the specification of grass-fed beef that LPMO established shall be used. These codes would apply from the next tender issued.

(c) Other issues which are set out in an exchange of letters between the LPMO and AMLC will be subject to further discussion.

5. Joint Study Team (JST)

(a) LPMO and NLCF encouraged the Australian industry to participate actively in the study.

(b) The Australian meat and livestock industry will notify the NLCF Chairman of the Australian co-chair for the joint study team in the near future, but no later than May 21, 1990. Composition of the joint study team and the topics for consideration by the team will be agreed as soon as possible.

(c) The first meeting of participants in the study team will take place in Seoul either in the week beginning June 11 or 18 June, 1990. The agenda for this meeting will include details concerning study topics, study methodology and study timetable.

ATTACHMENT 2

DEFINITIONS

For the purpose of this Record of Understanding and its Attachments:

1. "Beef" means meat of bovine animals, fresh, chilled or frozen. All tonnage specified in the agreement is given in boneless weight equivalent.

2. "Tourist hotels" and "tourist restaurants" mean tourist hotels and tourist restaurants as defined by the Korean Foreign Trade Act and related and referenced regulations.

ATTACHMENT 3

SIMULTANEOUS BUY/SELL SYSTEM

1. All imports of beef under the simultaneous buy/sell system will receive equal, non-discriminatory treatment without regard to country of origin and without regard to whether it is grass-fed or grain-fed; fresh, chilled or frozen; bone-in or bone-out.

2. Buyers and sellers will have sole responsibility for product specification, delivery and other terms of sales.

3. Buyers and sellers will simultaneously submit buy and sell prices to the LPMO to participate in the LPMO tender.

4. Details of successful bids including product type, quantity, price, and origin will be made public, promptly, once awarded.

5. The operation of the SBS system will be reviewed at the request of either party.

ANNEX 2

JULY 1993 RECORDS OF UNDERSTANDING*

RECORD OF UNDERSTANDING BETWEEN THE GOVERNMENT OF THE REPUBLIC OF KOREA AND THE GOVERNMENT OF AUSTRALIA ON MARKET ACCESS FOR BEEF

The Government of the Republic of Korea and the Government of Australia, recognizing the recommendations of the General Agreement on Tariffs and Trade (GATT) dispute-settlement panel report on Korean import restrictions on beef (L/6504) as well as the report of the GATT Balance-of-Payments Committee (BOP/R/183/Add.1) concerning Korea, and the May 1990 bilateral Record of Understanding between the Government of the Republic of Korea and the Government of Australia on beef, have agreed as follows:

I. GENERAL PROVISIONS

(a) The Governments of the Republic of Korea and Australia confirm that this Record of Understanding and its attachments (hereinafter referred to as "Understanding" will be implemented on a most-favoured-nation (m.f.n.) basis.

(b) Conditions and levels of importation and sale of imported beef and all other provisions provided for in this Understanding shall not be impaired or modified by either Government without prior consultation and mutual agreement.

(c) This Understanding is the second Understanding between the Government of the Republic of Korea and the Government of Australia on market access for beef. This Understanding reflects the desire of the Parties to implement the GATT dispute-- settlement panel recommendations and Balance-of-Payments Committee determinations. Consultations between the Parties regarding such measures will be held no later than 1 June 1995.

(d) Unless otherwise specified in this Understanding, all provisions of this Understanding shall become effective upon the date of the exchange of letters confirming this Understanding between the Gov-

* The three July 1993 ROUs are almost similar.

ernment of the Republic of Korea and the Government of Australia.

II. DEFINITIONS

For the purposes of this Understanding:

"Base amount" means the minimum annual amount, on a customs cleared basis, expressed in metric tonnes, of beef to be imported into the Republic of Korea.

"Beef" means all meat of bovine animals, fresh, chilled or frozen, as classified under HS 0201 and HS 0202. All tonnage specified in this Understanding is given in retail weight equivalent.

"Customer" means any individual private enterprise, firm, business or grouping thereof that under the terms of this Understanding has the right to import beef through NLCF and KCSC.

"End-user" means any individual private enterprise, firm, business, or grouping thereof, and/or their buying agents that has the right to import beef through any super-group except NLCF or KCSC.

"General tender system" is the import and distribution system for beef imported into the Republic of Korea, excluding that which is supplied through the SBS system.

"Large-scale outlet" means a store with a total sales space of 3,000 square metres or more and with more than 30 per cent of the total sales space operated by the owner.

"Mark-up" means the charge collected by the ROKG expressed as a percentage of the duty-paid c.i.f. price.

"Parties" means the Government of the Republic of Korea and the Government of Australia.

"SBS share" means the portion of the base amount that must be allocated through the SBS system.

"SBS sub-share" means the portion of the SBS share that must be allocated to a super-group.

"SBS system" means the system through which suppliers of beef imported into the Republic of Korea conduct business directly with super-groups, end-users, or customers.

"Super-group" means and organization or association of end-users that has the right to import beef under the SBS system and, as appropriate, allocate SBS sub- shares among its affiliated end-users, and shall include the following entities, subject to the conditions and terms specified in this Understanding: the National Livestock Co-operatives Federation and its subsidiary companies (NLCF); Korea Cold Storage Company, Ltd. (KCSC); Korea Tourist Hotel Supply Centre (KTHSC); Korea Meat Industries Association (KMIA); Korea Super Chain Association (KOSCA); and a Non-Tourist Restaurant Organization (NTRO) to be formed for the purpose of importing and allocating imported beef.

"Supermarket" means a retail store whose principal business is the sale of food and beverages.

"Tourist hotels" means tourist hotels as defined by the Korean Foreign Trade Act and related and referenced regulations.

"Tourist restaurants" means tourist restaurants as defined by the Korean Foreign Trade Act and related and referenced regulations.

"Wholesale market" is the market for auction and distribution of beef imported under General Tenders, other than that which is directed to NLCF and KCSC for further processing.

III. MARKET ACCESS - BASE AMOUNTS

(a) The base amounts are the minimum to be imported on a customs cleared basis for the three-year period beginning 1 January 1993, and ending 31 December 1995 and shall be as follows:

1993	99,000 metric tonnes
1994	106,000 metric tonnes
1995	113,000 metric tonnes

(b) These base amounts shall be divided between SBS shares in the SBS system, as specified in this Understanding, and the general tender system. The general tenders shall be published in domestic Korean newspapers, and the results of those tenders, when the results become known, shall be made available to any interested party upon request.

IV. MARKET ACCESS MEASURES - SIMULTANEOUS BUY/SELL (SBS) SYSTEM

A. *General*

1. NLCF, KCSC, and KTHSC; which participated under the 1990 Understanding, shall participate in the SBS system as super-groups under this Understanding. New super-groups, end-users, and customers will be added to the SBS system over the term of this Understanding as specified in this Understanding.

2. The SBS system, as specified in this Understanding, will be implemented not later than 1 August 1993. However, 1993 SBS shares and sub-shares will be allocated to super-groups not later than the date of the exchange of letters confirming this Understanding between the Government of the Republic of Korea and the Government of Australia.

3. The ROKG shall take no action to increase the price of beef entering under the SBS system above the price of similar beef imported under general tender.

B. *Framework for SBS system*

1. Annual SBS share and sub-share allocations

(a) The SBS annual shares are the amount to be allocated under the SBS system for the three-year period beginning 1 January 1993 and ending 31 December 1995 and shall be as follows:

1993	9,900 metric tonnes
1994	21,200 metric tonnes
1995	33,900 metric tonnes

(b) Annual sub-shares to be allocated to SBS super-groups shall be as follows (expressed in metric tonnes, retail weight equivalent):

	1993	1994	1995
NLCF	2,970	3,330	5,254
KCSC	2,970	3,330	5,254
KTHSC	3,960	4,664	5,424
NTRO		2,000	2,712
KMIA		4,676	7,118
KOSCA		3,200	8,138

2. Schedule for addition of new entrants

(a) In 1993 the SBS sub-shares will be allocated by the ROKG among the three super-groups (KTHSC, NLCF, KCSC), according to the schedule set out in Section IV.B.1.b of this Understanding. These super-groups shall import beef on behalf of affiliated end- users (except in the case of NLCF and KCSC) without the participation, direction, or other involvement of the LPMO or ROKG.

(b) Beginning 1 January 1994 NTRO and KMIA will have the right to participate as super-groups, and will each be allocated an SBS sub-share by the ROKG, according to the schedule set out in Section IV.B.1.b of this Understanding. KMIA and NTRO will allocate SBS sub-shares to their affiliated end-users and conduct transactions without the participation, direction, or other involvement of the LPMO or ROKG.

(c) Beginning 1 October 1994, KOSCA will have the right to participate as a super-group and will be allocated an SBS sub-share by the ROKG, according to the schedule set out in Section IV.B.1.b of this Understanding. The KOSCA super-group will allocated SBS sub-shares to its affiliated end-users and conduct transactions without the participation, direction, or other involvement of the LPMO or ROKG.

Criteria for determining eligibility for SBS participation of current and future KOSCA members are set out in Section IV.C.1 of this Understanding.

(d) Beginning 1 January 1995 any member of KOSCA not eligible to import through the KOSCA super-group, as outlined in Section IV.C.1 of this Understanding, shall have the right to participate in the SBS system as customers under NLCF and KCSC. For the sake of commercial convenience, such individual KOSCA members shall have the right to negotiate and place collective orders through NLCF and KCSC.

(e) Also beginning 1 January 1995, any butcher shops that are or become registered dealers of imported beef shall have the right to participate in the SBS system as customers under NLCF and KCSC. For the sake of commercial convenience, such individual butcher shops shall have the right to negotiate and place collective orders through NLCF and KCSC.

(f) Beginning 1 August 1993 and in 1994 and 1995, KTHSC, as a super-group, will administer the portion of the SBS system under which individual tourist hotels and restaurants, as end-users, have the option to purchase beef through KTHSC or directly from foreign suppliers.

C. Additional provisions for SBS system

1. KOSCA member participation in the SBS system

(a) Direct outlets of KOSCa member companies shall have the right to participate in the SBS system as end-users affiliated with the KOSCA super-group. Franchise outlets of KOSCA member companies that are or become registered dealers of imported beef shall have the right to participate in the SBS system as customers of NLCF and KCSC.

(b) Any outlet of a KOSCA member company that is a large scale outlet shall be excluded from SBS participation, except as provided for in sub-paragraph (c).

(c) Notwithstanding sub-paragraph (b), and notwithstanding whether a KOSCA member company outlet is affiliated with a large-scale outlet that is not a supermarket, such KOSCA member company outlets that are operated as supermarkets shall have the right to participate in the SBS system in the manner specified in Section IV.C.1.a.

2. Notification

The SBS sub-shares for a calendar year shall be divided by the super-groups into quarterly allocations in such a way as to reflect seasonal consumption patterns. These quarterly allocations shall be announced prior to the beginning of each calendar year. The allocations shall be expressed in metric tonnes, retail weight equivalent. SBS sub- share notifications shall be made available to any interested party on request.

3. Purchasing Authority

(a) End-users shall have the right to sign contracts and negotiate all terms of sale, including price, quantities, specifications, terms of delivery, etc. Customers shall have the right to negotiate all terms of sale, including price, quantities, specifications, terms of delivery, etc.

(b) End-users or their designated agents, and customers, shall have the right to apply to the appropriate super-group for import authorization amounts under the SBS sub-share. Such authorization shall be granted by the super-groups upon request. End-users and customers shall be granted such access to sub-shares through super-groups, as established in this Understanding, until the sub-share is exhausted. Once an end-user or customer receives authorization to import, there shall be no further involvement by the super-group in the commercial transaction with the exception than NLCF and KCSC will purchase and import beef on behalf of their customers.

(c) Direct or indirect charges imposed by super-groups for importing beef on behalf of their customers shall not exceed reasonable administrative costs and expenses associated with such importation. Direct or indirect charges imposed by super-groups for administering the allocation of SBS sub-shares to end-users shall not exceed reasonable administrative costs and expenses associated with such allocation. Super-groups shall make details of all such administrative costs and expenses available to any interested party upon request and shall not extract profits beyond the extent of such costs and expenses.

4. Allocation of SBS sub-shares by super-groups to end-users

(a) The allocation of sub-shares to end-users shall be the sole responsibility of super-groups. The procedures and criteria for allocation of these sub-shares shall be fair, equitable, transparent, and implemented in good faith. These criteria must be announced and published. To facilitate orderly marketing and development of normal commercial relationships between end-users and foreign suppliers, super-groups shall implement an allocation system that encourages stable, long-term commercial relationships between end-users and foreign suppliers while making provision for the entry of new end-users. Anticipating the addition of new end-users, the super-groups must have agreed procedures and criteria for distributing SBS sub-shares among their affiliated end-users.

(b) Unused end-user sub-shares must be reallocated, prior to 1 October of the calendar year, by the super-group.

5. NLCF and KCSC super-groups and importation of beef on behalf of their customers

Notwithstanding Sections IV.C.3 and IV.C.4, not later than 1 October 1994, NLCF and KCSC will set and announce the standard by which they will purchase beef on behalf of their customers. This standard will be equitable, established in a transparent manner, and based on the following principles: NLCF and KCSC, taking into account their SBS shares and the number of their customers, will determine an appropriate ceiling for each customer and import on behalf of the customer amounts requested under the ceiling, and in doing so shall not discriminate unfairly against any customers. As long as a customer's request meets the standard thus established, NLCF and KCSC will carry our the importation on behalf of their customers without imposing further conditions.

6. Importation, utilization, and distribution of SBS product

(a) Except as otherwise specified in this Understanding, there shall be no restrictions placed by the ROKG or any super-group on beef (regardless of country of origin, product type, or specification, whether grass-fed or grain-fed or whether fresh, chilled or frozen) imported under the SBS system, including processing requirements, labelling, pricing, marking or packaging requirements or other barriers to legitimate importation, distribution, and sale, that create unnecessary obstacles to trade or otherwise undermine the objectives of this Understanding. Beef imported under the SBS system must be distributed and sold through legal channels in conformance with Korean regulations.

(b) Any SBS sub-share that it not fully used by a super-group in any of its quarterly allocations shall be transferred to that super-group's allocation for the subsequent quarter, except that any SBS sub-share that is not fully utilized by a super-group by the end of the third calendar year quarter shall be reallocated to all other super-groups on a *pro rata* basis, in proportion to their respective entitlements under the SBS system, for their use in the final calendar year quarter. Such reallocation shall be made no later than 15 October. With regard to any such *pro rata* share that is reallocated to KTHSC, any part of that reallocation used by KTHSC end-users shall be subject to the percentage mark-up specified in Section IV.C.7. of this Understanding.

(c) Neither the ROKG nor LPMO shall take any action to discourage super-groups and their end-users or customers from importing or using their SBS shares or sub-shares, as appropriate, as allocated under the terms of this Understanding.

7. SBS mark-up

(a) A single, uniform percentage mark-up shall be applied to all types of beef purchased under the SBS system and shall be equal to the difference between the duty-paid price, c.i.f. Korea, and the price for all boneless cuts of imported grain-fed high quality beef, based on the purchases of the Livestock Products Marketing Organization (LPMO) sold in the general tender system. Such prices shall be determined by calculating the average prices over the immediately preceding three-month period. The mark-up shall be recalculated monthly. This mark-up shall be publicly announced and published prior to becoming effective. However, in the event that the mark-up in any month is in excess of the current percentage mark-up in the general tender market, the mark-up in the SBS system shall be recalculated weekly on a uniform basis using the latest available c.i.f. and general tender price data for the immediately preceding month.

(b) The mark-up applied to beef subject to a contract shall be the mark-up in effect on the date of the contract.

(c) Notwithstanding sub-paragraph (a), in further implementation of the findings of the GATT dispute settlement panel on beef, during 1993 the mark- up on beef shall not exceed 100 per cent of the weighted average percentage mark-up applied to imported bone-less grain-fed high quality beef during calendar year 1992, as derived from data in Attachment I. During 1994, the mark-up on beef shall not exceed 95 per cent of the weighted average percentage mark-up applied during calendar year 1992. During 1995, the mark-up on beef shall not exceed 90 per cent of the weighted average percentage mark-up applied during calendar year 1992. There shall be no minimum mark-up.

(d) Notwithstanding sub-paragraph (a), the mark-up for beef imported by KTHSC for tourist hotels and restaurants shall be no more than 2 per cent of the duty-paid c.i.f. price, except for cuts of beef specified in Attachment II.

(e) In the event that there are significant difficulties arising from discrepancies between the mark-up for bone-in beef in the wholesale market and the SBS mark-up in accordance with Section IV.C.7 of this Understanding, the Parties will consult with each other with a view to addressing and resolving such difficulties.

(f) The Republic of Korea, LPMO, and super-groups shall neither directly nor indirectly exert any influence on pricing decisions of end-users aside from the mark-up agreed upon in this Understanding.

8. Samples

The importation of samples will be allowed under the SBS system, and the sample quantities shall be counted as part of the SBS share. Samples shall not be subject to the mark-up. All super-groups shall be responsible for establishing their sample import systems.

9. Bid and performance bonds and letters of credit

The utilization of bid and performance bonds and/or letters of credit shall be at the option of SBS participants.

10. Short-weight claims

Short-weight claims shall be resolved between buyers and sellers.

11. Minimum purchase unit

There shall be no governmental restrictions on the minimum purchase unit of beef imports.

12. Product coverage

Product coverage for the SBS system shall be the same as for the overall Understanding, as defined in Section II for the term "beef" and shall include all product classified under HS 0201 and HS 0202.

13. Purchasing frequency

There shall be no governmental restrictions on the timing of purchases by customers, end-users, or their designated agents.

14. Record-keeping

Approved super-groups shall administer record-keeping of purchases to ensure compliance with the annual and quarterly SBS shares.

15. Delivery periods

Delivery shall be determined between the end-user or customer and seller. Delivery of products purchased under quarterly SBS shares may be shipped in subsequent quarters as long as deliveries are completed within sixty days following the end of the calendar year in which the product was purchased.

V. GRASS-FED BEEF MARKETING

(a) The ROKG will evaluate in a transparent manner the impact on beef marketing and consumer preferences of the 1993 trial imports of grass-fed beef into the wholesale market from July to September 1993.

(b) Giving due consideration to the results of the trial marketing of grass-fed beef in the Korean wholesale market, the ROKG will allow gradually increasing tonnages of grass-fed beef to be distributed in the wholesale market upon the completion of the trial run. In the event that any difficulty arises in the market either during the process of the trial or after its completion, the Parties will have due recourse to the consultation provision in Section VII of this Understanding for taking appropriate measures to address and resolve such difficulties.

VI. RELATIONSHIP TO THE GATT

(a) With regard to beef, the ROKG reaffirms its undertaking to eliminate its remaining import restrictions or otherwise bring them into conformity with GATT provisions as provided in the conclusion of the report on the GATT Balance-of-Payments Committee on consultations with the Republic of Korea adopted by the GATT Council on 7 November 1989.

(b) Notwithstanding the above, both Parties reserve their rights under the GATT.

VII. CONSULTATION PROVISION

(a) The Parties agree to consult promptly at the request of either Party on any matter relating to this Understanding.

(b) The Parties shall consult quarterly to ensure full implementation of this Understanding. The first such consultations shall take place not later than 1 October 1993. The agenda for these consultations may include, *inter alia*, problems caused by employing the mark-up specified in Section IV.C.7.a of this Understanding and problems in access for end-users and super-groups under the SBS system in accordance with requirements of this understanding.

ATTACHMENT I

LPMO DATA FOR CIRCULATION OF 1992 AVERAGE MARK-UP

Wholesale Price, Duty-Paid Price, c.i.f. for Imported Beef

		92.1	92.2	92.3	92.4	92.5	92.6	92.7	92.8	92.9	92.10	92.11	92.12	AVG
Chuck Roll	Wholesale price (A)	6,038	6,407	6,510	7,581	7,419	6,811	7,021	7,182	6,802	7,524	9,730	9,757	7,235
	c.i.f. + tariff (B)	3,804	3,756	3,886	3,916	3,897	3,764	3,514	3,537	3,521	3,695	3,829	3,829	3,726
	(A)-(B)	2,234	2,651	2,624	3,665	3,522	3,047	3,507	3,645	3,281	3,929	5,901	5,928	3,509
	Volume	3,885	1,335	1,945	1,681	2,414	2,211	2,281	3,362	3,029	1,895	1,397	1,916	2,279
Shoulder Clod	Wholesale price (A)	5,936	5,759	5,285	6,039	5,979	5,606	6,008	5,793	5,451	6,094	7,526	7,312	6,132
	c.i.f. + tariff (B)	2,682	2,677	2,750	2,749	2,732	2,886	2,946	2,926	2,912	2,912	2,902	2,900	2,812
	(A)-(B)	3,254	3,082	2,535	3,290	3,247	2,720	3,060	2,867	2,539	3,182	4,624	4,412	3,320
	Volume	77	129	238	185	179	19	43	44	93	196	272	27	125
Knuckle	Wholesale price (A)	6,349	6,087	6,520	6,983	6,500	5,731	6,002	6,100	5,661	7,627	8,332	8,858	6,600
	c.i.f. + tariff (B)	3,507	3,587	3,643	3,667	3,740	3,766	3,654	3,628	3,605	3,509	3,675	3,674	3,646
	(A)-(B)	2,842	2,500	2,877	3,316	2,760	1,965	2,348	2,472	2,056	4,018	4,657	5,184	2,954
	Volume	832	287	303	518	702	727	666	1,135	893	306	473	688	628
	Wholesale price (A)	6,133	5,941	5,664	6,395	6,349	5,650	5,559	6,136	5,725	6,833	7,263	7,279	6,211

		92.1	92.2	92.3	92.4	92.5	92.6	92.7	92.8	92.9	92.10	92.11	92.12	AVG.
Top Round	c.i.f. + tariff (B)	3,385	3,419	3,522	3,576	3,649	3,696	3,797	3,754	3,799	3,682	3,729	3,731	3,643
	(A)-(B)	2,748	2,522	2,142	2,819	2,700	1,954	1,762	2,382	1,926	3,151	3,534	3,548	2,569
	Volume	332	137	227	108	158	186	127	223	353	220	309	56	203
Short Ribs	Wholesale price (A)	10,072	10,095	9,881	10,340	10,120	10,291	10,900	11,741	11,671	13,629	12,709	11,422	11,041
	c.i.f. + tariff (B)	4,803	4,855	4,788	4,724	4,689	4,667	4,708	4,707	4,669	4,678	4,796	4,797	4,739
	(A)-(B)	5,269	5,240	5,093	5,616	5,431	5,624	6,192	7,034	7,002	8,951	7,913	6,625	6,302
	Volume	1,071	484	687	535	738	748	654	1,171	788	453	751	692	731
Average	Wholesale price (A)	6,781	7,059	7,050	7,830	7,639	7,217	7,453	7,825	7,250	8,356	9,797	9,854	7,749
	c.i.f. + tariff (B)	3,900	3,881	3,943	3,933	3,951	3,930	3,749	3,789	3,719	3,781	3,944	3,986	3,867
	(A)-(B)	2,881	3,178	3,107	3,897	3,688	3,287	3,704	4,036	3,531	4,575	5,853	5,868	3,882
	Volume	6,197	2,372	3,400	3,027	4,191	3,891	3,771	5,935	5,156	3,070	3,202	3,379	3,966

Note: Prices are for Won/kilogram, US$1=798.3 (as of 7 May 1993)
Volume is in metric tonnes.
Average is weighted average and may slightly differ, due to rounding.

Mark-up = (A)-(B)
Mark-up expressed as a percentage of duty paid import price

$$\frac{(A)-(B)}{B} = 3882/3867 = 100.38\%$$

Source: MAFF/ROKG

ATTACHMENT II

CUTS OF BEEF IMPORTED BY KTHSC

The following five cuts of beef, as defined in the National Association of Meat Purveyors Meat Buyers Guide and the Handbook of Australian Meat, imported by KTHSC for tourist hotels and restaurants shall be subject to the mark-up level specified in Section IV.C.7.a of this Understanding.

	Meat Buyers Guide Reference	Handbook of Australian Meat Reference
Shoulder Clod	114, 114A, 114B	2300 (Blade, Clod)
Chuck Roll	116A	2275 (Chuck Roll) 2270 (Chuck-Square Cut)
Short Rib	123, 123A, 123B, 123C	1690-1694: Bone-in 2235-2238 (Rib ends): Boneless
Knuckle	167, 167A, 167B	2060 (Thick Flank) 2070 (Knuckle)
Top Round	168, 169	2000 (Top Side) 2010 (Inside)

All other beef imported by KTHSC for tourist hotels and restaurants shall be subject to the mark-up level specified in Section IV.C.7.d of this Understanding.

ANNEX 3

DECEMBER 1993 RECORD OF UNDERSTANDING

RECORD OF UNDERSTANDING BETWEEN KOREA AND THE UNITED STATES ON AGRICULTURAL MARKET ACCESS IN THE URUGUAY ROUND

Pork

Pork shall be liberalized by July 1, 1997, with nothing but a bound duty (minus appropriate DFA reductions) remaining. During the interim period (January 1995 through June 1997), Korea will provide access quotas for imported frozen pork* in the amounts specified below. Duties applied on the quota amounts shall not exceed the bound duty, with any charges or fees applied in conformity with GATT Article VIII. Korea shall show a base rate of 37 per cent reduced to a bound rate of 25 per cent in 10 equal instalments in its Uruguay Round country schedule. The applicable tariff rate at the time of liberalization shall be 33.4 per cent.

1995	21,930 MT CWE
1996	29,240MT CWE
1997**	18,275 MT CWE

* HS 0203.21.0000, HS 0203.22.0000, & HS 0203.29.0000

** January through June

Chicken

Chicken shall be liberalized by July 1, 1997, with nothing but a bound duty (minus appropriate DFA reductions) remaining. During the interim period (January 1995 through June 1997), Korea will provide access quotas for imported frozen chicken* in the amounts specified below. Duties applied on the quota amounts shall not exceed the bound duty, with any charges or fees applied in conformity with GATT Article VIII. Korea shall show a base rate of 35 per cent reduced to a bound rate of 20 per cent in 10 equal annual instalments in its Uruguay Round country schedule. The applicable tariff rate at the time of liberalization shall be 30.5 per cent.

1995	7,700 MT RTC
1996	10,400 MT RTC
1997**	6,500 MT RTC

* HS 0207.21.0000 & HS 0207.41.1000

** January through June

Dairy

Korea shall liberalize the following dairy items on January 1, 1995, at the applied rates, minus appropriate DFA reductions.

HS 0406.30.0000	processed cheese	40 per cent
HS 0406.90.0000	other cheese	40 per cent
HS 1901.10.1010	preparations for infant use	40 per cent*
HS 1901.90.2000	other food preparations	40 per cent*

* Bound rate of duty is 60 per cent; 1993 applied rate of duty is 40 per cent.

Korea shall liberalize whey powder (HS 0404.10.1000) and other whey (HS 0404.10.9000) on January 1, 1995, and shall establish a tariff rate quota for calendar year 1995 of 23,000 MT with an annual growth rate of 10 per cent. The in-quota tariff rate shall be bound at 20 per cent. Korea shall bind in its Uruguay Round country schedule a ceiling binding of 99 per cent and shall reduce such rate by no less than 50 per cent over the implementation period.

Fresh Oranges

Korea shall liberalize fresh oranges on July 1, 1997. Korea shall provide access quotas for imported fresh oranges* in the amounts specified below. The quota shall be expanded from the 1997 base of 25,000 MT at an annual growth rate of 12.5 per cent. The in-quota tariff shall be bound at 50 per cent. Korea shall bind in its Uruguay Round country schedule a ceiling binding of 99 per cent and shall reduce such rate by no less than 50 per cent over the implementation period.

1995	15,000 MT
1996	20,000 MT
1997	25,000 MT

* HS 0805.10.0000

Orange Juice

Orange juice shall be liberalized by July 1, 1997, with nothing but a bound 60 per cent duty (minus appropriate DFA reductions) remaining. During the interim period (January 1995 through June 1997), Korea will provide access quotas for imported orange juice* in the amounts specified below. Duties applied on the quota amounts shall not exceed the currently applied rate of 50 per cent, with any charges or fees applied in conformity with GATT Article VIII.

1995	50,000 MT
1996	55,000 MT
1997**	30,000 MT

* HS 2009.11.1000, HS 2009.11.9000, HS 2009.19.1000, HS 2009.19.9000 & HS 2009.30.9000

** January through June.

Beef (not covered by the current ROU)

Beef jerky (HS 0210.20.0000) shall be liberalized by July 1, 1997, with nothing but the applied 30 per cent duty (minus appropriate DFA reductions) remaining.

Beef offal (HS 0206.29.0000) shall be liberalized by July 1, 1997, with nothing but the applied rate of 20 per cent (minus appropriate DFA reductions) remaining.

Beef

YEAR	*QUOTA AMOUNT* (MT RWE)	*DUTY* (%)	*MARK-UP* (%)	*PER CENT SBS* (%)
1993	99,000	20	100	15
1994	106,000	20	95	20
1995	123,000	43.6	70	30
1996	147,000	43.2	60	40
1997	167,000	42.8	40	50
1998	187,000	42.4	20	60
1999	206,000	42	10	70
2000	225,000	41.6	0	70
2001	-	41.2	0	-
2002	-	40.8	0	-
2003	-	40.4	0	-
2004	-	40	0	-

All balance-of-payments restrictions on beef shall expire no later than December 31, 2000. In the year 2001, there shall be no quota, no mark-up, no LPMO involvement, and complete private sector autonomy regarding product quantity, price, quality, and supplier. There shall be no government restrictions on product utilization.

The current July 15, 1993 Record of Understanding (L/7270) shall continue to apply except as modified to incorporate the provisions of the new understanding.

NON-SENSITIVE UNLIBERALIZED BALANCE-OF-PAYMENTS ITEMS

Korea shall liberalize the following balance-of-payments items on January 1, 1995 or January 1, 1996, at the currently applied 1993 tariff rates.

HS CODE	DESCRIPTION	APPLIED RATE
0806 10 0000**	Grapes, fresh	50
0808 10 0000*	Apples, fresh	50
2009 60 0000*	Grape juice	50
2009 70 0000**	Apple juice	50
2202 90 2000*	Beverage of fruit juice	10

* Korea agreed to liberalize these products in 1995.

** Korea agreed to liberalize these products in 1996.

DUTY REDUCTIONS. UNITED STATES MARKET ACCESS REQUESTS FOR THE REPUBLIC OF KOREA

HS TARIFF LINE	PRODUCT
0802 12 0000	ALMONDS, SHELLED
0802 32 0000	WALNUTS, SHELLED
0805 30 0000	FRESH LEMONS AND LIMES
0805 40 0000	FRESH GRAPEFRUIT
0806 20 0000	RAISINS
0809 20 0000	FRESH CHERRIES
0813 20 0000	PRUNES
1001 90 9000	WHEAT, OTHER (NOT DURUM)
* 1005 90 1000	FEED CORN
* 1005 90 2000	POPCORN
1101 00 1000	WHEAT FLOUR
* 1105 10 0000	POTATO FLOUR AND MEAL
* 1105 20 0000	POTATO FLAKES, PELLETS, ETC.
* 1108 12 0000	CORN STARCH
* 1202 20 0000	PEANUTS, SHELLED
1507 10 0000	SOYABEAN OIL, CRUDE
1507 90 1000	SOYABEAN OIL, REFINED
1512 11 1000	SUNFLOWER OIL, CRUDE
1512 19 1010	SUNFLOWER OIL, REFINED
1512 21 0000	COTTONSEED OIL, CRUDE
1512 29 1000	COTTONSEED OIL, REFINED
1601 00 1000	PORK SAUSAGES, INCLUDING HOT DOGS
1904 10	BREAKFAST CEREALS
2004 10 0000	FROZEN FRENCH FRIES
2005 80 0000	SWEET CORN, NOT FROZEN
2009 20 0000	GRAPEFRUIT JUICE
2104 10	SOUP AND BROTH
2304 00	SOYBEAN MEAL
2309 90 1010	MIXED FEEDS, FOR PIGS
2309 90 1020	MIXED FEEDS, FOR FOWLS
2309 90 1040	MIXED FEEDS FOR BOVINE ANIMALS

The duties on the products shown above shall be reduced by 40 per cent, for each individual tariff line, from the duty levels applied in 1993 and shall be bound at the reduced levels. These reductions shall be implemented in ten equal instalments, from 1995 to 2004.

* These products (HS 1005.90.1000, 1005.90.2000, 1105.10.0000, 1105.20.0000, 1202.20.0000 and 1108.12.0000) are subject to tariffication; the reduction commitments on these products shall be made on the in-quota tariff rates.

ANNEX 4

(Korea's Exhibit 45)

Detailed information on the Sales loss of LPMO by beef cuts in 1998

(Unit : Won/kg, Ton, boneless bases)

		sales volume	sales price(a)	duty paid CIF	import price(b)	(a-b)
Jan	Chuckroll	377	6,428	4,459	5,003	1,425
	butt and rump	74	6,022	4,712	5,254	768
	short-rib (choice)	58	10,052	7,099	7,684	2,368
	short-rib (select)	0	0	0	0	0
	grain fed (bone-in)	69	6,463	4,743	5,486	977
	grass fed full-sets	196	5,821	4,441	4,981	840
	grass fed (bone-in)	1,645	3,526	3,900	4,549	-1,023
	sub-total(avg)	2,419	(4,481)	(4,157)	(4,778)	(-297)
Feb	chuckroll	169	6,039	4,693	5,382	657
	butt and rump	7	6,012	5,198	5,892	120
	short-rib (choice)	11	9,213	8,882	9,613	-400
	short-rib (select)	0	0	0	0	0
	grain fed (bone-in)	62	6,476	4,879	5,839	637
	grass fed full-sets	125	5,290	4,584	5,268	22
	grass fed (bone-in)	1,278	3,483	4,403	5,262	-1,779
	sub-total(avg)	1,652	(4,042)	(4,496)	(5,327)	(-1,285)
Mar	chuckroll	327	5,567	4,949	5,545	22
	butt and rump	10	6,004	5,589	6,193	-189
	short-rib (choice)	19	8,766	10,253	10,881	-2,115
	short-rib (select)	0	0	0	0	0
	grain fed (bone-in)	63	6,472	5,417	6,254	218
	grass fed full-sets	174	4,905	4,584	5,175	-270
	grass fed (bone-in)	1,598	3,518	4,614	5,355	-1,837
	sub-total(avg)	2,191	(4,076)	(4,739)	(5,447)	(-1,371)

		sales volume	sales price(a)	duty paid CIF	import price(b)	(a-b)
Apr	chuckroll	649	5,000	5,027	6,569	-1,569
	butt and rump	9	6,001	5,589	6,247	-246
	short-rib (choice)	20	8,645	10,561	11,233	-2,588
	short-rib (select)	0	0	0	0	0
	grain fed (bone-in)	73	5,925	5,509	6,411	-486
	grass fed full-sets	209	4,818	4,583	5,225	-407
	grass fed (bone-in)	833	4,249	4,891	5,709	-1,460
	sub-total(avg)	1,793	(4,713)	(4,996)	(5,727)	(-1,014)
May	chuckroll	694	4,574	5,047	5,637	-1,063
	butt and rump	6	5,906	5,704	6,344	-438
	short-rib (choice)	10	8,335	10,595	11,252	-2,917
	short-rib (select)	0	0	0	0	0
	grain fed (bone-in)	85	5,857	5,507	6,384	-527
	grass fed full-sets	193	4,794	4,583	5,207	-413
	grass fed (bone-in)	884	4,018	4,906	5,694	-1,676
	sub-total(avg)	1,872	(4,416)	(4,984)	(5,685)	(-1,269)
June	chuckroll	981	4,432	5,047	5,750	-1,318
	butt and rump	16	4,907	5,704	6,451	-1,544
	short-rib (choice)	20	7,307	10,595	11,363	-4,056
	short-rib (select)	0	0	0	0	0
	grain fed (bone-in)	73	5,857	5,507	6,560	-703
	grass fed full-sets	156	4,736	4,583	5,330	-594
	grass fed (bone-in)	253	4,497	4,904	5,865	-1,368
	sub-total(avg)	1,498	(4,587)	(5,077)	(5,847)	(-1,260)

		sales volume	sales price(a)	duty paid CIF	import price(b)	(a-b)
July	chuckroll	2,465	4,054	5,047	5,508	-1,454
	butt and rump	23	4,336	5,704	6,219	-1,883
	short-rib (choice)	45	5,733	10,595	11,108	-5,375
	Short-rib (select)	1	5,344	11,384	11,914	-6,570
	Grain fed (bone-in)	52	5,857	5,507	6,239	-382
	grass fed full-sets	157	4,808	4,583	5,106	-298
	grass fed (bone-in)	60	4,497	4,904	5,551	-1,054
	sub-total(avg)	2,802	(4,169)	(5,122)	(5,597)	(-1,428)
Aug	chuckroll	4,306	3,953	5,015	5,303	-1,350
	butt and rump	202	3,863	5,704	6,012	-2,149
	short-rib (choice)	279	5,124	10,595	10,937	-5,813
	short-rib (select)	136	4,807	11,384	11,738	-6,931
	grain fed (bone-in)	41	5,857	5,507	6,001	-144
	grass fed full-sets	213	4,818	4,485	4,841	-23
	grass fed (bone-in)	374	4,009	4,583	4,990	-981
	sub-total(avg)	5,551	(4,082)	(5,431)	(5,736)	(-1,654)
Sep	chuckroll	2,040	4,563	4,982	5,296	-733
	butt and rump	239	4,156	5,703	6,023	-1,867
	short-rib (choice)	416	5,336	8,767	9,115	-3,779
	short-rib (select)	217	5,006	11,385	11,735	-6,729
	grain fed (bone-in)	69	5,858	5,507	5,991	-133
	grass fed full-sets	454	4,578	4,436	4,781	-203
	grass fed (bone-in)	1,273	3,981	4,453	4,866	-885
	sub-total(avg)	4,708	(4,494)	(5,460)	(5,811)	(-1,317)

		sales volume	sales price(a)	duty paid CIF	import price(b)	(a-b)
Oct	chuckroll	451	5,133	4,982	5,394	-261
	butt and rump	38	4,629	5,705	6,046	-1,417
	short-rib (choice)	186	5,929	8,767	9,225	-3,296
	short-rib (select)	8	5,366	11,373	11,832	-6,466
	grain fed (bone-in)	72	5,857	5,507	6,123	-266
	grass fed full-sets	239	5,099	4,437	4,890	209
	grass fed (bone-in)	1,283	4,042	4,453	4,944	-902
	sub-total(avg)	2,278	(4,596)	(4,992)	(5,462)	(-866)
Nov	chuckroll	716	5,384	5,071	5,454	-70
	butt and rump	0	0	0	0	0
	short-rib (choicc)	290	6,444	6,895	7,286	-842
	short-rib (select)	0	0	0	0	0
	grain fed (bone-in)	67	5,857	5,507	6,038	-181
	grass fed full-sets	265	5,608	4,447	4,841	767
	grass fed (bone-in)	1,893	4,149	4,374	4,820	-671
	sub-total(avg)	3,232	(4,784)	(4,784)	(5,208)	(-424)
Dec	chuckroll	1,220	5,254	5,165	6,049	-795
	butt and rump	0	0	0	0	0
	short-rib (choice)	279	6,306	5,518	6,415	-109
	short-rib (select)	0	0	0	0	0
	grain fed (bone-in)	54	5,751	5,507	6,754	-1,003
	grass fed full-sets	271	5,485	4,386	5,281	204
	grass fed (bone-in)	1,997	4,164	3,899	5,058	-894
	sub-total(avg)	3,821	(4,785)	(4,479)	(5,514)	(-729)

		sales volume	sales price(a)	duty paid CIF	import price(b)	(a-b)
total	chuckroll	14,395	4,511	5,015	5,472	-961
	butt and rump	624	4,431	5,577	5,956	-1,525
	short-rib (choice)	1,633	6,056	8,256	8,747	-2,691
	short-rib (select)	362	4,965	11,384	11,739	-6,774
	grain fed (bone-in)	780	6,010	5,382	6,177	-167
	grass fed full-sets	2,652	5,044	4,493	5,034	10
	grass fed (bone-in)	13,371	3,911	4,377	5,086	-1,175
	total(avg)	33,817	(4,428)	(4,965)	(5,535)	(-1,107)

(Note)

Grass fed beef (bone-in quarter cuts) is the portion supplied by the LPMO for military use and for processing.

Other beef cuts and grass fed full-set (bone-less) are the portion auctioned by NLCF at the wholesale market.

Total loss is produced by total sales volumes multiplied by total (a-b).

ANNEX 5

(Korea Exhibit 27)

Estimated sales amount of imported beef

(Unit: M/T)

Year	Total	Retail store	Prepack-aged	Processor	Restaurant	Military	Whole-sale market
1	2	3	4	5	6	7	8
1995	146,495	18,697	27,203	7,299	9,683	12,369	71,244
1996	149,201	37,116	15,801	7,420	15,149	14,397	59,318
1997	134,225	45,501	14,612	10,498	17,758	11,288	34,568
1998	85,416	31,505	10,502	13,609	6,485	5,454	17,861

Notes:

Numbers in column 3 purchased through Super groups. Sales portion of retail store is as follows:

household (37.9 per cent), other imported beef sales outlets (17.8per cent), restaurant (44.2per cent).

Numbers in column 5 purchased through Super groups.

Numbers in column 6 purchased through Super groups.

Those imported beef that the LPMO imported and sold at wholesale markets are purchased by retail stores, processors and restaurants, but data on their share in the total volume of imported beef marketed are not available.

Source: LPMO.

ANNEX 6

(Australia, 1st Submission, paragraph 3.6)

CHART 1 Imported beef distribution in Korea - 1999

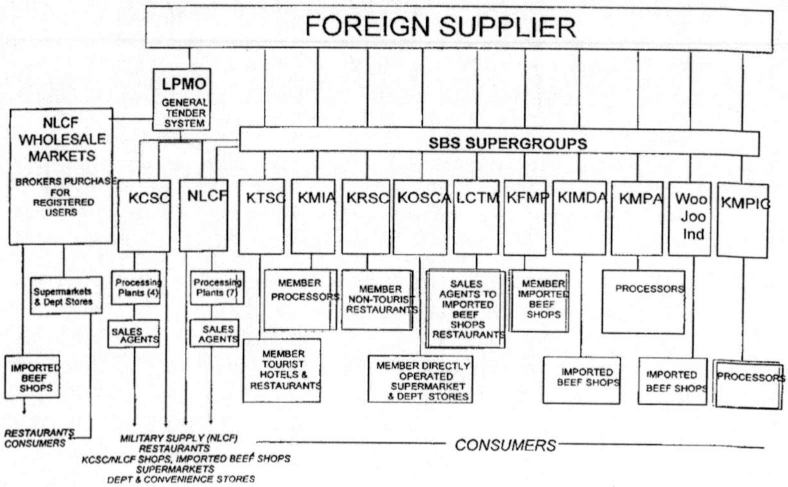

ANNEX 7

(Korea Exhibit 19)

Import and target prices for 1997

	Chuck roll				Ribs			
	1.1- 3.31	4.1- 6.30	7.1- 9.30	10.1- 12.31	1.1- 3.31	4.1- 6.30	7.1- 9.30	10.1- 12.31
import price	4,246	4,332	3,971	4,311	4,793	4,815	4,804	5,994
target price	3,800	3,800	3,800	3,800	3,340	3,340	3,340	3,340

Import Price = C.I.F.+DUTY+SELLING EXPENSES

ANNEX 8

(Korea Exhibit 39)

LPMO Stocks, Sales volume and Average exchange rate

	Stocks	Sales volume	Average exchange rate
	MT		Won/US$
Oct 1997	9,024	5,636	921.9
Nov 1997	14,130	4,519	1025.6
Dec 1997	17,061	3,701	1484.1
Jan 1998	16,600	2,419	1706.8
Feb 1998	18,293	1,652	1623.1
Mar 1998	18,837	2,191	1505.3
Apr 1998	18,475	1,793	1392.0
May 1998	17,011	1,872	1394.6
Jun 1998	15,514	1,498	1397.2
Jul 1998	12,717	2,802	1300.8

Note: Sales volume includes imported beef sold through wholesale market, for military use and as prepackaged.

ANNEX 9

(US Exhibit 60)

Slaughter Statistics for Korea

1000 Head

	1989	1990	1991	1992	1993	1994	1995	1996	1997	1998	1999
Hanwoo	397	311	302	345	488	576	580	640	887	1,023	912
Dairy Cattle	158	234	233	182	182	187	189	193	213	234	171
Other	12	9	10	10	17	15	11	17	25	25	12
Total Slaughter	567	554	545	537	687	778	780	850	1,125	1,282	1,095
% Dairy Cattle/Total	27.87	42.24	42.75	33.89	26.49	24.04	24.23	22.71	18.93	18.25	15.62

Source: NLCF

ANNEX 10

(New Zealand, Annex 7, Table 13)

Livestock numbers and meat production

	Livestock					Meat Production		
	Cattle	[Beef Dairy]	Pigs	Chicken	Total	Beef	Pork	Chicken
		1,000 Head				1,000 MT		
1980	1,541	[1,361 180]	1,784	40,130	423	93	235	90
1985	2,943	[2,553 390]	2,853	51, 081	588	116	345	126
1989	2,051	[1,535 515]	4,801	61,689	730	90	485	155
1990	2,126	[1,622 504]	4,528	74,463	773	95	506	172
1991	2,269	[1,773 496]	5,046	74,855	804	98	499	207
1992	2,527	[2,019 408]	5,463	73,324	932	100	601	231
1993	2,814	[2,261 553]	5,927	72,945	987	130	618	239
1994	2,945	[2,393 552]	5,955	80,569	1,006	147	614	245
1995	3,147	[2,594 553]	6,461	85,800	1,057	155	639	263
1996	3,395	[2,844 551]	6,516	82,829	1,143	174	692	277
1997	3,280	[2,736 544]	7,096	88,251	1,196	237	699	260

Source: MAF, Statistical Yearbook of Agriculture and Forestry (1998) and MAI (1998).

ANNEX 11

(Korea Exhibit 35)

Beef Import value, Import volume and Total consumption as compare to other products

	Technical means for distinction existing	Import value ($ million)	Import volume (1000 MT) (A)	Total consumption (1000 MT) (B)	A/B(%)
Beef	NO	247	91	345	26.3
Sesame seed	Yes	45	54	90	60
Pork	NO	137	52	700	7.4
Rice	Yes	21	61	5,041	2.4
Garlic	Yes	10	25	440	5.6
Potato flakes	NO	0.000057	0.00025	NA	-
Milkow (domestic)	Yes	-	28	345	8.1
Frozen chicken	NO	15	12	260	4.6
Safflower seed	Yes	0.033	0.041	NA	-
Grapes	Yes	2	1.1	399	0.27
Orange	Yes	28	36.6	36.6	100

Note: Import volume, import value and total consumption in 1998.

ANNEX 12

(Australia Attachment 17)

Cattle prices and beef supply & demand trends

1. Beef supply & demand trend as at 19 July 1999

		1998 Accrued stock	1999 Purchases	1999 Sales	Stock	Forecast Purchases
LPMO	Imported	67,934	14,343	20,753	61,524	47,457
	Domestic	12,723	-	6,354	6,369	-
	Subtotal	80,657	14,343	27,107	67,893	47,457
SBS		9,568	58,387	48,442	6,240	85,813
TOTAL		90,225	72,730	75,549	74,133	133,270

NB: 1. Of total stock accrued from 1998, 49,474 tonnes has not yet cleared customs.
2. LPMO 1999 quota 61,800 tonnes, SBS 1999 quota 144,200 tonnes.

2. Cattle prices and beef consumption

Cattle price

(Unit: '000 won)

	December 1998	June 1999	Early July 1999	20 July 1999
Large steer	2,129	2,098	2,199	2,404
Calf	743	887	929	1,033

Cattle yardings

(Unit: head, %)

	December 1998	January 1999	June 1999	Early July 1999
Offered	299	271	248	211
Traded	84	83	87	88

Daily consumption of domestic beef

(Unit: tonnes)

	December 1998	June 1999	Early July 1999	19 July 1999
Daily	867	704	749	1,034

UNITED STATES – IMPORT MEASURES ON CERTAIN PRODUCTS FROM THE EUROPEAN COMMUNITIES

Report of the Appellate Body

WT/DS165/AB/R

European Communities, *Appellant/Appellee*
United States, *Appellant/Appellee*
Dominica, *Third Participant*
Ecuador, *Third Participant*
India, *Third Participant*
Jamaica, *Third Participant*
Japan, *Third Participant*
St. Lucia, *Third Participant*

Present:
Bacchus, Presiding Member
Lacarte-Muró, Member
Taniguchi, Member

TABLE OF CONTENTS

I. INTRODUCTION

1. The European Communities and the United States appeal from certain issues of law and legal interpretations in the Panel Report, *United States – Import Measures on Certain Products from the European Communities* (the "Panel Report").[1] The Panel was established under the *Understanding on Rules and Procedures Governing the Settlement of Disputes* (the "DSU") to consider a complaint relating to measures taken by the United States with respect to certain imports from the European Communities.

2. The background to this dispute is set out in detail in the Panel Report.[2] On 25 September 1997, the Dispute Settlement Body (the "DSB") adopted the reports of the panel and the Appellate Body in *European Communities – Regime for the Importation, Sale and Distribution of Bananas* ("*European Communities – Bananas*").[3] The DSB recommended that the European Communities bring its banana import regime into conformity with its obligations under the *Marrakesh Agreement Establishing the World Trade Organization* (the "*WTO Agreement*"). On 1 January 1999, the period of time for implementation, established under Article 21.3(c) of the DSU, expired. At the DSB meeting of 2 February 1999, the United States alleged that the European Communities had failed to bring its banana import regime into compliance with the recommendations and rulings of the DSB in this dispute, and requested authorization to suspend the application of concessions or other obligations in accordance with Article 22.2 of the DSU. At the same meeting, the European Communities requested that the level of the suspension of concessions or other obligations proposed by the United States be referred to arbitration by the original panelists, in accordance with Article 22.6 of the DSU.

3. In accordance with the 60-day time-frame provided for in Article 22.6 of the DSU, the decision of the arbitrators appointed under Article 22.6 was to be circulated on 2 March 1999. On that date, the arbitrators informed the United States and the European Communities that they were unable to circulate their decision, and requested additional information from the parties.[4] On

---

[1] *United States – Import Measures on Certain Products from the European Communities* ("*US – Certain EC Products*"),WT/DS165/R and Add. 1, adopted 10 January 2001, as modified by the Appellate Body Report, WT/DS165/AB/R. (the "Panel Report").

[2] Panel Report,paras. 2.1-2.37.

[3] Panel Reports, *European Communities – Regime for the Importation, Sale and Distribution of Bananas* ("*EC – Bananas III*"), adopted 25 September 1997, *Complaint by Ecuador* WT/DS27/R/ECU, DSR 1997:III, 1085; *Complaint by Guatemala and Honduras*, WT/DS27/R/GTM, WT/DS27/R/HND,DSR 1997:II, 695; *Complaint by Mexico*, WT/DS27/R/MEX, DSR 1997:II, 803; *Complaint by the United States*, WT/DS27/R/USA, DSR 1997:II, 943 and Appellate Body Report, *European Communities – Regime for the Importation, Sale and Distribution of Bananas* ("*EC – Bananas III*"), WT/DS27/AB/R, adopted 25 September 1997, DSR 1997:II, 591. The complaining parties in the dispute were Ecuador, Guatemala, Honduras, Mexico and the United States.

[4] WT/DS27/48, 2 March 1999.

4 March 1999, the Director of the Trade Compliance Division of the United States Customs Service issued a memorandum entitled "European Sanctions", in which he instructed Customs Area and Port Directors to take certain action with respect to designated products imported from the European Communities, with effect from 3 March 1999.

4. The Article 22.6 arbitrators circulated their decision on 9 April 1999.[5] On 19 April 1999, the United States requested, and received, authorization from the DSB to suspend the application of concessions or other obligations in the amount determined by the arbitrators. Subsequent to this authorization, the United States imposed 100 per cent customs duties on designated products imported from the European Communities, an action referred to in this dispute as the "19 April action".

5. The Panel identified the measure at issue in this dispute as the "increased bonding requirements" imposed by the United States on a list of products imported from the European Communities as of 3 March 1999, and called this the "3 March Measure". In its Report circulated to Members of the World Trade Organization (the "WTO") on 17 July 2000, the Panel concluded:

> Although the 3 March Measure is no longer in existence, we conclude that:
>
> (a) The 3 March Measure was seeking to redress a WTO violation and was thus covered by Article 23.1 of the DSU; when it put in place the 3 March Measure the United States did not abide by the rules of the DSU, in violation of Article 23.1.
>
> (b) By putting into place the 3 March Measure, the United States made a unilateral determination that the EC implementing measure violated the WTO, contrary to Articles 23.2(a) and 21.5, first sentence. In doing so the United States did not abide by the DSU and thus violated Article 23.1 together with Article 23.2(a) and 21.5 of the DSU;
>
> (c) The increased bonding requirements of the 3 March Measure as such led to violations of Articles II:1(a) and II:1(b), first sentence; the increased interest charges, costs and fees resulting from the 3 March Measure violated Article II:1(b) last sentence. The 3 March Measure also violated Article I of GATT; and
>
> (d) In view of our conclusions in paragraph (c) above, the 3 March Measure constituted a suspension of concessions or other obligations within the meaning of Articles 3.7, 22.6 and 23.2(c) imposed

[5] Decision by the Arbitrators, *European Communities – Regime for the Importation, Sale and Distribution of Bananas – Recourse to Arbitration by the European Communities under Article 22.6 of the DSU* ("*EC – Bananas III (US) (Article 22.6 – EC)*"), WT/DS27/ARB, 9 April 1999, DSR 1999:II, 725.

> without any DSB authorization and during the ongoing Article 22.6 arbitration process. In doing so the United States did not abide by the DSU and thus violated Article 23.1 together with Articles 3.7, 22.6 and 23.2(c) of the DSU.[6]

The Panel recommended that the DSB request the United States to bring its measure into conformity with its obligations under the *WTO Agreement*.[7]

6. On 12 September 2000, the European Communities notified the DSB of its decision to appeal certain issues of law covered in the Panel Report and certain legal interpretations developed by the Panel, pursuant to Article 16.4 of the DSU[8], and filed a Notice of Appeal with the Appellate Body, pursuant to Rule 20 of the *Working Procedures for Appellate Review* (the "*Working Procedures*"). On 22 September 2000, the European Communities filed an appellant's submission.[9] The United States filed its own appellant's submission on 27 September 2000.[10] Both the European Communities and the United States filed appellee's submissions on 9 October 2000.[11] On the same day, Ecuador, India, Jamaica, and Japan each filed separate third participant's submissions, while Dominica and St. Lucia filed a joint third participant's submission.[12]

7. The oral hearing in the appeal was held on 18 October 2000.[13] The participants and the third participants presented oral arguments and responded to questions put to them by the Members of the Appellate Body Division hearing the appeal.

II. ARGUMENTS OF THE PARTICIPANTS

A. *Claims of Error by the European Communities – Appellant*

1. *The Measure at Issue*

8. The European Communities submits that the measure at issue in this dispute, to which the Panel refers as the 3 March Measure, included not only an increase in bonding requirements imposed on a list of products imported from the European Communities, but also an increase in the duty liability incurred upon the importation of the listed products. The European Communities considers that an increase in bonding requirements is, by necessity, based on an increase in the underlying customs duties, since a bonding requirement is ancillary to, and cannot be legally separated from, the underlying primary obligation.

---

6 Panel Report, para. 7.1.
7 *Ibid.*, para. 7.3.
8 WT/DS165/10, 12 September 2000.
9 Pursuant to Rule 21 (1) of the *Working Procedures*.
10 Pursuant to Rule 23 (1) of the *Working Procedures*.
11 Pursuant to Rules 22 (1) and 23 (3) of the *Working Procedures*.
12 Pursuant to Rule 24 of the *Working Procedures*.
13 Pursuant to Rule 27 of the *Working Procedures*.

9. According to the European Communities, there is no difference, in law or in fact, between a "contingent" increase in duty liability that is operated with the uncertain prospect of a return to bound rates at some later occasion, and an unqualified increase in duty liability. The European Communities argues that nothing changed in real terms for the products which remained on the reduced list published on 19 April 1999: their legal situation remained the same as before that date in that they were subject to an increased duty liability, with the only difference being that it was no longer called a "contingent" one.

10. The European Communities disagrees with the Panel's finding that the 19 April action, i.e., the imposition of 100 per cent duties, was not included in the Panel's terms of reference. The European Communities contends that the 19 April action and the 3 March Measure are not legally distinct measures and that, in fact, the 19 April action is a continuation of the 3 March Measure, and, therefore, falls within the terms of reference of the Panel. The European Communities submits that its request for the establishment of a panel referred specifically to the 19 April action.

11. Finally, the European Communities contends that, in addition to the incorrect and artificial distinction the Panel makes between the 3 March Measure, and its confirmation on 19 April 1999, the Panel also erred in finding that "the 3 March Measure is no longer in existence".

2. *The Mandate of Arbitrators Appointed under Article 22.6 of the DSU*

12. The European Communities submits that the Panel erroneously considered that the WTO-consistency of an implementing measure can be determined in arbitration proceedings under Article 22.6 of the DSU. In the view of the European Communities, the reasoning of the Panel creates basic systemic problems which severely affect the carefully balanced results of the Uruguay Round.

13. The European Communities submits that the text of Article 22.7 charges the arbitrator with one main task, and two more possible tasks. The main task is to determine whether the level of the suspension of concessions or other obligations is equivalent to the level of nullification or impairment. The arbitrator may also determine whether the proposed suspension of concessions or other obligations is allowed under the covered agreements, and whether the principles and procedures set out in Article 22.3 of the DSU have been followed.

14. The European Communities asserts that the Panel's reading of the relevant procedural provisions of the DSU entirely ignores the fundamental difference between the role of the parties to a dispute in a panel procedure to determine the WTO-consistency of a contested measure, and the role of the parties in an arbitration procedure under Article 22.6 of the DSU. The European Communities also argues that the Member requesting an arbitration procedure under Article 22.6 would have its rights of defence seriously undermined if it had to develop a fully fledged defence of the WTO-consistency of its measure. Further, the Euro-

pean Communities notes that there can be no appeal from an Article 22.6 arbitrator's decision. The European Communities also submits that panel and Appellate Body procedures provide for the active participation of third parties, unlike arbitration proceedings. The European Communities also notes that decisions of arbitrators are not subject to adoption by the DSB. The European Communities, therefore, submits that Article 22.6 arbitration proceedings ensure none of these procedural rights and guarantees, and the Panel's interpretation should be reversed.

15. The European Communities also considers that the interpretation by the Panel of the terms "these dispute settlement procedures, including wherever possible resort to the original panel", in Article 21.5 of the DSU, is incorrect. According to the European Communities, a panel procedure is the ordinary "dispute settlement procedure" in the sense of Article 21.5. In the view of the European Communities, it is apparent that the terms "including wherever possible resort to the original panel" constitute nothing other than an adjustment of the ordinary panel procedure.

3. *The Effect of DSB Authorization to Suspend Concessions or Other Obligations*

16. The European Communities submits that the Panel incorrectly considered that, as a general rule, once a Member imposes DSB-authorized suspension of concessions or other obligations, that Member's measure is *ipso facto* WTO-compatible because it has received DSB authorization. According to the European Communities, DSB authorization is a necessary, but not sufficient, condition to legally implement the suspension of concessions or other obligations.

B. *Arguments of the United States – Appellee*

1. *The Measure at Issue*

17. The United States submits that the Panel was correct in finding, as a factual matter, that the 3 March Measure consisted only of increased bonding requirements legally distinct from the 19 April action, which imposed increased customs duties. The United States contends that, while this factual finding is beyond the scope of appellate review, it is amply supported by the evidence of the actual legal status of the 3 March Measure under United States law.

18. The United States asserts that, on 4 March 1999, the European Communities requested consultations with respect to the 3 March Measure. On that date, the United States had not yet taken the 19 April action. According to the United States, the 19 April action could, therefore, not have been the measure identified in either the request for consultations, or in the subsequent request for the establishment of a panel. As a result, the 19 April action could not have been within the terms of reference of the Panel.

19. The United States submits that, in arguing that WTO law does not distinguish between an increase in "contingent" duty liability and an increase in actual duty liability, the European Communities incorrectly assumes, with no evidence in United States law or regulation, that the 3 March Measure increased the actual duties, and that the only changes made on 19 April 1999 were to remove duty liabilities already imposed. Moreover, the European Communities assumes, with no basis in United States law or regulation, that "contingent liability" exists under United States law.

20. Finally, the United States submits that, before the Panel, it explained that the increased bonding requirements of 3 March 1999 were removed for entries of merchandise which were not to be included on the 19 April 1999 list within a few days of the arbitrators' decision of 9 April 1999, and were removed on 19 April 1999 for all remaining products. The United States, therefore, submits that the Panel's statement that the 3 March Measure "is no longer in existence" is correct.

2. *The Mandate of Arbitrators Appointed under Article 22.6 of the DSU*

21. The United States contends that the Panel need not, and should not, have reached the issue of the relationship between Articles 21.5 and 22 of the DSU. Firstly, the United States points out that Members of the WTO broadly recognize that this relationship requires clarification. The United States considers that it is for the membership of the WTO to provide such clarification. Secondly, the United States argues that the Panel need not have reached the issue of the relationship because this issue is not implicated by the measure at issue, nor by the Panel's analysis of how a violation of Article 21.5 is established.

22. The United States submits, however, that, while the Panel need not, and should not, have reached the issue of the relationship between Articles 21.5 and 22, it ultimately reached the correct substantive conclusion, namely, that an Article 22.6 arbitrator can determine the WTO-consistency of an implementing measure in determining the equivalent level of suspension of concessions or other obligations.

23. The United States asserts that an analysis of the text of Article 22 supports the Panel's finding. The text of Article 22.2 contains no reference to either Articles 21 or 23 of the DSU. Had the drafters intended to make the suspension of concessions or other obligations conditional upon the completion of another proceeding, they "would not have written the text of Article 22 to refer all deadlines under Article 22 back to the end of the 'reasonable period of time' for implementation" provided for in Article 21.3 of the DSU.[14]

24. The United States submits that Article 21.5 does not qualify the phrase "these dispute procedures", with the exception of providing for resort to the

[14] United States' appellee's submission, para. 48.

original panelists, wherever possible, and establishing an upper limit of 90 days for proceedings. There is, thus, no basis for excluding any dispute settlement procedure that could be used to determine the WTO-consistency of an implementing measure.

25. The United States argues that, if, as the European Communities suggests, Article 21.5 requires that "ordinary" dispute settlement procedures apply, except as specifically provided in Article 21.5, this would lead to the absurd result that "referral to the panel" under Article 21.5 would have to be preceded by consultations, adding an additional 60 days to the process. Even without consideration of this additional time, the 90-day time-frame provided for in Article 21.5 would render inoperative the negative consensus rule in Articles 22.6 and 22.7 of the DSU, if Article 21.5 were read to require separate proceedings under Article 21.5 before a WTO Member could invoke Article 22.

26. The United States argues that the European Communities' arguments on "procedural rights and guarantees", that is, its arguments relating to burden of proof, notice requirements and third party rights, are policy, and not legal, arguments. In making these arguments, the European Communities objects to the text as it stands, and does not explain how the Panel read that text incorrectly.

3. The Effect of DSB Authorization to Suspend Concessions or Other Obligations

27. The United States submits that the Panel's statement on this point, like other of its statements and conclusions on the mandate of arbitrators appointed under Article 22.6, was not germane to the dispute at hand. Accordingly, the United States submits that it was not necessary for the Panel to reach the issue of the WTO-consistency of DSB-authorized measures suspending the application of concessions or other obligations. The United States argues, however, that the decision to authorize the suspension of concessions or other obligations is within the sole authority of the DSB, and it is, therefore, impossible to draw any conclusion other than that a suspension of concessions or other obligations which has been authorized by the DSB is WTO-consistent.

C. Claims of Error by the United States – Appellant

1. Articles II:1(a) and II:1(b), First Sentence, of the GATT 1994

28. The United States appeals the Panel's finding that the increased bonding requirements are inconsistent with Articles II:1(a) and II:1(b), first sentence, of the GATT 1994. According to the United States, the Panel made its finding based, not on the conclusion that the bonding requirements themselves breached the obligations in question, but because the duties they might be called upon to enforce, if imposed, would breach those obligations.

29. The United States argues that this approach is inconsistent with the Panel's duty to base its analysis of a measure's WTO-consistency on the measure itself, and not to attribute to that measure the effects or breaches of another measure. Article II:1(a) requires each Member to provide treatment no less favourable than that provided for in its tariff Schedule. Article II:1(b), first sentence, exempts products listed in a Member's Schedule from "ordinary customs duties in excess of those set forth and provided therein," while the second sentence exempts such products from "other duties or charges". The additional bonding requirements in this dispute did not themselves impose additional duties even if, as the Panel concluded, they imposed additional costs.

30. The United States submits that the GATT panel reports cited by the Panel either do not support the Panel's position, or else provide no reasoning to support that position.[15] The United States submits that the Panel quoted a statement by the panel in *United States – Section 337*, but ignored the context of that statement and the nature of the analysis which followed it. In the view of the United States, the analysis in the panel report in *EEC – Minimum Import Prices* cannot be read to support the conclusion that a breach by a measure may be attributed to the measures enforcing it. With respect to the panel report in *EEC – Animal Feed Proteins*, the United States argues that the panel in that case provides no persuasive reasoning in support of its conclusion, and the Panel in this dispute should not have followed it.

2. *Articles 23.2(a), 3.7 and 21.5 of the DSU*

(a) Article 23.2(a) of the DSU

31. The United States submits that the Panel erred in finding that the 3 March Measure was inconsistent with Article 23.2(a) of the DSU, both because the European Communities neither requested nor argued for this finding, and failed to meet its burden of establishing a violation of this provision, and because the Panel based its finding on the erroneous conclusion that a "determination", within the meaning of Article 23.2(a), may be inferred from other actions.

32. The United States argues that the European Communities did not refer to Article 23.2(a) "outside of … passing references".[16] At no point in its statements or submissions did the European Communities ever request the Panel to make a finding with respect to Article 23.2(a). Throughout its submissions, the European Communities argued and presented a case only with respect to Articles 23.1 and 23.2(c).

---

[15] Panel Report, *United States - Section 337 of the Tariff Act of 1930* ("*United States - Section 337*"), adopted 7 November 1989, BISD, 36S/345; Panel Report, *EEC - Measures on Animal Feed Proteins* ("*EEC - Animal Feed Proteins*"), adopted 14 March 1978, BISD, 25S/49; Panel Report, *EEC - Programme of Minimum Import Prices, Licences and Surety Deposits for Certain Processed Fruits and Vegetables* ("*EEC - Minimum Import Prices*"), adopted 18 October 1978, BISD, 25S/68.

[16] United States' appellant's submission, para. 38.

33. The United States submits that, while the simple fact that the European Communities did not make a claim under Article 23.2(a) is sufficient for the Appellate Body to reverse the Panel's finding because the Panel relieved the European Communities of its burden in this dispute, the Appellate Body also should conclude that the Panel's finding under Article 23.2(a) should be rejected because of the inadequacy of the European Communities' panel request, and the prejudice to the United States which resulted.

34. The United States submits that the Appellate Body should also reverse the Panel's finding because the Panel relied on the erroneous conclusion that a "determination" within the meaning of Article 23.2(a) may be inferred from other actions. The United States considers that the Panel wrongly interpreted the term "determination". The United States submits that a "determination" is a formal decision that is made explicitly, as a result of a domestic legal process, and one which has some legal status.

(b) Article 3.7 of the DSU

35. The United States submits that the Panel erred in finding that the 3 March Measure was inconsistent with Article 3.7 of the DSU. The Panel improperly relieved the European Communities of its burden of establishing a violation of Article 3.7, because the European Communities neither requested nor argued for this finding. Furthermore, the United States argues that, even if the European Communities *had* argued that the 3 March Measure was inconsistent with Article 3.7, it is not clear how it could have demonstrated a violation, since the last sentence of Article 3.7 contains no obligation which might be breached. The United States considers that the last sentence of Article 3.7 is merely descriptive and does not contain an obligation, in the sense of providing that a Member "shall" or "shall not" undertake any action.

(c) Article 21.5 of the DSU

36. The United States submits that the Appellate Body should reverse the Panel's finding that the 3 March Measure is inconsistent with Article 21.5 because this finding is based on argumentation not presented by the European Communities, and on the Panel's erroneous conclusion that the 3 March Measure is inconsistent with Article 23.2(a) of the DSU.

D. Arguments of the European Communities – Appellee

1. Articles II:1(a) and II:1(b), First Sentence, of the GATT 1994

37. The European Communities agrees with the United States that the Panel erred when it found that the increased bonding requirements are inconsistent with Article II:1(a) and (b), first sentence, simply because they enforce a measure which is inconsistent with those provisions. The European Communities submits

that it did not claim that the bonding requirements "as such" are inconsistent with those provisions on that ground.

38. The European Communities submits that the error appealed by the United States stems from the Panel's mischaracterization of the 3 March Measure as consisting merely of an increase in the generally applicable bonding requirements. The Panel failed to recognize that such increase was only an ancillary measure to enforce the main decision taken by the United States on 3 March 1999, that is, the "contingent" increase of customs duties on listed products to 100 per cent *ad valorem*.

39. The European Communities asserts that, had the Panel properly characterized the 3 March Measure as also including that duty increase, it would necessarily have come to the conclusion that, as claimed by the European Communities, the duty increase is in breach of Article II:1 (a) and (b), first sentence, whereas the increased bonding requirements "as such" are inconsistent with Article II:1 (b), second sentence of the GATT 1994.

2. *Articles 23.2(a), 3.7 and 21.5 of the DSU*

(a) Article 23.2(a) of the DSU

40. The European Communities submits that in its request for the establishment of a panel, it cited Articles 3, 21, 22 and 23 of the DSU as being those provisions in respect of which the European Communities claimed violations.

41. The European Communities submits that the United States does not contest, and could not contest, that the European Communities' claim of violation of Article 21.5 of the DSU was raised sufficiently clearly in the present case. According to the European Communities, there is a very close link that flows from Article 23.2(a) of the DSU between the obligation to resort to Article 21.5 procedures in the circumstances of the present case, and the prohibition on making unilateral determinations concerning the WTO-consistency of a trade measure taken in order to implement an earlier DSB recommendation.

42. The European Communities submits that the Panel did not err in finding that a determination could be "implied" from the actions taken by the United States. The European Communities submits that, as determined by the panel in *United States – Sections 301-310 of the Trade Act of 1974*, a "determination" only constitutes a violation under Article 23.2(a) of the DSU when it is made in the context of seeking redress of a perceived WTO-inconsistency committed by another WTO Member.[17] An action seeking to impose trade retaliation must therefore be considered relevant when determining whether a breach of the obligations under Article 23.2(a) has been committed. The European Communities

[17] Panel Report, *United States – Sections 301-310 of the Trade Act of 1974*, ("*US – Section 301 Trade Act*"),WT/DS152/R, adopted 27 January 2000, DSR 2000:II, 815.

submits that, where a WTO Member concludes that another WTO Member has acted inconsistently with its WTO obligations, and this conclusion forms the basis of a measure seeking redress of the perceived WTO-inconsistency without following the dispute settlement procedures, such conclusion is a prohibited "determination", within the meaning of Article 23.2(a), in conjunction with Article 23.1 of the DSU.

(b) Article 3.7 of the DSU

43. The European Communities submits that Article 3.7, last sentence, of the DSU contains an obligation not to resort to the suspension of concessions or other obligations without authorization by the DSB. This provision is in line with Article 23.2(c) of the DSU, and the United States cannot argue that the European Communities did not make a claim of violation of the latter provision. A breach of the prohibition contained in Article 23.2(c) of the DSU entails by necessity a breach of the provision contained in Article 3.7, last sentence, of the DSU.

(c) Article 21.5 of the DSU

44. The European Communities submits that in its written submissions and oral statements before the Panel, the European Communities presented a claim and arguments according to which the United States violated Article 21.5 of the DSU when it applied the disputed measure, and requested the authorization of suspension of concessions in the absence of a finding that the European Communities' implementing measures were inconsistent with its WTO obligations.

III. ARGUMENTS OF THE THIRD PARTICIPANTS

A. Dominica and St. Lucia

1. The Measure at Issue

45. Dominica and St. Lucia submit that the European Communities' request for the establishment of a panel appears to cover sufficiently all the measures which gave effect to the United States' decision to impose 100 per cent retroactive duty liability, as of 3 March 1999, on selected products imported from the European Communities.

46. Dominica and St. Lucia argue that subsequent actions which modify the legal form, but confirm the substance of a previous measure identified in a panel request, may fall within a panel's terms of reference. According to Dominica and St. Lucia, the fundamental test is one of due process, that is, whether all parties received adequate notice of the claims raised. As such, subsequent actions merely modifying the legal form of an original measure that remains in force *in substance*, and that is the subject of a complaint, may fall within a panel's terms of reference.

2. *The Mandate of Arbitrators Appointed under Article 22.6 of the DSU*

47. Dominica and St. Lucia submit that the Panel erred in its conclusion that the arbitration procedure under Article 22.6 of the DSU constitutes a proper WTO dispute settlement procedure to determine the WTO-consistency of implementing measures, as mandated by the first sentence of Article 21.5 of the DSU.

48. According to Dominica and St. Lucia, an Article 22.6 arbitrator has authority to determine the "level of suspension equivalent to the level of nullification", while an Article 21.5 panel has authority to determine the WTO-consistency of an implementing measure. Their mandates are distinct, irrespective of the possibility that the members of the original panel may serve both on the Article 21.5 panel and as Article 22.6 arbitrators. Dominica and St Lucia further submit that the conclusions of the Panel raise serious systemic concerns.

B. Ecuador

49. Ecuador fully shares the Panel's opinion that Members of the WTO should not take unilateral action in the resolution of WTO disputes. Should a situation arise in which Members of the WTO disagree as to whether a WTO violation has occurred, the only remedy available is to initiate dispute settlement procedures under the DSU.

50. In Ecuador's view, the possible conflict between the time frames of Article 21.5 and those of Article 22 cannot be used as an excuse to take unilateral action, just as this conflict cannot serve as a basis for any Member's "losing its fundamental rights", such as the right to suspend the application of concessions or other obligations.[18]

C. India

51. India strongly disagrees with the Panel's finding that the WTO-consistency of measures taken by the implementing Member can be determined through an Article 22.6 arbitration procedure. India submits that the panel procedures which were designed to address and rule on the merits of disputes, involving substantive obligations of Members of the WTO, are fundamentally different from the arbitration procedures provided under Articles 21.3 and 22.6 of the DSU. These arbitration procedures are given the limited task of determining, in the case of Article 21.3, the "reasonable period of time" for implementation and, in the case of Article 22.6, the level of suspension of concessions and whether the procedures and principles of Article 22.3 were followed.

52. India submits that, if an arbitration procedure under Article 22.6 could be used to determine the consistency of implementing measures, Article 21.5 of the

---

[18] Ecuador's third participant's submission, para. 3.

DSU would lose its relevance and effect. India argues that, if the Panel's interpretation of Articles 21.5 and 22.6 of the DSU is allowed to stand, the use and relevance of Article 21.5 would be minimal, and Members of the WTO could conveniently bypass the procedures under Article 21.5, and proceed directly to Article 22.6.

D. *Jamaica*

53. Jamaica disagrees with the Panel's interpretation of the relationship between Articles 21.5 and 22 of the DSU, and supports the European Communities' grounds of appeal on this issue. Jamaica submits that the function of an Article 22.6 arbitrator is restricted to a specific role in a particular circumstance, namely to determine the appropriateness of the level of suspension of concessions or other obligations.

54. Jamaica submits that a new dispute over the WTO-consistency of implementing measures is to be resolved through "these dispute settlement procedures", as provided in Article 21.5 of the DSU. Jamaica submits that "these dispute settlement procedures" are the good offices, conciliation and mediation procedures in Article 5 of the DSU. Jamaica contends that "these dispute settlement procedures" are also the ordinary panel procedures, with the possibility of appeal to the Appellate Body. Jamaica requests that the Appellate Body find that arbitration under Article 22.6 of the DSU serves a specific and limited role which does not include any authority to determine the WTO-consistency of measures taken to comply with the recommendations and rulings of the DSB.

E. *Japan*

1. *The Mandate of Arbitrators Appointed under Article 22.6 of the DSU*

55. Japan supports the European Communities' appeal of the Panel's finding that the WTO-consistency of implementing measures can be determined in the course of arbitration proceedings under Article 22.6 of the DSU. Japan submits that Article 21.5 and Article 22.6 proceedings serve entirely different functions and are governed by separate procedural requirements. In the view of Japan, the Panel did not take into account the distinction between proceedings under Article 21.5 and those under Article 22.6, and thus disregarded the intended structure of the dispute settlement process.

2. *Articles II:1(a) and II:1(b), First Sentence, of the GATT 1994*

56. Japan does not support the United States' appeal of the Panel's finding that the bonding requirements imposed by the United States on 3 March 1999 violated Articles II:1(a) and II:1(b) of the GATT 1994. Japan considers that a bonding requirement is an integral part of the tariff collection process, and, therefore,

should not be considered separate and apart from the imposition of the tariff itself. Japan, therefore, agrees with the Panel's finding that the imposition by the United States of the increased bonding requirements violated Articles II:1(a) and II:1(b), first sentence, of the GATT 1994.

3. Articles 23.2(a), 3.7 and 21.5 of the DSU

57. Japan does not support the United States' contention that the Panel erred in finding that the 3 March Measure was inconsistent with Article 3.7 of the DSU because that provision does not set forth an obligation which can be breached. Japan considers that like Article 23.2(c), Article 3.7 indicates that Members of the WTO only have the right to suspend concessions on a discriminatory basis subject to authorization by the DSB. Japan submits that, as the 3 March Measure constituted a suspension of concessions or other obligations without DSB authorization, the United States acted inconsistently with Article 3.7.

IV. ISSUES RAISED IN THIS APPEAL

58. The Panel found that, by adopting the 3 March Measure, the United States acted inconsistently with its obligations under Articles I and II:1(a) and (b) of the GATT 1994 as well as Articles 3.7, 21.5, 22.6, 23.1, 23.2(a) and 23.2(c) of the DSU.[19] The United States appeals the Panel's findings of inconsistency with Articles II:1(a) and II:1(b), first sentence, of the GATT 1994, and Articles 3.7, 21.5 and 23.2(a) of the DSU. The United States does not appeal the Panel's findings of inconsistency with Articles I and II:1(b), second sentence, of the GATT 1994, and Articles 22.6, 23.1 and 23.2(c) of the DSU. In our view, therefore, the United States has accepted the conclusions of the Panel that, by adopting the 3 March Measure, the United States acted inconsistently with its obligations under Articles I and II:1(b), second sentence, of the GATT 1994, and with the obligation in Article 23 of the DSU not to take unilateral action in redressing perceived breaches of WTO obligations by other WTO Members. To us, the most significant aspect of this case may well be the Panel's conclusions, which were not appealed, about the failure of the United States to comply with the legal imperative found in Article 23.1 of the DSU[20], which states:

> When Members seek the redress of a violation of obligations or other nullification or impairment of benefits under the covered agreements or an impediment to the attainment of any objective of the covered agreements, they shall have recourse to, and abide by, the rules and procedures of this Understanding.

59. The following issues are raised in this appeal:

---

[19] Panel Report, para. 7.1.

[20] *Ibid.*, paras. 6.34, 6.87 and 7.1(a) and (d).

(a) Whether the Panel erred in finding that the measure at issue in this dispute is the 3 March Measure, which is the "increased bonding requirements as of 3 March on EC listed products", that this measure is no longer in existence, that the 19 April action is legally distinct from the 3 March Measure and that the 19 April action is not within the terms of reference of the Panel;

(b) Whether the Panel erred by stating that the WTO-consistency of a measure taken by a Member to comply with recommendations and rulings of the DSB can be determined by arbitrators appointed under Article 22.6 of the DSU;

(c) Whether the Panel erred by stating that "[o]nce a Member imposes DSB authorised suspensions of concessions or obligations, that Member's measure is WTO-consistent (it was explicitly authorised by the DSB)"[21];

(d) Whether the Panel erred in finding that the increased bonding requirements of the 3 March Measure are inconsistent with Articles II:1(a) and II:1(b), first sentence, of the GATT 1994; and

(e) Whether the Panel erred in finding that, by adopting the 3 March Measure, the United States acted inconsistently with its obligations under Articles 23.2(a), 3.7 and 21.5 of the DSU.

V. THE MEASURE AT ISSUE

60. The Panel found that the measure at issue in this dispute is the "increased bonding requirements as of 3 March on EC listed products"[22], and called this the 3 March Measure. The Panel found that this measure is "no longer in existence".[23] The Panel also found that the 19 April action, i.e., the imposition of 100 per cent duties on certain designated products imported from the European Communities, is a measure that is legally distinct from the 3 March Measure, and that the 19 April action, therefore, does not fall within the terms of reference of the Panel.[24] The European Communities appeals these findings of the Panel.

61. The Panel was established by the DSB on 16 June 1999.[25] In accordance with Article 7.1 of the DSU, the Panel had the following standard terms of reference:

> To examine, in the light of the relevant provisions of the covered agreements cited by the European Communities in document WT/DS165/8, the matter referred to the DSB by the European

---

21 Panel Report, para. 6.112.

22 *Ibid.*, para. 6.21.

23 *Ibid.*, para. 7.1.

24 *Ibid.*, para. 6.89 and 6.128.

25 WT/DS165/9, 18 October 1999 and WT/DS165/9/Corr.1, 5 November 1999.

> Communities in that document and to make such findings as will assist the DSB in making the recommendations or in giving the rulings provided for in those agreements.[26]

62. With respect to the measure at issue in this dispute, we note that the request for the establishment of a panel submitted by the European Communities refers to:

> *... the US decision, effective as of 3 March 1999, to withhold liquidation on imports from the EC of a list of products, together valued at $520 million on an annual basis, and to impose a contingent liability for 100% duties on each individual importation of affected products as of this date (annex 1). This measure includes administrative provisions that foresee, among other things, the posting of a bond to cover the full potential liability.*
>
> This measure has deprived EC imports into the US of the products in question of the right to a duty not in excess of the rate bound in the US Schedule. Moreover, by requiring the deposit of a bond, US Customs effectively already imposed 100% duties on each individual importation as of 3 March 1999, the return of which was uncertain, depending on future US decisions. ...[27] (emphasis added)

63. With respect to these "future US decisions", the European Communities stated in the panel request:

> When the US received WTO authorisation on 19 April 1999 to suspend concessions as of that date on EC imports of products with an annual value of only $191.4 million, a more limited list of products was selected from the previous list (annex 2). At the same time, the US confirmed, despite the prospective nature of the WTO authorisation, the liability for 100% duty on the products on the list in annex 2 that had entered the US for consumption with effect from 3 March 1999.[28]

64. The "US decision, effective as of 3 March 1999", to which the panel request refers, is contained in a memorandum, dated 4 March 1999, from Mr. Philip Metzger, Director, Trade Compliance Division, United States Customs Service, to the Customs Area and Port Directors and CMC Directors, regarding "European Sanctions" (the "Metzger Memorandum")[29], as clarified by a memorandum dated 16 March 1999.[30] The Metzger Memorandum provided:

---

[26] *Ibid.*

[27] WT/DS165/8, 11 May 1999.

[28] *Ibid.*

[29] Panel Report, para. 6.29.

[30] *Ibid.*, para. 6.30. This memorandum, entitled "Clarification of Bond Requirements for European Sanctions", was also sent to Customs Area and Port Directors and CMC Directors by Mr. Philip Metzger.

> Effective for all merchandise classifiable under the Harmonized Tariff Schedule (HTS) subheadings listed below, entered, or withdrawn from warehouse, for consumption, on or after March 3, 1999, and produced in the listed countries, Area and Port Directors must require a Single Transaction Bond (STB) equal to the entered value of the merchandise. The only exception to this requirement is, at the discretion of the Port Director, the importer of record may use a continuous bond equal to 10 per cent of the total of the entered value of the covered merchandise imported by the importer for the preceding year. Ports should process increased continuous bonds immediately.
>
> No entry shall be scheduled to liquidate earlier than the 314th day, thereby ensuring the withholding of liquidation as requested by USTR. ... [31]

65. It follows from the Metzger Memorandum that the "US decision, effective as of 3 March 1999", to which the panel request refers, concerned a change in bonding requirements and the withholding of liquidation on imports of certain products from the European Communities.

66. With respect to the withholding of liquidation, the Metzger Memorandum instructed United States customs authorities to withhold liquidation until at least the 314th day after entry of the designated products. The United States argued before the Panel that this was, in fact, already the usual practice of the Customs Service and, therefore, did not constitute a change in treatment.[32] The Panel did not view the withholding of liquidation as part of the measure at issue in this dispute.[33]

67. With respect to the change in bonding requirements, the Metzger Memorandum, as clarified by the memorandum dated 16 March 1999, instructed the United States customs authorities to change the bonding requirements with respect to certain designated products imported from the European Communities. The customs authorities were instructed to demand a *single transaction bond* equal to the entered value of the designated imports, or to add to the *continuous bond* an amount equal to 10 per cent of the entered value of the designated products imported by an importer during the previous year.[34] The Panel found that the

---

[31] The memorandum dated 16 March 1999, which clarified the Metzger Memorandum, stated:
If the importer of record provides a statement at the time of entry (release) certifying that it has reviewed its continuous bond and has added to it an amount equal to 10 percent of the total of the entered value imported by the importer for the preceding year of the merchandise presently subject to the sanctions, the Port Director will accept the continuous bond.

[32] See first written submission of the United States, para. 34, and the United States' responses to questions of the Panel and parties (13 January 2000), para. 11. The European Communities did not challenge this assertion.

[33] Panel Report, para. 6.21.

[34] *Ibid.*, paras. 2.24-2.25 and 6.29-6.30.

change relating to continuous bonds led to *increased* bonding requirements.[35] It is this aspect of the "US decision, effective as of 3 March 1999" that is in contention in this dispute. The Panel, therefore, found that "[t]he measure in the present dispute is increased bonding requirements as of 3 March on EC listed imports."[36]

68. As the request for the establishment of a panel by the European Communities refers to the "US decision, effective as of 3 March 1999" as the measure in dispute, and, as the contentious aspect of this decision is the increase in bonding requirements, we agree with the Panel's finding that the measure at issue in this dispute is the 3 March Measure, which is the "increased bonding requirements" that were imposed as a result of the Metzger Memorandum on designated products imported from the European Communities.

69. We note that, in its request for the establishment of a panel, the European Communities, after describing the "US decision, effective as of 3 March 1999" with respect to which the establishment of a panel was requested, refers to the fact that, after this "US decision" was taken, the United States received WTO authorization on 19 April 1999 to suspend concessions and, at the same time, "confirmed ... the liability for 100% duty on the products on the list in annex 2 that had entered the US for consumption with effect from 3 March 1999."[37] Undeniably, the panel request by the European Communities does refer to the 19 April action. Yet it is not possible for us to conclude on the basis of this *reference* alone that the measure at issue in this dispute is not only the 3 March Measure, but also the 19 April action. Therefore, it is not possible for us to conclude, on this basis *alone*, that the 19 April action is within the Panel's terms of reference.

70. Furthermore, we note that, in our Report in *Brazil – Export Financing Programme for Aircraft*, we stated that:

> Articles 4 and 6 of the DSU ... set forth a process by which a complaining party must request consultations, and consultations must be held, before a matter may be referred to the DSB for the establishment of a panel.[38]

The European Communities' request for consultations of 4 March 1999 did not, of course, refer to the action taken by the United States on 19 April 1999, because that action had not yet been taken at the time. At the oral hearing in this appeal, in response to questioning by the Division, the European Communities acknowledged that the 19 April action, *as such*, was not *formally* the subject of the consultations held on 21 April 1999. We, therefore, consider that the 19 April

---

35 Panel Report, para. 6.51. With respect to single transaction bonds, the Panel noted that the change in the bonding requirements did not lead to an increase in bonding requirements.

36 *Ibid.*, para. 6.21.

37 WT/DS165/8, 11 May 1999.

38 Panel Report, *Brazil – Export Financing Programme for Aircraft* ("*Brazil – Aircraft*"), WT/DS46/R, adopted 20 August 1999, DSR 1999:III, 1221, para. 131.

action is also, for that reason, not a measure at issue in this dispute and does not fall within the Panel's terms of reference.

71. We note the European Communities' contention, before the Panel as well as before us, that the 3 March Measure, in fact, includes not only an increase in bonding requirements, but also the imposition of a "contingent" liability for duties of 100 per cent on a specific list of products imported from the European Communities.[39] The European Communities argues that the 19 April action, which provides for the imposition of 100 per cent duties on a reduced list of products imported from the European Communities, is not legally distinct from the 3 March Measure, but rather is a "confirmation" of the 3 March Measure.[40] The European Communities sees the increase in bonding requirements effected on 3 March 1999 as inextricably linked with the imposition of 100 per cent duties on 19 April 1999. According to the European Communities, the 3 March Measure "is the basic measure by which the United States imposed sanctions on EC imports ... while the 19 April action is merely partly the confirmation, partly a withdrawal of a pre-existing measure."[41] According to the European Communities, "[t]he legal situation did not change" for products from the European Communities that were maintained on the second list "by the *19 April 1999 confirmation* of the increase in duty liability for those items".[42] (emphasis added)

72. The action taken by the United States customs authorities as of 3 March 1999 is set out in the Metzger Memorandum.[43] The action taken by the United States on 19 April 1999 is described in the notice of the United States Trade Representative on "United States suspension of tariff concessions", dated 19 April 1999 and published in the Federal Register (the "USTR Notice").[44] The USTR Notice stated that:

> The United States Trade Representative (USTR) has decided to suspend the application of tariff concessions and to impose a 100% *ad valorem* rate of duty on the articles described in the Annex to this notice ...
>
> The USTR has determined that, effective April 19, 1999, a 100% *ad valorem* rate of duty shall be applied to the articles described in the Annex to this notice ... and that are entered ... on or after March 3, 1999.

---

[39] European Communities' appellant's submission, para. 17. This list of products is contained in the Metzger Memorandum.

[40] The 19 April 1999 list of products is contained in the USTR Notice, dated 19 April 1999. The reduced coverage of the list was the result of the Decision of the Arbitrators, circulated 9 April 1999, that the appropriate level of suspension of concessions or other obligations was $191.4 million, rather than $520 million, the level proposed by the United States.

[41] European Communities' appellant's submission, para. 38.

[42] *Ibid.*, para. 26.

[43] See *supra*, paras. 64-65.

[44] 64 Fed. Reg. 19,209 (1999).

73. It cannot be disputed that the 3 March Measure and the 19 April action are related actions of the government of the United States, in as much as both measures were taken by the United States to redress what it saw as the failure of the European Communities to implement the recommendations and rulings of the DSB in the *European Communities – Bananas* dispute. We note that the official USTR press release of 3 March 1999 announcing the 3 March Measure and the letter from Mr. Peter Scher, Special Trade Negotiator of the USTR for Agriculture, to Mr. Raymond W. Kelly, Commissioner of the United States Customs Service, dated 3 March 1999, stated, respectively, that the 3 March Measure "imposes contingent liability for 100 per cent duties" and that the 3 March Measure was intended "to preserve [the United States'] right to impose 100 percent duties as of March 3, pending the release of the arbitrators' final decision".[45] However, these and other statements made by USTR officials do not, in and of themselves, allow us to conclude that the 3 March Measure and the 19 April action are not legally distinct measures. In order to determine the legal relationship between these two measures, we must examine, on the basis of factual findings of the Panel, what the United States actually *did* on 3 March 1999 and 19 April 1999, irrespective of how the United States described its actions publicly at the time.

74. As noted above, what the United States *did* on 3 March 1999 is set forth in the Metzger Memorandum; what it *did* on 19 April 1999 is described in the USTR Notice on "United States suspension of tariff concessions". On the basis of the Metzger Memorandum and the USTR Notice, it is clear that there are a number of differences between the 3 March Measure and the 19 April action. The most important of these differences is that the 3 March Measure provides for *increased bonding requirements* for certain designated products imported from the European Communities, while the 19 April action provides for the *imposition of 100 per cent duties* on some, but not all, of the designated products that were previously subject to the increased bonding requirements.[46]

75. Moreover, the 3 March Measure was a measure taken by the United States Customs Service and, as explicitly stated in the Metzger Memorandum, a measure taken on the basis of Section 113.13 of the Code of Federal Regulations (the "CFR"), Volume 19. The authority granted to the United States Customs Service under this provision of the CFR does not include the authority to increase customs duties. In contrast, the decision on 19 April 1999 to impose 100 per cent duties on certain designated products imported from the European Communities was an action by the USTR and, as explicitly stated in the USTR Notice dated 19 April 1999[47], an action taken pursuant to the authority granted to the USTR under

---

[45] Panel Report, para. 2.23.

[46] For the difference in product coverage between the 3 March Measure and the 19 April action, see *supra*, footnotes 39 and 40 of this Report.

[47] 64 Fed. Reg. 19,210 (1999).

Section 301 of the Trade Act of 1974.[48] This alone need not necessarily make the 3 March Measure and the 19 April action separate and legally distinct measures. It is perfectly possible for more than one governmental agency to be involved in taking a single measure. However, in our view, in this case, the fact that two separate agencies of the United States government acted separately on two separate occasions, and pursuant to two distinctly separate legal authorities, tends to reinforce the notion that the 3 March Measure and the 19 April action were two separate and legally distinct measures.

76. Furthermore, and more significantly, we note that nothing in the 3 March Measure in any way required the United States to impose 100 per cent duties on 19 April 1999. This measure was taken pursuant to Section 113.13 of the CFR. We note that there is nothing in this particular regulation that requires that increased bonding be accompanied by increased customs duties. Nor does Section 113.13 permit customs authorities to increase customs duties, irrespective of whether bonding requirements are increased or not.

77. We also note that the 3 March Measure was not in any way a prerequisite for the imposition of 100 per cent duties on 19 April 1999. The 19 April action was taken by the USTR under authority found in Section 301 of the Trade Act of 1974. We note that there is nothing in Section 301 that in any way requires an increase in customs duties to be preceded or accompanied by any change in bonding requirements. Moreover, we think it significant that there is no perceptible correlation between the amount of the increase in bonding requirements implemented on 3 March 1999 and the 100 per cent customs duties provided for by the 19 April action. The increase in bonding requirements implemented on 3 March 1999 was not calculated on the basis of the imposition of 100 per cent duties, but was fixed at an amount equal to 10 per cent of the entered value of the designated products in the preceding year.[49] All this, in our view, reinforces the legal distinctiveness of what the United States did on 3 March and what it did on 19 April 1999.

78. The European Communities has stressed, and we are mindful that, when the United States decided on 19 April 1999 to impose 100 per cent duties on certain designated products from the European Communities, that decision applied *retroactively* to those designated products imported on or after 3 March 1999. However, this retroactive application of duties as of 3 March 1999 does not mean that the United States had already decided, as a matter of law, on 3 March 1999, to impose 100 per cent duties. As we have just explained, under Section 301 of the Trade Act of 1974, the United States could just as easily have imposed the increased duties retroactively to 3 March 1999 without having increased the bonding requirements on 3 March 1999. Thus, unlike the European Communi-

[48] 19 U.S.C. § 2411.

[49] Panel Report, para. 6.47.

ties, we do not see this element of retroactivity as necessarily leading to the conclusion that the 3 March Measure and the 19 April action are one and the same.

79. Reinforcing this view is the fact that, as the United States explained to the Panel:

> ... the increased 3 March bonding requirements were removed for entries of merchandise not to be included on the April 19 list within a few days of the Article 22.6 Arbitrator's April 6 report, and were removed on April 19 for all remaining products.[50]

Thus, as of 19 April 1999, imports of the products from the European Communities on which 100 per cent duties are imposed were subject once again to the normal United States bonding requirements.

80. In the "Conclusions and Recommendations" section of the Panel Report, the Panel, on the one hand, found that "the 3 March Measure is no longer in existence"[51] and, on the other hand, recommended "that the Dispute Settlement Body request the United States to bring its measure into conformity with its obligations under the WTO Agreement."[52] We note that the European Communities appeals the Panel's finding that "the 3 March Measure is no longer in existence". As we have discussed, the European Communities contends that the 3 March Measure includes the imposition of the 100 per cent duties currently applied to certain designated products imported from the European Communities. For the reasons we have stated, we disagree.

81. We note, though, that there is an obvious inconsistency between the finding of the Panel that "the 3 March Measure is no longer in existence" and the subsequent recommendation of the Panel that the DSB request that the United States bring its 3 March Measure into conformity with its WTO obligations. The Panel erred in recommending that the DSB request the United States to bring into conformity with its WTO obligations a measure which the Panel has found no longer exists.

82. For all these reasons, we conclude that the Panel correctly found that the measure at issue in this dispute is the 3 March Measure, which is the "increased bonding requirements as of 3 March on EC listed products"[53], that this measure is no longer in existence, that the 19 April action is a legally distinct measure from the 3 March Measure and that the 19 April action is not within the terms of reference of the Panel.

---

[50] United States' appellee's submission, para. 23, referring to United States' second written submission, para. 11 and the United States' responses to questions by the Panel (8 February 2000), para. 21.

[51] Panel Report, para. 7.1.

[52] *Ibid.*, para. 7.3.

[53] Panel Report, para. 6.21.

VI. THE MANDATE OF ARBITRATORS APPOINTED UNDER ARTICLE 22.6 OF THE DSU

83. In paragraphs 6.121 to 6.126 of the Panel Report, the Panel stated, *inter alia*:

> ... We consider that the arbitration process pursuant to Article 22 may constitute a proper WTO dispute settlement procedure to perform the WTO assessment mandated by the first sentence of Article 21.5 of the DSU. ... [Article 22.7 of the DSU] gives the arbitration panel the mandate and the authority to assess the WTO compatibility of the implementing measure. Since the Article 22.6 arbitration was given the authority to determine "a level of suspension equivalent to the level of nullification", it has the authority to assess both variables of the equation.[54]
>
> ... Since the Article 22.6 arbitration process was given the authority to determine "a level of suspension equivalent to the level of nullification", it has the authority to assess both variables of the equation, including whether the implementing measure nullifies any benefit and the level of such nullified benefits.[55]
>
> ...
>
> ... we consider that the WTO compatibility determination mandated by the first sentence of Article 21.5 can be performed by the original panel or other individuals through the Article 22.6-7 arbitration process. ...[56]

84. The European Communities appeals these statements of the Panel. According to the European Communities, the WTO-consistency of a measure taken by a Member to comply with recommendations and rulings of the DSB cannot be determined by arbitrators appointed under Article 22.6 of the DSU.

85. In our view, the question that arises with respect to the Panel's statements on the mandate of Article 22.6 arbitrators is the following: was the issue of the mandate of arbitrators appointed under Article 22.6 of the DSU in any way pertinent to the Panel's determination of the claims relating to the measure at issue in this dispute?

86. The sequence of events that provides the background to this dispute is relevant to resolving this issue. On 2 February 1999, in the dispute in *European Communities – Bananas*, the United States requested authorization from the DSB to suspend the application of concessions or other obligations with respect to the European Communities pursuant to Article 22.2 of the DSU. On the same day,

---

[54] *Ibid.*, para. 6.121.

[55] *Ibid.*, para. 6.122.

[56] *Ibid.*, para. 6.126.

the European Communities requested, pursuant to Article 22.6 of the DSU, arbitration on the level of suspension of concessions or other obligations proposed by the United States. The arbitrators were unable to issue their decision on 2 March 1999, which was the deadline for the circulation of their decision, in accordance with the 60-day time-frame provided for in Article 22.6 of the DSU. On the following day, the United States took the 3 March Measure "as a retaliation measure", with the aim of redressing "a perceived WTO violation by the European Communities".[57] The arbitrators circulated their decision on 9 April 1999. On 19 April 1999, the United States requested, and received, authorization from the DSB to suspend the application of concessions or other obligations in the amount determined by the arbitrators. Subsequent to this authorization, the United States took the 19 April action.

87. This sequence of events is not contested by the parties. In particular, it is not contested that the United States took the 3 March Measure *before* the Article 22.6 arbitrators had issued their decision. Thus, the issue of whether it is within the mandate of arbitrators appointed under Article 22.6 to determine the WTO-consistency of implementing measures was not, and could not have been, relevant to the Panel's determination of the claims relating to the 3 March Measure. This issue could only be relevant with respect to claims relating to the 19 April action, a measure taken *after* the decision of the Article 22.6 arbitrators and the subsequent authorization of the DSB based on that decision.

88. However, as we have already concluded, the Panel correctly found that the measure at issue in this dispute is the 3 March Measure and that the 19 April action is not within the terms of reference of the Panel.

89. Having found that the 3 March Measure is the measure at issue in this dispute, and that the 19 April action is outside its terms of reference, the Panel should have limited its reasoning to issues that were relevant and pertinent to the 3 March Measure. By making statements on an issue that is only relevant to the 19 April action, the Panel failed to follow the logic of, and thus acted inconsistently with, its *own* finding on the measure at issue in this dispute. The Panel, therefore, erroneously made statements that relate to a measure which it had *itself* previously determined to be outside its terms of reference.

90. For these reasons, we conclude that the Panel erred by making the statements in paragraphs 6.121 to 6.126 of the Panel Report on the mandate of arbitrators appointed under Article 22.6 of the DSU. Therefore, these statements by the Panel have no legal effect.

91. In coming to this conclusion, we are cognizant of the important systemic issue of the relationship between Articles 21.5 and 22 of the DSU. As the United States correctly points out in its appellee's submission, the terms of Articles 21.5 and 22 are not a "model of clarity" and the relationship between these

---

[57] Panel Report,paras. 6.33-6.34.

two provisions of the DSU has been the subject of intensive and extensive discussion among Members of the WTO.[58] We note that, on 10 October 2000, eleven Members of the WTO presented a proposal in the General Council to amend, *inter alia*, Articles 21 and 22 of the DSU.[59]

92. In so noting, we observe that it is certainly not the task of either panels or the Appellate Body to amend the DSU or to adopt interpretations within the meaning of Article IX:2 of the *WTO Agreement.* Only WTO Members have the authority to amend the DSU or to adopt such interpretations. Pursuant to Article 3.2 of the DSU, the task of panels and the Appellate Body in the dispute settlement system of the WTO is "to preserve the rights and obligations of Members under the covered agreements, and to *clarify the existing provisions* of those agreements in accordance with customary rules of interpretation of public international law." (emphasis added) Determining what the rules and procedures of the DSU ought to be is not our responsibility nor the responsibility of panels; it is clearly the responsibility solely of the Members of the WTO.

VII. THE EFFECT OF DSB AUTHORIZATION TO SUSPEND CONCESSIONS OR OTHER OBLIGATIONS

93. The European Communities appeals the following statement of the Panel:

> Once a Member imposes DSB authorised suspensions of concessions or obligations, that Member's measure is WTO compatible (it was explicitly authorised by the DSB).[60]

94. The European Communities argues that this statement is incorrect and should be reversed. According to the European Communities, DSB authorization to suspend concessions or other obligations does not have the automatic and unrebuttable effect of rendering a measure suspending the application of concessions or other obligations WTO-consistent. The European Communities argues that DSB authorization is a necessary, but not a sufficient, condition in order to implement legally a suspension of concessions or other obligations.

95. We note that the claims before the Panel, as they related to the 3 March Measure, were that the United States had suspended the application of concessions or other obligations *without* DSB authorization. Thus, the issue before the Panel was that of the *absence* of DSB authorization.

96. The statement of the Panel relates to the effect of DSB authorization, *once granted*. In the context of this dispute, the issue of the effect of DSB authorization, *once granted*, could only arise with respect to the 19 April action, which is a measure taken to suspend concessions *after* the United States had *received* DSB

---

58 United States' appellee's submission, para. 39 and footnote 85.

59 WT/GC/W/410.

60 Panel Report, para. 6.112.

authorization. However, as we have already established, the Panel correctly found that the measure at issue in this dispute is the 3 March Measure, and that the 19 April action is not within its terms of reference. Having found that the 3 March Measure is the measure at issue in this dispute, and that the 19 April action is outside its terms of reference, the Panel should have limited itself to issues that were relevant and pertinent to the 3 March Measure. By making a statement on an issue that is only relevant to the 19 April action, the Panel acted inconsistently with its *own* finding on the measure at issue in this dispute. The Panel erroneously made a statement that relates to a measure which it had *itself* previously determined to be outside its terms of reference.

97. For these reasons, we consider that the Panel erred by stating that "[o]nce a Member imposes DSB authorised suspensions of concessions or obligations, that Member's measure is WTO compatible (it was explicitly authorised by the DSB)".[61] Therefore, this statement by the Panel has no legal effect.

VIII. ARTICLES II:1(A) AND II:1(B), FIRST SENTENCE, OF THE GATT 1994

98. The Panel found that:

> ... the increased bonding requirements of the 3 March Measure, as they provided a treatment less favourable than in the United States' Schedules, violated Article II:1(a) of GATT. The 3 March Measure also violated Article II:1(b), first sentence, as it was guaranteeing and, therefore, enforcing tariffs above their bound levels.[62]

99. The Panel also found that:

> ... any additional interest, charges and costs incurred in connection with the lodging of the additional bonding requirements of the 3 March Measure violated Article II:1(b) of GATT.[63]

100. The United States does not appeal the Panel's finding of inconsistency with Article II:1(b), second sentence, of the GATT 1994. During the oral hearing in this appeal, the United States conceded that it follows from this finding of the Panel that the increased bonding requirements are inconsistent with Article II:1 (b), second sentence. We agree.

101. The United States appeals only the Panel's findings that the increased bonding requirements of the 3 March Measure were inconsistent with Article II:1(a) and the first sentence of Article II:1(b) of the GATT 1994. In support of its appeal, the United States submits that:

---

[61] Panel Report, para. 6.112.

[62] Panel Report, para. 6.59. See also Panel Report, para. 6.72. We note that one panelist disagreed with this majority view, see Panel Report, paras. 6.60-6.61.

[63] Panel Report, para. 6.67. See also Panel Report, para. 6.72.

> [t]he Panel ... made its finding[s] based *not* on the conclusion that the bonding requirements themselves breached the obligations in question, but because the duties they might be called upon to enforce (if imposed) would breach those obligations.[64]

102. The Panel's findings on the inconsistency of the increased bonding requirements with Article II:1(a) and the first sentence of Article II:1(b) are based on the reasoning that the increased bonding requirements were linked to the collection of 100 per cent duties, insofar as the increased bonding requirements were imposed at a level that would guarantee the collection of these duties. Thus, the Panel reasoned that:

> The 3 March additional bonding requirements were established at a level which would guarantee the collection of 100 per cent duties. We have found that the bonding requirements should be assessed together with the rights/obligations they purport to protect, being in this case, the right to collect tariffs at bound levels. The 3 March Measure imposed additional bonding requirements to guarantee collection of 100 per cent tariff duty. The 3 March additional bonding requirements increased the contingent tariff liability for EC listed products above their bound levels, all of which are much lower than 100 per cent *ad valorem* (the highest is 18 per cent). In fact, on 3 March, with the additional bonding requirements on EC listed imports, the United States began 'enforcing' the imposition of 100 per cent tariff duties on the EC listed imports, contrary to the levels bound in its Schedule.[65]

The Panel, thus, found that the increased bonding requirements of the 3 March Measure are inconsistent with Article II:1(a) and also with the first sentence of Article II:1(b) of the GATT 1994 *because* the 100 per cent duties to which they were linked, would, if imposed, be duties above bound levels, and thus, inconsistent with these provisions.

103. We have previously upheld the findings of the Panel that the measure at issue in this dispute is the increased bonding requirements imposed by the 3 March Measure and that the 19 April action, which imposes 100 per cent duties, is not within the terms of reference of the Panel.[66] The task of the Panel, as the Panel had itself defined it in its finding on the terms of reference, was, therefore, to examine the GATT 1994-consistency of the increased bonding requirements; the Panel's task was not to examine the GATT 1994-consistency of the imposition of 100 per cent duties.

104. Nevertheless, the Panel examined the GATT 1994-consistency of the increased bonding requirements *in the light of* the GATT 1994-consistency of the

---

64 United States' appellant's submission, para. 5.

65 Panel Report, para. 6.58.

66 See *supra*, para. 82.

imposition of 100 per cent duties, and concluded, on the basis of this examination, that the increased bonding requirements are inconsistent with Articles II:1(a) and II:1(b), first sentence, of the GATT 1994. As the Panel had previously concluded that the imposition of 100 per cent duties and the increased bonding requirements were legally distinct measures, and that the imposition of 100 per cent duties was not in the Panel's terms of reference, the Panel could not, based on this reasoning, have come to the conclusion that the increased bonding requirements are inconsistent with Articles II:1(a) and II:1(b), first sentence, of the GATT 1994.

105. We, therefore, conclude that the Panel erred in finding that the increased bonding requirements are inconsistent with Article II:1(a) and Article II:1(b), first sentence, of the GATT 1994, and we reverse these findings of the Panel.

IX. ARTICLES 23.2(A), 3.7 AND 21.5 OF THE DSU

106. The Panel found that, by adopting the 3 March Measure, the United States acted inconsistently with its obligations under Articles 3.7, 21.5, 22.6, 23.1, 23.2(a) and 23.2(c) of the DSU. The United States appeals the Panel's findings of inconsistency with Articles 23.2(a), 3.7 and 21.5 of the DSU.

(a) Article 23.2(a) of the DSU

107. We first examine the appeal of the United States relating to Article 23.2(a) of the DSU. The Panel found that:

> ... the 3 March Measure constituted a unilateral determination contrary to Article 23.2(a) ...[67]

108. The United States contends that the European Communities' request for the establishment of a panel referred only to Article 23 of the DSU, and that the Appellate Body should reverse the Panel's finding of inconsistency with Article 23.2(a) on the basis that the panel request of the European Communities was insufficient to "present the problem clearly" as required by Article 6.2 of the DSU. The United States also argues that the European Communities "never requested or argued for" findings under Article 23.2(a), and that the European Communities failed to meet its burden of establishing a *prima facie* case of inconsistency with Article 23.2(a) of the DSU. The United States further submits that the Panel incorrectly found that a "determination as to the effect that a violation has occurred", within the meaning of Article 23.2(a) of the DSU, could be "implied" from the actions taken by the United States.

109. The request for the establishment of a panel of the European Communities stated:

---

[67] Panel Report, para. 6.107.

The European Communities considers that this US measure is in flagrant breach of the following WTO provisions:

- Articles 3, 21, 22 and 23 of the DSU;
- Articles I, II, VIII and XI of GATT 1994.[68]

110. Article 23 of the DSU states, in relevant part:

1. When Members seek the redress of a violation of obligations or other nullification or impairment of benefits under the covered agreements or an impediment to the attainment of any objective of the covered agreements, they shall have recourse to, and abide by, the rules and procedures of this Understanding.

2. In such cases, Members shall:

(a) not make a determination to the effect that a violation has occurred, that benefits have been nullified or impaired or that the attainment of any objective of the covered agreements has been impeded, except through recourse to dispute settlement in accordance with the rules and procedures of this Understanding, and shall make any such determination consistent with the findings contained in the panel or Appellate Body report adopted by the DSB or an arbitration award rendered under this Understanding; ...

111. Article 23.1 of the DSU imposes a general obligation of Members to redress a violation of obligations or other nullification or impairment of benefits under the covered agreements only by recourse to the rules and procedures of the DSU, and not through unilateral action. Subparagraphs (a), (b) and (c) of Article 23.2 articulate specific and clearly-defined forms of prohibited unilateral action contrary to Article 23.1 of the DSU. There is a close relationship between the obligations set out in paragraphs 1 and 2 of Article 23. They *all* concern the obligation of Members of the WTO not to have recourse to unilateral action. We therefore consider that, as the request for the establishment of a panel of the European Communities included a claim of inconsistency with Article 23, a claim of inconsistency with Article 23.2(a) is within the Panel's terms of reference.

112. However, the fact that a claim of inconsistency with Article 23.2(a) of the DSU can be considered to be within the Panel's terms of reference does not mean that the European Communities actually made such a claim. An analysis of the Panel record shows that, with the exception of two instances during the Panel proceedings[69], the European Communities did not refer *specifically* to Arti-

[68] WT/DS165/8, 11 May 1999.

[69] In para. 42 of its oral statement at the second Panel meeting, the European Communities cites Article 23.2(a) in support of its argument in para. 43 that "the revised EC banana regime ... was

cle 23.2(a) of the DSU. Furthermore, in response to a request from the United States to clarify the scope of its claim under Article 23, the European Communities asserted only claims of violation of Articles 23.1 and 23.2(c) of the DSU; no mention was made of Article 23.2(a).[70] Our reading of the Panel record shows us that, throughout the Panel proceedings in this case, the European Communities made arguments relating only to its claims that the United States acted inconsistently with Article 23.1 and Article 23.2(c) of the DSU.[71]

113. The Panel record does show that the European Communities made several references to what it termed the "unilateral determination" of the United States.[72] However, in those references, the European Communities did not specifically link the alleged "unilateral determination" to a claim of violation of Article 23.2(a) *per se*. The European Communities' arguments relating to the alleged "unilateral determination" of the United States were made with reference to the alleged failure on the part of the United States to redress a perceived WTO violation through recourse to the DSU as required by Article 23.1 of the DSU. At no point did the European Communities link the notion of a "unilateral determination" on the part of the United States with a violation of Article 23.2(a).

114. On the basis of our review of the European Communities' submissions and statements to the Panel, we conclude that the European Communities did not specifically claim before the Panel that, by adopting the 3 March Measure, the United States acted inconsistently with Article 23.2(a) of the DSU. As the Euro-

---

never determined to be incompatible with the EC's WTO obligations in a dispute settlement procedure initiated by the US". In para. 86 of its second written submission, the European Communities argues that Articles 23.1 and Article 23.2(a) "specify that such a [determination] can only be made under the rules and procedures of the DSU".

[70] In its response to the United States' request for clarification, the European Communities explained as follows:

> As we have already explained in detail in our first written submission, the US measures that are the subject matter of the present complaint by the European Communities were taken in flagrant violation of the obligations of all WTO Members to respect the provisions of Article 23 of the DSU...
>
> The guiding principle of Article 23 is contained in its para. 1 which also governs the more detailed provisions of para. 2 . . .

The European Communities then quoted Article 23.2(c) of the DSU in full and argued:

> The EC submits that the measures complained of in the present case are obviously in breach of this explicit provision concerning the sequence between the procedures under Article 22 of the DSU and the recourse to the suspension of concessions or other obligations.

See paras. 13-15 of the European Communities' oral statement at the first Panel meeting.

[71] The two specific references to Article 23.2(a) of the DSU, in para. 42 of the European Communities' oral statement at the second Panel meeting and in para. 86 of the European Communities' second written submission (see *supra*, footnote 70), were made in the context of the European Communities' arguments on its claim of violation of the general obligation in Article 23.1 of the DSU.

[72] European Communities' first written submission, paras. 5, 10, 20, and 28; European Communities' second written submission, para. 30; and European Communities' oral statement at second Panel meeting, Addendum to the Panel Report, p. 44.

pean Communities did not make a specific claim of inconsistency with Article 23.2(a), it did not adduce any evidence or arguments to demonstrate that the United States made a "determination as to the effect that a violation has occurred" in breach of Article 23.2(a) of the DSU.[73] And, as the European Communities did not adduce any evidence or arguments in support of a claim of violation of Article 23.2(a) of the DSU, the European Communities could not have established, and did not establish, a *prima facie* case of violation of Article 23.2(a) of the DSU.[74]

115. For these reasons, we conclude that the Panel erred in finding that the United States acted inconsistently with Article 23.2(a) of the DSU. Therefore, we reverse this finding of the Panel.

(b) Article 3.7 of the DSU

116. We next examine the appeal of the United States relating to Article 3.7 of the DSU. In paragraph 6.87 of the Panel Report, the Panel found that:

> ... the 3 March Measure constituted a suspension of concessions or other obligations within the meaning of Articles 23.2(c), 3.7 last sentence and 22.6 last sentence, ... Having reached the prior conclusion that the 3 March Measure was a measure seeking to redress a WTO violation within the meaning of Article 23.1, we find that when it put in place the 3 March Measure, prior to any DSB authorization ... the United States did not abide by the rules of the DSU - violating Articles 23.2(c), 3.7 and 22.6 of the DSU ...

117. We recall that the United States does not appeal the Panel's findings of inconsistency with Articles 22.6 and 23.2(c) of the DSU. Instead, the United States appeals the Panel's finding of inconsistency with Article 3.7 of the DSU. The United States argues that the European Communities "never requested or argued for" findings under Article 3.7 of the DSU.[75] Furthermore, the United States submits that the Panel erred in concluding that Article 3.7, last sen-

---

[73] We note that in addition to the 3 March Measure, the European Communities referred in its submissions and statements to the Panel, to various public notices published in the United States' Federal Register (first written submission, para. 18, and oral statement at first Panel meeting, paras.10-11), as well as to statements made by the Deputy USTR at a press conference held on 3 March 1999 (first written submission, para. 15). However, the European Communities has not argued, let alone demonstrated, that any of these notices or statements constitute a "determination as to the effect that a violation has occurred" within the meaning of Article 23.2(a).

[74] We recall that in our Report in *EC Measures Concerning Meat and Meat Products (Hormones)* ("*European Communities - Hormones*"), we held that:

> ... a *prima facie* case is one which, in the absence of effective refutation by the defending party, requires a panel, as a matter of law, to rule in favour of the complaining party presenting the *prima facie* case.

See WT/DS26/AB/R, WT/DS48/AB/R, adopted 13 February 1998, DSR 1998:I, 135, para. 104.

[75] United States' appellant's submission, para. 56.

tence, contains a specific obligation which can be the subject of a dispute under the DSU.

118. Article 3.7, last sentence, of the DSU states:

> The last resort which this Understanding provides to the Member invoking the dispute settlement procedures is the possibility of suspending the application of concessions or other obligations under the covered agreements on a discriminatory basis vis-à-vis the other Member, *subject to authorization by the DSB of such measures*. (emphasis added)

119. Article 3.7 is part of Article 3 of the DSU, which is entitled "General Provisions" and sets out the basic principles and characteristics of the WTO dispute settlement system. Article 3.7 itself lists and describes the possible temporary and definitive outcomes of a dispute, one of which is the suspension of concessions or other obligations to which the last sentence of Article 3.7 refers. The last sentence of Article 3.7 provides that the suspension of concessions or other obligations is a "last resort" that is subject to DSB authorization.

120. The *obligation* of WTO Members not to suspend concessions or other obligations *without* prior DSB authorization is explicitly set out in Articles 22.6 and 23.2(c), not in Article 3.7 of the DSU. It is, therefore, not surprising that the European Communities did not explicitly claim, or advance arguments in support of, a violation of Article 3.7, last sentence. The European Communities argued that the 3 March Measure is inconsistent with Articles 22.6 and 23.2(c) of the DSU. We consider, however, that if a Member has acted in breach of Articles 22.6 and 23.2(c) of the DSU, that Member has also, in view of the nature and content of Article 3.7, last sentence, necessarily acted contrary to the latter provision.

121. Although we do not believe that it was necessary or incumbent upon the Panel to find that the United States violated Articles 3.7 of the DSU, we find no reason to disturb the Panel's finding that, by adopting the 3 March Measure, the United States acted inconsistently with "Articles 23.2(c), 3.7 and 22.6 of the DSU".[76]

(c) Article 21.5 of the DSU

122. Finally, the United States appeals the Panel's finding of inconsistency with Article 21.5 of the DSU. The United States argues that this finding was based on "argumentation" that was not presented by the European Communities and on the "Panel's erroneous conclusion" that the 3 March Measure is inconsistent with Article 23.2(a) of the DSU.[77]

---

[76] Panel Report, para. 6.87.

[77] United States' appellant's submission, para. 64.

123. This appeal by the United States raises the question whether a panel is entitled to develop its own legal reasoning in reaching its findings and conclusions on the matter under its consideration. In our Report in *European Communities - Hormones*, we held:

> Panels are inhibited from addressing legal claims falling outside their terms of reference. However, nothing in the DSU limits the faculty of a panel freely to use arguments submitted by any of the parties - or to develop its own legal reasoning - to support its own findings and conclusions on the matter under its consideration.[78]

The Panel in this case exercised its discretion to develop its own legal reasoning. Contrary to what the United States argues, the Panel was not obliged to limit its legal reasoning in reaching a finding to arguments presented by the European Communities. We, therefore, do not consider that the Panel committed a reversible error by developing its own legal reasoning.

124. The United States further argues that the Panel's finding under Article 21.5 should be reversed because, in making this finding, the Panel relied on its "erroneous Article 23.2(a) finding".[79] According to the United States, the Panel did not undertake any analysis separate from that under Article 23.2(a) in finding a violation of Article 21.5. The United States submits that the Panel:

> ... simply quoted the language of Article 23.2(a), stated that this provision prohibits "unilateral determinations" and that the 3 March Measure "necessarily implies" such a unilateral determination, and concluded that this unilateral determination was "contrary to Article 23.2(a) and 21.5 of the DSU".[80]

125. The Panel stated in relevant part:

> We consider that the obligation to use the WTO multilateral dispute settlement mechanism (i.e. as opposed to unilateral or even regional mechanisms) to obtain any determination of WTO compatibility, is a fundamental obligation that finds application throughout the DSU. For us, the prohibition against unilateral determinations of WTO violation contained in the first sentence of Article 21.5 of the DSU is comparable to that of Article 23.2(a) of the DSU.[81]
>
> We conclude, therefore, that Article 21.5, first sentence is another DSU obligation (similar to Article 23.2(a)) which, although not

78 Appellate Body Report, *European Communities – Hormones, supra*, footnote 74, para. 156.
79 United States' appellant's submission, para. 66.
80 *Ibid.*
81 Panel Report, para. 6.92.

> explicitly listed in Article 23.2, is covered by Article 23.1, when the measure at issue was seeking to redress a WTO obligation.[82]
>
> ... when the United States put in place the 3 March Measure, no WTO adjudicating body had determined that the EC implementing measure was WTO incompatible. The United States, therefore, when it put in place the 3 March Measure violated Article 21.5 of the DSU ...[83]

126. Our reading of the Panel Report does not lead us to conclude that the Panel based its finding of the inconsistency of the 3 March Measure with Article 21.5 on its conclusion that the measure was inconsistent with Article 23.2(a). Although the Panel considered that the obligation under Article 21.5 was "comparable" and "similar" to the obligation under Article 23.2(a), it explicitly stated that "Article 21.5, first sentence is another DSU obligation ... which, although not explicitly listed in Article 23.2, is covered by Article 23.1 ...".[84] The Panel's references to Article 23.2(a) cannot be construed as the basis upon which the Panel reached its conclusions under Article 21.5. On the contrary, the Panel based its finding of inconsistency on the uncontested fact that, when the United States put in place the 3 March Measure, the WTO-consistency of the European Communities' implementing measure had not been determined through recourse to the WTO dispute settlement procedures as required by Article 21.5 of the DSU.[85]

127. We, therefore, uphold the Panel's finding that, by adopting the 3 March Measure, the United States acted inconsistently with its obligations under Article 21.5 of the DSU.

X. FINDINGS AND CONCLUSIONS

128. For the reasons set out in this Report, the Appellate Body:

(a) upholds the Panel's findings that the measure at issue in this dispute is the 3 March Measure, which is the "increased bonding requirements as of 3 March on EC listed products", that this measure is no longer in existence, that the 3 March Measure is legally distinct from the 19 April action and that the 19 April action is not within the terms of reference of the Panel;

(b) concludes, for the reasons stated in paragraph 89 of this Report, that the Panel erred by stating that the WTO-consistency of a measure taken by a Member to comply with recommendations and rulings of the DSB can be determined by arbitrators appointed un-

82 Panel Report, para. 6.129.

83 *Ibid.*, para. 6.130.

84 *Ibid.*, para. 6.129.

85 *Ibid.*, para. 6.130.

der Article 22.6 of the DSU, and, thus, concludes that the Panel's statements on this issue have no legal effect;

(c) concludes, for the reasons stated in paragraph 96 of this Report, that the Panel erred by stating that "[o]nce a Member imposes DSB authorised suspensions of concessions or obligations, that Member's measure is WTO compatible (it was explicitly authorised by the DSB)", and, thus, concludes that this statement has no legal effect;

(d) reverses the Panel's findings that the increased bonding requirements are inconsistent with Articles II:1(a) and II:2(b), first sentence, of the GATT 1994; and

(e) reverses the Panel's finding that, by adopting the 3 March Measure, the United States acted inconsistently with Article 23.2(a) of the DSU, finds no reason to disturb the Panel's finding that the United States acted inconsistently with "Articles 23.2(c), 3.7 and 22.6 of the DSU", and upholds the Panel's finding of inconsistency of the 3 March Measure with Article 21.5 of the DSU.

129. As we have upheld the Panel's finding that the 3 March Measure, the measure at issue in this dispute, is no longer in existence, we do not make any recommendation to the DSB pursuant to Article 19.1 of the DSU.

9 780521 829786